The French Property Buyer's Handbook

The French Property Buyer's Handbook

Everything you need to know about buying a house
and moving to France

Natalie Avella

HARRIMAN HOUSE LTD

3A Penns Road
Petersfield
Hampshire
GU32 2EW
GREAT BRITAIN

Tel: +44 (0)1730 233870
Fax: +44 (0)1730 233880
Email: enquiries@harriman-house.com
Website: www.harriman-house.com

Second edition published in 2006 and again in 2007
First published in Great Britain in 2004

ISBN: 1-8975-9773-8
ISBN 13: 978-1-897597-73-6

British Library Cataloguing in Publication Data
A CIP catalogue record for this book can be obtained from the British Library.

Printed and bound by Biddles Ltd, Kings Lynn, Norfolk.

Contents

Detailed contents

About the author

Natalie Avella is a part-time design writer and full-time francophile. She lives in London, fortunately close to Waterloo and an easy hop to the south of France.

Acknowledgements

The author would very much like to thank all the kind people that contributed their stories to this book. In particular she'd like to thank Gaynor and John Wingham who, in the early stages, kindly invited her round to their south London home to discuss the purchase of their house in Normandy, and gave her some good pointers in the right direction. Thanks also to Alison Eckett for her help with the statistics and *région* information. Lastly thanks to Nick Inman for providing the excellent illustrations.

Preface

What the book covers

The book covers everything a non-French person needs to know about:

- **Buying a house in France**

  What area to choose, what type of house style, where to look for a house, building your own house and, finally, how to negotiate the property transaction.

- **Moving to France**

  Congratulations! You've bought the house. You now need to know about moving into the house, living in France and, if you need to, working there.

The book explains the above in straight forward language, supported by a wealth of tables and contact details for further information.

Whether you're looking to buy an old country farm, a new house, an apartment, share a property or set up a *gîte* complex, this book covers you all the way.

Who the book is for

The book is aimed at non-French people who are looking to buy a house in France to use as a:

1. holiday home,

2. retirement home, or

3. to work from.

The book assumes no prior knowledge of France, the French language or of the French property market.

Therefore, it is hoped the book will prove useful to the whole range of ages: from young people looking to move to France and start a new life, to older people planning to retire to France.

The book can be used as an active reference guide when 'on the ground' in France getting up early for that 8am appointment with an *immobilier*. But it can also be used by people thinking about moving to France in the future, but who are not quite ready to make the move yet. This book highlights the issues you need to consider.

Finally, the book should also be useful to people who have already moved to France, but who are now looking to carry out some building work, become part of the French social security system or who decide to start working.

How the book is structured

The book is designed to take a reader gently, but comprehensively, through all the stages of buying a house and moving to France. As such, the chapters in the books follow the logical pattern that most people will follow. The order of the chapters, and their contents, are described in more detail below.

- **It's a big decision – what to consider first**

  First, we look at the issues to think about before starting the great adventure, including: is France right for you?

- **Overview of the French property market**

  Then there's a quick overview of prices of property in France, and how these compare with those in the UK. We also look at the profile of the French market, including houses in the country and the growth of secondary residences.

- **Choosing an area**

  Whether to buy on the Brittany coast, inland near the Mediterranean, deep in the countryside in South West France, near the channel ports in Normandy, or lost in the Auvergne – there's quite a choice. This chapter provides an overview of all *régions* in France, and explains how France is divided into *communes, départements* and *régions*.

- **What type of property**

  Having chosen a *région*, the next decision is what type of property you are looking for. An old property, a new one, an apartment, a shared property or a timeshare? Or would it be best to start renting for a period? All these are explained, with information in each case on likely costs and issues to think about.

- **Building your own house**

  Many people have an image of their dream house in France: a property in a certain location, with certain features just right. But looking around, it can be difficult to find a property that is exactly what you have in mind. If this is the case, why not build your own dream house, with everything to your exact specifications? This section explains how to go about this; from finding and managing architects and builders, to building a swimming pool. This section will be useful to anyone carrying out building works on their property on any scale.

- **How to find that perfect property**

  OK, you have an idea where and what type of property you're looking for. Now for the fun part – looking at the houses! But where do you start? Do you contact a UK-based agent, go directly to one in France, look at some websites, or what? This chapter guides you through all the various methods for finding your perfect home in France.

- **The property transaction**

  Not the most exciting section, I'll admit, but essential nevertheless. I've tried to explain the whole legal process as simply as possible, so you know what to expect, and when. I cover surveys, contracts and conveyancing, what fees you can expect, and where to get a mortgage if you need one.

- **Moving in**

  At last, you're ready to move into your new home. One question, how are you going to get all your furniture there? I give some tips on making the move as painless as possible.

- **Living in France**

  You're in your new home, and life is one long cycle of hot croissants for breakfast, fresh bread for lunch, an afternoon siesta by the pool, and then a local aperitif as the sun goes down. Easy, wasn't it? Yes, although I hate to mention it, but we haven't finished quite yet. Here's some advice on banks, tax, social security, education, cars and pets.

- **Working in France**

  If you're hoping to work in France, this section is for you. Advice on running a *gîte* or *chambre d'hôte*, finding a job or setting up your own business.

Although the information is as detailed and thorough as possible, it's important to remember that France is such a huge country, with many regional differences and quirks, and that the experience of buying property is unlikely to be the same for everyone. We also include in the book several interviews with people who have bought property in France, where they can tell their own stories. For some the process has been fairly simple and for others it has, at times, been traumatic... what's interesting is that even if realising their dream has been a rocky journey, not one of them has regretted it.

Supporting website

www.harriman-house.com/frenchproperty

Introduction

France has always been a popular destination for buying a second home and it's easy to understand why. It's a huge country with beautiful landscapes and a diverse climate.

The attractions of France

It has qualities to attract all sorts of people, whether they enjoy painting, golf, walking, horse riding, climbing, drinking fine wine, or gorging on haute cuisine. All the coasts of France – from the long empty white stretches of the Aquitaine, to the sandy stretches and pretty coves of Brittany and the Western Loire, or the sun-baked Mediterranean – are superb for swimming, surfing, sailing or bathing in the sun. Even deep inland you need never be far from water as there are many rivers and lakes for fishing and watersports, as well as extensive canal networks for those who like to potter around on boats.

The spectacular mountains of the Alps and Pyrenees are winter wonderlands to which people from all over the world flock to ski, but which, once the snow has melted, are carpeted with meadow flowers and are perfect for hiking.

Architecture and history enthusiasts will find no end of perfectly intact medieval and renaissance town and village centres, as well as fine *chateaux*. And, even though France is one of the world's most popular tourist destinations, it is so large, with still so many remote areas, that there are plenty of places to discover off the beaten track.

And it's so close to the UK

For UK residents, France is the perfect place for a holiday home as it's so easily accessible. You needn't be dependent on flying to get there, as for many it's an easy jaunt by boat or train. For families it's ideal as you can pack all your belongings and kids in the car, making for a much easier and cheaper trip abroad. If you do decide to fly, there are budget airlines serving many French destinations which offer one way journeys, sometimes for just a few pounds. It's often cheaper for anyone based not far from Stansted to fly to Montpellier than to take a train to Manchester. Some people even manage to commute to the UK from France – working in the UK during the week and returning to their families in France at weekends.

 Warning: **Don't become too dependent on the budget airlines. The takeover of budget airline Buzz by Ryanair meant the closure of several less profitable routes (and lots of very disappointed, and some pretty much stranded, regular users).**

A new life abroad

As well as remaining a popular destination for a holiday home, France is increasingly becoming a destination for those searching for a new life abroad. Increased mobility between EU member states means that it is easier than ever for EU nationals to switch to another country to find work and set up home. If you are unemployed in the UK, you can even continue claiming benefits in France.

Many people give the following reasons for wanting to move permanently to France:

- Being able to afford a much more appealing home in France (unlike, for instance, in the UK where prices are extortionate and most of your life is spent chained to a very hefty mortgage).

- Desire to live in a better climate.

- A slower, more relaxed lifestyle that revolves around home and family rather than careers. In many French towns and villages, the shops still close for several hours during the day while everyone, including the schoolchildren and working adults alike, returns home to eat with their families.

- Better healthcare. Even though the UK has some of the finest surgeons and medical staff in the world, many people feel that – with long waiting lists, dirty, overcrowded hospitals and overworked staff – the NHS is in a severe state of decline and that France has a much better and more reliable standard of healthcare.

- Food direct from the growers. Many people move to France to escape the supermarket culture that has a monopoly in the UK. They wish to live close to good local markets where they can buy fresh food direct from the farmer, food that isn't cosmetically or genetically modified or shipped in freezer containers from the other side of the world. Also, with delicious cheese and many of the world's best wines, France is a delight for foodies.

Warning: **Vegetarians beware – in most restaurants you are very limited in your choice of meat-free dishes! Unless you eat fish, you may well be limited to an omelette and tomato salad every time you eat out. (Vegans will have a very difficult time.) Fortunately many of the larger towns have good North African, Chinese and Indian restaurants. Vegetarians and vegans should check out Alliance Végétarienne's website:**

www.ivu.org/avf/

Another food warning: **If you're leaving a big UK city to move to the French countryside, you may find yourself desperately missing Indian and Chinese takeaways and pizza deliveries!**

But France is not a Utopia

Of course it's wrong to imagine France as a Utopia. France also has its problems and probably one of the first frustrations you'll encounter is what seems like a wall of bureaucracy. Some *départements* are worse than others and it will seem very difficult to get things done.

France has its fair share of racial tensions, poverty, and corruption in all tiers of government and the legal professions. It has an appalling record for road accidents and not everywhere is traffic-free and unpolluted (even the valleys of the Alps suffer from terrible road pollution). The 'laidbackness' that so appealed to you from back home may well drive you crazy when you're trying to get your house built in time for you to move in. You may even realise that there are many good things about your own country that perhaps you took for granted (television may be one of them – it's awful in France!)

Vive la difference!

Then again, discovering such differences, be they good or bad, is not such a negative thing. Moving to a foreign country is a great way to learn about the culture you're leaving – just as much as about the one you're moving to. Your perspective on the world and on yourself will be challenged and changed. A move abroad will, without a doubt, be a great adventure that enriches your life.

1

It's a big decision – what to consider first

A checklist of things to think about before starting to look for a property.

If it's a second home, do you really need it?

1. Will you get enough use from the property? It's one big initial expense and after that will continue to be a year round expense. Perhaps you should consider sharing a property with friends?

2. Will you be happy going to the same place on holiday? Why not go to the same rented *gîte* for two weeks each year? If you are worried about feeling too tied to a property or place but still wish to buy then you could always consider holiday home swapping. Try renting a place for a couple of months first, as you never know, the novelty might well wear off.

3. It's not worth buying a second home if you only intend visiting it for a week or two each year, leaving it empty for the rest of the year. Although you could consider letting it out as a *gîte* when you're not using it.

If you are moving permanently:

1. How will you make a living?

2. How much will you miss your family and friends back home?

3. Are your language skills good enough to enable you to get a job or make new friends? Even if the local people are extremely friendly and go out of their way to befriend you, you could soon get bored of speaking like a child!

Accessibility from the UK

1. If you're buying a holiday home, are you close to rail, air and ferry links? Think about the accessibility of your property by car. Once you leave the airport or ferry port, do you really want to spend hours travelling in a car? And if you don't have a car based in France what will you do? Rural areas are very poorly served by public transport and are only worth considering if you have a car.

2. Will the travelling put you off going there? Will you get bored of the journey?

Rural or urban?

1. If you live in a remote hamlet you won't be able to indulge in some of the things most of us love about France – such as popping along to the *boulangerie* for a baguette in the morning, joining the locals at the bar for a glass of *eau de vie* (it's worth noting that villages with bars tend to be the easiest in which to integrate), or perhaps participating in a game of boules. On the other hand, you might want the complete seclusion that you never found when you lived within the M25 back home.

2. If you love eating out and enjoy a glass of wine, perhaps you should consider living near a large town where there are plenty of restaurants and also taxis to get back home when you've had one glass too many.

3. What local health and social services are provided? You might need a doctor or a pharmacy close at hand. If you're thinking of one day retiring to your second home, a remote rural village might not be such a good idea. You will need a good school if you're moving there permanently with your children.

4. What shopping facilities are there? What if you have no shops within walking distance and your car broke down?

Appropriate for your hobbies

If you enjoy golf, are there golf courses nearby, or if you fish are there rivers and lakes? If you're a landscape artist, are you surrounded by scenery you'd never tire of? For art lovers, are there plenty of cultural/historical opportunities? Cities such as Bordeaux and Toulouse have fine galleries. If you enjoy eating out then it's no good living in the middle of nowhere.

Size of property

1. What size property do you want? Do you need extra bedrooms for visiting friends and family? (A word of warning though: don't say to everyone you know 'oh you must come and visit me' as they might just do that . . . one after another, and you'll end up as a tourist guide/guest house host with *no* time to relax!)

2. As you get older you may not want to look after so much space.

3. Do you need much land? After all, even though you might love gardening, who will do it in your absence?

4. How much time are you prepared to devote to repairs and decorating?

5. Will you let others use the property in your absence? Perhaps you'd consider letting it out?

Language

Is your French adequate for day-to-day communication? If it isn't then you may face some difficult times ahead.

Climate

If you're moving to a place permanently and climate is a priority then it's important to find out what it's like all year round. Languedoc-Roussillon has hot sultry summers, but winter can be freezing when the ice cold winds come howling down from the mountains. Because of the narrowness between the gulf of Gascony and the gulf of the Lion (the 'French isthmus'), France is at a crossroads of climatic influences: mountain, oceanic, continental and Mediterranean.

The chart below shows the average daily maximum and minimum temperatures throughout the seasons (all in centigrade).

Table 1.1 – Average seasonal temperatures for selected French cities

	Spring	Summer	Autumn	Winter
Bordeaux	17/6	25/14	18/8	9/2
Boulogne	12/6	20/14	18/8	6/0
Lyons	16/6	27/14	16/7	5/-2
Nantes	16/6	24/14	16/8	8/2
Nice	17/6	27/18	21/12	13/4
Paris	16/6	26/15	16/7	6/1
Strasbourg	16/5	25/13	14/6	2/-2

 Tip: A useful website to find out more about the French climate and to check the daily forecast is 🖳 www.meteo.fr

Where to buy

This will be a major question for most people, as almost every *région* in France has its own distinct and captivating charm.

Many people decide to move to France after spending years holidaying or touring different parts of the country. It's possible that you may be lucky enough to have seen enough of it to know for certain which part you'd like to buy a property in. For those that have visited France and fallen in love with several places, it can be more difficult to come to the right decision.

Later in this book is a regional guide which should help, but the best way to find your area is, obviously, just to get over there, drive around and get a feel for the different *régions* yourself.

Getting to France

By tunnel

Eurostar

Eurostar trains run directly from London to Paris frequently throughout the day. The journey is only three hours, so catching a Eurostar just after 08h15 from Waterloo easily gets you into Paris in time for lunch. Trains also stop at Lille which is becoming more popular as a weekend and short break destination. If you're heading for Lille the journey time is even shorter at only two hours.

💻 www.eurostar.com

Eurotunnel

You can take your vehicle across the channel via Eurotunnel. There are regular 35 minute crossings from Folkestone.

💻 www.eurotunnel.com

By sea

Brittany Ferries

Brittany Ferries operates ferries between Portsmouth and Caen, and Portsmouth and St Malo. Ferries also run between Poole and Cherbourg and Plymouth and Roscoff, as well as between Cork and Roscoff.

☎ +44 (0)8703 665333

🖳 www.brittanyferries.com

Condor Ferries

Condor Ferries operates between Weymouth and St Malo, Poole and St Malo, and Portsmouth and Cherbourg. Crossings take as little as four hours.

☎ +44 (0)845 345 2000

🖳 www.condorferries.co.uk

Hoverspeed

Hoverspeed operates between Dover and Calais.

☎ +44 (0)8702 240 8070

🖳 www.hoverspeed.co.uk

Norfolk Line

Operating between Dover and Dunkerque, Norfolk Lines is primarily a freight carrier, but also takes passengers. Because it is not as well-known and marketed to passengers as other companies, it's possible to find some very good deals (especially for camper vans).

☎ +44 (0)870 8701020

🖳 www.norfolkline.com

Norse Merchant

Those travelling from Northern Ireland should take a look at Norse Merchant. You can travel on the Norse Merchant ferry from Belfast to Birkenhead, then drive down to Dover and take the Norfolk Line to Dunkerque.

☎ +44 (0)870 6004321

🖳 www.norsemerchant.com

SeaFrance

SeaFrance operates ferries between Dover and Calais.

☎ +44 (0)8705 711 711

🖳 www.seafrance.com

Speed Ferries

Speed Ferries offers low-cost 50 minute ferry crossings between Dover and Boulogne.

☎ +44 (0)870 2200570

💻 www.speedferries.com

P&O Ferries

P&O operates ferries between Dover and Calais, and Portsmouth and Le Havre.

☎ +44 (0)8705 9803332

💻 www.poferries.com

Transmanche Ferries

Ferries between Newhaven and Dieppe.

☎ +44 (0)800 917 12 01

💻 www.transmancheferries.com

By air

Ryanair

Ryanair is a budget airline operating flights from Stansted to Bergerac, Biarritz, Carcassonne, Dinard, Grenoble, La Rochelle, Limoges, Montpellier, Nantes, Pau, Perpignan, Poitiers, Rodez, St Etienne, Toulon and Tours.

Flights from Luton go to Brest and Nîmes. There are also flights between Liverpool and Bergerac, Carcassonne, Limoges and Nîmes. Ryanair also runs flights from Glasgow to Marseille and Paris.

Ryanair Direct Booking Line: United Kingdom +44 (0)906 2705656

💻 www.ryanair.com

Easyjet

Easyjet operates budget flights to the following destinations:

London Gatwick to Grenoble, Marseille, Nice and Toulouse
London Luton to Grenoble, Nice and Paris Charles de Gaulle
London Stansted to Lyons and Nice, Paris Orly and Toulouse

💻 www.easyjet.co.uk

FlyBMI

FlyBMI offers budget deals between several British cities and Lyon, Nice, Paris and Toulouse

💻 www.flybmi.com

bmibaby

bmibaby offers budget deals from London, Manchester and Norwich to Nice, Paris, Perpignan and Toulouse.

🖥️ www.bmibaby.com

Air France

🖥️ www.airfrance.fr

British Airways

🖥️ www.ba.com

Hiring a car

The following car rental companies operate in France:

Alamo

🖥️ www.alamo.com

Avis

🖥️ www.avis.com (or in French only – 🖥️ www.avis.fr)

Budget

🖥️ www.budget.com

Europcar

🖥️ www.europcar.com

Hertz

🖥️ www.hertz.com (or in French only – 🖥️ www.hertz.fr)

Thrifty

🖥️ www.thrifty.com

Interview with a property buyer

David bought a house in Normandy, but came across some odd houses while looking, including an all-stone house.

Q. *Tell me about how you found your house in France.*

A. We have had a house in Normandy for 15 years now but we found the most bizarre things while looking around, especially when looking at property that has been left to several members of the same family and not all want to sell, especially to 'foreigners'. We went to look at many places before we bought but some stand out.

The first house we looked at was basically derelict. My wife and I went upstairs on our own while the agent attempted to force open the downstairs back door. We discovered a lovely, fully tiled luxury bathroom upstairs which was in stark contrast to the rest of the house. The agent came running upstairs and told us to get out of the bathroom as it was 'not included in the sale'. As the only access to this bathroom would be through 'our' house, we asked why not. It was apparently one son's share of the property and he did not want to sell and wanted to retain the right to come in and use 'his' bathroom at any time day or night. Needless to say we passed on that one and the agent was very surprised at this and actually took exception to my wife and I laughing till we cried at the absurdity of it all.

Another one was the house with three parts. Two cottages at either end of the row which were in a fair state and a derelict garage section stuck in the middle. Two brothers wanted to sell, the one with the middle bit did not, presumably he was a bit hacked off about getting the booby prize in the family giveaway and was going to make the other two pay for this by making their bits of the property unsaleable.

Lastly, we were told by the agent we were going to see a 'particular' house. We thought the choice of adjective a bit bizarre, but when we got there, with a bit of Franglais, we realised he meant 'peculiar' not particular. The entire house was made of stone. How nice, I hear you say, but actually I mean the inside, not the outside. Stone kitchen units, stone table, stone bathroom including a bath made of concrete and lined with pebbles. It would have taken £200 a week to heat the house. We found out the reason was the owner worked at a quarry and was obviously helping himself to what was lying around at work.

Still, we found our house eventually and have had it ever since. We have many wonderful French friends now and all this from a twin town football trip (Coutances/Ilkley in Yorkshire) at Easter 1986.

2

Overview of the French property market

Table 2.1 shows the average house prices in each *région* during the years 2004 and 2005. As properties are advertised by the square metre rather than by number of rooms, the figures show the average cost per metre in each region. The table is based on figures collated by FNAIM (*Fédération Nationale de l'Immobilier*).

From the table you will see that:

- The most **expensive *régions*** to buy property in France are *Provence-Alpes-Cote d'Azur* (PACR), *Ile de France* (the small but heavily populated *région* that incorporates Paris) and Rhône-Alpes. These *régions* have the best employment opportunities, good transport links and are generally well known for the good quality of life enjoyed by inhabitants.

- The **cheapest *régions*** are *Champagne-Ardenne, Limousin, Auvergne* and *Lorraine*. These *régions* are areas which have suffered severe depopulation, there are few large towns and very little in the way of industry. Parts of these *régions* are extremely remote and have poor transport links.

From their statistics FNAIM worked out that for €121,300 you could buy a:

- one bedroom apartment in the Ile-de-France,
- 3 bedroom/68m² property in Brittany, Languedoc Rousillon, Nord-Pas-de-Calais and Rhônes-Alpes, or
- 4 bedroom/111m² property in Burgundy, Champagne-Ardenne or Limousin.

Table 2.1 – Regional property prices in 2004 and 2005

	Avg price per m² (euros)	Avg price per m² (euros)	Avg annual increase %	Avg annual increase %	Avg annual increase %
Alsace	1828	1981	8,3	9,4	3,3
Aquitaine	1648	1812	10,0	12,5	8,1
Auvergne	1337	1527	14,1	8,2	7,0
Basse-Normandie	1397	1578	13,0	10,2	8,2
Bourgogne	1318	1420	7,7	12,0	5,7
Bretagne	1592	1798	12,9	14,0	8,2
Centre	1416	1575	11,2	7,7	7,5
Champagne-Ardenne	1260	1375	9,1	6,0	5,8
Corse	1925	2123	10,3	21,6	7,7
Franche-Comté	1401	1578	12,6	8,0	8,5
Haute-Normandie	1515	1715	13,2	11,0	7,2
Ile-de-France	2495	2708	8,6	16,0	6,2
Languedoc-Rousillon	1967	2188	11,2	9,5	8,9
Limousin	1206	1296	7,5	15,1	6,2
Lorraine	1353	1525	12,7	4,1	6,0
Midi-Pyrénées	1626	1802	10,9	23,0	8,6
Nord-Pas-de-Calais	1520	1691	11,3	11,7	8,2
PACA	2797	3020	8,0	9,9	9,0
Pays de la Loire	1643	1821	10,8	11,7	7,3
Picardie	1490	1653	10,9	11,5	6,1
Poitou-Charentes	1 350	1529	13,2	13,9	6,2
Rhône-Alpes	2 050	2198	7,2	13,5	6,0
France entière (average across entire country)	1 838	2 019	9,9	12,5	7,8

Source: FNAIM, January 2006

Comparing UK and French property markets

French property prices have risen in the last ten years, but it has been a very steady rise when compared with the British market which has seen some huge jumps in prices.

Note: **The UK statistic is based on all property, rather than just the above statistics on older houses, as used by FNAIM. One of the problems with comparing statistics from different countries is that they are not all based on the same criteria.**

If you sold a property in the UK ten years ago in order to buy one in France, then you would be seriously out of pocket if you decided to move back to the UK. It's even possible that you would not be able to afford to move back, or at least without considerably downsizing. This is certainly something to bear in mind, especially when people say to you, "don't worry – if it doesn't succeed you can always move back home". Unless you are 100% certain that a move to France is right for you, then do consider letting out your property in the UK and renting in France first. Alternatively, consider buying a small property in the UK to let out, as well as a place in France, so that you always have a foothold on the ladder back home.

So why are the markets so different?

Britain – a nation obsessed with property

Britain is a nation obsessed with property, and people are prepared to take out very high mortgages at low interest rates without, it seems, the concern that the very next month their mortgage payments could double. For this reason the UK has experienced some serious booms and, just as serious, busts. In the last decade, buyers have been riding the boom, people have seen buying property as a better and more stable investment than buying shares. This is changing: in 2005 there was a huge slowdown in the market and in early 2006 British lenders are no longer offering the low interest buy-to-let mortgages that they were a couple of years ago.

More stability in the French property market

In France there is a much less competitive mortgage market to lure consumers. There are codes in place to prevent lenders from giving borrowers more than they can afford – you cannot borrow more than a third of your salary – and if a lender does give you more then they will face penalties. Importantly, almost all mortgage rates tend to be fixed for their entire duration rather than just the first couple of years.

Consequently, French borrowers aren't given the bait of very low rates for the first few years, followed by a high variable rate (which is great for first time buyers when they're first finding their feet after saving for years for a deposit, but for everyone else it's a false economy). Long term fixed rates in France (which in recent years have compared favourably against UK variable rates) means that there is much more stability in the French property market.

Renting is more common in France . . . but this is changing

Another difference is that, until very recently, there has not been the same urgency to buy, buy, buy in France. Owning property in Britain is very much tied to status and renting is seen as the domain of flat-sharing students and twentysomethings. In France – which is not really any less materialistic, as they do love their clothes, cars, holidays and gadgets as much as we do – renting (as in most of continental Europe) is much more socially acceptable. People from all backgrounds are quite happy to spend their entire lives renting.

This, however, is changing as, according to recent research published by the *Institute Nationale de la Statistique et des Etudes Economiques (INSEE)*, there is a growing trend of people wishing to own their home. In 1996, 32% of tenants seeking to move wanted to become homeowners, and in 2002 this number had risen to 41%. Other INSEE research found that although more tenants want to own property, the proportion of tenants has remained stable since the beginning of the 90s (although tenants are highly mobile with two-thirds occupying their dwelling for less than four years). It found, however, that the proportion of young people living in private housing is rising, therefore indicating a new trend towards ownership.

There's simply more space in France

Despite the difference in market forces in France and the UK, France will always be cheaper simply because land is at much less of a premium; it is physically three times the size but with a similar sized population as the UK. It is still true that in many areas you can pick up an old ruin for less than €40,000 or swap your three bedroom semi in Croydon for a *château*.

Old properties traditionally have not appealed to the French

Another reason older property is cheaper in France than in the UK is that most French people are completely disinterested in renovating a wreck, and would balk at the expense of maintaining and heating an old large property – even if they could afford the building. Aesthetics of character property have long been less important than the comforts of a nice modern home with all mod cons and comforts. For some reason the French have long loved newness, although this is certainly changing and many are beginning to appreciate what can be done with older property. In recent years they have even caught the British obsession with DIY! INSEE reported that there is an increasing number of purchases of older houses, which made up three-quarters of sales from 1998 to 2002.

Unlike many foreign buyers looking for a holiday home, the French will have more pragmatic reasons for buying property – they'll be looking for homes close to employment, schools, services and transportation. The very cheap run-down but attractive property that appeals to foreign buyers is usually found in more remote areas, where there are less employment opportunities, services and transportation links (as reflected in the table above), as well as remote pockets of the more expensive *régions*.

La France profonde

House hunters in these remote areas will learn a lot about rural poverty in France. Many elderly people live alone in appalling conditions without modern heating or sanitation, many still without indoor toilets. Today there are grants available for the poor and elderly to modernise their homes, but these opportunities have still not been taken up by (or perhaps even been made known to) everyone.

The countryside wasn't always so poor and empty. During the golden age of rural France – the years 1800 to 1860 – it was dotted with thriving autonomous yet interconnected communities. Then a series of disasters struck which carried on well into the 20th Century:

- first, the countryside witnessed the phylloxera disaster (a vine disease that spread all over France, destroying the economy and resulting in the loss of many types of precious vines); then

- there was the flight of workers to the towns during the industrial revolution; and later came

- the immense human losses of World War I and II.

 Note: **In 1931, the urban population exceeded the population of the countryside for the first time.**

In 1968 agriculture still employed over 3 million people, but in 1977 it was employing no more than 2 million workers. The decline in agriculture resulted in many deserted farms and hamlets, villages and small towns and for decades many properties remained empty.

Today people are returning to the empty properties, although they are mainly being renovated as second homes (*residences secondaires*) for city dwellers and foreigners.

It is the first time since the late 1960s that the percentage of unoccupied dwellings in the total stock of housing has been so low: just under 7%. Although, these 2,000,000 unoccupied homes aren't all beautiful old wrecks waiting to be renovated; 51% of them are apartments in cities and towns.

Secondary residences

INSEE research found that there has been a marked upturn in the stock of secondary residences and occasional dwellings – 50,000 per year were purchased between 1997 and 2002. Between these years, 20,000 secondary homes were built, the same as between 1992 and 1996, but less than in the boom years of the 1980s.

This is not quite so good news for foreign buyers as they now have to face increased competition from French nationals when buying second homes and property for renovation.

 Note: **According to estimates by INSEE there were 3 million second homes in France at the end of 2002, meaning 8% of French households now own one.**

INSEE puts this increase in second home purchasing down to several factors:

- more importance is placed on leisure time and there is more free time thanks to the new 35 hour week;
- a low base rate on loans;
- the availability of grants to renovate property; and
- a lack of trust in the stock market which has resulted in people putting money into their homes instead.

Research conducted by nationwide estate agent Century 21 found that preferred areas for buying second homes were those by the sea and in four main areas:

- south west (Biarritz, Bayonne);
- south east (all of the Cote d'Azur);
- Brittany; and
- Normandy.

Second homes not necessarily leading to regeneration of country areas . . .

To some extent the buying of second homes is good news for the countryside as it means that derelict empty buildings are being restored and coming to life again. Although it does not necessarily mean that the economy of the countryside is being regenerated. Most people only occupy their second home during the summer months and the occasional week or weekend here and there. This seasonal and weekend business is not enough to sustain small shops and businesses.

. . . so think about your own impact when you buy a house

Such an issue should be an important ethical concern for people buying a second home: it's a good idea not to buy in small villages that have existing shops and bars, as you will not be able to support their existence if you're hardly ever around. It is better to buy somewhere either completely remote or in a busy town or resort that won't suffer because of your absence.

Those wishing to move permanently into a depopulated zone will get lots of support – financial and other – from local departmental and regional development bodies (and in some cases the EU). Such areas are crying out for new blood, energy, ideas and long term day-by-day commitment.

Interview with a property buyer

Pat swapped a house in Scotland for a house in Gers to be near the Pyrenees.

Q. *Why did you decide to move to France?*

A. People have so many different reasons for deciding to take the plunge and move over to France. From my reading and conversations with those who have done so, it seems that most people spent some time getting to know the country, and slowly fell in love with the French way of life. But this is too much of a generalisation, and there will be as many reasons as there are people.

Q. *Did you already know France well?*

A. We knew very little about France when we decided to buy a house here. As a family we had always enjoyed walking, progressing from the Peak District to the Lakes and then the Scottish Highlands. We started camping, then youth hostelling, then B&B, then eventually bought a small house in the Scottish Highlands, where we went as often as possible. After several enjoyable years there, suddenly came the terrible foot and mouth plague, and Scottish farmers banned walkers from their land. Instead, that year Eddie decided to fulfil a long-held dream and went walking in the Pyrenees. I took a *gîte* nearby with one of our children.

Q. *How did you make the jump?*

A. To cut a long story short we decided to sell our Scottish house, and settled on the Gers as the place we wanted to be. We now have a house and three hectares of land in this beautiful area of rolling hills and picturesque farms and villages.

Q. *How will you use your house?*

A. Now we are here it has become more than a holiday house, and though we still have our house in England, we spend most of our time here, loving the slower pace of life and the time to enjoy the changing seasons. We are near enough to the Pyrenees to go there for the day, skiing in the winter and walking in the summer. Our family can come and stay with us, as the airports aren't too far away.

Q. *Any major problems with the move?*

A. Although there have been problems, on the whole our life is satisfying and exciting, with so many new things to discover. We see it as possibly our last big adventure before slipping into old age.

3

Choosing an area

Understanding France's *communes, départements* and *régions*

For the purposes of administration and local government, France is geographically broken down into three tiers:

- *commune*
- *département*
- *région*

The town of Bordeaux, for example, is a *commune*, with its own elected council and local authority. But it also belongs to a greater local authority, the Gironde *département*, which in turn belongs to another, still larger local authority, the Aquitaine *région*. Both the *département* and the *région* each have an elected council. Each level of local authority (*région*, *département* and *commune*) is (like the State) a distinct legal entity responsible for exercising general powers over circumscribed geographical areas.

Communes

Dating from before the French Revolution, *communes* are the oldest form of local authority in France. They continue to exist following various constitutional reforms and their current structure dates from 1884. Every city, town or village in France, whatever its size, is considered as an independent authority with an elected assembly and a mayor. This means that there are over 36,000 communal authorities in France, the large majority of which represent less than 1,000 habitants.

In some areas, especially those affected by conurbation, another tier of local government has occurred called *Inter-Communal Authorities*. Often these are needed when a number of *communes* share the same facilities (such as airports or industrial zones) and it makes sense that *communes* work together in developing and controlling the area. In 1999 these areas were given definitions:

- *Communauté d'agglomération* (Urban)
- *Communauté urbaine* (Metropolitan)
- *Communauté de communes or Pays* (for rural areas)

Départements

Introduced in 1789, a year after the French Revolution, *départements* were created to replace the feudal division of France (Counties, Duchies, etc.) The *département* was a means of imposing national laws over territories that were previously governed by communal or feudal rule. They are roughly the same size and, where possible, square in shape.

There are currently 100 *départements*: 94 in mainland France, two in Corsica and four in French Overseas Territories. Each *département* has a name, but can also be identified by a two-digit number (e.g. 75 for Paris, 64 for Pyrénées-Atlantiques). The number also serves administrative purposes and is included on postal (zip) codes, vehicle registration and social security numbers. *Départements* are numbered according to their alphabetical order (with a few exceptions).

Each *département* has a local authority called the *Conseil Général* and an elected Council that, in turn, elects a *Président*. A governor, called a *Préfet*, is also appointed to each *département* by central government and the principal town or city of a *département* is known as the *Préfecture*. Today the powers of the *Préfet* are largely reduced and executive power is exercised by the *Président* of the *Conseil Général*.

Régions

The 100 French *départements* are grouped into 27 *régions*. There are 22 *régions* in mainland France, a *territoire régional* for the island of Corsica and four *régions* for French overseas territories.

Régions were created by the 1982 Decentralisation Act and elections of France's first regional assemblies were held in 1986. Many functions previously belonging to central government were devolved to regional authorities by the Act – in particular the promotion of economic and social development, education and culture. Like *départements*, *régions* have their own public authority, the *Conseil Régional*, with an elected council, and a *Président* and a *Préfet* appointed by central government. The *Conseil Régional* is based in a regional capital, which is usually the major city of all the *départements* it represents.

French *régions* are important centres of decision-making and action in terms of regional planning, education, occupational training, transport, culture and research, but they are not autonomous in the same way that 'states' of other countries are. They have, for instance, no power to pass laws over the territory they cover.

(For a detailed description of all France's *régions* see the reference section in the appendices.)

Interview with a property buyer

Lesley moved to Limousin to farm in 1989, but it didn't work out as she'd hoped.

Q. *How did you come to move to France?*

A. We'd heard about Brits who were farming in France and so I started making enquiries. We visited the French Consulate in London and got information on property sale and purchase procedures, employment and taxes etc. 'Farmers Weekly' magazine had installed a couple of British farmers in France, so I wrote and they sent me copies of their previous articles on the subject. These articles are extremely informative and detailed and cover buying a farm, setting up the business and difficulties encountered. We also contacted the Dutch consultant that 'Farmers Weekly' had used and decided to use him ourselves. We decided Limousin was the best area for us to farm sheep and beef and the farm prices were within our means. Then we saw a TV programme on some Brits who were already farming in France, and that was it. The next thing I knew I was on a ferry (neither of us had been to France in our lives before!) and we bought a farm – in three weeks! This was in March 1989.

Q. *How did find your farm?*

A. We couldn't see the point of using an estate agent, so we set off looking for ourselves and visited several *notaires* to see what they had to offer. We even visited SAFER (Société d'Aménagement Foncier et d'Etablissement Rural), who looked at us as if we'd landed from Mars and sent us off to look at a bog! We looked at five farms in all, but ADASEA (Association Départementale de l'Aménagement des Structures d'Exploitation Agricoles) came up with the one we bought. The consultant was with us every step of the way and helped us with all the paperwork, negotiations, authorisations, bank accounts, loan applications, grant applications, translating, interpreting, etc. Setting up in farming is much more than just buying the farm and we never regretted paying for his services.

We also arranged to buy most of the farm machinery from the owner and all the hay that was in the lofts, but we did not buy his livestock.

Q. *How did the purchase go?*

A. The vendor wanted to use his usual *notaire* and not the one we had chosen, so we used both. We went straight back to England after the contract was signed.

In May, my husband went to France to take possession and start haymaking, even though we hadn't yet completed. This was allowed because otherwise the whole hay crop would have been lost and it was technically ours. My husband also attended a course run by the consultant's firm in collaboration with the Chamber of Agriculture (if I remember rightly) for foreign farmers setting up in France. He was supposed to learn French and how the agricultural system worked.

Q. *And the move went smoothly??*

A. Meanwhile, I had problems back in England. I'd put my house on the market as soon as we'd got back from France, but the housing market suddenly plunged. I had to carry on working to pay the mortgage and send him what I could for him to live. The completion date loomed and still the house wasn't sold, so I had to arrange an emergency loan to complete with and then took out a second mortgage. As I couldn't be present at the completion, which we had delayed by a month, my husband signed for me by proxy. That was in August 1989.

I finally managed to sell the house in February 1990 for £20,000 less than anticipated, which meant less money to invest in the farm. So, not having been married that long and having been separated for nine months (I did manage to go over and spend Christmas with him), with less money than planned and being stuck at Dover in a hired lorry crammed with furniture because the ferries were cancelled due to a hurricane, it wasn't a very good start. I spent the night in a freezing waiting room with a duvet rescued from the lorry.

Q. *How did you finance the purchase?*

A. The whole project was financed with capital from the two houses and loans for the rest. To get the loans we had to supply the bank with a detailed financial plan, and the loans were duly granted. My husband bought a flock of sheep and paid by cheque – which bounced. We then learned that French banks do not immediately credit your account with the loan money; instead, you have to go to the bank with the bill and they release the money to cover that bill only. It goes on like this until you have reached the loan limit.

Q. *How did things work out?*

A. To be honest, although our plans were completely viable, it was a no-no from the start. Although neither of us had been in farming before, we both had country backgrounds and I had worked on farms (with horses), so we weren't completely ignorant. The first year was mainly spent learning from our mistakes – unfortunately, my husband didn't seem to learn much. His idea of farming was swanning around with new machinery and letting the animals look after themselves. He lost interest after the first year when he realised that animals were hard work.

To cut a very long story short, I ended up doing all the work while he went out eating and drinking with his friends. There was no money and life was miserable.

The marriage ended very dramatically and I experienced how the gendarmes handle a 'domestic' – I wasn't impressed.

He stayed at the farm and I found a small house to rent just outside the village. I then started to learn about the French social security system. My ex-husband found he couldn't cope on his own and did a runner a few days before the first divorce hearing in March. He had sold our 18-month-old tractor (without my knowledge) and took the money with him, leaving me with huge debts to pay (as everything was in joint names and as we had no marriage contract, I was liable for everything should he default).

Q. *You had to sell the farm I suppose?*

A. I then had the task of winding up the business, selling the farm and machinery and paying off all the debts. It took me a long time to sell the farm because everyone was waiting for me to be declared bankrupt, then they would have been able to buy it at auction for little more than the total debts. I was amazed that some people actually had the cheek to ask me how much I owed. Time went by with plenty of offers to rent, but none to buy. Then, as if by magic, I suddenly started getting offers. Not magic really, they'd just realised that after two years it was obvious I wasn't going to be declared bankrupt. I ended up with three matching offers and I couldn't decide which one to go for. As none of them would go any higher, I let the SAFER sort it out for me. The farm sold for £5,000 less than we paid for it.

Q. *What happened then?*

A. The next problem was finding a way to earn a living. I was on RMI – *Revenue Minimum d'Insertion*, equivalent to income support. To qualify for RMI, you have to make a contract with a plan for getting back to work – and stick to it. My contract for the first year was to wind the farm up – the social worker recognised I was in no fit state to do anything else.

Towards the end of the year, I started looking for work. Anything would have done (except cleaning – I can't even keep my own house in order) but there were no jobs to be had anywhere. I wasn't surprised at all because there is a reason why property is cheap around here – there is no work. I decided I would really like to train to be a translator, so I asked my social worker if I could take a university degree course. I couldn't. But she did have an idea. She'd heard there was a new headmaster at the local *Collège* (secondary school) who wanted to set up some sort of internet project, maybe he could use me. Internet?! I was a middle-aged technophobe!

Q. *Did you get the job?*

A. I went to see the headmaster and came out with a job. Not a proper job, but a CES (*Contrat Emploi – Solidarité*), a government sponsored get-you-back-to-work type of thing, part time and very low-status. The project was to set up an internet site about the area and I would translate it all into English.

I stayed for two years and thoroughly enjoyed it. The staff were wonderful and I was more or less left to myself to get on with it. While doing this job, I went on a course to learn how to use the computer and another course to brush up on French grammar. Extremely useful stuff and I had the luxury of practical translation experience with no deadlines. This was it, this was what I wanted to do. When my CES finished they asked me to stay on as a CEC (*Contrat Emploi – Consolidé*). This would have given me another three years of work with more hours, but I'd reached a crossroads by this time. I wasn't getting any younger and I'd have been on the scrap heap when the contract finished, so I said no, I was going freelance.

I then did a two-month intensive course at the Chambre de Métiers on setting up in business. I could have done the same course at the Chambre de Commerce which was two weeks shorter, but they skipped the accounting. It was hard work but I thoroughly enjoyed it.

Q. *And what are you doing today?*

A. I live in the same little rented house I moved into temporarily in 1996, I am a struggling freelance translator/interpreter (French to English), and I still have my two horses from the farm. I work during July and August as a receptionist and *régisseur* (responsible for the register and the money) at a camping site owned by a syndicate of communes. I am also a local councillor. I'm broke but happy. Oh yes, I almost forgot, I'm now 50.

So that is my story. I really don't know if it's going to be of any use to you because it's mostly an account of my experiences of ordinary life – stuff which could have happened anywhere, it just happens to be France.

4

What type of property

Old property

The different styles of old property

Great diversity can be found in the rural architecture of France – not only from one *région* to the next, but also within each *région*. Many different building materials are used, the roofs have different pitches and volumes, doors and windows are located in different places (some façades are extremely symmetrical while on others the location of the openings seem very random), and a host of differing decorative features are applied. Despite the different façades and materials used, the basic floor plans tend to be more generic and these plans cross both regional borders and even countries. The plans can often be narrowed down to these categories:

The single roomed house

This was the home of the agricultural worker tied to a large estate, who didn't have any land, equipment or livestock of his own. It consisted of a single room, closer to a square than a rectangle in shape, single-storeyed, with a hearth and oven at one of the gables. The façade, generally in the longer wall, had two simple openings: a doorway and a small window. The entire furnishings would have consisted of a table, benches, beds and a wardrobe. A single family, often a large one, lived there and its loft provided overspill sleeping accommodation. Although the labourer's house usually stood isolated, twin or conjoined houses, or even whole terraces of houses, were not an uncommon sight (good examples can be found in the Orléans *région* and Berry).

These houses sprang up in large numbers during the first half of the 19th Century, in response to a population boom in rural areas. As their tenants acquired smallholdings, a few dependent buildings were added such as barns and wine-cellars, and these turned into small farms. However, the exodus to urban areas in the second half of the 19th Century was to bring about their gradual desertion and today they have almost totally disappeared from the countryside.

Longère

These buildings extend lengthwise along the direction of the roof ridge and have low ceilings and openings along the long walls rather than on the gable walls at the sides. They are mostly found north of the river Loire, particularly in Brittany. This house, built for the smallholder or craftsman, had a simple kitchen with an integrated dining corner, bedroom and small stable.

The earliest agricultural *longère* was a single room shared by both man and beast. Livestock was confined to the end opposite to the hearth and the floor sloped to prevent liquid manure running into the human living area. A wooden partition separated the lower-end stable from the upper-end living room.

The interior layout was rudimentary: a fireplace against the gable wall and an outside oven and a sink was set into the long wall next to the entrance. The furniture consisted of a table, covered or curtained beds, a kneading-trough, a chest (in which clothes and valuable items were put away), a dresser, a wardrobe and benches or chairs (the latter becoming common only after 1850).

Later a barn/stable was attached separately to the building. Eventually this barn/stable became a freestanding building.

Salle haute

The *salle haute* (high rooms) style was a building where living accommodation was confined to the upper floor and the ground floor was used for production and storage. Entry to the upper floor is by an external staircase and landing which are normally set against a long wall and protected by overhanging roof eaves supported by pillars or posts.

Once home to village leaders, wealthy rural tradesmen, artisans such as blacksmiths and vineyard owners, this property fell down the social scale with the advent of the industrial age, and in the first decades of the 19th Century became home to the small peasant. A stable or cow shed and barn was then added to its length. Only a few examples of *salle hautes* still exist in Northern France, but large numbers of this type can be found throughout the rest of the country, notably in wine-growing areas (higher Quercy, the Rhône and the Saône valleys, Touraine, etc.)

The central corridor plan

A typical house of this kind has a façade with its openings symmetrically placed round a central entrance and its elevation rising two, sometimes three, storeys high under the eaves of an imposing roof pierced by dormer windows. Internally, rooms are evenly distributed on either side of a central corridor.

This house was originally built for the upper classes during the Renaissance period but gradually spread to the lower levels of the social hierarchy. It first reached the urban and rural bourgeoisie and then the middle classes in the 18th and 19th centuries, resulting in the *maison de maître*.

The depthwise house with nave and aisles

This house extended in depth (i.e. perpendicularly to the axis of the roof ridge), with a load-bearing structure consisting of pairs of wooden posts supporting trusses, thus forming a nave flanked by two aisles or, more rarely, a single aisle. It contained both dwelling and farming functions under the same roof, sheltering humans, cattle, implements and crops at the same time. Houses with nave and aisles were built to house agricultural tenants, first by aristocratic or ecclesiastical landlords and later by the merchant middle classes.

The earliest surviving examples date back to the 16th Century, the latest to the 19th. Some houses of this style were originally aisled barns belonging to large estates under the Monarchy. This type is encountered in relatively large numbers in the Landes and the Basque country, and in lesser numbers the Agen, Charente, lower Quercy and Lorraine. A few surviving examples are found in Burgundy, Champagne, Berry and Perigord.

Property terms to look out for

If you are looking for an older property you may come across descriptive terms that you were not previously familiar with. Terms such as: *belle demeure, chai, colombage, maison bourgeoise* or *mas*.

A glossary of these terms can be found in the appendices.

Buying an old property

Ruins

When you see a crumbling old barn in a beautiful setting on the market for as little as €15,000, it's very tempting to think that with a bit of time and energy you could turn that property into your dream home. 'A bit of' though is normally a vast understatement. Renovating property is hard enough work in the UK, let alone in a foreign country.

You must, and no doubt you will, take into account how realistic the project is. There may well be a reason why that old cottage halfway up the mountain hasn't been renovated – it may be because it's impossible for any large vehicle to get anywhere near it. If a property is too remote it may be difficult to find a builder or *artisan* (tradesperson) who'll go out of their way.

Do you want the stress?

Extensive building work can cause a lot of stress. Ask yourself:

- Do you want every **holiday** for the next couple (or more) years to be a hard and dirty slog? Surely you'd rather be lounging by the pool of a rented villa than breaking your back lugging slabs of stone and dirt bags around.

- If you have **children**, will they be happy to entertain themselves while you're doing the work?

- Do you have enough **money** – plus a significant sum on the side for the almost inevitable over-run in costs?

- Have you got the **patience** and diplomacy needed for dealing with builders? While some are very reliable, others have a habit of disappearing for days on end or taking three-hour lunch breaks.

- Can you find one enterprise to do the work? if not then a number of different artisans will be needed. Realistically, you cannot **supervise** the building during the odd week or two every few months, you need to be there most of the time. It's impossible to supervise a project that's 400 miles away. Can you afford to employ someone else to supervise the project for you?

When you start house-hunting in France you'll see that there are plenty of half-renovated properties on the market. These are properties that have simply become millstones around their vendor's necks.

But for some, renovation can be very rewarding

Despite highlighting the downsides, there are many people who spot a ruin and go about – much to the bemusement of locals who think they are mad – turning it into a wonderful home. Many of these Francophiles restore French properties more lovingly and sympathetically than the French themselves.

Restoring an old house is a wonderful way to learn, not just about the background of the building, but also about the history of the area that you move into. You'll also learn about the geology of the area as many rural homes built before the mid-19th Century were made from materials close at hand such as timber from local woods, stones cleared from the fields, straw stubble from the recent harvest, or mud and clay. If your home was built from the late 19th Century onwards, it will reflect the growing wealth among the agricultural communities, new materials and transportation of these materials. The opening of quarries, setting up of brickworks and lime-kilns, and the development of railway and waterway transport meant that wider access was gained to materials like fired clay bricks and tiles and quarried slates that had previously been reserved for the richer classes. Half-timbered buildings with their in-fill of a cake of mud, straw and clay began to be replaced by houses built from mass-produced bricks. Coverings of thatch and stone tiles gave way to roofs of slate extracted from quarries. Looking at and getting to know a building is a great way to understand the socio-economy of the people that lived not only in the building, but in the *région*, before you.

For instance, if you buy a cottage on one of Brittany's islands you'll realise what a tough life the first inhabitants there had. Here, where storms reached speeds of up to 185km/h, the tiny cottages with pebble walls were built with small openings to withstand the elements. The chimney could be closed up to keep the wind out. A lack of wood on the islands and a maritime culture meant that very basic lofts were built and these were modelled on the structure of boats. The single entrance door leads to an entrance hall; two identical rooms are on the left and right and a staircase leads into the loft. Renovation work often involves installing windows into the slate roofs to make the rooms lighter.

Restoring an old building will bring you in touch with the whole nature of a place (its geology, climate and socio-economic history) much more than if you were moving into one where the work is completed. It's easy to take a building for granted and forget that it had a life beyond you and your own needs – and will continue to have a life long after you have departed.

Renovating an old property

Renovation or restoration?

Renovation, *restoration* and *historic restoration* are terms that are often confused or carelessly used, but which have very different meanings.

- **Renovation** usually means a team of contractors coming in and covering or replacing anything old or dated, for instance knocking out the old windows and putting in vinyl windows anywhere and everywhere, carpeting drafty old boards, installing a fitted kitchen and covering outside walls with cement. Renovation, means renewing, but does not necessarily mean conserving, or respecting, precious architectural details. Many features that make the property unique and tie it with its past are sadly lost or destroyed through renovation work and cost-cutting quick-fix solutions.

- **Historical restoration** is the polar opposite. Instead of covering it up, the old and dated are explored and revealed. Here, layers of wallpaper and plasterwork are examined to discover original colours and treatments, floorboards are removed and then reinstalled last so they aren't damaged during the work, and old window frames are sanded carefully to the first thin layer of paint so as not to remove any wood.

Unless you don't mind spending evenings reading by candlelight, going to the loo in an outhouse or being subjected to the dangers of lead paint, it is possible to find a balance between renovation and historical restoration.

Simple restoration

Simple restoration is a compromise between saving the old and installing the new. It respects the structure of the house and the materials it is made of. An old house can be restored back to its original architecture, yet still embrace the modern with the installation of electricity, heating, plumbing and even air conditioning. Yes, your house should be a home and not a museum, but with careful planning it can be comfortable and modern while conserving its heritage for future generations to admire and learn from.

When you start house-hunting you'll see many renovated houses in which owners have rushed ahead and imprinted their own idea of 'restoration'. Often they turn their home into a gaudy, Disney-like pastiche of its former self. This is often because they haven't done their homework. Working on old structures necessitates a relearning of skills and a rediscovering of knowledge that has often been lost because, having been replaced by modern building techniques, it's no longer transmitted from builder to builder. Take the time to learn about your building's history. Read books about local architecture and visit local museums. If you act in haste then mistakes could be made that are irreversible.

The best way to learn about your building, and about construction techniques and materials in your area, is to speak to a local historian or a specialist on local vernacular architecture.

Maisons Paysannes de France

A good way of getting in touch with such local enthusiasts is to contact your departmental representatives of *Maisons Paysannes de France*. This organisation was founded in 1965 and has 10,000 members, grouped in 70 delegations across France, who are all passionate about old country houses. Maisons Paysannes de France feel that buildings should be treated like living beings and believe that to respect an old house you must repair without modifying.

Here's some of the advice given on their website:

The façade:

To let in more light you can open one or two picture windows. Never enlarge a window. Instead knock out another close to the first, always at the same height.

The vertical slats of wood that make the shutters should be joined by two or three horizontal bars, a 'Z' shape was hardly ever used.

Do not varnish shutters or add decorative black painted iron features.

Apart from in some areas, your house will detest symmetry. Do not try to force it on the façade.

On the roof:

You wish to convert the attic. Put in one or two skylights, but don't put too many. Think about opening a window in the gables instead . . .

Do not make the surface of the roof too rigid. The old roofs were not perfectly smooth.

On masonry:

As your house is a living entity, you must definitively reject the use of cement in the masonry. This prevents the house from breathing and keeps all the humidity inside.

The organisation also runs short courses (2-5 days) in traditional restoration techniques and on the conservation of rural buildings. These classes are open to professionals, architects and artisans, but also to owners who wish to learn skills applicable to their own projects. Their website gives details about the courses and provides the contact details of representatives in each *département*.

Maisons Paysannes de France

✉ 8, passage des Deux Soeurs, 79009 Paris
☎ +33 (0)1 44 83 63 63
Fax +33 (0)1 44 83 63 69
@ maisons.paysannes@wanadoo.fr, or president@maisons-paysannes.org
⌨ www.maisons-paysannes.org

Architectural heritage in France

Today there are about 41,000 protected monuments in France, of which one third is *classified* and two thirds *inscribed*.

- *Sites classés* – these sites are the most important properties and they can't be altered.
- *Sites Insrits* – modifications of these sites can be made only if *Architectes des Bâtiments de France* (state-employed architects and architectural advisors) are consulted and agree that the plans will not be detrimental to the historical value of the property.

Half of these protected monuments belong to private owners, of which 5,000 are classified as 'castles or manors'. In the past, heritage conservation focused on more 'elite' projects such as castles, palaces and religious monuments. Recently there has been a shift in focus and the importance of conserving examples of domestic vernacular architecture has been realised. Your simple village house could even be a *Monument Historique*!

Monuments Historiques

Around 400 of the 13,000 *Monuments Historiques* are financed by the *Ministère de la Culture et de la Communication*. The state commits itself to the conservation, maintenance and security of these sites. Most of these are open to the public and entrusted to the *Centre des Monuments Nationaux*.
(⌨ www.monum.fr).

Strict regulations affect buildings within a 500 square metre periphery of a *Monument Historique*. These buildings must not be altered without prior permission from the authorities.

ZPPAUP

Other large areas such as city centres and rural landscapes are sometimes designated as *Zone de protection du patrimoine architectural urbain et paysager,* abbreviated to ZPPAUP, (urban and countryside protected heritage zones). These should not to be confused with the *secteurs sauvegardés* (safeguarded sectors) which are ensembles of buildings in the centres of old towns or villages, whose historic character and aesthetic appeal justifies their restoration and protection.

If you think that your property is a *Monument Historique* then you should contact an *Architecte des Bâtiments de France* – a state-employed architect based at your local CAUE (*Conseil d'architecture, d'urbanisme et d'environnement*). Your CAUE will also be able to advise you on any grants available to improve the condition of older properties or to convert properties into tourist accommodation. If your home is in a village of historic interest then you may have a good chance of getting funding. You are also very likely to receive funding if you live in a depopulated *région* where tourism is being encouraged so as to boost the economy and encourage people back into the area.

Anyone can contact CAUE for advice – whether you are seeking to renovate an old building or you are about to build a new property from scratch.

Conseil d'architecture, d'urbanisme et d'environnement (CAUE)

CAUE is an organisation of architects, urban and country planners, economists and ecologists that seeks to enhance our habitats by promoting both modern architecture and a respect for architectural heritage. They also seek to contribute to the quality of the environment. A lot of their work is focused on community projects but they will also freely give advice to individuals and on the quality of the architecture and its impact on the environment.

If you believe your building is one of historical interest and justifies financial aid, or if you wish to convert it into a *projet d'hébergement touristique* (tourist accommodation) such as *gîtes*, *chambre d'hôtes*, *tables d'hôtes* or *fermes auberges*, then CAUE will help you seek funding to make it possible. CAUE will visit the building and evaluate its possibilities and study the feasibility of your intended project. They will help you put together a dossier of information (photos, sketches, plans) and give advice on technical drawing, costs and architecture. They will see whether your property justifies belonging to the criteria *bâti de caractère* (character property).

CAUEs have close working relationships with partners that include:

* *Comité Départemental du Tourisme* (CDT);
* *Relais Départmental de Gîtes de France* (see section on *Gîtes*);
* the departmental and regional cultural institutions SDAP (*Services departmentaux de l'architecture et du Patrimoine*); and
* DRAC (*direction régionale des affaires culturelles*).

CAUEs also get involved in allocating money from the European Union's *Programme pour le Developpement des Zones Rurales* (PDZR).

For your local CAUE address consult the *Federation Nationale des CAUE* website: 🖳 www.fncaue.net

The central office is based at the Ministry of Culture and Communication, which deals with the protection of historic monuments and is at the following address:

Bureau Protection des monuments historiques

✉ 8, rue Vivienne, 75002 Paris, France
☎ +33 (0)1 40 15 80 00
Fax +33 (0)1 40 15 33 33

Looking for funding

When looking for funding you should first of all contact your local *mairie* and your CAUE (discussed above) to find out what funds are available. You might also benefit from *Loi Malraux*, which is a fiscal law that encourages people to renovate older properties in exchange for some fiscal benefits. To apply for this, the property must be of historic or architectural significance or situated in a conservation area. The cost of all renovations and interest on loans are tax deductible and any deficit after deductions can be taken from the tax applicable to the owner's global income. The owner must ensure that the property is only for residential use and is available to be let within twelve months of purchase.

Other heritage organisations

It's worth finding out about the various heritage organisations that offer grants to certain restoration projects. There are all sorts of obscure grants that can be applied for and which aren't widely publicised. Take Europa Nostra for instance.

Europa Nostra

Europa Nostra is a pan-European federation of more than 200 non-governmental heritage organisations. It is also supported by many national, regional and local authorities, cultural and educational bodies, business enterprises and by many individual members. Europa Nostra is presided over by HRH the Prince Consort of Denmark.

Each year, the federation hands out a prize to help restore part of a historic monument or to rescue a well known architectural or historical site that is in peril. Each year a different theme is announced. Recent annual prizes have gone to the restoration of an endangered orangery in Finland, restoration of 16th Century decorative plasterwork in a Czech castle and restoration of a decorative rococo ceiling in a Dublin convent. There are no restrictions on the type of owner who can apply, but the properties must be period properties.

Europa Nostra

✉   Lange Voorhout 35, 2514 EC The Hague, The Nederlands
☎   +31 70 302 40 51/55/57
Fax +31 70 361 78 65
@   office@europanostra.org
🖥   www.europanostra.org

For further advice on your restoration work you could even try contacting experts at colleges that specialise in teaching architectural heritage and traditional skills. You never know – you may get lucky and they could send a team of volunteers to work on your place! It may even be worth getting involved in volunteer projects yourself, as a way of learning more about French architecture (and a chance to do something worthy).

École d'Avignon

The *École d'Avignon* trains students to link the traditional building methods of old structures with the adaption of a building to modern needs. They explain:

"Quite different from pure restoration, here the economic framework, as well as the future uses of structures, become important criteria. For each site, the ideal solution must tie the essence of the old structure with its new life."

The *École d'Avignon* works toward this goal as project consultant, and provides on-site training in France and abroad. The school participates in study missions for the French Ministry of Culture, for the Provence-Alpes-Cotes-d'Azur *région* and for a number of international organisations such as the European Council, UNESCO and ICOMOS.

It also provides short training courses such as:

- decorative painting.
- painting with lime.
- preservation of window frames; and
- restoration of iron-work.

A three day course on general heritage building skills costs €330. These courses are mainly attended by professionals such as builders and architects, although some are open to all.

In 2005, after numerous demands from English-speaking individuals, it introduced its first course in English – a five day course in traditional lime renderings and washes.

École d'Avignon

✉ 6, rue Grivolas, 84000 Avignon, France
☎ +33 (0)4 90 85 59 82
Fax +33 (0)4 90 27 05 18
@ contact@ecole-avignon.com
💻 www.ecole-avignon.com

Centre de Hautes Etudes de Chaillot (C.H.E.C.)

This important school offers students two year courses in restoration and renovation. The courses are at an advanced level and targeted at those who already have some background in architecture. The school trains many of the architects and urbanists that go on to work for CAUE.

Centre de Hautes Etudes de Chaillot (C.H.E.C.)

✉ Palais de Chaillot -1, Place du Trocadéro – 75116 Paris, France
☎ +33 (0)1 47 04 39 88
Fax +33 (0)1 47 55 17 16
💻 www.archi.fr/CHEC/

Patrimoine Architectural Rural: Techniques Identification Restauration (Le Centre PARTIR)

This organisation, created in 1996, trains architectural students in restoration and renovation and is composed of architects, craftsmen, local and regional development agents, and all those who value architectural heritage. They run various courses in heritage, for example there's a course on the identification of old buildings and one on how to recommend which buildings should be titled as *monuments historiques*.

Centre Européen de Formation PARTIR

✉ 118 – 128 avenue Jean Jaurès, 75019 Paris, France
☎ +33 (0)153 72 84 54
@ centrepartir@9online.fr
💻 www.centre-partir.com

REMPART

REMPART– a federation of 170 local French associations – is an organisation that brings together teams of volunteers and co-ordinates restoration projects and training. During the last four decades its volunteers have restored 600 monuments. These monuments, which cover all epochs, include:

- military buildings (forts and towers);
- religious buildings (chapels, churches, monastries and priories);
- domestic and civilian (hamlets, farms, barns, habitats, troglodytes, mills; wash-houses and fountains);
- industrial buildings (railways, lime ovens, tileries, forges and laundries); and
- natural and planned landscapes (terraces and historic gardens).

One of the organisation's principal objectives is to study archaeological works and publish the research for use by professionals such as archaeologists, historians and scientists, as well as the larger public. They also open sites to the public and organise museum exhibitions, and develop educational activities.

Their mission is not only to safeguard and to restore but also to bring a building back into use: a medieval ruin becomes a place of spectacle, a rural house is transformed into a *gîte*, or a museum is installed in an old mill.

REMPART

✉ 1, rue des Guillemites, 75004 Paris, France
☎ +33 (0)1 42 71 96 55
Fax +33 (0)1 42 71 73 00
@ contact@rempart.com
💻 www.rempart.com

Demeure Historique

This organisation is for owners of private historic monuments. As explained earlier, half of the protected monuments belong to private owners, of which 5,000 are classified as 'castles or manors'. Just over half these private owners are members of the *Demure Historique*. More than a thousand are open to the public and welcome more than seven million visitors a year.

Founded in 1924 by Doctor Joachim Carvallo, creator of the Gardens of Villandry, the Demeure Historique was acknowledged as a public utility in 1965. It is one of the oldest associations for the defence of French heritage and is managed by volunteers. Demeure Historique members open their buildings to the public on the third weekend of September. For this simple inconvenience owners are exonerated of inheritance tax. Any money made at the openings goes to help continue raising awareness of the properties. As well as tax exemption, owners are also given support and advice on insurance, security, and maintenance. It's certainly a benefit to the owners and well worth considering if you don't have any moral qualms about your heirs not paying the tax that those who live in much less beautiful surroundings must pay. *Perhaps we should all lobby to open our homes (even if it's a 1990s kit house) to the public so as to benefit from this scheme!*

Demeure Historique

⊠   Hôtel de Nesmond, 57, quai de la Tournelle, 75005 Paris, France
☎   +33 (0)1 55 42 60 00
Fax   +33 (0)1 43 29 36 44
@   contact@demeure-historique.org
▭   www.demeure-historique.org

Vieilles Maisons Françaises (VMF)

Founded in 1953, VMF promotes the preservation and restoration of historical buildings and also promotes the training of craftsmen in traditional building and restoration skills. The association has 18,000 members in France, and 95 local delegates (all *départements* are represented). The association publishes a magazine to promote historic houses (mainly prestigious castles and *chateaux*) and offers free consulting services to members (4,000 of which own property on the Historic Monuments list) on fiscal issues, restoration, property security and insurance. The association also lobbies the government for the preservation of old historical buildings and their surroundings.

VMF also has a directory of prestigious French property for rent for film shoots, a picture library and they give an annual prize (funded by corporate sponsorship) to reward an exceptional restoration.

VMF

⊠   1, chemin de Pirey – 25000 Besançon, France
☎   +33 (0)3 81 80 94 44
Fax +33 (0)3 81 80 94 29
@   hc.cellule-vol-vmf@wanadoo.fr
💻   www.vmf.net

Subsidies for modernisation of property

Agence Nationale pour L'Amelioration de l'Habitat (ANAH)

Government organisation ANAH provides grants to improve security, comfort and sanitation of properties. It helps with updating equipment, adapting properties for those with disabilities and also contributes to the costs of improving heating and noise insulation. ANAH provides owners with up to 20% of the cost of works up to €13,500. An ANAH office will be situated at your local *Directions Départementales de l'Equipement* (DDE).

Any additional costs that you can't afford can be met by interest free loans (*Prêt 0%*). Find out from your DDE whether you qualify.

In 2003, the French Building Federation (*La Fédération Française du Bâtiment*) and ANAH presented results of research into the average cost of the most common improvements that ANAH contributes to.

Here are their findings:

- Replacement of **façade coating**: €34.6 per m²
- Replacement of **exterior joinery**: €437.4 per m²
- Heating **insulation**: €27.1 per m²
- Installation of a **washbasin**: €202.2
- Installation of a **toilet**: €311.5
- Installation of **gas central heating**: €4,515.6

These are just average costs (that do not include tax) and can vary from *région* to *région*.

Agence Nationale pour L'Amelioration de l'Habitat

💻 www.anah.fr

New property

When you buy a property that's less than ten years old, you must make sure that the previous owner has kept an *assurance dommage-ouvrage* – a ten-year building insurance. Your *notaire* must obtain copies of the insurance policies, and following signature of the *acte de vente* you can decide whether you want to keep with these policies or terminate them.

With a property that has only recently been built, the *notaire* will check that the *certificat de conformité* has been delivered. This certificate confirms that the property has complied with local planning permission and that the final building conforms to the plans which enabled it to be given a *permis de construire* (building permit). Do not buy a property that does not have a *certificat de conformité*.

The ultimate in buying *new* is to buy a property *sur plan*.

Buying off-plan (*sur plan*)

If you are a complete DIY-phobe and like the idea of a brand new home already furnished to your taste before you even first walk over the threshold, then buying a property *sur plan* (one that is yet to be built or completed) is for you.

Ideal for retirement or second homes

Many of these developments tend to be in a good position, such as on the coast, in the mountains or next to a golf course and so make ideal holiday homes. They are also ideal for retired people who are looking for a good quality of life. Often they have a shared swimming pool and well-kept landscaped gardens maintained by an appointed management company (*Syndic de Copropriété*). So apart from paying contributions to the upkeep, you don't have to worry about weeding and mowing grass or cleaning pools – which is especially convenient if it's a second home.

Houses and apartments bought *sur plan* are often built to high specification with superb insulation, ventilation and security. Building in France is strictly regulated and most new properties must be covered by a ten-year warranty against structural defects while other systems and equipment have a minimum two-year warranty. Before signing anything ask to see a copy of the *assurance dommage-ouvrage*, an insurance policy which covers any serious damage that occurs in the ten years following its completion.

What's included

New homes are delivered 'ready to move in' with standard specifications including a fitted bathroom, floor and wall coverings and electric heating.

Smaller properties may include a fitted kitchen corner (sink, hob, fridge and unit) whereas in larger properties, the fitting of the kitchen units and appliances is normally left to the purchaser to arrange. Plumbing and electrics are provided in the kitchen. The choice of decor tends to be limited and neutral. Buyers get a choice of wall colour, tiles and carpets. Buying early often means more flexibility with the decor, and with more expensive properties there is normally more choice.

Schedule of payment

Properties tend to be sold six to eight months before construction begins. Payment is conducted in stages as the building work progresses. The payment schedule will be predefined and detailed in the contract. The developer cannot ask for any more money than is stipulated in this contract. In general you will pay 5% deposit followed by 30% once the foundations have been laid, with the remaining payments following at different stages of completion. The local independent *bureau de control* should provide you with confirmation that the appropriate stage has been reached before you make each payment. Some developers will not ask for stage payments, but will ask for money on completion, instead charging an additional amount of around 3% to take into account the fact that you have had the use of your money rather than them.

Contracts

The *acte de vente* or completion papers are normally signed once the foundations are laid. A firm completion date should be laid out in the contract – although this is usually not a specific day but a quarter. Buyers have to accept that setbacks could occur such as bad weather or problems with subcontractors delaying proceedings. In the south of France delivery problems can be caused because the scale of new building works means that there are not enough plumbers, tilers, electricians, etc to go round. Building in the Alps is prone to delays because of severe weather conditions. In recent years building has stopped in many Alpine towns as planning permission has become necessarily more stringent. Development in and around Les Gets for instance has been prevented for three years because there is not enough drinking water to support an enlarged community.

 Warning: Check that the developer has obtained planning permission before committing to a property, otherwise you could expect a frustrating delay.

If building work hasn't started within two years of the reservation contract being signed then the contract is declared null. To avoid frustration ask a solicitor to incorporate a delay and compensation clause in your contract, so that after the two years is up you are not left with completely empty dreams.

There are financial advantages to buying new such as less property tax and because the *notaire* doesn't have to get involved in examining the history of the property lower conveyancing charges. New properties are also popular with investors because they are often highly rentable and need nothing done in the way of refurbishment. Once a property is five years old the legal fees jump up, although there is a good market in re-sales.

 Warning: **Be cautious if a development is already built and largely unsold as there could be something wrong with it.**

Some people might find the wait (anything up to two years) for a property bought off-plan frustrating. It can also be daunting buying a property you haven't even seen. Try asking an agent who is more accustomed to looking at plans, which house or apartment is best. It is much better to be one of the first buyers on a development as there is then more choice and sometimes there's a chance of better pricing. The price often goes up as the developer sells more. It's important not to be taken in by the glossy brochures alone so visit the show flat and also look at other developments completed by the same builder. It's a good idea to visit the site in order to get a feel for the surroundings.

Most new property in France is sold in this way and as it is highly regulated; it is certainly not an option to be afraid of.

New development contacts:

Propriété 'Direct' France

Specialises in new developments in *Paris, Côte d'Azur* and golf resorts.

⊠ 72 rue du Faubourg St. Honore, 75008 Paris, France
☎ +33 (0)1 40 07 86 25
Fax +33 (0)1 40 07 80 40
@ pdf@wanadoo.fr
▱ www.pdfparis.com

Apartments (*copropriété*)

All apartments in France are sold freehold and buying one means that you'll own the interior volume of the property and also a share in the building or group of buildings in which it is situated. This share of the property is called *quote-part des parties communes* and includes elements of the building's structure (exterior walls, roofs), and common areas (corridors, landings, green spaces, lifts). Each owner, called a *copropriétaire*, has an interest in the building's upkeep and in keeping the harmony of the *copropriété* (the group of *copropriétaires*).

If you are buying an apartment check that the roofs, façades, lifts and common equipment such as heating, are in good condition. Beware of impressive entry halls, common gardens, concierges, fountains etc., as these can greatly increase monthly communal costs. Find out what works are to be done in the short term, as you may be obliged to participate in financing them. Has major building work been programmed for the future? (The cost of putting in an elevator, a new roof or a new façade is shared by all the co-owners.)

Collectively the *copropriétaires* belong to a syndicate known as a *syndicat de copropriété*. The members meet each year at an *assemblée generale* (general assembly) where they discuss and vote on various issues, decide which works need to be carried out and agree on their budget.

Management of the building

The *syndicat de copropriété* employs an individual or agency known as a *syndic professionnel* to manage the building. This professional will hold a card called a *gestion immobilière* which means that they are registered to do such work and are permitted to handle the sums paid in by the *copropriétaires*. If they disappear with your money or become bankrupt, then their third party civil and professional insurance will kick in and their financial institution will step in to complete the work. A contract (*contrat de syndic*) is drawn up between the *syndic* and the *syndicat des copropriétaires*. The *syndic* is given a three year maximum mandate (*mandat*) that the *coproprietaires* can renew for a further three years if they so wish.

In some circumstances, particularly when the building is so small that it is not economical to employ a professional, one of the *copropriétaires* can take on this managing and administrative role. Such a person is called a *syndic non professionnel*. They don't have to subscribe to third party insurance, although it's in their interest to, and the fees of this insurance will normally be paid by the *syndicat de copropriété*.

Responsibilities of the syndic

The *syndic's* mission is to execute any decisions put forth by the *assemblée generale*. The *syndic* also:

- administers **repairs** to the building;
- sees that **urgent works** are carried out;
- makes sure **water, electricity and gas** is provided;
- makes sure that the building **insurance** is in place;
- **recruit and manage personnel** such as caretakers, gardeners, etc;
- check that all **work is of good order** and that invoices are correct;
- ensure that **charges** are recovered from each *copropriétaire*;
- represent the *syndicat de copropropriété* in **court** if need be.

Since 1st June 2001, it has been law that the *syndicat* must establish and keep a notebook recording all **maintenance** that takes place in the building (this is called the *carnet d'entretien* and it is the responsibility of the *syndic* to keep it up to date).

The *syndic* is charged with establishing a provisional budget (*budget prévisionnel du syndicat*), which is limited to day-to-day maintenance and running expenses of the building. The budget is prepared by the *syndic* and voted by *syndicat* at the *assemblée generale*. The *syndic* must set up a bank or postal account in the name of the *syndicat* in which to keep this shared money.

On average each *lot de copropriété* (each apartment) must pay between €91,47 and €198,18 per year for the services of a *syndic*. Although, the larger the *copropriété,* the cheaper it will be.

A *conseil syndical*, composed of elected *copropriétaires*, assists and controls the *syndic* in its management throughout the year. The *syndicat* also votes for a *président*, who will overlook and lead the *assemblée generale* and liaise between the *syndic* and the *copropriétaires*. The *président* assists the *syndic* and controls the management and accountability of the *syndicat*, but has no judgement, no power to decide, nor capacity to take judicial action.

The *syndic* is obliged to consult the *conseil syndical* on any contracts of expensive works to be done that haven't featured in the budget. The written advice of the *conseil syndical* is notified to the *copropriétaires*.

 Note: When you buy a *copropriété* make sure you keep aside some money for major works that come up, especially any unexpected works.

It's sometimes possible to pay your share of a bill for major works over a period of ten years, although this is subject to interest. You are obliged to participate in financing the management and repairs of all the building, but remember that these payments will be on top of your mortgage and such expenses can make owning an apartment even more expensive than being a tenant.

Annual meeting between owners

The *assemblée générale* meets once a year and is representative of all the *copropriétaires*. Everyone has a right to participate and it is in each person's interest to do so.

You must be informed of the date, location and time of the meeting by letter at least fifteen days before. In principle it is the *syndic* that organises it and sends out the letter. The questions and order of the day will be asked for and notified by the *syndic*. The letter will also indicate what will be on the agenda. Owners who wish to place their own items on the agenda must notify the person organising the meeting before six days of it taking place. Then the organiser will notify the *copropriétaires* of these extra issues and questions, by letter, five days before the date of the meeting. Questions must be precise, and directed so that either a positive or negative vote can be called.

If you cannot make the meeting it is possible to give a mandate to someone – either another *copropriétaire* or an outsider – to represent and vote for you (*un pouvoir en blanc*). One person cannot represent more than three *copropriétaires*. You cannot choose the *syndic* or anyone related to this *syndic* to represent you.

The *syndic* assumes the function of *secretaire de séance*, writing down the verbal process and taking a list of all present. The verbal process is authentified by the signature of the president of the assembly and a transcript is registered and kept in the office of the *syndic*. The *syndic* must notify the *copropriété* of the decision of the *assemblée générale*, normally by a copy of this transcript, within two months. Decisions taken in relation to management and works of the building are abridged and posted in a communal area.

If a *copropriétaire* strongly objects to a decision made at the meeting, it is possible to have a *tribunal de grande instance*, whereby a lawyer can be asked to intervene.

How charges are divided between apartments

In some circumstances, when apartments are of equal size, then charges can be split equally. For instance, ten apartments would each have to pay one-tenth of all bills.

Not all buildings are so uniform. When a studio is next door to a three-bedroom apartment, it's only fair that the bachelor girl or boy living in the former will not have to pay the same amount as the neighbouring family of six. The latter will inevitably consume more hot water, use the lift six times as much and will add extra wear and tear to all communal spaces.

Normally, those living on the ground floor do not have to pay towards the maintenance and upkeep of lifts. Inhabitants of the top floors will have to pay proportionately more towards the maintenance of lifts than those on the lower floors, as they will be consuming more electricity to reach their level.

When you buy a *copropriété* you will be given a descriptive state of your particular lot which will include your *tantième*, a percentage of the entire building which is worked out as a proportion of 1,000 or in some cases 10,000. Your *tantième* will enable you to work out your *quote-part* share in the property and the proportion of the amount of the charges you have to pay.

An example of charges for a building owned by four *copropriétaires*:

Example taken from *lemoneymag.fr*:

Lot 1: *un local à usage commercial situé au rez-de-chaussée du bâtiment et comprenant une boutique avec vitrine, une arrière-boutique et une réserve. Est attachée à ce lot une quote-part de 2554/10,000.*

Lot 1: commercial premises situated on the ground floor of a building, comprising of a shop with a shop front window, a back-shop and a stock room. Attached to this lot is a share of 2554/10,000.

Lot 2: *un appartement d'habitation situé au 1er étage et comprenant une entrée, un séjour donnant sur un balcon, deux chambres, une cuisine, une salle de bains et des toilettes indépendantes. Est attachée à ce lot une quote-part de 2678/10,000.*

Lot 2: a residential apartment situated on the first floor that includes a hallway, a sitting room opening onto a balcony, two bedrooms, a kitchen, a bathroom and separate toilet. Attached to this lot is a share of 2678/10,000.

Lot 3: *un appartement de cinq pièces situé au deuxième étage du bâtiment et comprenant une entrée, un séjour, un bureau, deux chambres et une cuisine, une salle de bains, des toilettes indépendantes. Est attachée à ce lot une quote-part de parties communes à hauteur de 2678/10,000.*

Lot 3: a five room apartment situated on the second floor of the building and comprising a hallway, sitting room, study, two bedroms, a kitchen, a bathroom, and independent toilet. Attached to this is a share of the higher communal parts of 2678/10,000.

Lot 4: *un appartement de trois pièces situé au troisième et dernier étage du bâtiment et comprenant, outre la pièce principale, deux chambres, une salle d'eau avec toilettes, une entrée, une penderie. A ce lot est attachée une quote-part de parties communes à hauteur de 1257/10,000.*

Lot 4: an apartment of three rooms situated at the third and top floor of the building and comprising, other than the principal room, two bedrooms, a shower room with toilet, a hallway, a wardrobe. To this lot is attached a share of higher communal parts 1257/10,000.

Total: 10,000 / 10,000e

Clearly an A-level in maths will give you an advantage here!

The proportion that you pay is relative to the proportion of your value of your *tantième*. The higher your *tantième*, the more weight your vote will have at the *assemblée generale*. The value of your *tantième* is equal to the value of your vote. It's not an equal vote for each owner and those with larger apartments will have more push than the owners of studios in the block. So, rather than counting raised hands at a general assembly, the *tantièmes* are all added together.

Example of weighted voting at the *assemblée generale*

Here's how a simple majority decision is decided:

The total voices will be 1000/1000.

- Those present and represented at the meeting: 600/1000
- Those abstaining from voting: 150/1000
- Voting for: 250/1000
- Voting against: 200/1000
- Majority required (450/2) +1 = 226/1000
- The decision is adopted

Le Réglement de Copropriété

The vendor or *notaire* will provide you with information called *le reglement de copropriété* when you are in the process of buying the property. Not only will it tell you the size of your *quote-part* and the surface area of your apartment (see below), but it will lay down the rights and obligations of each *copropriétaire*, and determine the way private and public areas of the communes are used.

Here's some typical rules:

- No bikes in the hallways.
- No barbeques on the communal gardens unless permission is sought from other *copropriétaires*.
- No football on the staircases.
- No laundry hanging from the balconies.
- Professional activity is not permitted.
- Do not park your car in the access ways.
- Only park your car in your allocated space.
- Keep noise levels low.
- If you rent out your apartment you must inform your lodger or tenant of these rules. You will be responsible for any trouble your lodger or tenant causes.

Some syndicates can be more draconian than others. It's a good idea to meet your neighbours before committing to an apartment. Your idea of having a couple of friends over and playing a few records could be the grumpy sociopath with his ear to the wall's idea of a late night rave.

The area of your *copropriété*

The area (excluding cellars and garages) of which it is at least equal to $8m^2$ must obligatorily figure in the *avant-contrat* and the *acte authentique* (explained later).

If the area (*superficie*) isn't mentioned in the *acte de vente* the buyer can ask for the *acte* to be annulled, or if it isn't mentioned within a month of signing the *avant-contrat* can demand that the *avant-contrat* is annulled without waiting for the *acte de vente*.

A law, called *Loi Carrez*, rules that if the real area turns out to be smaller by more than 5% of the area figure indicated in the *acte*, the buyer can, within a maximum of one year, ask a judge to intervene and lower the price according to the number of m^2 missing.

For example, an *acte de vente* says that the surface area of the apartment for sale at €150,000 is $100m^2$. The area is then measured and it's found to be $94m^2$. The buyer has the right to ask for the price to be lowered by 6% which is equal to – €9000. If the area measures 95 m² then the price can't be lowered.

The calculation of the floor space excludes separating walls, stairs, terraces and balconies as well as any floor space that has a ceiling lower than 1.80 metres. So, an *apartment de charme* (a name given to a bijou flat with lots of character) which has slanted ceilings, a mezzanine, a staircase etc., which is 60 m², might actually be only 30 m² according to the *Loi Carrez*.

The *Loi Carrez* does not apply to houses or lots of less than 8 m².

Other information to feature in the acte de vente

Other details that must be indicated in your *acte de vente* include a declaration if termites, lead pipes and paint (present in certain areas) and asbestos, especially in false ceilings is known to be present. If there's been a test for the presence of these in the previous three years the *notaire* must make the results known to the buyer. This is explained later in the section on conveyancing.

A *copropriété*-owned building that is more than fifteen years old must have a report of good health (regarding the solidity of walls, roofs, pipes, etc.) known as a *diagnostic technique*.

If the property has natural gas installed, then a servicing of the installation (*le diagnostic de l'installation de gaz*) should have been established in less than a year of the *acte-authentique*.

Before writing up the *acte de vente* the *notaire* will tell you the eventual payments the new owner can expect and the levels of charges that you have to support as new *copropriétaire*.

Prior to signing an *avant-contrat* you can ask the owner about charges of at least the last two years in order to evaluate what you'll be encumbered with. You can get the transcripts of at least the last three *assemblées generales* in order to find out what sort of work is envisaged. It is sometimes possible to make an agreement with the vendor that they will pay for any near future works after the sale. The *syndicat* is not against this sort of arrangement, but it is up to you to go back to the vendor when the time comes to obtain reimbursement of the sums they engaged to pay.

 Tip: Ask the owner to show you the *carnet d'entretien* which will detail all previous works.

The *carnet d'entretien* must contain the address of the building, the identity of the *syndic*, and information on the insurance policies. It will give you the date that payment was made for works and maintenance, the year works took place, the identity of the enterprises that carried out the work, the references of the *contracts d'assurance dommages-ouvrage*, the maintenance contracts of the communal equipment and an indication of their guarantees.

If one exists, ask to see the date schedule of work planned by the *assemblée générale*.

Summary

Prior to signing the *avant-contrat*, ask the *agent immobilier, notaire* or owner to provide you with the following:

- The *Reglement de Copropriété*.

- The amount of charges paid over the former year.

- The date when future funds will be collected.

- Transcripts of the last three general assemblies.

- The last provisional budget.

A useful website – set up by the government to aid *copropriétaires* in difficulty – is www.coproprietes.org.

Shared ownership (*bi-propriété*)

Many people consider buying property with friends or family. Sharing a property (known as *bi-propriété*) is a chance to have access to a property that you would not otherwise be able to afford on your own.

There is no limit to the number of people that can share a property but in order to limit the likelihood of disputes fewer shares is better than more. Any more than say four or five individuals or couples means that if you plan to divide the occupation between you throughout the year, then you'll each have less time to spend in the property. If you're exceptionally close, get on well and the property is large enough (and you agree not to argue about who gets the ensuite bedroom with the terrace and views) then you'll probably be able to spend holidays together. This would be the utopian scenario – but it's more likely that you'll start getting on each others nerves after the first day and spend the rest of the time door slamming.

Another option is to start a co-operative – whereby you get some land with a number of buildings and you and your friends occupy different parts. This is good because you'll each have your own private space and there'll be no limitations on time spent at the property. You could also consider buying a large house to share and dividing it into separate living quarters. Be careful as large French houses are very expensive to maintain, especially to heat, during the cooler months.

Bi-propriété is a much better idea than timeshare (although it demands a much larger sum up front, especially if only a few of you are sharing) because you can always make money on the property's equity.

Forming an SCI

If you are considering sharing a property with friends or family it is very important to consider how the property is to be owned prior to looking. The best idea is to form an SCI (*Société Civile Immobilière*) which is a French property-owning company. Members of an SCI own shares in the company rather than shares in the property. This arrangement helps owners to avoid the problems of inheritance (explained later in more detail). It's not mandatory that owners have equal shares. If one owner wishes to sell then they must give the others first refusal. If the others refuse and a new owner can't be found then the property must be sold.

Sources of possible disputes

After the initial excitement of buying with friends has died down, it's wise to consider the possible problems that might arise.

- **Decor** – much to your distaste one of your fellow sharers insists on putting teddy bears on the bed or their collection of antique thimbles on the shelves and one of their kids puts up posters of the latest teen idol all over a bedroom wall. Perhaps it's a good idea to agree on neutral colours and no personal knick-knacks.

- **Cleanliness** – the sharers that stayed the weeks before you have left the place a complete tip. Think about hiring a cleaner.

- **Heating** – if you're staying in the summer do you have to share the expense of the very high heating bill of those that stayed in the winter?

- **Works** – you think the window frames could do with a lick of paint but everyone else is too strapped for cash and thinks it can wait a few years. Perhaps you should all consider putting a sum of money into a joint fund to cover costs.

- **Selling up** – what happens when you want to sell up but the others aren't so keen. Do you know plenty of people interested in buying your share?

- **Time allocation** – if a group of sharers all have children then it's likely that you'll all need the property at the same time – during the school holidays. How can you work this out?

- **Renting** – one of you wants to make some extra income from renting your portion of time at the property but the rest aren't happy about having strangers coming into the house. Agree on whether sub-letting is permissible from the start.

How will all this be co-ordinated?

One of the biggest problems will be finding the property in the first place. Who co-ordinates it all? Just organising a holiday with friends can be a headache . . . but finding a property! You may think you share the same taste with your friends but differences will soon emerge when you're working so closely together. Do you all go to view the properties together. The best idea would be for one of you to find a property and then sell the shares in it afterwards. By doing this you are of course inadvertently setting yourself up as being the chief co-ordinator if anything goes wrong. You could begin to resent the other owners for not putting in as much effort as yourself.

Outsourcing co-ordination

If you find you don't have the time or patience to co-ordinate it all, but the idea still appeals to you, or perhaps you don't know any potential sharers, then it could be worth contacting *The OwnerGroups Company*. This company, based in the UK, works at bringing people together to form groups to buy not only property, but also planes, boats and cars. It finds a small number of people with similar requirements and puts together a detailed agreement between them as to what it is they actually want and how they want the group to work, before any specific property or asset is considered. An agreement is set up between the members which is unique to each group and is called the Shareholder's Syndicate Agreement. This agreement ensures that every member of the group has his or her rights fully protected, and that the mutual obligations of the members are fully understood, before significant amounts of money change hands.

Once a legally binding framework has been put together for the group, the company goes out and finds what they are looking for, then sorts out all the purchase paperwork for the group. They also help run the group – from accounts and maintenance right through to running a time allocation system to ensure its use is shared out fairly. If, after a couple of years, the group decides they no longer need the company's involvement and can manage the property on their own then they are free to do so. The company does not at any stage own any equity in the property, the property is entirely owned by the group.

Groups that have already independently formed can also use The OwnerGroups Company to act as their agent to acquire property. This scheme can also provide existing property owners the opportunity to release capital from their property, by selling shares. This is ideal for owners whose circumstances have changed and they do not spend as much time at the property as they used to yet are too attached to it to sell up completely.

Examples from The OwnerGroups Company

Here are some examples of shares on offer by groups put together or represented by The OwnerGroups Company:

- **For £30,000**: A share in a 3-4 bedroom cottage on the coast near Brest in Brittany. Four current member couples are looking for a fifth owner. Each owner has a 20% share in the property, giving each ten weeks usage a year.

- **For £100,000**: A one-sixth share in a luxury 3-bed villa with a pool on the Cotes d'Azur close to St Tropez. The share price is equivalent to buying a small apartment there. Owners of this share will get nine weeks use of the property each year. The annual running cost (which includes utilities, taxes, staff costs, a reserve fund for maintenance), is expected to be £10,000. This works out at £1,700 per member per year (at £140 monthly this seems quite a lot, but the company asks potential buyers to compare this figure to that which similar properties are rented out – £1,400 per week high season, £900 low season).

The OwnerGroups Company

✉ The Barn, Hill Farm Road, Marlow Bottom, Bucks, SL7 3LX
☎ +44 (0)1628 486 350
Fax +44 (0)1628 486350
@ info@ownergroups.com
💻 www.ownergroups.com

Timeshares

When most of us think of timeshares, we think of sun-baked Brits on the Spanish Costas snared by Del-boy type geezers who bully them into forking out thousands for a week on a building site in the middle of winter. Despite the odd tout with dodgy products still chancing it here and there, and a number of constantly evolving scams to be on the alert for, the timeshare industry is today very tightly regulated and most potential buyers have wisened up to the hard sell techniques. If you're careful, timeshare is potentially a great idea.

 Note: Timeshare, known as *multipropriété* or *résidence en temps partagé* is not the same as buying a property.

You are not the owner or even the joint owner of that property, you simply have the right to stay there on a certain week for anywhere between 3 and 99 years. You are not buying the bricks and mortar and you will in no way benefit from the property increasing in value. A timeshare is not a good financial investment in the way that buying property is. You can resell your timeshare but it's unlikely you'll make a profit on it. Also, timeshares are very difficult to resell. As the Timeshare Consumer Organisation points out:

"Very few owners have made a profit out of a timeshare – and certainly none of those who bought at highly inflated prices from hard-sell developers. There are a great many good reasons for buying a timeshare – but financial investment is definitely not one of them."

The attractions of timeshares

Having said all this, timeshares can be a good idea, especially for many people who dream of owning a property abroad but cannot afford to. The majority of timeshares are on well-kept resorts with good facilities such as swimming pools, bars, restaurants, tennis courts or golf courses. Each year you pay a small fee to a management company that takes care of the property, so you can be assured that the leisure facilities and accommodation are kept in good condition.

Timeshare owners tend to treat the apartments or villas with much greater care than renters and so furniture and fittings are often of a higher standard than that usually found in other self-catering accommodation. Crystal glass, sophisticated kitchen equipment and fine fabrics often help to create a luxurious living environment. You also don't have to worry about finding your way there as you do on other holidays and there's the potential of forming close friendships with the other people who have a week at the resort at the same time as you. You'll get to see familiar faces and your children will find friends that they can meet up and play with every year.

Costs of timeshares

It costs between £1,000 and £2,000 to construct a week of timeshare – including the land, infrastructure and leisure facilities shared between all the weeks on the resort. So, allowing for reasonable marketing costs and profit, a week would be expected to sell for between £2,000 and £3,000 – which is the price range in which most owners eventually resell. It will cost more if your date is during the high season – Christmas, New Year, summer and school holidays. A week in a winter sports resort will cost more in February than May.

Example timeshare prices

Here are some examples of French timeshares recently seen on the market:

- **Paris** – a classic suite for two people lasting twenty years in *la résidence Paris, rue de Berri*, in the *8th arrondissement*. €14,787,55 (€739,38 each year).
- **Saint-Tropez** – a bungalow that sleeps four people, for eighteen years. €6,860,21, (€293,88 each year).

Timeshares are cheaper in less prestigious areas and it's easier to find bargains if you go directly to a resale broker rather than to a new developer. Some of these brokers offer timeshares by people that need a quick sale. Responsible resale brokers charge a commission (generally between 15% and 25%) to the vendor only after a sale is made and do not take any form of up-front fee for their resale service. Avoid any resale broker who asks for a 'listing' or 'registration' fee or any other form of advance payment.

Timeshare exchange

Timeshares are often perceived as potential millstones and it's widely thought that owners are stuck visiting the same property year after endless year, long after the novelty's worn off. This is not true as most timeshare owners belong to exchange schemes giving them the chance to swap their week for other weeks in property all over the world. A week skiing in Meribel can be exchanged with a week in places as far-flung as, for example, Hawaii, Mexico or Las Vegas.

Of course, exchanges need to be of equivalent value in terms of the size of living unit, the season (whether high, medium or low) and availability. A week bought in July on the Côte d'Azur will be more easily exchangeable against a week in Miami, than a week bought in November in le Finistère. Owners can also rent out their week or take up a rental of a week at another resort. They can also choose to visit their own timeshare on a different week. Another advantage of these schemes is that they give owners the security that the foreign resort will be to a similar standard to their own resort.

The two largest exchange companies are *RCI* and *II* (who together have over 2.7 million adherents across the world). Each charge around £75 a year for membership, but two or three free years may come as part of the initial timeshare purchase price. On top of this is an exchange fee, ranging from £50 to £300. Owners still have to pay their own management fees. Sometimes there is the incentive of free use of a week in a resort somewhere else in the world – or even in your own resort at a different time of the year.

Note: **Once all these figures are tallied together then a timeshare is not necessarily cheaper than many of the last minute deals that can easily be found (especially outside the school holiday season). If you're planning on getting a timeshare for the exchange facility then it's really only worth getting one that's at a very good resort and is during the peak season, so that it is easily exchangeable with other good timeshares.**

Although smaller than the two exchange companies mentioned above, UK-based *Dialanexchange*, is a company worth looking into. They do not charge a membership fee, only £69 for every exchange they arrange. They also deal with exchanging properties with private owners, which is good because if you have a timeshare on a resort you may get the chance to spend a week or more in a private property in France. Alternatively, if you have a private holiday home you could exchange it for a totally different experience – staying at a resort with lots of facilities, such as pools and bars.

Timeshare law

Any business selling new timeshare in a European Union country must allow buyers a 'cooling-off' period following the signing of a purchase agreement. This allows the buyer to back away, without any penalty, within ten days if you are buying from a broker or developer in France or within fourteen days if you are buying in the UK. You must not pay any deposit before the time is up. If you are asked for any payment of any sort at the time of the sale then walk away, because if you eventually decide to cancel, the chances of seeing your deposit again are very slim. According to the Timeshare Consumer Organisation up to half of the people who agree to buy a timeshare actually cancel within the cooling-off period.

Full details must be disclosed

The seller must disclose full details of the developer, the resort, the purchase contract, rights of cancellation, management fees, etc. The resort, amenities and operation of the Club and Management Fees must be accurately described or the Trade Descriptions Act may be breached. The contract has to be in the language of the purchaser or the Member State in which the purchaser resides and be accompanied by a translation of the contract in the language of the Member State where the resort is situated. If it is 'temporarily out of print' or 'not in your language' walk away.

Any purchase using a credit card automatically makes the credit card company (or issuing bank) jointly responsible, with the seller, in ensuring that the product or service materialises as promised. If you do not get what is promised you may be able to obtain repayment from the credit card company. But this is not the case if you make a cash withdrawal using your card to pay or you use your card as a debit card.

The Organisation for Timeshare in Europe clearly explains this law on their website.

Note: Sales between private individuals are not regulated by the Timeshare Act nor are sales of periods of three years or less – such as 'Holiday Plans' and similar sounding short-period purchases.

Avoiding the hard sell

Whether it is a 'hard' or 'soft' sell, expect a presentation of at least one hour as a reasonable length of time is needed to understand the resort, the exchange system and the club arrangements. If however you're approached by someone promising 'only 90 minutes' and you're still with them, locked into a hard sell six or seven hours later, then you know you've been snared by a tout. Such a tout will keep the 'punter' captive until they have cajoled and bullied you into saying yes to a purchase.

Popular persuasion techniques include comments such as:

- 'the last week left';
- 'prices go up tomorrow'; or
- 'everyone else buys – what's wrong with you, can't you afford it?'

Some touts are intentionally rude in an attempt to frighten buyers into saying 'yes'.

High costs of marketing

Many developers admit to having selling costs that exceed 50% of the sales price. You may be asked for £8,000 for a week, but £4,000 of that may have gone on promotions, gifts, commissions etc. for the nineteen couples that 'walked away' before they sold to you. This does not argue well for the future resale value of what you have just bought.

Other scams include incapacitating a person through drinks and/or drugs and getting them to pay up with their credit card. They only discover what has happened once they get home and find out it's past the card's cancellation period.

Reputable developers do not need to rely on scams and hard sell to persuade people to buy their product – the product sells itself and the price is clearly reasonable. The presentation is still needed to explain the timeshare process – but the prospective buyer is not pressurised into buying – if you want to go away and think about it they'll say 'that's ok – just call me when you've made up your mind'.

Owners clubs

Most, but not all, timeshare resorts have an owners club or association that enable owners to influence the way the resort is run, the continuing quality of the facilities and the costs.

The good resorts have democratically run clubs where owners can elect their own representatives to directly influence the management of the resort. Many resorts, however, are still controlled – directly or indirectly – by the developer keen to continue milking profits from owners. Buying into one of these resorts can mean lowering quality standards and increasing management fees. Sales people may say 'you become a member of the owners club' but you may not know just how democratically that club is run.

 Note: **Never buy into a resort unless you are automatically enrolled as a member of a democratically run owners club or association.**

If the resort is not in the complete control of the owners, ask questions to satisfy yourself that the club has substantial influence over the running of the resort.

Timeshare industry contacts:

Organisation for Timeshare in Europe

The official trade association of the timeshare industry in Europe. It's a non-profit organisation with lots of information on timeshare law.

- ✉ Oak House, Cours St Michel 100/3, B-1040 Brussels, Belgium
- ☎ +32 2 533 3061
- 💻 www.ote-info.com

Timeshare Consumer Organisation

- ✉ Hodsock, Worksop, Notts, S81 0TF
- ☎ +44 (0)1909 591 100
- @ info@timeshare.org.uk
- 💻 www.timeshare.org.uk

Exchange clubs

RCI

- @ info@rcicommunity.com
- 💻 www.rci.com

Interval International

- ✉ Coombe Hill House, Beverly Way, London, SW20 0AR
- ☎ 0805 639957
- 💻 www.intervalworld.com

Dialanexchange

- ✉ 21 High Street, Gargrave, Skipton, North Yorkshire, BD23 3RA
- ☎ +44 (0)1756 749 966
- @ info@dialanexchange.com
- 💻 www.dialanexchange.com

Renting

Prior to buying a property and moving permanently to France it is worth considering renting for a while.

Renting is widespread in France, and nearly always involves unfurnished property, which can be a problem if you're not quite ready to lug all your stuff over. Another problem is that not all (in fact most) rental properties do not even come with an oven, gas-rings, a refrigerator or a washing machine. (You could look into buying second-hand furniture and equipment.) If you are taking your furniture with you make sure that you'll be able to get large items into the property if it's an upper floor apartment. Even if there's an elevator, it may be small and some furniture may have to be lifted by ladder from outside the building.

Short term lets can be difficult to find

Most rental periods are for three years, although it is possible to find shorter term furnished rentals, especially in Paris and the larger cities. Outside these cities, and especially in small towns, finding short term furnished rental accommodation can be difficult. If you wish to rent for less than six months and your time coincides with the non-tourist seasons, then you could consider working out a deal with a *gîte* owner. As many *gîtes* are empty for most of the year, you'll probably be able to get a good price. Check that there's adequate heating if it's during the winter months – even some of the hottest areas can be bitterly cold in the winter and many *gîtes* aren't equipped for this.

Whether to use an agent or not

The majority of people looking for rental property go through an *agence immobilière* (estate agency). Agencies command a fee of one month's rent, which is split between the new *locataire* (tenant) and the *propriétaire* (owner), who is also called a *bailleur* (lessor), on completion of the deal. Always check what the fees are in advance. If you approach an *agence immobilière* to find a property for you but none is found, then no fee is charged. The only way to bypass this fee is by dealing directly with an owner, but watch out because it may involve less protection for you as a tenant. In all circumstances you can choose for a *notaire* to act as an intermediary.

If the rental contract (*contrat de location*) is written up between you and the *bailleur* then it's called an *acte sous-seing privé* which is a simple document signed by both parties; if it's written up by a *notaire* then it's an *acte authentique*, which has the seal of the State. If you are new to letting in France, it's a good idea to get a *notaire* to intervene, as you can then be assured that all your rights are carefully outlined in the document. The *notaire* also has an obligation to make sure you fully understand what you are signing.

Property for rent directly from the owner is usually advertised in the local, and sometimes the national, press. The weekly national magazine *De Particulier à Particulier*, which literally means from 'individual to individual', is full of private property ads. Most concern sales but there are also hundreds of rentals each week.

Contracts and letting periods

The common rental agreement includes an owner's pledge of three years, called *un bail de trois ans*. During this three years the owner cannot ask the tenant to leave, except if the tenant reneges on the terms of the agreement laid out. The tenant is free to leave whenever they wish, subject to terms of a two or three month notice period. Within the agreed *bail*, it will state that the tenant cannot be ousted for the property to be sold or if the owner wishes to re-occupy. All agreements are renewable at the end of the term of contract. If you are offered a *bail* of only one year, it's likely that you will probably be turfed-out at the end, as such a short term is indicative that the owner is not committed to renting out longer term. For a period shorter than three years, the owner must confirm the agreed date of the end of the contract, by letter, two months prior to the end. Without this confirmation the contract will proceed for a further three years.

As you can see from the above, French law offers a great deal of protection to the tenant. It's very difficult to evict tenants: eviction is prohibited during long winter months and the evictions procedure is very complicated and includes rights of appeal. These restrictions have been blamed for the recent nationwide reduction in the offer of rentals, which has particularly affected Paris. French *propriétaires* are therefore very cautious before concluding a deal and go to great lengths, and through reams of paperwork, to obtain the assurance that the potential *locataire* can and will pay the rent.

Proof of status

The demands on you for proof of your status are very stringent, restrictive even. You'll be asked to provide:

- **Pay slips**, usually for the previous three months, and your monthly income must be at least three (in some cases as much as four) times the monthly rent.
- If you are self-employed and cannot provide pay slips, you will be asked to provide your previous year's **tax payments** as an indication of what you earn.
- You can expect to be asked for proof that you are **not just employed for the short term** or close to retirement. It's difficult for those in contract fields like entertainment, as agencies will not let you rent their properties unless you can provide third-party financial guarantees.

- You'll also be asked to provide a letter, from one or even two people to act as a **guarantor** if you fail to pay your rent.
- **Proof of identity** will be asked in the form of a *carte de séjour* (residence permit), although sometimes a passport is acceptable.
- You'll be expected to provide a **telephone or electricity bill** as further proof of your current address.

New arrivals in France

For new arrivals such requirements can cause problems. A good idea is to get a bank guarantee, but this will require blocking a large sum of money. Since you're not a French resident, you'll probably be asked to supply details of a resident who will act as a guarantor. This person will have to sign a form (and provide some documents) and will be responsible for absolutely all costs arising.

Deposits and property condition

A deposit (*chèque de caution*) for the sum of two or three times the rent must be paid on signature of the contract. This is returned to you at the end of the rental period, subject to it being partially or totally used to fix any damage you are responsible for. Some agencies have a mandatory cleaning charge that they deduct. You will not receive interest on the sum and it is repayable to exactly the same amount, even if it's returned to you ten years later. It will only be refunded after you've left, as a guarantee of no hidden damage.

A written evaluation of the property's condition is carried out in mutual agreement with the owner or agency after a rental agreement has been reached and before the tenant moves in. This is called an *état des lieux* which both *locataire* and *bailleur* (or *agence immobilière*) must sign. Carefully observe the details of the written evaluation prior to moving in. Go around the house or apartment looking for any possible flaws that are not in the agreement but that you could later be held responsible for, such as a broken tile on the kitchen floor, marks on the paintwork or scratches on the parquet. Make sure that all these details are clearly written in the report.

 Tip: **A good idea is to take photos of the property during the** *état des lieux* **as proof.**

As a condition of the contract you will be required to take out a home insurance policy and subsequently show the owner proof that you have done so.

Communal charges

Renting an apartment will involve contributing to the communal charges for the regular upkeep of the building. These are sometimes included in the rent, in which case the rental sum will be described as *charges comprises*. If charges are not included, it will be described as *charges non comprises*. The charges are worked out as a monthly average based on the previous year and cover things like the cost of the *concierge*, gardeners, common water supplies and general repairs throughout the year. If the charges are not included, make sure you know what was paid the previous year, or whether any unusual costs can be expected in the coming year. You do not want to find yourself having to contribute thousands of euros to the construction of a new roof, if you are only intending on staying for a year. (See also the section on *co-propriété*.) If charges are included, and during your first year the common spending was less than the previous year, then you'll be refunded accordingly.

The tenant occupying the apartment on January 1st each year is responsible for a local tax, *taxe d'habitation,* which is an annual charge varying greatly from *département* to *département*, that is broadly calculated on the size of your property. Heating, electricity and water are usually not included in the rent. You usually have to pay these directly to the appropriate utilities company. Before entering into an agreement, the agency or owner should be able to give you an accurate account of what you are likely to pay.

Interview with a property buyer

Gillian moved to Normandy, but had problems with the agent and the *mairie* (town council).

Q. *How did your move to France work out?*

A. We first moved to Normandy in 1989. When we arrived at our property we found that all the ceiling lights had been cut off with scissors through the cable and we had raw sewage pumping onto the land even though it was sold as having a septic tank. One year later some men came onto our land and chain-sawed some of our oak trees saying we had not purchased them with our property. The gendarmarie wouldn't stop them sawing and the *notaire* said the contract states trees on our land but didn't state which ones were ours (even though they were all on our land). We cleaned up the stream on our side only to be told that we were not allowed to do so without asking permission first even though it was our bit of soil, our stinging nettles, etc.

Q. *So, did you stay there for long?*

A. We were so fed up that after six years we sold it and got ripped off by an agent. He actually arranged the sale of our place to go through on the same day as he sold it for £12,000 more. This agent also did the dirty on some other English people up in the village who sold their place fully furnished but he cleaned it out before the new people moved in.

Q. *After all that, what would your advice be to to others?*

A. My advice is go to the local *mairie* and, if they are are friendly and welcoming, you are half way there to finding a place to buy. If they are unwelcoming then don't buy in that commune because they make or break you.

Q. *Did you try again in France?*

A. We bought a small cow shed the second time, around 50 miles further west, nearer to Granville.

Q. *And the neighbours?*

A. Our new place has only four neighbouring houses and as our luck goes the old boy next door doesn't like the English but we get on well with the others. But we had so much abuse from him that we had to take him to court and he has been bound over to keep the peace.

Q. *What are your plans for the future?*

A. All is now calm but during the lengthy court case we decided to buy a boat and go onto the canals instead for some peace and quiet. The trouble is the boat is in England and we have some work to do on it before we take it over to France. We haven't decided to stay in England for good as we do like France more than England, and our son has now married a French girl and they have three children now and live at Flers 61100. All in all we have learned so much and gained a lot from our adventure.

5

Building your own house

Architects

If the net surface area to be built exceeds 170 m² (an area that does not include the attic or underground area, roof terraces, balconies, the driveway and area taken up by technical installations such as heating systems) then you must call upon the services of an architect.

This architect must be a registered member of the *Ordre des Architectes*. You can look for an architect or check whether the one you are using is registered by looking at the *Ordre des Architectes* website (🖥 www.architectes.org) and clicking on *Vous recherchez un architecte*. Alternatively call the *Conseil Régional de l'Ordre des Architectes* in your *région*. A registered architect will have *assurance de responsabilité décennale* – an insurance that will cover any faults or malfunctions to the structure of the property in the ten years following its completion.

An architect can be involved during all stages of a project: from finding an appropriate plot through to the day that the work is complete (*la réception*). They can manage the contracts of the builders and artisans involved and can act as a supervisor (*maître d'œuvre*), visiting the site regularly to make sure all is going according to plan.

 Tip: **If you do want the architect to be more hands-on then make sure you hire one that is based near your site. If your plot is more than forty minute's drive away then the likelihood of frequent visits diminishes.**

What comes first: the plot or the plan?

This depends on whether the style of your building or the location is more important to you.

If you're a big fan of highly contemporary glass and steel buildings but have a plot that is squeezed between two traditional *colombage* houses, the aesthetics just might not work. Well . . . many people would think a blend of New York cool with Normandy quaint is very exciting but your neighbours and mayor may well not belong to this more radical school of thought. If style is of the essence then find the plot first. If you have an architect on board from the start then they will help you choose this plot. It will be much easier to find a plot and get planning permission for a more traditional (conservative!) design.

Using an architect

Architects see the big pictures – they don't just design four walls and a roof but create total environments, both interiors and exteriors, that are functional and exciting places in which to live or work. An architect will not sell you a standardised plan, but will listen to you and will take into account your needs, your tastes, your way of life and the possible evolution of your family. An architect will not try to impose his or her taste onto you, although it is best to find an architect whose work you have seen and like. You also want an architect who will enjoy designing your project and working with you.

Many architects have online portfolios. Check out the architect's previous work and if possible try to visit any properties they have worked on before. Most architects have their own design philosophies. Some, for instance, are keen environmentalists. Some architects like to work with wood and other renewable sources, others with glass and steel. If you are creating an extension to a medieval house then the second type of architect may not be ideal (unless, of course, juxtaposition is what you're after).

You do not have to be rich to hire an architect

The architect will propose a project compatible with your financial means. The cost of using and managing your house will depend on the quality and conception with which the works are realised. A good architect will save you money during the building process, for instance they will make sure that all materials are correct, that there is as little wastage as possible and that workmanship corresponds with the plans. They will have many good contacts and will help you source the best builders and will deal with them should problems occur.

A building designed for maximum energy efficiency can reduce bills for many years to come. Space will be planned efficiently. A well-designed building can reduce initial costs and also increase its long-term value.

Fees

Architect's fees are normally between 8 and 12% of the final project. The contract that you sign with your architect must clearly explain the mode of remuneration that will determine the fees. The remuneration will depend on the cost of materials, the building's size, its complexity and the duration and difficulty of the mission with which they have been confided. It's impossible to know the exact cost of the construction, as an estimate will only be known once the builders have given their quotes. It is possible to put a clause in the *contrat d'architecte* stipulating that if your project costs a lot more than the budget that you have given the architect then the architect's cost will be lowered. There is often a margin (*margin de tolerance*) between the amount estimated and the real cost, and the remuneration of the architect is less if the real cost goes over this margin. This margin is usually less or equal to 10% of the estimation.

Methods of calculating architect's fees

There are three ways of calculating the fees:

1. *La remuneration au forfait (fixed or set price)*
   This applies if the job is clearly defined before the project starts. Fixed prices tend to be used for smaller projects, for instance those under 170m², such as extensions and conversions.

2. *La remuneration au pourcentage du coût des travaux (remuneration at a percentage of the cost of works)*
   This is an architect's preferred way of charging clients. Normally the nature of the project is known in advance, but the cost of construction isn't.

3. *La remuneration a la vacation horaire (an hourly rate)*
   Most architects have an hourly rate for consultation, advice or expertise.

On some projects the above modes of remuneration are combined.

An architect's fees can seem like a huge expense but doing without one, in order to save money, is often a false economy.

Questions to ask an architect's firm

A checklist of questions to ask an architect before signing a contract:

1. Who will be designing your project? Who will you be dealing with directly? Is the person you'll be communicating with the same as the one designing the project?

2. What is the architect's design philosophy?

3. What are the steps in the design process?

4. How busy is the architectural firm?

5. How interested is the architect in this project?

6. What sets this architect or achitectural firm apart from the rest?

7. How does the architect/architecture firm establish fees? What would the architect expect the fee to be for your project?

8. How does the architect organise the process?

9. What does the architect expect you to provide?

10. What is the architect's experience in obtaining planning permission?

11. What will the architect show you along the way to explain the project? Will you see models, drawings or computer images?

12. Inevitably there are changes that occur with any project. How does the architect handle changes? Who pays for changes?

13. If the scope of the project changes later in the project, will there be additional fees? How will these fees be justified?

14. What services does the architect provide during construction?

15. How often can they guarantee they'll visit the site during construction?

16. Can the architect/architecture firm supply a list of clients with whom they have worked in the past?

Tip: **If at any stage you are unsure of your architectural plans and want a separate opinion you can consult the *Conseil d'architecture, d'urbanisme et d'environnement* (CAUE) (explained in a previous section). In some régions you will also find representatives of the *Maisons de l'architecture* who you can contact for advice.**

Contacts: finding an architect

🖥 www.Architectes.org

(The official website by the *Ordre des Architects*. Here you'll find sample contracts.)

🖥 www.architectes.com

This website provides a list of architects by region.

🖥 www.archifrance.com

For a list of architects that specialise in creating 100% environmentally-friendly homes contact *Construction de l'Environnement et Econome en Energie (CREE)*. The annual of these architects can be found on their website:

🖥 www.cr3e.com

Another good site is:

🖥 www.eco-logis.com

If you already have architectural plans

Will your home fit in with surrounding buildings in terms of style, size and value?

If you are buying a parcel of land in a *lotissement* (see below), can you be sure people buying the parcels of land surrounding yours will be building properties that you find aesthetically appealing or acceptable? You may be building a unique property, but your view may be of very unimaginative kit houses.

Will building codes allow you to build a house the size and shape you want? You may want to create something extraordinary but find that the local authorities have more conservative tastes to your own. Sometimes it's necessary to be sympathetic to the local style and even though the property might look great to you – to others it will be a major blot on the landscape. The *certificate d'urbanisme* will tell you the characteristics that you must include and the architectural constraints effecting the shape of the roof, windows, and the colour of the tiles. Check what surface and width the façades must be.

And then of course, there are more personal issues you need to address:

- Even though you love the land and the price is right, is this an area where you want to live?
- Is it a good location for children? Is it near schools?
- Are shopping areas as close as you'd like?
- How far are the nearest emergency services? For instance if you have suffered a heart complaint, a stroke or chronic asthma in the past it is likely you'll want to live reasonably close to a hospital.
- If you plan to use public transportation, is it close by? Or will you be completely car-dependent?
- Is the view what you want?
- Is it private enough to suit you? Or perhaps it's far too isolated.
- Will you be able to resell it easily one day? It may make a delightful remote hideaway but if you decide to move on will anyone else appreciate such solitude. As an indicator of its desirability, find out how long the plot has been on the market so far.

Land

Finding land

The following factors should be considered when looking for *terrain à bâtir* (land to build upon). Many of the issues listed below will be addressed by the *Certificate d'Urbanisme* (outline planning permission). You are instantly at an advantage if you look at plots with planning permission already in place.

Things to consider:

Power

Is power connected? Is connection underground or overhead? In most rural areas of France connection is to an overhead power supply. Pylons are not aesthetically pleasing and could potentially obstruct a pretty view but it is less expensive than the installation of underground cables. The longer the distance from the house site to the underground connection point, the more costly the connection will be. Will EDF (*Electricité de France*) be willing to extend the supply to your plot?

Telephone

Is there a telephone service to the area? Will *France Télécom* be willing to extend its cables to your site? And in this age of the internet: is ADSL available, or cable?

Water

Is the site connected or close to mains water, or is supply by tank, spring or well? Will the water board be willing to extend pipes to your plot? Do roads need to be dug up in order to lay pipes to reach your land? If so then you'll be looking at a big expense.

Waste water

Is town sewerage available? Or will a *fosse septique* (septic tank) be necessary?

Water drainage

Assess whether water will flow across your land from neighbouring land. Be careful, you don't want everyone else's septic systems to end up flowing onto your property.

Access for construction work

Will the site cause difficulties during construction (e.g. with storage of materials, side boundary access, access by heavy machinery, wet weather)? If you are far from any large commune, will builders and artisans want to travel such a long distance to work?

Access to the final property

Do you have direct access to a road or will you have to pass through someone else's property? Will you have to build a driveway to your property? How long will it need to be? You will have to work this into your budget as it could be a big expense. If you share a track to the plot with someone else then who is responsible for road maintenance and how is maintenance managed?

Trees

Will trees need to be removed for access and safety purposes?

Soil

Will the soil support the house without settling? The consistency of the soil (for instance, hard or soft) will impact significantly on excavation and foundation designs. It's worth getting this checked before buying the land, as dealing with problems such as instability, dampness, sloping, or the presence of hard rock, will add to the building cost. Contact the *Bureau de Recherches Géologiques et Minières* (💻 www.brgm.fr) or the *carriéres* (quarries) specialists of your *département* to get an expert to study the earth.

Slope of the land

The slope of the block will affect the design of the house. Foundations, especially, are more complicated and expensive on sloping ground.

Outlook

Is there a view? If you build on this plot, will your house face the direction you want it to? Think about the direction of the light and whether the rooms you spend the most time in such as your sitting room, kitchen and study will have good light during the day. Your fantastic view might be to the north, but that's not where the best light will be. The trees close to the house may be beautiful but will they envelope the property in constant darkness? Check that you're not in the shadow of a large hill, building or the neighbour's leylandii. Will the view last forever or might vegetation or other construction in the future alter it? Find out who owns the land around your house and if they intend to sell it and for what use. The town hall should let you know whether any plans to build an autoroute, airport, or any other such eyesore next to your property, are foreseen in the near future.

Servitudes

Are there servitudes attached to the land that will create obstacles for your project? For instance, does the neighbouring farmer have rights to graze his sheep on the property, can walkers use it as a passage, are you unable to build there because there was a previous agreement that no building work would be undertaken that would obstruct a neighbour's view? It could be that the land is limited to a particular use, such as cattle farming. You wanted somewhere to put your feet up and potter around, pruning the roses and weeding here and there, instead you could find yourself knee-high in cow dung for years to come.

What if there is no way out to the main road? Articles 682 and 683 of the French Civil Code say that an owner must be allowed out by the shortest route to the public road. So if you buy a plot next to one with no access, you could well find your neighbour's tractor passing outside your front door every morning.

In some areas new legislation has been brought in to protect against urban sprawl meaning that it is unlikely that you'll get permission to build on the edge of some existing villages.

Rights of pre-emption

Check that there are no *Droits de Préemption*. This means that either the local *mairie* (town council) or SAFER (*Société d'Amenagement Foncier et Etablissement Rural* – an organisation that manages the rural environment) can claim the property or land to use it for planned public works, such as building a road or a leisure centre. Also, a farmer who has tenanted or worked on the land for the last three years or more will have first rights to buying the land.

Boundaries

Are the boundaries clear? Will you have to put up fences or plant a hedge? The *avant-contrat* and the *acte de vente* (discussed in the chapter on conveyancing) must precisely indicate the length and location of the boundaries as worked out by a *bornage* (kilometre-marker). The vendor is obliged to measure the boundaries before putting it on the market.

If there are two neighbouring properties or your property is in a *lotissement* (see below) then this operation must be carried out by a geometric expert. This expert will not give you the surface area but you should be able to calculate this from the figures given.

It's in your interest to establish where the boundaries are and what the surface area of your land is. The cost of hiring a geometric expert to verify the details can either be included in the price of the land or can be shared with your neighbours. If the estimates originally given are wrong then you should ask the vendor to pay for the cost of an expert.

Conservation areas

If the land is within 500 metres square of a *Monument Historique*, in a *secteur sauvegardé* (an ensemble of character properties in towns and villages) or in a landscape designated as a *Zone de protection du patrimoine architectural urbain et paysager* (ZPPAUP), you will be severely restricted in terms of the style of building. It's also more than likely that you won't get permission to build at all and in the process of seeking permission you'll face so much of the famous French beaurocracy that you'll probably end up wishing you'd never set eyes on the place.

Lotissements

A *lotissement* is a division of land into at least three plots.

It's likely that you will either view a *lotissement* plot that is within an existing housing state or a large area of unbuilt upon land that has been divided into plots to create a future housing estate. Check that the *lotisseur* (the person selling the land) has been granted permission to sell the land in this way. He or she will have applied for permission at the town hall and there would have been a public notice on the site for two months.

Existing planning permission . . . but that does not mean that anything goes

The advantage of many *lotissements* is that they come with planning permission and the *lotisseur* will provide guarantees of the constructibility of the land. The constructibility of the land does not mean that you can construct any building you like on it and that you can start building straight away. You will still have to apply for a *permis de construire*. There are no guarantees that you'll be able to build the type or building you like and you may also be limited by the *reglements de lotissement*. Rules may apply that dictate the maximum and minimum surface area and height of your construction, the look of its façade, the colour of materials and paint used. Find out what your obligations are concerning plants, trees and the nature of walls and fences, the use of communal space, and the number of parking spaces you are allowed. Check where the water drainage from other properties and your own is. Other rules may relate to your personal use of the property. For instance, washing lines could be forbidden in the garden. If you intend to start a small home-based business, then be careful as professional or commercial activities could be forbidden.

Communal facilities

Lotissements often have communal facilities – such as lawns, driveways and water features. If there are more than five lots in the *lotissement* and equipment is shared between them, then the *lotisseur* must create a syndicate called an *association syndicale libre* so that the communal space and facilities can be jointly managed. Each owner in the syndicate contributes to a fund called a *cahier des charges du lotissement* that pays towards the upkeep. They will have an annual general meeting where they together decide on the budget and each must participate in payments, respect the majority vote and ensure that all repairs are carried out. The *association syndicale* must subscribe to an *assurance responsabilité civile* which is an insurance covering any accident and injury that takes place on the shared land and facilities (such as a falling tree damaging a car or a swing breaking and injuring a child).

Management of the *lotissement*

In practice the syndicate is managed by the *lotisseur* who reserves the role of *administrateur provisoire*. This person must call a general meeting within one month of the day that half of the lots have been sold or at least one year after the first lot has been sold. The running charges tend to include fees for management, works, communal electricity for lighting and water for plants and lawns. It will also include the insurance and general costs attached to administrating the syndicate (postal stamps, photocopies, etc.) The amount of the *cahier des charges* can be modified at the *assemblée générale*. Modification of the charges or the rules depends on either two-thirds of the owners who own at least three-quarters of the land or three-quarters of the owners who own two-thirds of the land, asking for or accepting the change. Up until the syndicate is five years old, modification to the charges or rules can only happen if the *lotisseur* (if they have retained at least one lot) agrees to it.

Membership of the syndicate applies to the property only and will pass on to the new owner of the plot once you move. Once all works have been completed, the commune can decide to claim the shared areas of this *lotissement* as public domain and take charge of the upkeep and management. If this happens then the syndicate will be dissolved and all shared facilities and ground become publicly owned and managed. The transfer is made by an *acte administratif de vente* carried out by a *notaire*. If the *lotissement* is destined to remain private then you will be informed prior to the signature of the *acte de vente* when purchasing the land, and in this case the *association syndicale* will always be maintained.

Planning permission

There are two stages:

1. First you will have to get a **certificat d'urbanisme** to find out if you are able to build on the land and that there are no restrictions, such as servitudes, that will hinder the project. It is highly recommended that you achieve this before you buy the land (put a *condition suspensive* in your *avant-contrat* saying that this must be achieved before you sign the final deeds).

2. Once you receive this certificate, you still do not have permission to build your property. For this you will have to apply for a **Permis de construire** (building permit) by submitting your architectural plans.

The process is explained below:

Le certificat d'urbanisme

There are two types of *certificat d'urbanisme*:

1. The **certificate de simple information** is, as the name says, a simple document that you can ask for that will give you some general information on local planning and regulations but won't tell you anything specific about the plot or building you are hoping to buy. It will simply help you plan your project before applying for the main *certificate opérationnel*.

2. You will need the **certificat opérationnel** in order to find out whether your project can be achieved. This planning certificate specifies the provisions of town planning in relation to the land, the rights of ownership and any limitations imposed on you if you buy the land. It determines whether you can construct on the land or not and under which lawful conditions a construction can be carried out. It will also inform you of taxes applicable to this land, details of public equipment existing or planned, and limitations such as servitudes (public rights of way, or the existence of the pre-emption rights – discussed in the conveyancing section).

Your application for a *certificate opérationnel* must provide a clear explanation of the project you have planned, with a description of the future building, including its area and the surface area of the building and of the land around it, characteristics of the land, and the density of any existing construction. You will have to include a plan of the plot and a map showing the location of the building in the commune.

Send this application to the *maire* (mayor) of your commune. On the *maire's* authority, the application is passed to the departmental planning office known as the *Direction Départmentale de l'Equipement (DDE)*. Given their final approval the mayor will issue you with the required certificate. If your property is close to a *monument historique* or is in a protected zone, the application will also have be considered by an *Architecte des Bâtiments de France*.

From the date of application it should take two months until you get your final response. The certificate will enable you to establish whether the project you envisaged is realisable or not, or whether it will be limited by the restrictions imposed. The *certificat d'urbanisme* is free.

If you decide that you are able to go ahead with your plans then you must deposit a request for a *permis de construire* (building permit) during the time of the *certificat d'urbanisme's* validity. The *certificat d'urbanisme* is valid for one year from the date of issue and is renewable for a further year if need be, although the extension must be applied for.

Note: The *certificat d'urbanisme* isn't an authorisation to build, it doesn't replace the *permis de construire*.

Permis de construire

Application for a *permis de construire* is free and must be applied for by yourself or by a representative applying in your name, such as the builder, architect or the *maître d'œuvre*. The process should take up to two months.

The application should be sent with your architectural plans, to the *mairie* or the *Direction Départmentale de l'Equipement* (DDE) at the town hall. The plans must show the scale of the building, its surface area, the style and surface of its façades and maps showing its exact location on the plot and its location in the commune. Your architect will advise and help you put together the required dossiers to be sent with the application.

Within fifteen days of sending your application, the town hall will write to give you your registration number and to inform you of the date by which you can expect to receive a decision. This letter says that if you receive no reply by that date then you can assume that approval is granted.

Tip: Nevertheless, if you don't receive a reply it's in your interest to chase them up on this, as you certainly don't want your building work interrupted by a negative decision (perhaps, for instance, because a refusal was sent but lost in the post).

A notice of the permit will be placed in the town hall and on the plot and, during the two months following, a dossier will be publicly consultable at the DDE. If a neighbour wishes to contest your building application, they must do so within the two months following the posting of the notice at the town hall or on the land.

They must do so by letter written to the mayor or president of the administrative tribunal and to the beneficiary of the permit.

Given that you obtain approval, tacit or written, you have two years to carry out the works approved. A twelve-month extension can be obtained upon application. When you finally get started you must advise the authorities that you have done so and you must post a sign giving the details of your authorisation.

Permis de construire (building permit) or *déclaration de travaux* (declaration of work)?

If you intend to do only minimal building work to an existing property, then you do not necessarily need a *permis de construire* and only need to ask for *une note de renseignement d'urbanisme* (a note of information on town planning). Here are the general requirements:

*   *permis de construire*

    needed for all major building work and work that modifies the appearance, changes the use (for instance, from an agricultural building to a residential) or creates additional levels within any existing construction.

If your work is of low importance, you will have to deposit a simple *déclaration of travaux* (declaration of work).

*   *déclaration de travaux*

    needed for outdoor swimming pools or for all the works whose ground surface is less than 2m² and the height does not exceed 1.5 metres. Likewise no permission is needed for walls of less than 2 metres which are not used as fences or for terraces of less than 60cm in height.

Below is a simple table explaining what's needed.

Table 5.1 – Building work licences

	Permis de construire	Déclaration de travaux
Construction or extension under 2m² and height < 1.5 m	No	No
Construction or extension 2m² to 20m²	No	Yes
Construction or extension 20m² to 170m²	Yes	No
Construction or extension over 170m²	Yes	No
Non-covered swimming pool	No	Yes
Building a fence	No	Yes

Interior work and *taxe d'habitation*

Unlike in the UK, planning permission is not needed if you alter the interior of your house but it's important that you declare any changes to your living area as your *taxe d'habitation* depends on the *surface habitable* of your house. Attics, and cupboards do not count as living space but if these are converted into extra bedrooms then you will pay more tax. The number of rooms does not make a difference and only living areas count (hallways, entrances and staircases do not count).

Some people go so far as to build two storey houses but board up the first floor windows so you can't tell from the outside that there's another floor – their reason being that they will convert the first floor into a living area when they later have the money, but until then they don't want to pay extra tax.

Declaration d'ouverture de chantier (opening the building site declaration)

Once your request for a *permis de construire* is accepted, you must declare that your plot has become a building site, an action called *declaration d'ouverture de chantier*. This declaration must be lodged at the town hall of the commune where the building site is located.

The *permis de construire* must be posted, very visibly, on the land. If the *permis* isn't posted then anyone has the right to object to your building work during any time in the 30 years that follow.

The posting must remain in place and will name the architects and construction firms involved. Any defect of posting is liable to a fine. For the first two months of the posting anyone can object to the building work and, within reason, insist that it is stopped.

Builders

Choosing a builder

The best method for finding good professionals is by word of mouth and references. Your *notaire, maire* and new neighbours will probably be able to recommend good local builders and artisans. It's worth asking your *agent immobilier*, but be careful as some take commission for passing on customers. If you're using a local architect to draw your plans then they will certainly have good contacts, or as part of their fees will do all the consulting for you. Unless they are new to the *région*, the best builders don't need to advertise as they get a constant stream of work through personal recommendation. The only problem with good builders is that they are always busy and you may have to wait many months (years even) until they are available to work on your project.

> *Tip*: Get quotes from two or three builders and ask to visit other properties that they have worked on. If possible try to arrange your first meeting with a builder on his current work site so that you can see them and their workers at work. Compare prices, services, and the length of time you'll have to wait until it gets started.

Depending on your budget and the amount of time (as well as energy and patience!) you have to co-ordinate and supervise building work yourself, you have several options.

You can choose between hiring:

* A **building consortium** (*entreprise*) that will provide the plans and build the entire house for you for a fixed sum.
* A builder or building consortium (*entreprise*) that will build the entire house for a fixed sum but **using plans that you supply**.
* A number of **independent tradespersons** (artisans) – plumbers, joiners, plasterers etc. – and perhaps one main entreprise to carry out the major works and supervise the work yourself.
* A **supervisor**, known as a maître d'œuvre, to bring together the independent artisans and to oversee the work on your behalf.

Each of these options is described in more detail further on.

Choose local builders

It is better to use local builders and artisans rather than a builder or *entreprise* from further afield (such as those from your own country even). Local people will appreciate you supporting their economy, and insularity wins few friends. You'll benefit from the local knowledge and skill of such builders: they'll understand planning regulations and limitations, and if you are renovating an older property they will be familiar with the structure and the materials used. They may know local builders merchants with whom they have struck deals or get reductions, the savings of which could be passed on to you.

One of the main reasons for choosing a builder from your own country is because there is no language barrier to overcome. If you are to use French artisans then some working knowledge of the language is of course needed, but if you cannot speak a word of the language this can be overcome by recruiting a bilingual *maître d'œuvre* to overlook the project for you. A building site is probably a good place to start learning the language (especially if you want to get well-versed in local slang and swear words).

Checking the quality of a builder

Anyone is free to enter the construction trade and there are no professional regulations, therefore it's difficult to evaluate in advance the quality and integrity of a professional. Certain qualifications (*Qualibat, Qualifelec, Qualisol*) can give some indications but these qualifications aren't obligatory and not having one does not necessarily mean that the builder or enterprise is bad.

If your builder is local you will be able to see previous houses they have worked on and perhaps do some knocking on doors and find out if their previous clients are content with the job done. Some national building consortiums and coalitions of builders have set up independent quality benchmarks backed by their own 'labels' such as the label *NF maison individuelle*. Inspectors visit the building sites and finished projects to check that everything conforms to a charter which carefully follows building laws, regulations and ethics. The enterprise you decide on does not have to belong to such a group, and not belonging to one doesn't mean that its work is of a lesser quality.

Kit houses

Builders that have subscribed to these benchmarks tend to be those that also supply the architectural plans of the individual house. Such houses – many call them 'kit' houses – are not to everyone's taste. Choosing such a house involves sifting through a catalogue. They are often a 'one size fits all' (although plans can often be adapted to fit your tastes and needs) and the materials used are not unique to the *région*. Such houses are not designed with the surrounding environment in mind and are often alien to the local building styles and materials. This can be a major flaw of such properties: a house designed for the Mediterranean coast would be freezing on the west coast of Brittany during a blustery wet winter. You're as likely to find an identical 'kit' house in both Lorraine and Languedoc.

An architect will visit the site and will design the property with not just the building plot in mind, but the whole area. The materials chosen, unless completely innovative, will be from the local terrain so that they blend with the environment and adapt appropriately to the local climate. Although it may blend in, your building will be unique. It's much more exciting to get a unique property – designed to your own specification.

Siret number

All *entreprises* and *artisans* must be registered at the local town hall (*mairie*) and have a *siret* number. This is issued by the *Chamber of Commerce* and signifies TVA (VAT) registration. You have no recourse in French law if you use someone who is undeclared or works clandestinely (*travaille au noir*). The *siret* number should be on all contracts and documentation.

Using a foreign builder

Builders from outside France will also have to be registered and have a *siret* number. This ensures that they are paying the appropriate TVA (VAT) and have all the necessary insurances in place.

A foreign builder providing goods or services to an end customer in France must charge VAT at the French rate and will need to register with the *Centre des impots des non-résidents* (CINR) to obtain a TVA (VAT) registration number. He or she will need to be VAT registered in the UK first.

Centre des impots des non-residents (CINR)

(Tax for non-residents)

✉   9 rue d'Uzes 75094 Paris Cedex 02, France
☎   +33 (0)1 44 76 19 07
Fax +33 (0)1 44 76 19 43

Contracts

Before signing a contract with an *entreprise* or *artisan* you must own the land or at least have signed an *avant-contrat* (such as a *compromis de vente*). Do not pay any sum before signing a contract!

If you have only signed an *avant-contrat* for the land then you should insert a *condition suspensive* – a get-out clause – in the contract with the builder or *artisan* saying that if the sale does not follow through then the contract will be annulled and all monies paid will be reimbursed.

If you are dependent on loans the contract should state this and should contain a *clause suspensive* saying that if the financing isn't forthcoming the contract will be annulled and any sums paid by you will be returned. From the signing of the contract you have a month at minimum to obtain the loans. Even if this clause doesn't figure in the contract, you'll still be protected by a law enabling you to reclaim the sums if the loan doesn't come through (Consumer code: art L. 312-1.) If you finance the works *without* a loan, you must put a handwritten note in the contract indicating that you have knowledge of the protections of this law regarding loans but that you renounce these benefits.

Before signing the contract, ask for a copy and take some time to examine its contents, consider the consequences and get advice from *Agence Départementale d'Information sur le Logement* (ADIL). Don't pay any sum of money to a professional, *entreprise* or builder before signing a contract. Don't forget that all signatures on a document constitute an engagement.

Mandatory guarantees and insurances

There are a number of mandatory guarantees and insurances specific to your property that either you or the people working on the property must provide. You must check that they have the appropriate certification and your contract should state that these guarantees have been subscribed to. Ask to see the builder or artisan's insurance documents (*attestations*).

- *Garantie de livraison*

  This is a mandatory insurance that the builder must subscribe to. It is a guarantee that if the builder goes bankrupt or abandons the site during the building process, their insurance company will step in to complete the project.

- *Assurance Responsabilité Civile*

  This is third party insurance and provides cover in case the builder accidentally causes damage to the house during the course of renovation works.

- *La garantie de parfait achèvement*

  During the twelve months following the completion (*la réception*) of the works, the builder has an obligation to repair any disorders that occur.

- *Garantie de bon fonctionnement/assurance biennale*

  In the two years following completion (la *réception*) of works this guarantees that all your equipment that is not actually a part of the building work but which has been installed (for instance, central heating, electricity or plumbing installation) will function perfectly. If not, it will be fixed or replaced.

- *Garantie décennale*

  All professionals involved must have a *Garantie décennale*. This is a ten year insurance that covers them in the event of any major disorders that occur to the property due to their workmanship. This insurance policy covers the ten years following the day of *la réception* of the property. Any artisan that starts on a job without subscribing to this insurance is liable to severe penalisation. The numbers of their insurance policy (*la police d'assurance*) and the name of their insurance company should be on their contract. If it is not then ask to look at their *contrat d'assurance* on the day that their work begins.

- *Assurance Dommages-Ouvrage*

  Prior to opening the building site you – the client – must subscribe to *assurance dommages-ouvrage*. This insurance guarantees payments of any faults in the ten years following completion (*réception*) of the works. It kicks off only when the building work is complete. It covers vices and malfunctions which occur that threaten the solidity of the construction, such as problems with the foundations, the roof or the thermal insulation, also the solidity of equipment which cannot be dissociated from the work.

> *Note*: It is very important, and your responsibility alone, to ensure that this insurance is in place.

If you have a *contrat de construction d'une maison individuelle avec or sans fourniture de plan* (explained further on) then it is conditional that you subscribe to such insurance. The *assurance dommages-ouvrage* enables you to obtain, in principal, rapid payment of repairs for works without waiting for results of tribunals with individuals. The individuals will be protected by their *garantie décennale* but without your own insurance you will have to wait for a tribunal determining the responsibilities of the workers involved.

> *Note*: This insurance is especially needed if you intend to sell the property within ten years. Otherwise you will be personally responsible for any default that occurs to the house within ten years of it being built.

Call around for different quotes. Your builder may be able to recommend an insurance company. You can also contact the *Fédération Française des Sociétés d'Assurance* (🖥 www.ffsa.fr).

You may also want to consider taking out insurance against bad weather that could effect the property both during work and afterwards, such as hailstorms or flooding. This policy is called *assurance contre les intempéries*. The moment the roof is up you should consider getting fire insurance (une *polie incendie*). Such risks are not covered by *l'assurance-dommages*. In principal, your builder should be insured against these problems, but this does not always happen.

Here is a good site where you can obtain building insurance quotes:

💻　www.assuranceconstruction.com

Builder problems

If, while work is going ahead, you are not happy and see that the solidity of the structure is in jeopardy because of shoddy workmanship then you may have to demand that work is stopped. You will then need to address your *tribunal de grande instance* (local county court) to ask for a judge to intervene. This action should only be taken in extreme and urgent circumstances.

If work stops for no apparently good reason (good reasons being bad weather, atmospheric conditions, illness or death) you will need to call or write to your builder reminding them of the date of the *réception* and warn them that you will cease all payments until work continues. If you get no response then consult the *tribunal* and they will implement a fine for each day that work does not take place.

When the work is finished

La réception

La réception is the day that the work is complete and many of the above mentioned guarantees kick into effect. Normally your builder will inform you of its date. You, the client, must be present along with all the builders and artisans involved (if it's an *entreprise* then just the presence of its representative is okay). The *réception* cannot happen without you.

You should get an expert (a *professional habilité*) to assist you such as an architect, a *maître d'œuvre* with architectural qualifications or an engineer. They will check the functioning of the windows, ventilation, installation of heating and water, etc. Inspect everything very carefully – examining the materials used, turning taps on and off, opening and closing windows, switching on lights, checking sockets and making sure the heating works. You must take great care because at the end of the inspection you must agree that:

* *the works have been achieved*

   that they conform to the plans, that the materials used are correct and the quality of the equipment is good (and in some circumstances, the colour of the walls and carpet conform to what you agreed).

- *that the execution is good*

  if there are any disorders you can discuss them with the builder. If you don't mention any obvious problems on the day then you risk not getting them repaired.

If you are **not** assisted by a professional then you have eight days in which you can find any changes or repairs to be made.

Pointing out any disorders or things to amend doesn't restrict you moving into your house (as long as there are no risks to your safety).

If, on the day of *la réception*, you find that the work is not completed or needs to be amended then you will have to agree on a new date. If the builder or artisan refuses to make amendments then you will need to address a *tribunal de grande instance* (local county court).

La déclaration d'achèvement des travaux

Once the work is complete and you are happy with the results, you must send the town hall a *déclaration d'achèvement des travaux* (a declaration that the work is completed) within 30 days.

The *entreprise* with whom you signed a *contrat de construction d'une maison individuelle avec fourniture de plan* (a type of contract explained on the following page) will often complete this formality for you (and charge you for doing so). An inspector will be sent and if the works conform to the *permis de construire*, a *certificat de conformité* will be delivered within three months.

Types of contracts

Employing one builder or building consortium (*entreprise*) for the whole project

A good idea is to use a builder that has their own workforce and little or none of the work is subcontracted.

They will build the entire house for you from the foundations to the roof as well as take care of all internal work and the implementation of utilities (the plumbing, electrical installation, plastering, joinery, etc.) for an agreed price. Such *entreprises* (sometimes individual builders are called *entrepreneurs*) will even help you with obtaining the *permis de construire*.

Alternatively there are *entreprises* that simply do the major works (foundation, walls, roof, windows and doors) and it will be up to you to complete the plumbing, electrical installation, etc.

The advantage of using such an entreprise is that once the work starts there is less likelihood of delays occurring because all the workers are in one place. The builder will oversee everything and you can hold him or her accountable if anything goes wrong. It frees you from the hassle of looking for each separate artisan, getting numerous quotes, weighing them up and then setting up separate contracts. In this case only one contract is made.

There are two types of contract:

1. When the **builder provides you with architectural plans** you both sign a *contrat de construction d'une maison individuelle avec fourniture de plan*.

2. When **you provide the builder with your own architectural plans** then the contract will be a *contrat d'une maison individuelle sans fourniture de plan*.

These are explained in greater detail below.

Le contrat de construction d'une maison individuelle avec fourniture du plan par le constructeur (contract for constructing a house based on architectural plans provided by the building enterprise)

The builder will provide you with a plan of the house you have chosen (often from their catalogue), as well as a detailed written description of the house which includes the number and type of rooms, surface area, etc. Before signing the contract the builder will verify that this project is adapted to your particular plot and you will be informed of the supplementary costs if it's found necessary that the foundations need to be reinforced.

From the date you receive the contract and plans you are entitled to a seven day cooling-off period (*délai de rétraction*) during which you can reflect on the plans and the contract. During this time study the plans attentively:

1. Check whether it will be suitable for your family by considering the area of the rooms, partitions, communication between rooms, orientation, etc.

2. If you're able to see a property they have already worked on check the technical quality and finishing, the aesthetics of the house, heat insulation, etc.

3. Check the presence of labels, guarantees and plans.

If you decide not to go ahead, then you must inform the builder by the end of this seven day period.

Charges and penalties

The contract will mention the fixed cost of the house (TVA – VAT – should be included), the costs of adapting the plans, the fees for examining the land, the cost of guarantees and assurances. This price cannot increase, save if the contract has to undergo a revision. The conditions of revision must be explained clearly in the contract. The contract also indicates the penalties the builder will pay if the delivery is delayed. These penalties can be as little as 1/3000 of the full price per day of the delay.

Starting date

The opening date of the building site will be in the contract. The contract will state that work only begins once:

1. the final deeds of the land have been signed;

2. the *permis de construire* is obtained;

3. the assurance *dommages-assurance* has been subscribed to (by yourself); and

4. the *garantie de livraison* has been subscribed to by the builder.

Payment schedules

On signature of the contract and before opening the building site the builder can ask you for a percentage of the cost. If they have given a guarantee of reimbursement (*attestation de la garantie de remboursement*) you can give the builder up to 5% of the price and then a further 5% at the delivery of the *permis de construire*. This attestation guarantees that all money will be reimbursed if the *conditions suspensives* aren't realised, if you retract in the seven days cooling-off period, or the building site doesn't open on the day it says in the contract.

If the builder hasn't given you a *garantie de remboursement* then you mustn't pay more than 3% of the price. This percentage mustn't (as with all the payments) be paid unless the contract has been signed. This sum is blocked in a special account opened in your name (usually opened by the credit association lending you the money) until all the *conditions suspensives* have been met. All sums must be reimbursed if the conditions aren't realised.

The payment schedule will be as follows:

15% of the total sum at the **opening** (percentage includes sums paid before starting the works) of the building site.

25% once the **foundations** have been laid.

40% once the **walls** have gone up.

60% once the **roof and water-proofing** has been put in (a stage called *hors d'eau*).

75% once the **partitions** and enclosed – doors and windows are in (a stage called *hors d'air*).

95% once **all other works**, the plumbing, joining, lighting and heating is implemented.

If the sums are paid directly by your lender to the constructor then you will have to give your written accord before each payment is released. The builder cannot prevent you from visiting the building site before each payment.

The final 5% balance will be paid at *la réception* – the day (explained above) when the works are complete and you can assess whether you are happy with the complete job or whether work still needs to be completed or repairs and alterations made.

Le contrat de construction d'une maison individuelle sans fourniture de plan (contract for constructing a house based on your own architectural plans)

Le contrat de construction d'une maison individuelle sans fourniture de plan is when the client provides the plans and approaches one building entreprise to carry out at least the major works (*gros-œuvre*), that is to say, the foundations, walls, roofs, windows and doors.

This contract is less regulated than the contract *avec fourniture de plan* described above however, if the same mandatory insurances and guarantees are mentioned in the contract, then you should have as much protection.

The mode and amount of payments can be negotiated. You can pay according to the advancement of the project in the way outlined above.

The contract must include:

- a description of the land and how the property will be situated on this land;
- a description and characteristics of the work involved;
- the fixed and definitive price, how payments will be paid and a timetable for making them, a clear explanation of the circumstances under which revisions of cost can be made;
- the date for the work's completion;
- an agreement that you will subscribe to the *assurance dommages-ouvrage*; and
- an indication of whether or not you will be assisted at *la réception* by a *professional habilité*.

It will note that you will be holding back a part of the price in case you have any reservations about the work on the day of *la réception*. This sum, normally 5%, is known as *la consignation d'une partie du prix en cas de reserves a la réception*.

You will then benefit from a *délai de rétraction*, a cooling down period of seven days, during which you must analyse the contract and reflect on your decision to use this builder. If you change your mind you must inform the builder before the seven days expire.

Using a *mâitre d'œuvre* (master of works)

An independent *mâitre d'œuvre* (and one that does not supply the plans) will cost between 8 and 10% of the project. In some cases a *mâitre d'œuvre* (master of works) is trained in architecture and can provide you with the plans or get involved with structural alterations. The *mâitre d'œuvre* can help you put together your application dossier for the *permis de construire* and will guide you through the legal, financial and administrative processes. They will help you select the *entreprises/artisans* (builders, roofers, plumbers, plasterers, electricians and so on) to carry out the works and will then go about employing and co-ordinating them. This person will not be on the site full-time but will visit it several times to check that everything is going according to plan and that the workmanship is good and materials used are correct.

 Note: The *mâitre d'œuvre* is not a builder so do not expect to see them getting their hands dirty on site! The closer the *mâitre d'œuvre* is based to the site the better, as they are then more likely to pay more frequent visits.

Contracts

More than one contract will be involved:

- The client signs the *contrat de mâitrise d'œuvre* with the *mâitre d'œuvre*.
- If the architect is taking on this role then you will sign a *contrat d'architecte* within which their supervisory role will be outlined.
- On top of this contract you will sign a *contrat d'entreprise* with each individual *entreprise* and a *marché de travaux* with each *artisan*. Each contract applies strictly to the worker's determined task.
- If one building consortium is involved in the *gros œuvres* then you will sign with them the *contrat de construction d'une maison individuelle sans fourniture de plan* which is described above.

Role of the *mâitre d'œuvre*

The *mâitre d'œuvre* can guide you in your choice of workers but cannot choose them for you. The ultimate decision must be made by the client.

The *mâitre d'œuvre* will not be able to engage in the cost of the construction, but will respect the budget that you have indicated. They must organise consultations with, in general, up to three *entreprises* or three *artisans* of each trade, and discuss with you the ones that they believe should realise the work.

The *maître d'œuvre* will then liaise with the chosen *entreprises* or *artisans* for you and will provide them with plans and descriptions of the work, will make sure that they follow a timetable for works and that all costs are kept to. The *maître d'œuvre* will assist you at *la réception*.

> *Tip*: When the *maître d'œuvre* holds meetings at the building site, it's in your interest to participate, especially at each important stage of works such as those when payment is due.

The *contrat de maîtrise d'œuvre* must give a clear and precise definition of the *maître d'œuvre's* mission. For instance, it will state whether they will be co-ordinating your application for a *permis de construire*. You mustn't presume that they will be doing this.

The contract will give a precise definition of your project explaining where it is to be built, the number and nature of the rooms, the particular equipment (e.g. the type of heating to be implemented), and the materials to be used (down to the wall covering and floors). You must provide the *maître d'œuvre* with the plan and the contract must include an agreement that this plan will be precisely followed.

Fees will either be negotiated or fixed, according to the percentage of the amount of the works.

The *maître d'œuvre* will receive a budget called an *envelope financière* and you will entrust them to co-ordinate payments and check all invoices. It will be impossible to determine the definitive cost of the construction until all the *artisans* have been found and their quotes collated. You should give a cost limit in the contract and include a *clause de résiliation aux torts of the maître d'œuvre*, which allows you to back out if the definitive cost of the works goes past the foreseen amount. Some contracts give a margin above the definitive cost that you can dip into in case of urgency.

> *Tip*: Don't begin work before knowing the full cost of the project; you won't know this before you have a signature on all the *marchés de travaux*.

As a number of independent builders and tradespeople are involved the timetable will need to be more flexible. At each stage of the building work the *maître d'œuvre* must have your permission to carry on.

The *maitre d'œuvre* and each *tradesperson* will need to subscribe to the various mandatory guarantees outlined above.

Employing independent tradespeople and supervising the entire project yourself

A task not to be undertaken lightly

Employing a number of independent builders and *artisans* and supervising the entire project yourself will be hard work. You will certainly need to speak good French and it will help to have some building experience. Any mistakes could lose you a lot of money and your inexperience could even cause structural problems. Even if you do have experience, there are certain skills and materials used that will be very different in France to your homeland. Don't just presume that you can transfer your set of skills to another culture – you may even have to relearn your skills and adapt your ways of dealing with people.

It will be time-consuming looking for the right people and then setting up individual contracts. You will also have to be on site most of the time so that your inexperience isn't taken advantage of and to insure that everything is going smoothly. Supervising the project will certainly test your diplomacy. If, however, you're familiar with the building trade, you have a good grasp of the French language and good managerial skills (and an ability to adapt to a different working culture) and are up to it, then this is a good way to save money.

Contracts

With each tradesperson you will have to write up a *contrat d'entreprise* or a *marché de travaux*.

Don't sign a contract with any *artisans* or *entreprises* without first having obtained the *permis de construire*. If you haven't obtained it, at the moment of signing the contract, introduce a note that says the contract will only become definitive on the day you are granted the *permis* or, if a *permis* is refused, the contact will be annulled and you will recuperate any money you've handed over.

The contract must have precise details of the works to be taken out and instructions on the materials to be used by the *entreprise* (if they are to be supplied by the *entreprise*) and an estimate of the price. You are also able to ask for a fixed and non-revisable price (*un prix forfaiture et non révisable*). If the contract has a fixed but revisable price (*prix forfaiture et révisable*) it must explain precisely under what conditions this is likely to change.

Payment schedule

It is a good idea to make clear in the contract at what stage of the works the builders or *artisans* will be paid. Payment is negotiable but it is best if you can arrange it so that the worker is paid once the work is complete. To guarantee that the work is well-executed you are entitled to hold back a sum of no more than

5%. This sum can held by a third party (such as a bank, *notaire* or bailiff) until *la réception* is complete and you are content with the finished work. Make sure that the builders are fully aware of how and when you are paying them before their work begins.

In case of damage or a problem with the construction, you must research the responsibility of each *entreprise* individually.

Contacts: construction

- Union Nationale des Constructeurs de Maisons Individuelles (www.uncmi.org)
- Confédération de l'Artisanat et des Petites Entreprises du Bâtiment (www.capeb.fr)
- Fédération Française du Bâtiment (www.ffbatiment.fr)
- Syndicat National des Architectes, Agréés en Architecture et Mâitresd'œuvre en Bâtiments (www.synaamob.com)

Tip 1: **If you know an exceptionally good and trustworthy builder then get him or her to co-ordinate the works. A *maître d'œuvre* is not always necessary. You could get an architect to draw up the plans for the *permis de construire* only, which will cost around about €3,000 to €6,000 for an average sized house (but prices vary considerably).**

Tip 2: **Keep all receipts for building work so that these costs can be set against the perceived gain on the resale of the property for French capital gains tax. All receipts from materials and labour should also be kept in order to prove that TVA has been paid on the works.**

Contacts: kit houses

If you are interested in a 'kit' house here are a few companies to contact:

- Maisons de Qualité (www.maisons-qualite.com)
- Mikit (www.mikit.fr)

Building an environmentally-friendly property

If you wish to build an environmentally-friendly property or restore an older building in an ecologically-sound way then you should contact CREEE – *Construction Respectueuse de l'Environnement et Econome en Energie*. Their website is an excellent resource listing over 2,000 providers of environmentally-kind products and service providers. You can search by *région* or *département*. Via their website you can subscribe to *La Maison Ecologique*, a magazine on ecological building and decorating that comes out every two months.

CREEE

✉   Pégase-Périgord – Froidefon, 24450 Saint Pierre-de-Frugie, France
☎   +33 (0)5 53 52 59 50
Fax +33 (0)5 53 55 29 99
@   creee@wanadoo.fr
💻   www.cr3e.com

eco-logis.com

Another good website is 💻 www.eco-logis.com – here you can purchase goods such as non-toxic natural paint and wool insulation. The site also has lots of informative articles and interviews.

It's possible that you will benefit from subsidies if you build an environmentally-friendly home, especially if you are installing solar panels for heating.

Building a swimming pool

If your property is used as a family holiday home or let out as a *gîte* to others, then it's likely that you'll want to install a swimming pool. A swimming pool will certainly boost your *gîte's* letting potential.

The average pool size in France is 4.70m x 9.50m. 60% are made with panels and liner, the rest with concrete or polyester. In the private family pool sector, there is a trend towards smaller but better equipped pools with easier maintenance due to automation. There are two types:

•   A **liner pool** which is by far the cheapest option and can be installed by anyone.

•   A **concrete and tiled pool** which will require a team of builders so will cost much more.

If you specifiy non-standard designs, materials or equipment, then obviously costs will rise.

Cleaning

The sophistication of equipment is advancing rapidly and nearly all pools today have an automatic cleaning system. Nearly a quarter of pools each year are equipped with a device to electrolyze salt – this is a cost-effective method of producing chlorine in a regular and controlled way which reduces the amount of maintenance time and ensures safer pool water. There has also been increasing demand for products without chlorine (i.e. active oxygen, PHMB). Many manufacturers provide cleaning and water maintenance through their after-sales service. Cleaning services should also include the checking of water chemical dosage.

A small 3 x 6m liner pool can cost as little as €5,000, but if you have a large family or guests then you may need to spend more in order to get the right size. Think about how many bathers will be using the pool and the size needed to fit them all comfortably. If you have more than one dwelling, such as a *gîte* complex, then sharing the pool will be classed as *demi-commercial* and you will be required by the Ministry of the Environment to have faster water turnover and more precise sanitisation than the conventional domestic pool.

Remember all the added extras, such as automatic vacuums and sterilisation systems, heating equipment (heat pumps), security covers and wave-making machines which all add significantly to the basic cost. If you want to increase the annual utilisation of your pool then consider installing heaters.

Pool fences

On January 1st 2004, a new law that all new open-air pools must have a fence built around them, was implemented. The aim of the law is to minimise the large number of drowning incidents of young children each year. As of January 1st 2006, all pools – old and new – must be fenced in. Many property owners are not happy with this new legislation because often pools were built to enhance; barriers around the edges of such pools will inevitably ruin the vista.

Guarantees

Most swimming pools come with the following guarantees:

- **Ten year** guarantee covering:
  - Traditional work with concrete (pre-fabricated, or industrialised in-ground construction).
  - In-ground pipes.
  - The liner (however, the time frame of the guarantee is decreasing and it often depends on the quality of the welding).
  - Waterproof system by reinforced timbering in synthetic resin.
- **Two year** guarantee covering:
  - Visible pipes.
  - Paintwork.
- **One year** guarantee covering:
  - Electrical motors (such as filters, technical accessories, heating devices).

Contacts: swimming pools

Annuaire de la Piscine, Spa, Sauna et Hammam

They produce a brochure and also have contacts online and an English section.

☎   +33 (0)4 90 68 87 63
@   Infos@piscine-pro.com
💻   www.piscine-pro.com

National swimming pool distributors:

- 💻 www.carrebleu.fr
- 💻 www.everblue.com (section in English)
- 💻 www.lagon.fr

Builders merchants and DIY shops

Builders merchants

Many of the builders merchants and DIY shops below have lots of building and DIY advice on their websites as well as online catalogues.

- **Cedeo** (🖥 www.cedeo.fr)

  A major distributor of plumbing and heating materials with more than 140 branches throughout France. Website provides an online catalogue.

- **CGE Distribution** (🖥 www.cge-distribution.com)

  The main brand of the Sonepar group (a leading French company dealing in electrical products distribution). 118 branches throughout France.

- **Comptoir des Peintures Gauthier** (🖥 www.peintures-gauthier.tm.fr)

  With more than 130 branches in France, they provide a large range of painting and decorating products.

- **Lapeyre** (🖥 www.lapeyre.fr)

  European leader in manufacturing and distributing doors, windows, kitchens and bathrooms, and many other household accessories.

- **Point P** (🖥 www.pointp.fr)

  The leading builders merchant in France. Point P has over 700 branches serving all professionals in the building industry.

- **Seigneurie** (🖥 www.seigneurie.tm.fr)

  The first professional paint manufacturer in France, with more than 80 branches and an online catalogue.

DIY (bricolage) shops

- **Brico Depôt** (⌨ www.brico-depot.com)
  This store, under the same ownership as Castorama below, often has good promotions.
- **Bricomarché** (⌨ www.bricomarche.com)
  There is a more limited range than the store above but prices can be cheaper.
- **Bricorama** (⌨ www.bricorama.fr)
  You can find good deals but the quality is not necessarily the best.
- **Castorama** (⌨ www.castorama.fr)
  Cheaper than Mr. Bricolage (although its recent takeover by the Kingfisher group could mean prices changing).
- **Leroy Merlin** (⌨ www.leroymerlin.fr)
  Good quality but higher prices than Castorama or Mr. Bricolage.
- **Mr. Bricolage** (⌨ www.mr-bricolage.fr)
  This popular store has a good website with lots of tips and advice.

Interview with a property buyer

Carole and Patrick bought a house in a village in Normandy to be close to England.

Q. *Tell me about yourself*

A. Mid-40s married 21 years ago. No kids, though a succession of labradors, first two of which were given to us by my parents as a wedding present. Also a succession of cats: due to old age and encounters with cars, none currently.

Our Wiltshire village mirrors almost precisely in size and amenities the Normandy village where we've bought a home. There are about 250 inhabitants, there are no village shops and both villages have churches. In Wiltshire we have a pub and a thriving village school – mainly populated by children from outside the village; in Manche there's no bar for 4 kms and the kids are bused to Sourdeval. In Manche much of the village is inhabited 24 hours a day; in Wiltshire – located a few miles from the M4 which provides easy links to Bristol, Bath, Swindon Reading – it is very much a commuter village.

In Wiltshire, the land around is farmed but the vast majority of the inhabitants have nothing to do with farming and no understanding of it. It's a pretty place to live. Our quality of life is excellent apart from the British/American disease of working too many hours to take the time to appreciate what we have. Patrick left farming some years ago and is self-employed as a builder; I've had a career in sales and marketing in a number of industries, currently educational publishing.

Q. *What tempted you to buy a house in France?*

A. The usual, touring holidays gave us time to appreciate the scale and space of France. There was the unassuming welcome extended to us wherever we were in France – including Paris – no matter how poor our French was. Okay, the property prices were appealing too, but that just made the idea possible as opposed to initiating and motivating it.

We switched from touring holidays to *gîte* holidays about 10 years ago. We both love cooking – our waistlines confirm this – and I reached the point where standing in the middle of a French market (Cahors) full of mid-September local produce (and only being able to justify buying a bag of apples and some cheese for lunch) caused me serious stress. I desperately wanted to buy mountains of glowing peppers, tomatoes, aubergines, earthy mushrooms and local dried meats, cheeses . . . and the home grown chickens, guineafowl and rabbits . . . and take them home to cook. We decided that *gîte*-renting was the answer!

We discovered that renting a *gîte* for a week or two meant we could build up a routine, get to know the local shops, the best boulangerie, take a pastis in the local bar once (or twice) a day; we almost became part of the village fabric for that short time. And we wanted more. A house of our own was the logical next step. Nice idea. Then my sister died. She was 37, younger than me, and (amongst other things) it brought home to us that if you have a dream or desire, don't assume you've got another 10, 20, 30 years in which to achieve it.

We'd decided we wanted to move to France for a different way of life, perhaps a quieter, maybe more insular way of living, but one where we could "enjoy the day now" rather than give it an appointment in two weeks time – and then find it was raining and I had a headache anyway. So our decision was based on: do we assume we'll make 60/65 and then make the move? Or do we have the balls to do something now, find a way of making our ideas a reality? We decided on the latter.

Q. *Have you spent much time in France before?*

A. We toured most of France over a number of years and then rented *gîte*s in a number of *départements*.

Q. *How did you choose your area of France?*

A. The year after my sister died, as the anniversary of her death approached in September, we wanted to give my parents an additional, different event to think about. This event took the form of a week in France in October in a snug *gîte* set up for winter lets. We chose Normandy, an area we hadn't really explored previously because, perversely, it was too close to home! But that suited my parents as they didn't want a long car journey. We explored the towns nearby, really liked Vire and Sourdeval and decided to return, which we did, several times in the next few years before buying.

The area of France we most like is the Haute Loire *région* – around Le Puy-en-Velay, particularly to the north of the town which has a lot of broadleaf woods and forests. That, we decided, wasn't practical for a first-time move as I needed reasonably easy access to my parents in southern Wiltshire and my nieces and nephew in Warwickshire. Therefore, southern Normandy fit accessibility and other criteria. But the southern Auvergne is the retirement plan.

Q. *Tell me a bit about the area and what you've discovered about it.*

A. The area is rural, very hilly, classic Normandy bocage. Agriculture is mostly small-scale farming. Shorthand to describe the area is the Cotswolds without the pretensions, the cars and the antique shops.

Since owning a home in the area, we've discovered just how popular it is with other English families (30 British-owned homes in the *commune* as of December 2002) and from reading and exploring we've realised more clearly how heavily this area suffered in the last war.

Q. *How long did you take to find a property and what was the process?*

A. We took about as long as it took to get half way down a bottle of red wine!

After the holiday with my parents, we planned to return to the area and did so the following June. We stayed in a tiny *gîte* down a farm track which we loved so much, we tried to book again the following year. Too late: everyone loved this little cottage and we couldn't get the June week we wanted. So we cast around and found another cottage a few miles away. On arrival, the caretakers had left a note on the door – "Key under the stone, let yourselves in." So we opened the door, then a bottle and took a look around the property.

We don't mind a *gîte* that's a bit low on comfy seating or lacking in stylish décor but we do love silence, relative isolation and good views, preferably mountainous (or in Normandy, hilly!) where we can sit and look down a valley, book in hand, a nice bottle of wine, some cheese. So we checked out the location and views. Not bad, we decided, rural Normandy, pretty hills and valleys, lots of woodland. Then we looked along the hill to the house in the next field. Better view from there, we thought, looks straight down the valley. Gets the evening sun too. Hmm. Doesn't look lived in. Looks quite . . . deserted in fact. By the time the caretakers arrived to take our deposit, we were half way down the first bottle and greeted them with a glass, some nibbles and a question: "Is the house over there empty and do you know who owns it?" They did know that it was empty – apparently the old lady that had lived there had died 5 years previously – but they didn't know who owned it. Which wasn't a problem. Later in the week, we wrote our script and walked, slightly nervously, around to the third house on the hill, on the other side of 'our' house, to enquire if they knew who owned the building.

The woman who came to the door – Renee, who is now our neighbour – did know who owned the house because the old lady had been her mother-in-law. She wrote down an address in the local town and the telephone number. We chickened out of phoning but back in the UK arranged for a friend, fluent in French, to write and enquire if the house was for sale. Three weeks later, the response was yes, in principle it was. Would we like to visit and view the inside? We were joining friends in the Auvergne for a week that October so met the owner – the old lady's daughter – at 10am one misty morning, straight from the overnight ferry.

We were startled to find the *notaire* there with a *compromis de vente*. Patrick and I got out of the car hissing: "don't sign anything!" at each other. So far, we'd not mentioned a price. The *notaire* was very pleasant, spoke some English which made communications between Madame and Monsieur Rault easier, and he explained where the boundaries were, how a spring-fed pond could be reinstated at the bottom of the field and what good producers the apple trees were – so long as cider was the end product. The interior of the house was very much as we'd expected having seen the exterior. Very basic, run down, with damp in the walls, but – pride of the premises – an inside loo. Adjacent to the kitchen sink. As Madame had been 99 when she died, I suspect the inside loo had been quite a step up in comfort for her.

We went back to the Rault's home with the *notaire* for coffee, Calva and sugar cubes and left for the Auvergne feeling slightly shell-shocked. That may have been the home-distilled Calva delivering an alcohol-fuelled sugar hit to the blood stream but we suspected it was shell-shock because – assuming we could agree a price – we were on the way to buying a house.

Q. *Once you found the property, how long did it take till you signed the Acte?*

A. Once we'd agreed a price with the owners, it took about three months. The owners accepted £12,000 negotiated down from £18,000. A good exchange rate finally brought it in at about £11,600. We estimate we'll need to spend about £60,000 on it.

Q. *How much did you pay in fees on top of that?*

A. Primarily *notaire's* fees – just under £3,000.

Q. *How did you finance the property?*

A. Voluntary redundancy payment from the company I'd worked for over the previous 8 years. Voluntary redundancy was a project I'd commenced 10 months previously and it came to pass in conjunction with completing on the house. How lucky was that!

Q. *Worst experience?*

A. No bad experiences, except about a week before we were due to sign the Acte, we were startled by the news that part of the corrugated roof had blown off in the gales of December 1999. This surprise was entirely our fault for not being sensible enough to visit the house between seeing it in October 1999 and completing the purchase mid-way through the following year. Duh!

However, final repairs were already written into the Acte de Vente as the responsibility of the previous owner to put right – via an insurance claim already in process. Roofers were at a premium in northern France in the year following the tempête, and the roof was finally nailed back on four months after we completed, with the previous owner on site to see that operations were carried out properly.

Of course, we've not started really renovating yet, so the worst surprise is probably yet to come!

Q. *Best experience?*

A. Lots of little best experiences.

Finding we had a barn owl in one end of the building – who unfortunately flew off to quieter premises once he realised the house was in use again.

Finding out how welcoming everyone in the village was – despite, as we later discovered – we were just one more English family!

The stunning silence, particularly at night, when you can lie in the garden at midnight and see the stars with such clarity and listen to the grasshoppers and crickets.

The little things we take for granted in the UK – going to France Telecom and arranging for a telephone line – including two new telegraph poles – to be installed and we – that would be Patrick! – conducted the transaction entirely in French.

Realising, as we put in a small, temporary hot water boiler that this was the first time in the house's history – part of it is probably around 350 years old – there'd been hot running water.

Q. *Biggest surprise along the way?*

A. Probably finding out that half the roof had blown off – see worst experience above.

Or maybe the cold, wet and windy Sunday afternoon when we'd retired to bed for a siesta . . . and things . . . after a large lunch at the local bar. The surprise came when an acquaintance from the village arrived unexpectedly to deliver an enormous, home-baked *tarte au pommes* which he'd baked as a treat for us. He had to come in to put the tarte on the dining table which, in our one-room living style – is currently at the foot of the bed. Patrick, who'd managed to put on a pair of trousers en route to the door, thanked him profusely and waved him goodbye without offering coffee or Calva. There's a limit to how hospitable you can be when your wife is hiding under a duvet trying not to shriek with laughter. We have a large, 7ft screen now which is opened out to provide a modicum of privacy should we retire to bed in similar circumstances.

Q. *Can you speak the language?*

A. Sufficient for basic communication but insufficient for animated discussion of the state of our respective nations in the local bar or to start a conversation about foot and mouth disease and agriculture today. Patrick is attending evening classes twice a week so is improving dramatically. I attend evening classes too – but travel a lot so work frequently prevents attendance. I'll improve too – I like talking too much not to eventually manage at least adequate French although I suspect my French will never be elegant.

Q. *Are you renovating the property?*

A. Oh yes! Major restoration/renovation plans – for which we now have been given planning permission. Eventually, the house will be four bedrooms, two bathrooms, double height, split-level kitchen. At the moment, we have two large rooms – a total of about 600 square ft – on the ground floor. One is a sitting room/dining room/bedroom. The other is a shower room/loo/kitchen. I describe it as luxury camping. We are planning the sale of our house in the UK which will then release funds, part of which will be used to renovate the house in France. We embarked on a notional 5 year plan when we purchased the property in 1999.

Q. *How have the locals taken to you?*

A. The people we've got to know in the village seem bemused to find that so many English people are so keen on buying homes in the area. Having said that, we are invited – usually via our neighbour, Renee – to all the village fetes and *soirées* and attend when we can. Renee has adopted us, introducing us to family and friends so we know more people in the village than owners who've been there much longer. We're consciously making the effort to be part of the community, even though we still live in the UK, so they respond by involving us in whatever is going on. The tickets for a four course *Poule au Pot soirée* in the village hall recently were about 9 euros each. Very good value for an evening of eating, drinking and a disco for 200 people. The cost of the weekend's ferry tickets increased the price to about 199 euros each, however, so this energetic participation in the events of our second home comes at a price. But it was a very good weekend!

Q. *Ultimately, are you glad you bought your home in France?*

A. Yes. It's not so much a dream as simply what we've decided is our next phase in life. And transition to that next phase is in the process of being fulfilled. So far, it exceeds our expectations. When we move permanently, finding a way to earn a living there will be a challenge, not so much because of any language problems but because of the amount of red tape and taxes involved in working legally. But we're confident that we will find a way to make it work. What we can't yet anticipate is how we will feel after a few years, or five, or ten, about leaving our culture behind. To lose that whole cultural shorthand we use – probably unconsciously – when interacting with new acquaintances. Still, if we're aware of the possibility of 'culture shock', I think we should be able to surmount it.

6

How to find that perfect property

The internet

The best way to start your search is to look at property on the internet. This will give you a good idea of what's out there and the types of properties and areas that match your budget.

The IFP site (💻 www.french-property.com) has a database of several thousand properties and is updated daily. There are various criteria that one can use to search the database, such as *région, département*, price, date added to the database, or you can search by keyword. In addition there is a service that will alert you by email of new properties added to the database that satisfy your criteria.

You can also use one of the general internet search engines such as Google (💻 www.google.com), Yahoo (💻 www.yahoo.com) or MSN (💻 www.msn.com). Type in a keyphrase like:

* 'property for sale in Normandy'; or
* 'property near Montpellier'.

and you're off! There'll be hundreds of references.

Be warned though – looking at French property on the internet is addictive!

You'll start off looking for a small cottage as a second home, but when you realise that for the price of your terraced house in south London you can buy a small *château* then you'll probably start considering putting your principal residence on the market. If you're looking while at work then expect the pile on your in-tray to get bigger and bigger as you spend all your time day-dreaming of your escape to France.

Agent immobilier (the estate agent)

Estate agencies can be found, like their UK equivalents, in town and village streets with properties displayed in their shop-front windows. Note:

* an **agence immobilière** is the agency; and
* an **agent immobilier** is an agent that works within the agency.

If you search for property using an *agent immobilier*, make sure that they possess a *carte professionelle*. The *carte professionelle* permits them to propose one or a number of properties for you to rent or buy, to negotiate costs and to put in place all the conditions necessary to conclude the transaction. It also means they are covered by indemnity insurance. Often larger agencies employ negotiators called *agents commercials*. They act under the auspices of a registered agent's *carte professionelle* and it's not unusual to find small family-run agencies consisting of the *carte* holder and their wife or husband.

Professional bodies

Most dependable agents belong to one of the two professional bodies:

- **Federation Nationale de l'Immobilier** (FNAIM); or
- **Syndicat National des Professionnels Immobiliers** (SNIL).

These associations are independently-run bodies and provide back-up services for their members, such as computer programs for property databases and updates and seminars on property legislation. Membership of such an organisation is not compulsory, but an agent belonging to one of these tends to be more up to date in their field.

A *marchand de bien*s (translated as a 'trader in goods') is a property developer and speculator. They buy property simply to sell on. They aim for a quick turnover, although are only legally permitted to sell property they have owned for at least three months.

Before showing property to potential buyers the agent must get a mandate from the vendor which can either be:

- a **mandat exclusif**, meaning that they are the vendor's sole agent; or
- a **mandat simple**, which means that the vendor is selling with one or more agents.

Property buyers often turn up for a viewing only to find that the property has been sold by another agent – the vendor not bothering to tell other agents involved. This can be very frustrating for those that have made a trip to France especially to view a property. It's even worse if you have seen the property and have decided to put an offer in.

Paranoia rules

If you search via an *agent immobilier* don't expect to walk into the estate agency and be given lots of printed particulars to take away and mull over. Instead you'll have to sit with the agent while they show you photographs, usually by leafing through details collated in a ring-bound folder. It's unlikely that you'll be told the address and sometimes you won't even be told the village it is in. For a long time estate agents have been paranoid that buyers will go and make a private offer to the seller or that the seller will be approached by other agents, although this has begun to ease. Where such attitudes still exist, it can be very frustrating, especially for property hunters who want to travel around and get a feel for an area first.

Under French law, the agent entitled to the commission on the sale is the one who first showed or provided details of the visit. Sometimes estate agents may ask you to sign a *bon de visite* (visiting permit) which simply protects their commission as it proves that they were the first to have introduced you to the house.

Most agents expect at least a full day's notice before taking you to view a property. When you view you will almost always be accompanied by the agent. Don't be surprised if mid-way through a viewing schedule the estate agent insists on returning to town for his two-hour lunch break. Even if they know you are on a flying visit!

When looking at a property it's a good idea to make notes, take photographs or even record your visit on digital or video camera. Photocopy a 'tick list' to take to each property which makes you look at each feature, for example check the quality of roof, joinery, plastering and tick 'good', 'moderate' or 'bad', look for the presence of cracks and tick 'yes' or 'no', number of sockets tick 'enough' or 'not enough'. If you're on a fleeting visit you may not be able to revisit a couple of days later after work, as you would do at home, so you need to take your time and pay as much attention to detail as possible.

Make sure you do not fit too many viewings into a day. You'll need plenty of time to thoroughly look at each property and you should also leave some spare time in case the agent wants to show you a property that has just come up.

Notaires

Around half of all property sold in France is sold through *agences immobilières*. The rest are sold privately. About 15% of vendors sell directly through their *notaire*.

Notaires (public officials – discussed further in conveyancing section) also sell property but, as they are state employees and their job is not primarily as estate agents, not all of them display property details in their office windows. Some *notaires* are more active in selling property than others and will list the properties for sale on the website 🖥 www.notaires.fr.

  Tip: It's certainly worth approaching *notaires* in the neighbourhood you wish to buy, in order to find out if they have any property that might interest you.

You can find out the address of local *notaires* through the *mairie* (town hall). When a *notaire* is the selling agent, his 'agency' commission is not included in the asking price and is paid by the buyer. This doesn't cost the buyer any more, as the estate agent commission is included in the asking price.

UK-based agents

UK-based agents work by establishing a number of *agent immobilier* and *notaire* contacts in a *région* or number of *régions* of France. From these contacts they collate property that would be of interest to English buyers, particularly properties with lots of character, those that would make interesting restoration projects or any that have a great location, such as by the sea, a golf course, in the mountains, or those with fantastic views.

This sort of service can save you a lot of legwork and won't cost you any more as the UK-based agent will get a share of the estate agent's commission (sometimes as much as 50%) if the sale goes ahead. UK-based agencies often provide a much more detailed description of properties than the agents based in France. The UK agent will arrange a viewing schedule for you and confirm with the agent that the property is still for sale before you make the trip over to France.

UK-based agents are useful for people who speak little French and who find contacting French agents directly a daunting prospect. Having said that, an increasing number of French agents now offer services in English.

Case study

Gascony Property, based in Essex is a well-established agency started up by Pat Monk who fell in love with Gascony after spending family holidays there and has kept returning ever since. She now owns her own property in France and so fully understands the buying process and all the complications that can be involved. Pat responds to enquirers by forwarding details by email or post. She says:

"We then 'chase up' for visits and try to speak to them to arrange a sensible itinerary, if that is what they wish to have. We arrange the appointments and then off they go to France where our colleagues show them the properties. We often speak to them on their return to check how they got on and generally give advice etc. Our role technically ends once they are either 'off the books' no longer interested, or they have bought a property. To work in the UK there are no formal restrictions as in France – all our commissions are paid in France once TVA (French VAT) has been deducted."

If you have internet access, visit 💻 www.french-property.com to view a list of UK-based agents.

Personal property searchers

In recent years another breed of agent has emerged – a personal property searcher based in France.

Often these are people who have moved over to France and have discovered that finding property for others is not only a viable, but also rewarding way to make a living. The benefit of using a searcher is that they have been through the entire experience themselves and are able to share their wisdom with you. Most are fluent in French and have established good connections. They will offer you references before you agree to go ahead with them.

Two operations offering such a service are The Granny Network and Flying Visits. These are explained in greater detail below.

The Granny Network

Elayne Murphy works as part of The Granny Network – a group of personalised property searchers dotted over France. Elayne covers all areas of the Côte d'Azur and Provence from Menton to Montpellier, as far up as Orange and as far across as Ales.

Anyone that approaches her who is interested in purchasing a second home has to answer some preliminary questions over the phone or by email. She then sends clients a detailed questionnaire to really pinpoint what they want and assess whether their criteria are realistic. She says:

"I have been known to turn down a client because he has wanted a mansion in Peter Mayle country for the price of a barn in the Loire Valley – sorry no disrespect for the Loire!"

Once Elayne thinks they are being realistic she goes around all the agents, *notaires* and her various personal contacts in the area to find out what properties they have on their books. She eliminates those that do not come close and visits those that do. She says:

"I visit them personally and take loads of photos – anything between 12 and 30 depending on the size of the property. I also make a full report on both the good and bad ones, giving my own opinion for what it is worth, and then I let the client pick what they like. Usually they pick out half a dozen and I arrange the viewings. If they like nothing then I just keep on until I find several that they do like."

The client then comes over and Elayne joins them, if they wish, to visit the properties. She continues:

"I help out with all the paperwork, money transfers, etc. and even go to the signing of the compromis, do a translation and explain the various stages. In

between that and completion I help with bank accounts, transfer of utilities, in fact anything and everything. I help with house insurance, getting builders' quotes . . . whatever they need. The day of completion usually ends with my taking them back to my house for champagne!"

Her charge for this service is only €300, which is supplemented by a share of the commission from the agents. Not only does Elayne save clients time and wasted journeys looking at totally unsuitable properties – she holds their hand throughout it all.

The Granny Network

Contact: Sandie Marshall
☎   +33 2 51 98 23 96
@   vendeegranny@aol.com
💻   www.grannynetwork.info

Alternatively, if one of the following is based in the area you are searching, you can contact a 'granny' directly. Sandie Marshall was the first 'granny' and is based in the Vendee. The network has now expanded to include 'grannies' in Limousin, Poitou-Charente, Annecy, Normandy, Tarn, Dordogne, Loire, the Pyrenees and Elayne in Provence.

Provence: Elayne Murphy
@   Elayne@provencepropertysearch.com
☎   +33 4 90 20 39 50
💻   www.provencepropertysearch.com

Flying Visits

Flying Visits provides escorted 'just looking' tours in the Gers region. Over four days you'll be driven around and shown what the area has to offer, you'll view ten typical properties, meet English-speaking owners and talk to them about their experience of buying and moving to France, view plots and see renovation projects. Four nights, including three nights accommodation and food, costs £330 per person or £295 per person in a couple.

Flying Visits is run by two British couples who bought a house and *gîte* complex together in Gers in 2003 following many years of holidays together in France with their children.

Flying Visits

☎ +33 (0)5 62 67 09 21
@ info@flyingvisits.com
💻 www.flyingvisits.com

Other personal property searchers and businesses similar to Flying Visits can be found among the small adverts at the back of magazines such as *French Property News* (💻 www.french-property-news.com) and *Living France* (💻 www.livingfrance.com) – the first is subscription-only and the latter can be found on many newsagents' shelves.

Petites annonces (classifieds)

When you are in France it's worth buying or picking up some of the newspapers, free magazines (often found on stands outside estate agents) and weekly magazines that contain thousands of property advertisements (called *petites annonces*).

The best newspaper source is the national daily *Le Figaro,* which also prints a separate supplementary magazine *Résidences Sécondaires* which is packed with beautiful character properties for sale in all *régions* of France. There are also several specialised monthly magazines that can be found at any kiosk. Two of the most interesting are *Belles Demeures* and *Propriétés de France*, which specialise in *châteaux*, small farms, or *maisons de charme.*

For professional ads, try the two weekly specialist magazines, *L'Immobilier* and *L'hebdo Immobilier*, which both cover all of France. For the Paris area *A vendre/A louer* is a good source. For properties for sale by owner, the best and most popular source is a weekly paper called *Particulier à Particulier*, with over 20,000 classifieds each week covering every *région* of France.

In the UK, *French Property News* (subscription-only) has advertisements of property for sale.

On the internet, websites such as IFP (www.french-property.com) often have classified sections, where individuals can advertise their properties.

Understanding the *petites annonces*

The *petites annonces* can be confusing – they are often a minefield of abbreviations. Most homes, particularly apartments, are described in square metres. Some ads refer to the number of rooms by using the letter T meaning 'type' plus a digit, for instance T1 meaning Type 1 or T3 meaning Type 3. Kitchens, bathrooms, hallways and cellars are not included in the figure, so T4 could mean two bedrooms, a sitting room and a dining room or alternatively, three bedrooms and a sitting room.

The table overleaf has a list of common abbreviations.

Table 6.2 – Common abbreviations used in *petites annonces*

Abbreviation	In full	English
2P+C or 2P+K	2 pièces + cuisine	2 rooms, separate kitchen
2P+C équipée	2 pièces + cuisine	2 rooms, separate kitchen with some équipée appliances
2è	deuxième étage	second floor
60m²		surface area of 60 square metres
CA	Caution	damage deposit
DB	droit au bail	monthly rent tax of 2.5%
EDL	état des lieux	inspection fee
F2		2 rooms, separate kitchen
FA	frais agencies	agency fees
T2		2 rooms, kitchen as part of one room
Asc	ascenseur	elevator
balc	balcon	balcony
belles prestat	belles prestations	well appointed
bon état		good condition
calme		calm, quiet
cave		cellar, storage space
Cc	charges compris	charges included
cc	coin cuisine	small kitchen corner
cc (in another context)	commission comprise	agents' commission fees included
Ch	charges	monthly maintenance fees
chauf coll	chaufage collectif	whole-building heating (you pay a fraction of the building heating)
chauf ind	chaufage individuel	per-apartment heating (you pay according to your own use)
chf gaz	chaufage à gaz	gas heating
chf élec	chaufage électrique	electrical heating
coquette		cute (i.e. small !)
cuisine équipée	cuisine équipée	equipped kitchen
dble exp	double exposure	light exposure from both sides of residence
dble vitr	double vitrage	doubly glazed windows
digicode		numeric entry code at building entrance
env	environ	approximately
expo sud	exposition sud	looks South

Abbreviation	In full	English
FAI	Frais agence inclu	agency's fees included
HAI	honoraires agence inclu	agency's fee or commission included
Hon	honoraires	agency fees
HSP	hauteur sous plafond	high ceiling
imm bon stand	immeuble bon standing	prestige building
ISMH	l'Inventaire Supplémentaire des Monuments Historiques	a historically classified building
interphone		intercom at the building entrance
libre de suite		available immediately
meublé		furnished
part loue	particulier loué	privately rented (no agency!)
PdT	pierre de taille	stone building, often of the Haussmann era (if in Paris).
placards		cupboards
Prox	Proximité	close to
Rdc	rez-de-chaussée	ground level
Rdj	rez-de-jardin	garden level
refait à neuf		renovated
Rés	Résidence	group of apartments
SdB	salle de bains	bathroom
SdD	salle de douche	sink and/or shower only, implying that the W.C. is separate (and when in reference to a chambre de bonne, it's often down the corridor)
SH	surface habitable	living space
s/sol	sous-sol	basement
ss asc	sans ascenseur	without elevator
Séj	séjour	living room
Tb	très bon/beau	very good/pretty
Tcc	touts charges compris	all fees included (usually charges, heating, water)

Misleading descriptions to watch out for

coquette = cute, can also mean exceedingly small

studette = little studio, can be a broom cupboard, under 15m^2

kitchenette = little kitchen, is often a kitchen unit installed in the living room

décoration à revoir and rafraicheissement à prevoir = redecoration and repairs necessary, which may be quite costly

sur courette privative = on a private courtyard, often meaning a dark and dreary little inner courtyard

Examples of *petites annonces* for Paris apartments

Example 1

Rue Marx Dormoy. Agréable studio de 20,64m² ensoleillé (expo sud), calme sur cour avec vue dégagée, SdB avec fenêtre et kitchenette, Idéal 1er achat ou investiment. Charges raisonnables. €64,000

Rue Marx Dormoy. Pleasant studio of 20,64m², lots of sunlight (faces south), calmly situated on a courtyard with a clear view [for example, not looking directly into someone else's apartment], bathroom with a window and a kitchenette. Ideal first-time buy or investment. Reasonable charges. €64,000.

Example 2

Proche de Bastille. Très bel appt en 5è étage avec asc., 2 pièces en parfait état avec parquet, moulures, cuis. Amén. dble vitrage et cave, €161,000

Close to Bastille. Very attractive apartment on the 5th floor, with a lift, two rooms in perfect state with parquet, mouldings, fitted kitchen, double-glazed windows and cellar, €161,000.

Example 3

3ème – Beaubourg. Dans superbe imm. Au 5ème étage avec asc. 4/5P. de 103m² + balc., 3 chbres, dble séj., SdB., SdE., wc séparés, grde cuis. Beaucoup de caractère. €670,000.

Third arrondissement – Beaubourg. In a superb building, on the 5th floor with lift. 4/5 rooms of 103m² + balcony, 3 bedrooms, double lounge, bathroom, shower room, separate toilets, large kitchen. Lots of character. €670,000.

Example 4

Paris 12EME – Avenue Daumesnil. 3 pièces de 53m², 3ème étage dans immeuble. Double exposition, lumineux, Parquet, cheminée. Chauffage individuel gaz. Entrée, sejour, 2 chambres, cuisine, salle de bains, wc indépendants, placard. Cave. €251,000

Paris 12th arrondissement, Avenue Daumesnil, three roomed apartments of 53m², third floor in an apartment block, double exposure, lots of light, parquet flooring, fireplace, gas central heating, entrance, living room, 2 bedrooms, kitchen, bathroom, separate toilet, storage cupboard, cellar. €251,000.

Examples of *petites annonces* outside Paris

Example 1

Frais Réfuits Pour ce pavillon de 2001 situé à l'ouest de Bourgueil offrant cheminée, cuisine, 3 chambres sur 1,010 m² de terrain. €97,000

Reduced fees for this family house built in 2001 situated just west of Bourgueil offering working fireplace, kitchen and 3 bedrooms on 1,010 m² of land. €97,000.

Example 2

Touraine, proche d'Amboise, 10mn autoroute A10, maison du XVIIème siècle restaurée avec gout, d'une surface habitable d'environ 150m² comprenant salon-salle à manger, cuisine, salle de bains, lingerie chafferie. A l'étage, palier, 4 belles chambres, Petites dépendances, terrain d'environ 1 ha boisé et vallonné dans un site privilégié.

Touraine, close to Amboise, 10 minutes from the A10 autoroute, a 17th Century house tastefully restored, with a living area of around 150m² comprising a reception/dining room, kitchen, bathroom, heated linen room, boiler room, On the first floor, landing, 4 lovely bedrooms. Some small outbuildings and land of around 1 hectare, wooded and undulating and in a superior position.

Example 3

Lot-Quercy, dans un hameau en situation dominante, sur 2.9 ha, maison ancienne restaurée comprenant: sejour avec cheminé, cuisine, 2 chambres, dressing, salle d'eau, grenier aménageable, cave, grange 11 x 4 m sur 4 niveaux. 141,778e

Lot-Quercy, in a hamlet in a good location, an old restored house on 2.9 hectares, comprising a sitting room with fireplace, kitchen, 2 bedrooms, dressing room, shower, converted attic, cellar, 11 x 4 metre barn with four levels. €141,778.

Example 4

2h de Paris. Dans la campagne voisine de Honfleur, dans un très agéable, bello maison ancienne en brique et silex en excellent général sur terraine arboré d'environ 3,900 m² comprenant une cuisine, une salle d'eau avec wc, une belle pièce à vivre avec chem. À l'étage: 3 chbres. Edifiée sur une cave partielle. Excellent produit à découvrir. €137,900 F.A.I.

Two hours from Paris. In the countryside neigbouring Honfleur, in an agreeable location, beautiful old brick and flint house in an excellent condition on wooded land of around 3,900m² comprising a kitchen, a bathroom, a shower room with toilet, a beautiful living room with fireplace. On the next floor there are 3 bedrooms. Built on a partial cellar. An excellent find. €137,900 fees included.

Example 5

Nord-ouest Uzès. Dans village pittoresque, maison en pierres de pays rénovée avec soins offrant 220m² de surface habitable. Séjour, salon, cuisine, 4 chambres, bureau + appartement d'amis de 124m² de surface habitable. Belle cour close, piscine. 382,000 EUR

North-west Uzès. In a picturesque village, a traditional stone house sympathetically renovated offering 220m² of living space. Sitting room, drawing room, kitchen, four bedrooms, office and a guest apartment of 124m² living space. Beautiful enclosed courtyard, swimming pool. €382,000.

Auctions

In France property is auctioned through three distinct channels:

1. *Notaires* sell property that the owners have voluntarily decided to sell by this method. Sometimes it's because a quick sale is needed or because there is the need for transparency (a dispute between heirs could be a reason). *Notaires* also deal with properties that are unusual or have no real market. They are usually held in a room in the *département's Chambre des Notaires*.

2. **Tribunal de Grande Instance** (local county court) conduct law-enforced sales, called *ventes judiciaires* which concern properties that are mostly *saisie immobiliére* (mortgage repossession) sold on behalf of the creditor.

3. The **Domaine** (the State) auctions involve the sale of property belonging to the State, such as former public buildings the State no longer needs or wants to maintain. These auctions are good places to search for quirky buildings to convert into homes such as *phares* (lighthouses), *casernes* (barracks), *gendarmeries* (police stations), *bureaux de poste* (post offices) or old office buildings. Such sales also include *successions vacantes* (property that has passed to the State because no heirs have claimed it).

A cheap and quick way to buy property

The advantage of buying through any of these *ventes aux enchéres publiques* (auctions) is that, because a quick and easy sale is often called for, you are likely to get a property at less than the usual market value (depending of course on the demand and desirability of the property).

It is also the fastest process of purchasing a property in France – there's no conveyancing to be carried out and the buyer can, theoretically, take possession of the property eleven days after the auction. The downside is that you can only go by the information that's given to you and you cannot implement your own conditional clauses that will allow you to back away from the sale as, unlike with other sales, there is no preliminary contract between you and the vendor.

Viewing and information in advance

Some *notaire's chambres* publish an official auction programme three or four weeks before each auction session. Advertisements are also placed in the main regional, local or even national newspapers (under the property classifieds section) a few days before the property is open to viewing. The advertisement indicates the precise location of the property, its description, the reserve fixed price amount, the viewing dates and the contact details of the *notaire* in charge of the sale. The *Tribunaux* (local county courts) usually display the properties in the entry hall of the county court.

A sign is attached to the property and a detailed specification sheet called a *cahier des charges* is made available three to six weeks in advance. The specification sheet provides:

* details of the origin of the property;
* the town planning provisions;
* servitudes affecting the property;
* any charges (especially with copropriété); and
* details about whether lead piping, asbestos, or termites have ever been found present.

The sheet will also have the auction date, the opening bid price and the fees involved. Prepared and written by the *notaire* or, in the case of a *Tribunal de Grande Instance* by a clerk, it can be viewed in the office of the *notaire* or *avocat* (lawyer) in charge of the sale and has all the information you might require. It constitutes the sales document that you complete by establishing the purchase price.

Fixed days and hours for viewing the property will be given. Visit the properties that interest you, study the specification sheet, and then carefully consider and prepare your financing. Decide how much you want to spend, taking into account the added fees, and fix the maximum amount you will bid on the day of the sale. If you are getting a loan you will have to arrange in advance for the bank to lend you the money. Contact your bank as soon as possible before the sale. In almost all other sales you are protected by a clause which says that if you're unable to get a loan then the sale will be annulled. In this case, if you don't get a loan then you lose your deposit (the amount written in the *cheque de consignation,* see over the page). You will need to supply your bank with all the details of the property and the auction.

Before the auction date, thoroughly prepare your finances. Contact the *notaire* in charge of the sale in order to find out the estimated costs. The buyer at a *notaire's* auction is obliged to pay a share of the costs towards advertising and organisation costs of the auction, which amounts to 1% (before tax), with a minimum, for instance the Paris *notaire's* minimum of €387.50 (before tax).

When the sale is by a charitable association, the buyer must pay more towards the costs which is 2% (before tax) with a minimum of €775 (before tax). This cost will be mentioned in the *cahier des charges* and will be announced before the bidding begins.

You will also have to pay the standard taxes for transferring the property (see later section on conveyancing).

The day of the auction

Up to half an hour before the *séance* begins, all the *notaires* or *avocats* involved in the sales will be in a room called the *salle de consignation* which is outside the main auction room.

Here you must leave a *chèque de consignation* (deposit cheque) with the *notaire* or *avocat* who is in charge of your desired property's sale. After seeing some proof of identification, you will be given your *autorisation d'enchérir* (two documents giving you official permission to bid) and a number badge. The *chèque de consignation* is usually 20% but in some cases non-residents are asked to leave more, sometimes twice this amount. Check with the organisers of the auction in advance. Auctions are public and open to everyone, but only those bidders equipped with a badge can place bids and the badge number must be related only to the property on which they placed the deposit. You must display the numbered badge when you are bidding or the auctioneer will not accept any bids from you.

Once you are in possession of the documents and the badge you can enter the *salle de vente* (the auction room), also called the *chambre des criées*. The buyers are all gathered in the same room, each able to see their opposition and able to react accordingly. If you're worried about getting carried away by the excitement of the bidding you can be assisted by your own *notaire* or *avocat*. During the auction you can place your bids by the raising of your hand.

Let the bidding commence

At the start of the auction, the *Président* (chairman) of the sale announces the general conditions of sale that are common to all the lots. The properties are then presented for sale, usually following the order in the official programme. Before each individual sale the *notaire* of each vendor or the *avocat* (lawyer) representing the credit institution provides a brief description of the property. He or she indicates whether or not there are any tenants, the fixed price and the costs to be charged to the buyer. He or she informs the buyers of any information that may have been added to or amended in the specifications since they were signed by the vendor. At a tribunal there is often an independent *avocat inscrit au barreau* (barrister) present to oversee the sale and to guarantee that no one is advantaged above anyone else.

The method of sale *à la bougie* (by candle) is a custom dating back to the 15th Century that ensures bidders have an equal chance. Three small wicks are lit one at a time. When there are no more bids the first candle is lit and goes out after 15 to 30 seconds, then another is lit and if by the extinction of a third flame there are no further bids the winner is then announced. If anyone else bids during the succession of flames then the whole sequence must start again. The method is a more physically symbolic version of the verbal 'going once, going twice, gone' in British auctions. Beyond its symbolic and legal significance, this system allows for a sufficient period of reflection.

When the last bid has been placed and the final flame has gone out, the amount of the auction price and the badge number of the winning bidder are announced by the vendor's *notaire*. An advisory *notaire* present in the room then validates your bidding authorisation form by stamping *ADJUGE* (meaning AWARDED) and specifying the sale price on it.

You are then invited to the *salle de consignation* (the room where you left your deposit) by the *notaire* in charge of the sale, where you will be guided through the necessary formalities.

If you are not the winning bidder, you must also go to the *salle de consignation* in order to collect your cheque which will be returned to you, without costs, in exchange for your badge.

After the auction

Following the auction you either have 45 days (if it was a *notaire's* auction) or three months (if it was a *tribunal*) within which to pay the full purchase price as well as the costs and fees of the property transfer. If you are paying with a loan you must contact your bank immediately to get the ball rolling so that your payment deadline can be respected.

You cannot pay anything within ten days of the sale as during this time anyone can step in with a higher offer called a *surenchère*. The *surenchère* must be higher than your winning offer by at least 10% and the deposit cheque that the over-bidder must lodge generally represents 30% of the new opening bid. If this happens, a new and final auction must be organised. The new opening bid is equal to the price originally bid plus at least 10%. Once a *surenchère* is lodged, the *notaire* in charge of the sale must inform the person who was declared the winning bidder during the first auction and return to them their deposit cheque.

Finally, you are the owner

Without a *surenchère*, after ten days the winning bidder receives an *attestation* (certificate) to declare that they are the owner. You can pay the outstanding amount as soon as the overbidding deadline has expired, without waiting for the 45 days to pass, and therefore enabling you to immediately take possession of your property. The *cahier des charges* stipulates the different terms and conditions of transferring the property, taking possession of the property and information relating to the insurance of the property after the property has been awarded to the winning bidder. It normally specifies that the winning bidder must first of all pay the *prix d'adjudication* (the full agreed price) and the costs of the sale before taking possession of the property purchased. If you are buying an occupied property then you can collect rent or occupancy indemnities from that date.

In general all the extra fees and extra costs involved in auction sales do not exceed the equivalent costs you'd encounter in a more conventional sale through an estate agent. It normally works out at between 10 and 15% of the amount of the sale.

At a *tribunal* the deeds are not passed by an *acte* of a *notaire* but the *titre de propriété* is constituted by a document called *La Grosse* which is levied by the *avocat* after publication of the *adjudication*. If the buyer is unable to pay the full amount (*adjudication*) and the fees, the sale is called a *vente sur folle enchère* and the buyer loses his/her deposit.

If extra time is granted to the buyer to come up with the money then they will start being charged interest, after 45 days in the case of a *notaire's* auction or three months in the case of *tribunaux*.

Websites

There are a few websites concerning French property auctions, although not all are very clear and most lack photographs of the properties. The most informative website, which has a large and very good section in English clearly explaining the whole process, is that of the Paris *chambre des notaires*. The sequence of an auction can even be viewed on the website. It's certainly worth reading whether you are hoping to attend an auction in Paris or elsewhere.

The Paris Chamber offices

⊠   Place du Châtelet,12, avenue Victoria , 75001 Paris, France
☎   + 33(0) 1 44 82 24 82
@   encheres@paris.notaires.fr
💻   www.encheres-paris.com

Other websites with information on property auctions

- 🖥 www.directgestion.fr/immo-encheres
- 🖥 www.licitor.com/index.asp
- 🖥 www.immolegal.com
- 🖥 www.encheres-paris.com
- 🖥 www.info-encheres.com
- 🖥 www.realtrust.com
- 🖥 www.encheres-min.com
- 🖥 www.ventes-judiciaires.com
- 🖥 www.special-encheres.com
- 🖥 www.nouvellespublications.com

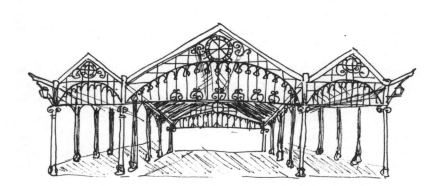

Interviews with agencies in France

Two interviews follow, the first with an agency based in France, the second with a UK-based agency.

Property agent interview 1

With Patricia Hamilton of Agence Hamilton, an agency based in Languedoc-Roussillon.

Q. *Recently there have been many TV programmes in the UK about buying property abroad – quite a few focusing on buying in France. Do you think these have had any effect on the market? Are there more British people coming over?*

A. The TV programmes had obviously put the idea into many people's heads of buying a property in France, some of these had perhaps previously only considered Spain as a location for a holiday home. However, they do paint a somewhat false picture as many English do not realise what a large country France is and how different houses and prices can be throughout the country. We have had many enquiries from clients wanting a farm house in good condition with outbuildings and land for £50,000 because they saw something like this on a programme. Unfortunately very few of them registered that it was in Bearn, which is a much cheaper area. The main reason for the influx of serious buyers has been the increasing number of cheap flights serving the area.

Q. *How about other nationalities? What proportion of Dutch, Italians, Germans etc would you say are looking in France? Do they look for different qualities in property?*

A. We have sold to many different nationalities: Finns, Swedes, Germans, Americans, Canadians, but the main market is still to the British. As an agency a very high proportion of our sales are to overseas buyers, with the British making up probably at least 60-70% of those sales. The different nationalities have very different views of what they look for in a house and the sort of area in which they wish to live. Generally speaking, Germans tend to be concentrated towards the coast, the Dutch more inland but in areas where there are other Dutch, Scandinavians want sun but more isolated properties with privacy and the English look for a house with a garden on the edge of a village with shops and not isolated.

Q. *Have property prices increased a great deal in the last couple of years? Could you tell me the typical cost of property in the régions you represent i.e. the cost of an old wreck, a village house, a detached property with land and in need of renovation, a modern villa?*

A. Property prices in Languedoc have risen in the last couple of years, mainly because of greater awareness of the area and easier accessibility. Typical prices are more difficult to pinpoint as, very unusually for a French agency, we cover a very large area and prices do vary quite considerably across the area.

Q. *What are the typical sorts of people looking for property in France? (e.g. young families, retired couples, people wanting to move permanently or those buying a holiday home.)*

A. All sorts of people, although I would say that nowadays probably 50 percent are looking to make a permanent move.

Q. *Do they tend to look for older homes they can renovate, complete wrecks or new property?*

A. The biggest demand is for a renovated older property in good condition with a garden, although new or recently built property is becoming more popular.

Q. *Why do estate agents in France give out none or such sparse details of the properties that they have on their books?*

A. A great many estate agencies in France are very small operations and do not employ a secretary, so have no-one to prepare the details. Also the French do not expect details of properties, they expect to be shown them. The final reason is that in the past overseas buyers had a very bad reputation in obtaining details of houses from agents and then going behind their backs direct to the owners, so that the agents did not get their commission.

Q. *Does gazumping happen in France?*

A. In theory it is not possible to gazump. Unfortunately the changes in French law have made it possible as now, in many areas, inspections to show whether there is any asbestos in the building or whether any of the paint has a lead content are obligatory and many *notaires* will not draw up the *compromis* until this has been done. If an offer has been made and accepted, the vendor is not in fact bound to that offer until such time as the *compromis* has been signed, so there is now a period where a higher offer can be accepted. However, the French generally speaking are very honest people and once they have given their word, we find they tend to stick to it.

Q. *Is there such a thing as closed bids? What if 10 separate buyers are interested in the same property and are all offering very similar offers?*

A. The first buyer to sign the *compromis* and to have that *compromis* signed by the vendor gets the house.

Q. *How do you go about making an offer? What's the lowest you can go beneath the price?*

A. Offers are generally made through the agent. We do not recommend offers in this area for the reasons given under gazumping. If an agent finds a buyer at the price shown in the mandate, the vendor is bound by law to accept that buyer. If an offer is made, the vendor can continue to show the property and look for another buyer. In Languedoc, it is a seller's market and there are more buyers than properties.

Q. *Do you think some estate agents up the price of the property for British people because they believe they are perhaps naive about the prices or it's perceived that they have a lot more money?*

A. An estate agent can only sell the property at the price shown on the mandate and not above that price. Therefore since virtually all agents in France are dealing with French clients as well as British clients they cannot increase prices for foreign buyers.

Q. *What type of British property buyer do French estate agents dread?*

A. The clients who try to buy from a distance and select properties to view weeks in advance. On the one hand they consider that if a property has been on the market more than 3 months there must be something wrong with it and on the other they expect to be able to select properties well in advance of their visit and expect them still to be available when they arrive. Also clients who expect to be able to arrive at a moment's notice without a prior appointment and cannot believe that the agent already has prior commitments or does not work on Sunday or public holidays – estate agents are people too!

Q. *What is the type of French estate agent that property buyers should dread?*

A. The agent who does not sit down with the client in their office to discuss in detail the client's requirements and the properties which may be suitable, but rushes them around the countryside showing everything and anything which might be suitable, wasting everyone's time.

Q. *Are there any cons or scams to watch out?*

A. No cons or scams that come to mind – or at least not involving British buyers.

Q. *If the vendor has agreed to sell exclusively through you but then you find out that he or she has sold through another agency, then what happens? Does this ever happen?*

A. The vendor cannot sell through another agency if he has given exclusivity. I believe it has happened, and that the courts have always found in favour of the 'exclusive' agency and awarded the commission to them, but I cannot quote cases.

Q. *Would you recommend that buyers get their own notaire to write up the compromis?*

A. It depends on the house and the *notaire*. Most *notaires* are totally trustworthy and competent and in theory are totally neutral. We always advise our clients on an individual basis whether or not we think it is necessary to appoint a second *notaire*.

Q. *What's the best advice you can give to someone about to embark on their property hunt in France?*

A. Find yourself a reputable agent, explain your requirements fully (nothing is more infuriating than spending a day showing a client houses only to be told at the end that none were suitable because there was not room for a pool – a fact which had not previously been mentioned), and then put yourself in the hands of the agent. Don't try to fill every minute of every day of your visit with appointments – this does not allow the agent flexibility to show you properties which may be new on their books or to show you the surroundings of any particular property.

Agence Hamilton

🖳 www.agence-hamilton.com

Property agent interview 2

With Bruce Claxton of Rural Retreats – a British-based agency that also specialises in property in Languedoc-Roussillon in France.

Q. *Firstly, can you give me a little background about Rural Retreats. How long have you been around? What service do you provide exactly? Which régions do you cover?*

A. Rural Retreats has specialised in the Languedoc-Roussillon *région* of southern France since 1989. It's aim is to assist prospective buyers with all aspects of acquiring a property in the *région* through its head office in the UK and its consultants and agents in France. Normally, this service is provided free of charge since the company is remunerated by the agency concerned in the event of a sale. Our keynote is a friendly and professional service based upon many years experience of the market and a thorough awareness of our clients' concerns.

Q. *Recently there have been many TV programmes in the UK about buying property abroad – quite a few focusing on buying in France. Do you think these have had any effect on the market? Are there more British people coming over?*

A. Yes to both your questions, although the downside is that sometimes these programmes fuel unrealistic expectations!

Q. *How about other nationalities? What proportion of Dutch, Italian, German etc. would you say are looking in France? Do they look for different qualities in property?*

A. I cannot quote statistics but certainly the British presently account for well over half the sales of properties to foreigners in this *région*. The Benelux (mainly Dutch & Belgian) are the second biggest group, followed by Scandinavians and then Germans. Italians are less interested in this area along with the Spanish. Until 9/11 the Americans accounted for probably 5% of our customers, now virtually zero.

Q. *Have property prices increased a great deal in the last couple of years? Could you tell me the typical cost of property in the French régions you represent for example, the cost of an old wreck, a village house, a detached property with land and in need of renovation, a modern villa?*

A. Yes, property in some cases has risen by as much as 30% p.a. Expect to pay upward of €50,000 for a modest village property requiring modernisation; a traditional stone property with land and outbuildings in need of renovation would start at around €250,000; a modern villa could be anything from €180,000 upwards depending upon size, plot, situation etc.

Q. *Your company also specialises in Italian properties. What sort of people are interested in Italy and what sort in France? Would you say there's a difference in terms of age, family status, second or permanent home seeking, socio-economic background etc?*

A. No, I would say that there is no marked difference, but remember that the area of Italy in which we are active (northern Lazio) is similar in many ways to the Languedoc. If our outlet was in Tuscany or Umbria where prices are generally much higher, the story might be different.

Q. *What proportion of people looking for property in France intend on making it their permanent home?*

A. I would say that more than 50% of our clients are seeking a property to move to permanently or to 'grow into' within a 5-year period.

Q. *Many people complain of turning up and finding property already sold? How can you avoid this happening?*

A. In a very active market, the simple answer is you can't. Which is why we always caution clients about getting too excited or set upon a particular property *before* they get to see it. A good agent will nevertheless aim to show only properties which conform broadly to a client's spec – which is why a company such as ours can be invaluable in briefing agents ahead of a client's arrival. Satisfaction can never be guaranteed but at least the client has a reasonable expectation of finding something suitable in the long run.

Q. *Why do estate agents in France give no or such sparse details on the properties that they have on their books?*

A. There is arguably a host of reasons, cultural, economic, historic, commercial and legal! I would say that there is now a tendency to provide more written information amongst certain agents, but still not to the extent that one finds in the UK and US for instance. My advice – don't spend too much time pouring over websites and magazines; instead plan a visit of at least 3 weekdays and see for yourself what's available.

Q. *Does gazumping happen in France?*

A. Only at the pre-preliminary contractual stage (i.e. the *compromis de vente*), and only then as a result of the import of aggressive real estate practices by foreigners such as ourselves!

Q. *Is there such a thing as closed bids? What if 10 separate buyers are interested in the same property and are all offering very similar offers?*

A. An agency is generally empowered by its *mandat* to accept an offer at the asking price on behalf of an owner. Offers at less (or more!) than this figure have to be referred to the owner for decision. In the past, an owner having accepted an offer at the pre-contract stage would stick to his word.

Q. *How do you go about making an offer? What's the lowest you can go beneath the price?*

A. Name your figure based upon a sum you can afford commensurate with an assessment of what a property is worth in comparison with others of similar category. If the asking price seems fair, don't try to get 'something off' as a point of principle – you'll probably lose the sale!

Q. *Do you think some estate agents charge more to British people because they are maybe naive about the prices or perhaps it's perceived that they have a lot more money?*

A. Not as a general practice, but certainly the plethora of foreigners wishing to buy has forced prices higher at a rate beyond that which would otherwise have occurred.

Q. *Would you recommend that buyers get their own notaire to write up the compromis?*

A. Not unless they know of a good *notaire* in the *région* or have a strong reason for doing so. Familiarity with the French language is often a major stumbling block however, which is why having somebody like us to help is often essential.

Q. *What's the best advice you can give to someone wishing to buy in France?*

A. Read up ahead of a visit, leave young children with their grandparents and don't try to combine a property search with a family holiday. Decide broadly upon the *région* most likely to suit (France is a *big* country), be motivated, stick to what you can afford, be realistic (it rains in southern France) but at the same time enthralled at the prospect of buying your own place in France. And be prepared to invest time learning something of the language. A tall order admittedly, but at the end of the day the property you choose must *excite* you, otherwise forget it and move on.

Rural Retreats

 www.rural-retreats.com

7

The property transaction

Surveys

Surveys are not common in France but this isn't to say you can't get one done.

There are simple checks that you can make yourself, for instance attentively examine the state of the roof, walls, heating, plumbing and electric installation. One thing you will become very familiar with if you have an older property is the *fosse septique* (septic tank) – certainly check that this is in good working order! If located near a waterway or in a valley check that the property is not prone to flooding. Verify that the property conforms to the description given to you: in particular the presence of equipment, measure the area (in some cases it must be written in the *avant-contrat* and the *contrat de vente*). If possible go accompanied by a building specialist (*specialist de bâtiment*) and get them to evaluate the importance and cost of eventual work.

There are a number of English-speaking surveyors based in France who advertise in magazines such as *French Property News*.

Contracts and conveyancing

The role of the *notaire*

The process of buying a house in France is very structured and subject to strict regulation. Whereas in the UK we appoint a solicitor to search the deeds and write up the documentation, in France the conveyancing is carried out by a *notaire*.

The *notaire* has no direct equivalent in the UK. There are about 8,000 *notaires* throughout France. The organisation and implementation of legal relations is at the heart of their profession. Their job, which mainly involves the writing up of legal documents and witnessing their signature, is considered a public service and they work directly for the State. About half of a *notaire's* activity involves real estate, but they're also involved in commercial, industrial, inheritance and land disputes, town planning and consumer law. It's a well-respected position and it takes many years of rigorous training to become a *notaire*.

Any document drawn up and signed by a *notaire* is an official document with legal weight and is known as an *acte authentique*. Such documents bear the seal of the State.

Two contracts are involved in the purchase of a property:

1. **avant-contract** (preliminary contract); and

2. **acte de vente** (the final sales contract).

Either a *notaire* or an estate agent can write up the *avant-contrat* (preliminary contract), but for the final contract, the *acte de vente*, only the signature of a *notaire* can seal the sale. An *avant-contrat* that is not written up by a *notaire* is known as an *acte sous seing privé*. The *notaire's acte* is the superior of course and if you decide not to use a *notaire* then you do so at your own peril.

Appointing a *notaire*

Even though the buyer is entitled to appoint the *notaire* (as the buyer is the one that picks up the bill) you may find that the person selling the property will want to use his or her own *notaire*. This has its advantages: if the *notaire* is already familiar with the vendor and the property, a lot of work could be avoided and the sale will go through more quickly. But you may wish to have your own *notaire*, one of the reasons being that although *notaires* are meant to be impartial, a *notaire* selected by yourself and independent from the person selling the property could be more rigorous in seeking out problems. If the buyer and vendor cannot agree on the choice of a *notaire* then you can each use your own and the fees will be divided between the two.

The preliminary contract *(avant-contrat)*

When you've found a property, the first stage is to sign a preliminary contract (*avant-contrat*), a legally-binding contract saying that you have agreed to buy the property and that the vendor has agreed to sell the property to you. The *avant-contrat* can be either:

- *promesse unilaterale de vente;* or
- *promesse bilatérale*, commonly known as a *compromis de vente*.

These are described below. Often in this book the *avant-contrat* will be referred to as the *compromis*, simply because that is the document you are more likely to be asked to sign.

Promesse unilaterale de vente

With such a document the owner agrees to sell the property to you and agrees to take the property off the market for a set period of time while the *conditions suspensives* (get-out clauses, explained later) are being checked. You are not obliged to buy the property, however you must pay 10% of the property price to the owner, which is returned to you if the *conditions suspensives* aren't met. If you back out in the agreed time limit, which is usually three months, then you lose your deposit.

Compromis de vente (promesse bilatérale)

This promise is binding on both the owner of the property and the buyer. The buyer agrees to go ahead with purchasing the property if the *conditions suspensives* are met. This promise is accompanied by a payment of a percentage of the property price. If you haven't changed your mind during the seven day cooling-off period and if the clauses are fulfilled then you are legally obliged to go ahead with the sale. If the vendor decides to withdraw then they forfeit a sum that can be double the sum of the deposit. Gazumping is almost unheard of in France thanks to such a legally-binding agreement.

Checks to make before the *avant-contrat*

Before the *avant-contrat* is written, get the estate agent to arrange a meeting with the vendor so that you can ask lots of questions about the property. The vendor is obliged to answer any questions to the best of their knowledge. If it is in a *copropriété* then find out about the amount of charges of the *copropriété*, how the block is maintained, about sound and heating insulation, etc. It's also important to confirm that fixtures and fittings will be staying as it's not unusual for a vendor to take with them the entire bathroom suite or kitchen units, or even to uproot and take the garden shrubs! Some vendors even take the light bulbs with them! You may want an inventory included in your final contract. In some situations a geometric expert will be needed to measure the land and to work out your boundaries.

Conditions suspensives

Your *notaire* will advise you on the *conditions suspensives* to be inserted into the *avant-contrat*, which allow you to break the agreement and recuperate your deposit if they are not met.

Examples of *conditions suspensives*:

- you will only go ahead if **planning permission** is found for building work you wish to carry out (especially important if land is being bought);
- that the presence of **termites, asbestos, lead piping and paint** is not found;
- verification that the person selling you the property does **own the property**;
- there are no **servitudes or droits de préemption** found that affect the property and limit your project; and
- that the **loans** you have applied for will be obtained.

Also included in the *avant-contrat* are the names of the buyer and vendor; the agreed price, and the date for completion.

On the signing of the *avant-contrat*, a deposit, normally of 10%, is paid by the buyer. Payments must be made in the form of a cheque or postal mandate and paid into a special bank account set up by the *agent immobilier* or the *notaire* where money is blocked until the *acte de vente* has been signed. **Never exchange money with either an agent or vendor directly, without first signing an avant-contrat.**

After you've signed the *avant-contrat*, your *notaire* will look at your passport, birth certificate and a copy of a utilities bill to establish your civil status.

Buying off-plan (*sur plan*)

If you are buying off-plan you will sign the *contrat de réservation*, which contains a description of the property (surface area, number of rooms, outbuildings, services), a description of building materials and quality, the site of the property and a list of collective equipment at your disposition. It also includes the sale price of the property, payment dates, timetable for completion, the completion date and penalties for non-completion. Both parties sign a copy of the floor plans and technical specifications. If you are buying an unbuilt property and there is to be a wait of one year then you will pay a deposit of 5% of the sale price, if there's to be a two year wait then 2% of the sale price will be asked for.

Seven days cooling-off period

After signing the *compromis de vente* you have a period of seven days in which you can reflect on your decision and change your mind without penalty. If you do change your mind, the estate agent must return your money within 21 days. During this waiting period you mustn't pay any more money to any of the parties involved.

After the seven days the *compromis de vente* becomes an *acte definitif* and from then on there is no turning back.

Checks made by the *notaire* following the *avant-contrat*

A period of, on average, three months will follow in which the *notaire* conducts all the checks. The *notaire* will find out the amount of taxes and duties that apply to the property and land, and will find out what your rights will be as owner.

If your property is *copropriété* then the *notaire* will examine the *Reglement de Copropriété* that provides details of the amount you must pay towards maintenance and works, as well as the rules that owners must abide by. They will check the reports of the last residents' meetings, and will inform you of charges that apply for proposed works, the nature of these works and how they will be carried out. The area of the house or apartment, which must be equal to or more than 8m², must be noted in the *avant-contrat*.

When a property is less than ten years old, the *notaire* will check that the owner has covered the property with the appropriate building insurance (the ten year *assurance dommages-oeuvres*). Your *notaire* must obtain copies of the insurance policies and after the sale you can decide whether you want to continue these policies or terminate them.

With a recently built property, the *notaire* will check that the *certificat de conformité* has been delivered. This certificate confirms that the property has complied with local planning permission and that the final structure conforms to the plans which enabled it to obtain a *permis de construire* (building permit).

The *notaire* is obliged to find out about:

- **Presence of lead** (for example, water pipes and wall paint)
  Lead piping and paint is most likely to be found in properties built before 1948 and some areas are more at risk of being exposed to it than others. The law obliges that when a house constructed prior to 1948 in such an area is on the market, then it must have a test for the presence of lead within the year preceeding the sale. You can find out if the property is in an area potentially at risk by contacting your local mayor or town hall.

- **Risk of the termite damage**
  In certain areas termites are a problem and a *constat parasitaire* must be carried out in the last three months and the results included in the *acte de vente*. In the absence of these tests the vendor remains responsible if you find termites. The vendor isn't obliged to seek out any other insects such as locusts, although you won't be prevented from sending someone in to look for these for yourself.

- **Presence of asbestos** (*amiante*)
  For all properties which the *permis de construire* (building permit) was delivered before 1 July 1997, a test for asbestos must be carried out and the results must be included in the final *acte de vente*.

The *notaire* is also obliged to find out for you the presence of *servitudes* and pre-emptive rights, explained below:

Servitudes

A *servitude* is a burden attached to an estate for the benefit of an adjoining estate or of some definite person. *Servitudes* are rights that are exercised over your property by others, be they neighbours, the commune or anyone else.

Some *servitudes* come into place following an agreement signed by owners of two neighbouring properties, such as an agreement that your neighbour can use your water well. In this case, along with the right to use the well, the right to cross your land to get to it is tacitly included. A *servitude* called *non edificandi* is when a neighbour covenants not to build on his land for your benefit, in order, for example, so that your view is maintained.

Other *servitudes* include:

- Those that originate from public regulations such as local authorities. If a new road will cut through your land then you do not have the right to plant a tree in the middle of the road or obstruct the road's use in any way.
- Certain *servitudes* originate from court orders.
- Others are needed to benefit neighbouring property for instance, pipes and cables that go under or over your property in order to service another property.

Servitudes are attached to the land and not to the owner who granted them. On the sale of a property or at the death of its owner, the property remains subject to the *servitude*. Therefore it will pass automatically to the new owner. It is possible to give a *servitude* a time limit – to set a date when use will come to an end.

 Tip: Be very careful about allowing anyone rights to your property.

As in the UK with squatters, if somebody occupies your property without being asked to leave, then, after a period of time, they gain the right to remain. For instance, the previous owner may have allowed the farmer to graze his cattle in an unused field for the last ten years. Beware, a *servitude* may have been unwittingly created obliging you to allow this to continue whether you now want to make use of the field for your own needs or not. Even if the *servitude* is not an immediate problem to yourself, it will bind future purchasers and thus could affect the value of your property.

A *servitude* can come to an end if it is renounced by its beneficiary, or that beneficiary becomes the owner of the property. It can also come to an end through non-use over a long period. In severe circumstances it can end if the property subject to the *servitude* is destroyed.

There are some rules that apply to all neighbouring properties. These are general laws, not *servitudes*:

- Rainwater (and snow) must drain onto your own property and not anyone else's.
- Your neighbour can oblige you to fence off your boundary with him or her and at common expense.
- If your neighbour's tree overhangs your land you cannot cut the branches nor collect any fallen fruit that lands on your garden. The tree is theirs and they must cut it and the fruit is theirs wherever it lands. This is the opposite to the law in England. (Your neighbour in France can of course give you permission to take the fruit.)

- If a neighbour's only access to the road is over your property then he or she has the right of way over your land.

- If your property borders a navigable river you must allow over 30 feet (9.75m) for haulage and a footpath. Be careful when buying property beside water as you may have no say in how the waterside foliage is kept.

Pre-emption rights (*droits de préemption*)

When property or land comes up for sale certain authorities have the right, called *droit de préemption*, to step in and purchase the property before anyone else. There are several ways in which this right may be exercised.

Droit de préemption urbain

This pre-emption right is held by the commune where the property is situated. The *mairie* usually exercises the right when the property or land is required for development purposes such as public works, for example the building of a sports centre, hospital or a new road. The vendor must notify the *mairie* of his or her intention to sell by sending a declaration called a *déclaration d'intention d'aliéner* (DIA). The DIA is usually drawn up by the *notaire* in charge of the sale of the property and sent to the *mairie*. The *mairie* then has two months to reply. If the *mairie* does not intend to purchase the land it will either not reply or will send the DIA back with the comment: *Droit non exerc* or *Droit n'existe pas*.

The *mairie* usually purchases property at a lower price than the purchase price indicated in the DIA. The vendor can choose whether to withdraw from the sale and keep the property, to accept the *mairie's* offer at the lower price, or let a judge fix the price at which the *mairie* purchases the property.

Droit de préemption by SAFER

Owners of agricultural land must send a letter of notification of the sale of the land to *Société d'Amenagement Foncier et Etablissement Rural* (SAFER), a governmental organisation that manages the rural environment. From receipt of this notification SAFER has two months to decide whether or not to purchase. If SAFER decides to purchase the property the same rules apply as to the *Droit de Préemption urbain*. The notification of the *droit de préemption* is published in a local or regional newspaper.

A farmer may have *droit de préemption* on agricultural land that comes up for sale where:

• They have been the sole user of the land.
• They have worked as a farmer on the land for three years.
• The total area of the land they use is over one hectare.
• The farmer commits him or herself to use the land continuously for nine years.

Droit de préemption protecting tenants

When the landlord sells occupied premises for the first time following the division of the property into a *copropriété*, they must send a notification to the tenant who then has one month to reply saying whether or not they wish to buy the property from the owner.

If the tenant wishes to buy the property they have two months to complete the purchase or four months if a loan must be obtained. If the lease is due to expire and the landlord wishes to sell, then the landlord must send a notification called a *congé pour vendre* to the tenant six months before the end of the lease and the tenant has two months within which to reply. Again, the sale must be completed within two months, or four months if a loan is to be obtained.

The law provides great security to tenants. If the landlord sells the property without notifying the tenant or sells the property at a lower price to someone else, then the tenant can, within one month following completion, take priority over the purchaser.

Droit de préemption by coindivisaires

If a number of people jointly own a property (usually because they have jointly inherited it) and one of them decides to sell their share, then the other *indivisaires* must have first rights to purchase the share. The vendor serves a letter written up by a *Huissier de Justice* on the other *indivisaires* and they have one month within which to answer. If the other *indivisaires* wish to purchase the share they must do so within two months.

The consequences of the *droit de préemption* are that the purchaser is obliged to let the *preémpteur* buy the property. He or she recovers all deposits made to the estate agent or the *notaire*.

Final contract (*acte de vente*)

Once all the checks have been made the final stage of sale is the signing of the *acte de vente* (the final deed of sale). This normally takes place at the *notaire*'s *étude* (the *notaire*'s office) with all parties present. Everyone tends to dress smartly for this formal occasion – so dust down your suit and polish your shoes!

If one party can't be present then they can send a representative power of attorney. This is common among buyers and vendors, especially by foreign buyers, and can be arranged by your *notaire*.

Tip: Ask to visit the property before the signing, so as to check that everything (including the kitchen sink) is there and that it is 'sold as seen' on that date. You don't want to sign the final deed and then find out the roof was blown away by a severe storm a couple of days before.

First, check the property

Go accompanied by a lawyer, if you have one, or by the estate agent. If anything is missing or broken then the *notaire* can hold back a portion of the final sum to pay for repairs or replacements. Do not go ahead with the sale unless this is confirmed as problems may be impossible to redress later. Owners who seem very trustworthy and sweet as pie at the signing (telling you not to worry and that all repairs will be made) have been known to do a Jekyll and Hyde as soon as the last page is signed and want nothing to do with the buyer or the property ever again.

At the signing

At the signing the *notaire* will read through the *acte de vente* and the buyer and the vendor will initial each page. The last page will be signed after writing in French *'bon pour accord'* which means that you have each understood and accept the terms of the document. If the *notaire* feels that your French is not good enough to fully understand what is being read out, he or she must find someone to translate. Although, be warned, this rarely happens and when it does the translation is normally nonsensical. If you lack confidence in your French then you should really take responsibility and find a trustworthy bilingual person to help you.

Congratulations – you're the owner!

Legal ownership is transferred, the outstanding amount is paid to the vendor (by banker's draft or bank-to-bank transfer into the *notaire's* account, in which case allow time for the money to transfer), and the *notaire's* fees and taxes are paid. After paying the money the *notaire* will give you an *attestation de propriété* which is a certificate saying that you own the place. You will also receive the long-awaited keys!

Proof of ownership is guaranteed by registration of the property at the land registry (*cadastre*) where the deed of sale will be stamped. The original deed is retained at the *notaire's* office for 100 years (after which it will be put in the public archives) and a certified copy is made available to the new vendor two to six months after completion.

Once the formalities are over all parties may go to the local bar to celebrate (even though you're probably dying to get to your new home and put that key in the door for the first time!)

If you are not happy with your *notaire's* work then write to the *notaire* or go to see him or her in order to get an explanation. If this doesn't work address your *Chambre Départementale des Notaires*.

Legal advice

Independent legal advice

There are many bilingual legal advisors based both in France and the UK from whom you can seek further advice or assistance. It is important that you are clear about what you are signing and that all necessary clauses have been inserted into your *avant-contrat*.

If you cannot be sure that you have understood everything with the *notaire*, then it's certainly worth seeking independent English-speaking legal advice. Remember, if you share your *notaire* with the vendor then he or she will be working for both parties. The *notaire* must make sure that you understand all issues but he or she must not necessarily give you advice. Another problem is that many *notaires* are not trained in English law, and in many cases will not be able to take into account the situation regarding your property in the UK. An independent advisor will look for solutions to your needs alone.

 Note: **It is very important that you get good advice on inheritance or taxation issues.**

Most legal advisors either charge a fixed rate or an hourly rate of between £170 and £250 an hour. It may seem expensive but if you're spending hundreds of thousands on a property it's a small sum to pay, and if, for example, you need advice on inheritance, then the advisor could save you a fortune in inheritance tax (as well as possible family disputes).

Contacts: UK-based legal advisors

John Howell & Co

⊠   The Old Glass Works, 22 Endell Street, London WC2H 9AD
☎   +44 (0)20 7420 0400
Fax +44 (0)20 7836 3626
@   info@europelaw.com
💻   www.europelaw.com

Prettys Solicitors

Contact: Matthew Cameron
⊠   Elm House, 25 Elm Street, Ipswich, Suffolk, IP1 2AD
☎   +44 (0)1473 232121
@   MCameron@prettys.co.uk
💻   www.prettys.co.uk

CBA Law

⊠   1 Beacon House, Landmark Business Park, Whitehouse Road, Ipswich, Suffolk IP1 5PB
☎   +44 (0)1473 464444
Fax +44 (0)1473 466844
@   emma.morris@cba-law.co.uk
💻   www.riddellcroft.com

Russell Cooke

Contact: Dawn Alderson

⊠   2 Putney Hill, Putney, London, SW15 6AB

☎   +44 (0)20 8789 9111

@   Aldersond@russell-cooke.co.uk

💻   www.russell-cooke.co.uk

Verifying legal details yourself

The French civil service has produced a superb website 💻 www.service-public.fr (some pages in English, but mostly in French) which is a mine of information on absolutely everything from neighbour disputes, inheritance issues, building contracts, visas, etc.

It has many FAQs relating to each issue and it's possible to download any application form you may need, for instance a *permis de construire* (application for a building permit). The entire civil service is involved in the production of this user-friendly site. It also tells you the relevant law or legal articles from which the information is gathered and has hyperlinks to the official descriptions of these articles at 💻 www.legifrance.gouv.fr.

Legifrance is a very useful French legal reference site. It provides free access to all the essential terms: all laws currently in force, selected regulations, an official Journal backdated to 1990, international treaties and agreements, jurisprudence, legal developments, etc. Sometimes even lawyers and *notaires* can give surprisingly contradictory information so it's always a good idea to read the official wording of an act of law yourself. Although be warned, even if your French is perfect, legal writing is about as far from vernacular as you can get; it can be quite gruelling to read and even nonsensical if you're not used to it.

Seeking advice from ANIL

L'Agence Nationale pour l'Information sur le Logement (ANIL) is a national agency well worth knowing about.

It's a national non-profit organisation (jointly managed by the Housing Ministry, local governments, representatives of housing and loan institutions and consumer associations) that gives out free information on housing to the general public. Your local representative of ANIL will be called ADIL – *Agence Départementale d'Information sur le Logement.*

Your ADIL makes information on housing (whether it's to do with buying, building or renting) available to the public, free of charge, on any aspects, financial, legal or other. If you have any concerns about your contracts then these are good people to approach. The majority of their employees are legal advisors.

Here are some of the topics they claim to deal with:

- Tailormade mortgage plans
- Legal, financial and tax advice
- Property and other taxes
- Housing benefits
- Contract law
- Improvement grants
- Building liabilities
- Building insurance
- Procedure for obtaining council property
- Planning permission and regulations
- Owner and tenant rights
- *Copropriété*
- Relations with the associated professions such as architects, builders, geometric experts, etc

ADIL is also a clearing house for information on newly-built properties and plots for sale and rent. ANIL and ADIL seek and collate feedback and carry out surveys on housing matters, especially housing policies and evolution of the market.

Find out the contact details of your closest ADIL from ANIL's website:
💻 www.anil.org

The website also has lots of useful information (some in English, German, Dutch, Spanish and Italian), especially that outlined in a number of downloadable PDFs (in French only) on how to deal with certain professionals.

Fees for purchasing the property

Notaire's fees

The buyer is required to pay the *notaire's* fees – *frais de notaire*. These fees pay for the *notaire's* services and also include certain taxes and registration fees. The *notarie's* fees are calculated according to a percentage of the value of the property being sold.

 Note: The *notaire's* fees are normally paid by the buyer and are based on the value of the transaction (not necessarily the price it was finally sold at).

Table 7.1 – *Notaire's* fees (approximate)

Value of transaction (EUR)	Fees
Below 50,000	10%
50,000 – 200,000	7%
Over 200,000	6.5%

Agent immobilier fees

The percentage that an *agent immobilier* claims as their fee isn't regulated but is often between 5 and 10% of the purchase price. The higher the price, the lower the percentage. Some agents will offer a flat fee, say, 6% for all transactions – although recently competition is encouraging some agents to charge just 3%.

The fee will be in the vendor's *mandat* to the agent and it will be made clear to potential buyers before they sign the *avant-contrat*. In principal, it is the vendor that pays the estate agent, although in some circumstances the buyer is asked to pay, or the cost is shared between the two. Who pays must be made precise in the *avant-contrat*.

Notaire as selling agent

If the *notaire* is responsible for selling the property then his or her fees are paid by the buyer. The percentage of fees are:

*   €0 - 45,735: **5%**
*   then the remaining sum over €45,735: **2.5%**

> **Example: *Notaire* as agent fees**
>
> Assume a property is sold at €115,000, the remuneration would be worked out as:
>
> 1. 5% of €45,735 = €2,286.75
>
> 2. Plus 2.5% of €69,265 (115,000 minus 45,735) = €1,731.63
>
> The total is **€4,018.38**

Other payments

Whether a property is old or new *droits d'enregistrement* (stamp duty) must be paid. The *commune, département* and the State each take their slice of duty.

The added payments for an older property will include:

1. *Taxe communale* (tax paid to the *commune*) of **1.2%.**

2. *Taxe départementale* (tax paid to the *département*) which is around **3.60%** but can be as low as 1%.

3. *Prélèvement de l'État* (tax paid to the State) **2.5%** *taxe départementale.*

> An older property sold at €200,000 will have to pay the following:
>
> 1. *Droit départemental* at 3.60% = €7,200
>
> 2. *Taxe communale* at 1.20% = €2,400
>
> 3. *Prélèvement pour frais d'assiette* at 2.5% on €7,200 = €180
>
> The buyer must pay a total of **€9,780** in duty.

Properties less than five years old will only have to pay a stamp duty of **0.6%.**

For buildings less than five years old that have not yet been sold once or properties yet to built (*ventes dites en l'état futur d'achèvement* or *sur plan*) the duty will be less. TVA (Value Added Tax) of 19.6% is calculated on the price. On top of the TVA is added the *taxe départemental* at a reduced rate of 0,6 % plus the *prélèvement au profit de l'état* de 2.5% of the *taxe départemental*.

All fees are payable on completion of sale, although some may be asked for in advance.

Mortgages

Your preliminary contract (*compromis de vente* or *promesse de vente*) with the vendor *must* indicate whether or not the property will be bought with the help of a mortgage.

Tip: If you are seeking a mortgage you should confirm this by inserting a *clause suspensive* in your preliminary contract, as this will allow you to reclaim your 10% deposit (or 5% in the case of new builds) if the mortgage is subsequently declined.

If the preliminary contract mentions a loan, then a period of one month will be accorded to you to obtain the loan. Many vendors will be flexible with this time, as in practice it can take up to three months, but developers of new properties are unlikely to wait around if they have others interested. If you don't obtain financing during this time, the vendor must reimburse you with your deposit. After the 15th day of asking for reimbursement of the sum, you are legally entitled to start claiming interest on that sum. In order to avoid all problems of reimbursement you're advised not to pay anything before conclusion of the mortgage contract and to always give the deposit to a third party such as a financial establishment or *notaire*.

Where to get your mortgage?

Banks and credit institutions

If you have time and a decent command of French then you should contact as many banks and credit institutions as possible. Get them to send details of their latest deals and make comparisons between the deals taking into account duration, administration fees, mandatory insurances and any costs that could be hidden in the small print.

For those with a poor command of French, there is a growing number of French banks and credit institutions with a dedicated English-language service. The main ones are listed below. Some of those listed below have extremely useful English-language websites.

Contacts: Mortgage lenders offering English-language services

Barclays

☎ +44 (0)20 8973 2906
From the UK call: 0845 6755544

🖳 www.barclays.fr

CA Britline

✉ Credit Agricole of Calvados, 15, Esplanade Brillaud de Laujardière, 14050 Caen
☎ +33 (0)2 31 55 67 89
Fax +33 (0)2 31 55 63 99
@ britline@ca-normandie.fr
🖳 www.britline.com

CAFPI

✉ 80, Avenue de la Libération, 14000 Caen
☎ +33 (0)2 31 53 62 00
Fax +33 (0)2 31 53 62 09

🖳 www.cafpi.com

Crédit Foncier

☎ +33 (0)153 33 28 30
@ buying-france@creditfoncier.fr
🖳 www.credit-foncier.fr

Groupe CIC

☎ +33 (0)3 83 97 89 87
@ filbprod@cic.fr
💻 www.cic.fr

Société Générale

✉ International Private Customer Branch, 29, Boulevard Hausmann, 75009 Paris
☎ +33 (0)1 53 30 87 10
Fax +33 (0)1 53 30 87 30
💻 www.societegenerale.com

UCB BNP Paribas

☎ +33 (0)251 866 829
@ customerservice@ucb.fr
💻 www.ucb-french-mortgage.com

Credit Immobilier de France (CIF) is a major mortgage provider with offices in all *régions*:

💻 www.credit-immobilier-de-france.fr

There are many other specialised institutions for borrowing in France, see the chapter on banking for more contacts.

Mortgage brokers

Perhaps the quickest and easiest way to find a loan is to go through a broker.

There are a number of UK-based brokers, or British expatriate brokers based in France, who specialise in French mortgages. This is a good option for those lacking confidence in their language skills. Even if your command of French is good, you will benefit from the mortgage broker's close connections and experience and they will advise you throughout the entire process.

Many people feel sceptical about such a service, thinking that brokers will only offer deals from lenders that give them more commission, but this is not the case as the amount of commission does not really vary from lender to lender. Mortgage brokers are often able to offer more competitive rates than those publicised by the main lenders and some even offer a number of totally exclusive products.

Most brokers are paid only the commission they get from the lender, but many also charge a small fee to the borrower on top of this which takes into account the added services of translating forms, giving advice, negotiating with the *notaire* and sometimes going as far as setting up your bank account for you. In fact some mortgage brokers pretty much hold your hand and advise you throughout the entire property buying process.

Contacts: Mortgage brokers

Blakes Overseas Mortgages

- ✉ 81 School Road, Sale, Cheshire, M33 7XA
- ☎ 0845 434 0200
- *Fax* +44 (0)161 973 5455
- @ mail@blakesmortgages.com
- 💻 www.blakesmortgages.com

Charles Hamer Financial Services

- ✉ 87 Park Street, Thame, Oxfordshire, OX9 3HX
- ☎ +44 (0)1844 218956 or 7
- *Fax* +44 (0)1844 261886
- @ charleshamer@exchange.uk.com
- 💻 www.charleshamer.co.uk

Mike Lorimer SARL

- ✉ 17 Les Vert Clos, 594 Chemin des Combes, 06600 Antibes, France
- ☎ +33 (0)6 21 85 84 42
- *Fax* +33 (0)4 93 74 73 35
- @ info@mikelorimer.com
- 💻 www.mikelorimer.com

Olive Tree Mortgages

- ✉ 423 Route de Villecroze, Aups 83630, France
- ☎ 0871 900 8867 (from UK) or 0494 840865 (from France)
- @ info@olivetreemortgages.com
- 💻 www.olivetreemortgages.com

Templeton Associates

- ✉ *UK Office:* 3 Gloucester Street, Bath, BA1 2SE
- ☎ +44 (0)1225 422 282
- *Fax* +44 (0)1225 422 287

- ✉ *French Office*: 1217 av du Touring – Club, 40150 Hossegor, Landes, France
- ☎ +33 (0)5 58 41 74 33
- @ info@templeton-france.com
- 💻 www.templeton-france.com

PropertyFinance4Less

✉ 160 Brompton Road, London SW3 1HW

☎ +44 (0) 207 594 0555

Fax +44 (0) 207 594 0550

@ info@propertyfinance4less.com

🖳 www.propertyfinance4less.com

Epargne Logement (PEL or CEL)

If you are already domiciled in France and looking to buy a property in the future it may be worth looking into getting an *épargne logement*.

This is a scheme whereby you save a minimum amount with a savings bank or *La Poste* each month for up to four years and after this time you are guaranteed a mortgage. There are two types:

1. *Plan Epargne Logement* (PEL) and

2. *Compte Epargne Logement* (CEL).

These loans can also be used for works on your property (although not maintenance works). The works must be carried out by one enterprise and all bills must be kept.

PEL

You are able to borrow a lot more money with PEL but the initial commitment to save is longer. The money you place into a PEL is blocked and the only way of withdrawing any is by leaving the scheme. You can save for between four and ten years and each year your savings will gain interest (2.5% annually if you opened the account in January 2006).

Once you have saved for long enough (up to a maximum of €61,500) you will be guaranteed a mortgage. Currently (January 2006) the mortage rate offered is 4.20% and you can borrow up to €92,000.

CEL

Money can always be withdrawn from a CEL on the condition that you leave at least €300 in the account and that you make the minimum payments of €75. You can save a maximum of €15,300. CEL is ideal for placing money that you may need in the short term.

While your money is in the CEL there is a fixed rate of interest paid on it. In January 2006 this was 1.25% but the amount can be modified by the State at any time.

Once your initial saving period has been completed you will be allowed a CEL (in January 2006) giving you an eighteen month interest rate of 2.75% but on a generally modest borrowing amount of €23,000 (maximum). A CEL is ideal if you are saving to carry out works on your property.

You can have a combination of both PEL and CEL, but you cannot borrow more than €92,000. The duration of these loans can be between two and fifteen years.

If you already own property

If you already own a property a PEL can be used for:

*   construction of a building that will be your principal residence or the residence of your children, parents or partner;

*   buying a second home if it is new;

*   works (not maintenance works) for an occupant of a property that you own (and let out for instance);

*   buying a parking space; or

*   developing another part of your property or converting it into tourist accommodation. So, this is certainly a loan to consider if you have an outbuilding that you are not in a rush to renovate but wish to do so in the future.

Mortgage terms

How much can you borrow?

The amount that most lenders let you borrow will depend on how much you can afford to pay back each month.

Monthly payments for all loans should not exceed 30% of your single or 33% joint pre-tax income. There is no law stating that French lenders can't go beyond this, but as the French consumer code gives a great deal of protection to borrowers and is very severe on reckless lenders, credit institutions have to be particularly careful. French lenders only assess eligibility for a loan on the applicant's ability to service the loan and not on potential rental income from the property. A percentage of existing rental and investment income will be considered.

*   If you are **self-employed**, income is assessed as the average of the last three years' net income. If you have only recently become self-employed, or if your income fluctuates a great deal, then you may find it very difficult to obtain a loan.

- If you are **employed** a lender will base your income on your payslips and the amount that is credited to your account monthly. Outgoings such as mortgage/rent in the UK, personal loans and maintenance commitment are taken into account.

Maximum limits

1. If you are borrowing **up to €75,000**, and your main residence is not in France, then it is likely that you'll be able to borrow up to 80% of the net price (and up to 80% of any estate agents' fees) as a maximum.

2. If you are borrowing **over €75,000** then you may be able to borrow up to 85% of any net price (excluding all fees) or 80% of the net price and up to 80% of any estate agents' fees (excluding *notaire's* fees).

3. For clients of any nationality who are **already resident, working and paying tax in France** and who are buying their main home, then higher percentage loans of 95%, and even 100%, are possible.

The maximum sum available varies from lender to lender, and can also depend on the type of property or *région*. Some lenders have regionalised lending policies and guidelines, where both interest rates and terms available are directly dependent on regional location. Other lenders have no such criteria and terms apply equally across all of mainland France.

Joint applications

French property may be purchased on an individual or collective basis.

A non-earning partner can be included in a joint mortgage so long as they do not have serious credit problems. French lenders will not consider lending to UK companies but it is possible to create a French company expressly for the purchase of the property.

SCI

A *Société Civile Immobilière* (SCI) is a transparent, non-trading company and a minimum of two shareholders is required. Any loan is then made to the company (the SCI) and the individual shareholders stand as guarantors.

Note: This type of purchase has advantages for groups buying together and anyone who wishes to avoid French inheritance issues (see more in inheritance section).

Mortgage period

Most mortgage terms range from a minimum of 5 years to a maximum of 25 years, (although the majority of lenders offer terms of between 7 and 20 years).

- **Employed applicants** cannot borrow beyond state retirement age (currently 60) unless there is adequate verified pension or investment income in retirement.

- Those **already retired** may be able to secure a mortgage on the basis of pension income – terms are assessed on an ad hoc basis, but cases below €60,000 are not normally considered.

- **Self-employed applicants** are allowed a maximum term of 20 or 25 years provided this is not beyond age 70 (unless there is verified private pension income available, post-retirement). Loans must be repaid by the age of 70 for capital and interest loans, and age 75 for interest only loans.

Mortgage rates

You will be able to choose how your mortgage rate is set. The most common ways are the following:

Fixed rate

Until quite recently fixed rates were the norm in France, but variable rates are now becoming widely used, particularly by the specialised lenders. Unlike in the UK, fixed rates last for the whole duration of the mortgage, so you'll know exactly how much you will have to pay in Euros and how many payments you'll have to make. If you take out a fixed rate mortgage, the option to convert it to a variable rate mortgage at a later date is not available and there is a redemption penalty for early repayment of fixed rate loans.

Discount rates are often available for the first year. Here, a fixed percentage is taken off the bank's variable rate.

Variable rate

As in the UK, variable mortgage rates are linked to variations in the central bank lending rate. This central bank rate is called the *EURIBOR Index* in France and other countries with the Euro currency.

Note: EURIBOR (Euro Inter Bank Offered Rate) is the interest rate at which European banks can borrow money over a set period, for example over 3, 6 or 12 month periods. EURIBOR is effectively the wholesale cost of borrowing money by banks, as opposed to the retail cost at which the bank's customers borrow.

Most variable rate loans in France work by setting a fixed margin for the whole loan term on top of the EURIBOR rate. Banks often review the variable rate quarterly, in line with the three-month EURIBOR rate, although in some cases it will be in line with the twelve-month EURIBOR rate.

Example: variable rate mortgage

If, for example, 1.2% is their fixed margin and 3.3% is the current EURIBOR rate and you have chosen a variable rate that is reviewed every 3 months, then for 3 months you will be paying an end rate of 4.5% (3.3% EURIBOR base rate + 1.2% your bank's fixed margin).

If the EURIBOR goes up or down after 3 months then your rate will change accordingly.

The 1.2% in the above example represents the lender's gross profit. Often the lender will give a lower fixed margin if you have a larger deposit.

Tip: Be sure that you know the basis of how your lender calculates its variable interest rates.

In the UK (which has LIBOR – London Inter Bank Offered Rate – as its equivalent of EURIBOR) this type of interest rate setting scheme is referred to as *Base Rate Tracker*. These mortgages are extremely popular with borrowers because of their visible pricing structures.

Lenders, on the other hand, are not so keen. In the past many key UK lenders were very quick to put their mortgage rates up but slow at bringing them down when money markets rates fell. Instead they used their discretion on traditional variable interest rate timing to maximise profits, at their captive customers' expense, whilst offering brand new customers much cheaper mortgage rates. This cannot be done with an index tracking mortgage scheme, such as a scheme linked to EURIBOR or LIBOR or to other similar money market indices.

There is normally no redemption charge for early repayment of standard variable rate mortgages and you can convert to a fixed rate mortgage to extend or reduce the term of the loan.

Note: Just because EURIBOR'S interest rate is less than the LIBOR rate in the UK, do not assume that there are better deals in the Eurozone. Britain has the most competitive mortgage market in Europe, which helps keep rates down, at least for the preliminary years of a mortgage on a UK property.

For more information on EURIBOR: 🖳   www.euribor.org

To find out the latest EURIBOR base rate:
🖳 www.finfacts.com/Private/dbn/dbn.htm

Arrangement fees (*frais de dossier*)

Arrangement fees are high when compared to the UK. Normally fees are 1% of the mortgage amount but this is subject to each lender's minimum and maximum level, which could be less or more than this 1%. Most lenders have a minimum of around €700 and a maximum of €1,500.

This amount cannot be worked into the mortgage and is not payable until the mortgage offer is accepted.

Life insurance

Life insurance is mandatory when getting a mortgage.

Often a medical examination is required with your life assurance application and can be carried out by a doctor in your country. Depending on the lender, life insurance premiums can be included in your mortgage payments.

Buildings and contents insurance

Buildings and contents insurance is also mandatory.

Your first annual buildings and contents insurance premium is due at the very start of your mortgage, as soon as you have signed the final deeds. Subsequent annual premiums are due on the anniversary of date of completion of your sale.

Getting the process going

You will need to get your preferred lender to give you an application pack. The application will involve filling in a form with all your personal and financial details. The form will ask you what the loan is for (i.e. the purchase of an existing property, new property, land for construction or an older property to renovate) whether it's for renovation/improvement, whether it's for the purchase of a main residence, or if it's equity release.

Your application will need to be accompanied by some, if not all, of the following documents:

Employed applicants

- Letter from employer(s) specifying your professional status, length of service and gross annual income.
- Copy of your most recent salary slips and most recent P60.

Self-employed applicants

- Photocopies of the last 2 or 3 years certified balance sheets and profit and loss accounts.
- Photocopies of the last 2 or 3 years personal tax returns (complete) and the most recent notice of assessment.

Income details

- Statement of any income other than from principal employment (including rental income: tenancy agreements and bank statements showing the rental income).
- Statement of investment income declared.
- Statement of pension.

Other personal documents

- Photocopies of each applicant's passport showing photograph and personal details, and *carte de séjour* if resident in France.
- Photocopy of birth certificate, marriage certificate or divorce decree.
- Life assurance application form(s).
- Completed direct debit form with full bank account details for a French bank account.
- Last rental statement (if you are a tenant).
- Most recent statements for existing loans/mortgages and credit cards.
- Photocopies of the 3 most recent months' continuous bank statements showing income, loans, mortgages and regular outgoings.

Property documents

- For a **property to be built**:
  - Property title or preliminary sales agreement for the land.
  - Building licence – building contract and plans.
  - Photocopies of all the quotations and insurance certificates for the builders.
- For **existing property**, completed constructions or off-plan properties sold under VEFA (*Vente en l'Etat Futur d'Achèvement* – Sale of property for future completion) contract:
  - Sales agreement or reservation contract.
- For **renovation or improvement works** to be carried out:
  - Professional estimates or invoices.
- For **re-mortgage or equity release**:
  - Title deed.
  - Loan deed.
  - Complete repayment table (current).

Once the lender has received a completed application form with all the requested supporting documents a decision will usually take around two weeks. Once the loan offer is issued there is a legal cooling-off period of ten days during which you can reflect on the offer and decide whether you want to go ahead and accept it. Once this time is up you can sign the forms and send your arrangement fee.

> *Note*: **Don't pay anything until the wait is over and don't sign any cheque before accepting.**

The day that you receive the offer letter does not count in the ten-day wait. You must accept the offer within 30 days or it will expire.

Once you have accepted the offer, the lender will send details of the mortgage offer to your *notaire* so that he or she can prepare for the deed of sale to be signed.

Valuation appraisal

Lenders do not insist on structural surveys although you will probably want to consider one to protect your own interests. In some cases lenders arrange for a professional valuation to be carried out for their own internal use. This is not the same as a mortgage valuation carried out in the UK. The appraisal is undertaken by a valuer as opposed to a professionally qualified surveyor and, in many instances, an inspection of the property is not undertaken. Structural defects may therefore not be identified. The purpose of the valuation appraisal is for internal risk assessment and the results are not released to applicants. The cost of the valuation is included in the application fee.

 Note: To ensure all formalities run smoothly for completion a minimum six-week period should be allowed.

Your loan only becomes definitive if the *contrat de vente* for which it is underwritten is concluded within four months from the date of the offer. If the contract isn't concluded in this timeframe the loan is annulled.

Interview with a property buyer

David inherited some money and bought a second home in Carcassonne. He now works part of the year there as a freelancer.

Q. *Tell me about yourself.*

A. 40 years old, married 15 years, living in Banbury, Oxon. I work freelance in music publishing, my wife is a part-time teacher. I inherited some money from a relative and decided to buy a second life (after persuading the missus). Did a lot of looking on the internet, made an appointment with VEF who were near Carcassonne at the time. Chose the Carcassonne area because of access via Ryanair and cost – it seemed cheaper than other Med type areas)

Q. *What was your reason for buying a house in France?*

A. Seemed like a fun project.

Q. *Had you spent much time in the Carcassonne area before? How did you choose or discover this area? Why not any other area of France?*

A. I'd never actually been to Carcassonne before, though I'd spent some time in the Narbonne/Sete area busking in my youth.

Q. *Can you tell me a little bit about this area in France and what you have discovered about it since moving there? What are its pros and cons?*

A. It's quite a sparsely populated area, particularly the Montagne Noire (where we are). 50% of the houses in the village are French maisons secondaires. It's very quiet in the winter, and becomes rather bourgois in the summer. It has a small shop open for a couple of hours in the morning. You'd struggle to live there without a car. The area seems quite windy, and over the last couple of years, wet! Though the locals say the weather isn't what they'd expect. It's easy to get to the coast as the motorway passes Carcassonne, easy to get to Toulouse (and IKEA). We've found the food to be a bit disappointing, but maybe that's cos I'm a 'hobby cook'. There's an excellent Saturday market at Revel (full of Brits!).

Q. *Did you rent for a while before buying? Or did you hop back and forth to the UK?*

A. Nope! We went over for a weekend to look at one particular property (which was magically sold the day before – but that's another story!) and ended up buying another on impulse.

Q. *What type of property were you looking for and why?*

A. We weren't sure, something within our budget, I'd have liked a farmy sort of place, but they were too much work and money. We wanted somewhere near water if possible.

Q. *How long did it take you to find a property and what was the process of finding it like?*

A. Most of the looking was done on the internet. The one we bought was for the 'wow' – effect attic. It's massive, and is now our living room. My video commentary is rather 'uninterested' till I go into the attic, then it's much more positive on the way down! It has a lovely small river running by in front of the house. We rejected others for price (agents trying it on), location, 'feel' and one because the owners allowed their dogs to use it as home (it was unoccupied). We called this one 'the house at poo corner' as it had piles of poo everywhere. . . absolutely disgusting! Uck!

Q. *Did you find the property through an agent immobilier?*

A. We went through a hand-holding agent based in the UK but with regional agents.

Q. *Once you found the property how long did it take you until you finally signed the contract and had the keys?*

A. About two months I think, though I'd stayed in it before as it wasn't secured! I managed to get the keys from the agent anyhow.

Q. *What did you pay for your property?*

€18k + fees, about €23k altogether.

Q. *Could you tell me about the renovation process.?*

A. It's been an interesting renovation project! If I knew when I started what I know now, I would have done things differently I think. I rejected the local builders fairly soon as they seemed uninterested in the project and then sent me an estimate that was three times the price of the house! It had a new roof which was good, but nearly everything inside otherwise needed gutting.

I used a couple of English guys who advertised in one of the English/French magazines for some of the bigger jobs, a friend for the wiring/electrics, local labour for other stuff and the local plumber (the only one to give a receipt!).

There are about 5 or 6 DIY and builders merchants in Carcassonne; I've used them all, and the local sawmill for timber.

Q. *How have the locals taken to you? How do you find them?*

A. We've made some friends in the village, and a lot of acquaintances but on the whole they tend to leave us to get on with it. There are Brits in other villages we see sometimes, but mainly it's the locals, and the local bar two villages away.

Q. *Can you speak the language? If not how did you get with on filling forms and general communication?*

A. I'm OK-ish with French, Alison not too confident. She has days when she won't go out into the village 'cos she can't be bothered to struggle!

Q. *Overall worst experience?*

A. The ongoing (but not mentioned at the moment) row with the woman next door about where our drainage for the downstairs loo/shower is going to join the main drainage pipe. And a car crash on the first weekend.

Q. *Best experience?*

A. Loads. The lake, the beach, the sun, food, drink, friends, and the local village fetes.

Q. *Biggest surprise along the way?*

A. The French really aren't like us at all.

Q. *Any regrets?*

A. I sometimes think we maybe didn't get the right house/location but, hey, we can always move!

Q. *How often do you visit the property?*

A. I spend about four months of the year there, Alison about two and a half. I work feelance and take my work with me. I have a computer and internet connection there too. I put the phone here on divert, and people don't even have to know I'm there. . . great.

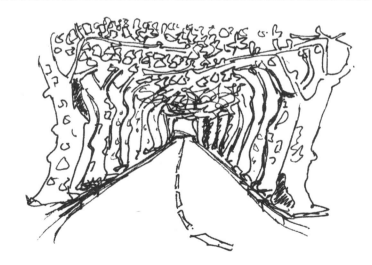

8

Moving in

Removals

Moving all your belongings to France can be a major expense, so if possible limit the amount of furniture, and other large objects, that you're taking over. If you don't have too much to move, consider taking the objects yourself in a self-drive hire van. This will be a lot cheaper than hiring a removal firm. Even if you do need a removal firm it's still good to limit the amount you're taking because the quote they give you will be in cubic metres and everything adds up. If you only have a few objects then it's possible your items can go as a part load along with other people's removals.

 Tip: **Remember, it's worth getting rid of your old furniture and buying new or second hand furniture once in France, as foreign furniture can look strange and out of place in a French home.**

It's also healthy to get rid of stuff in order to make as clean a break as possible, although there will inevitably be some objects with sentimental value that you'll wish to take. Be ruthless with yourself about what you really need.

The British Association of Removers (BAR) has a dedicated BAR Overseas Group with fewer than 100 members in the whole of the UK that can claim to meet the stringent membership criteria and high standards required for moving loads overseas. All BAR members are specially trained to deal with all sorts of packaging, including dealing with unusual, awkward and precious objects. Members will take care of everything: packing, collection, heavy lifting, storage and delivery. They will also be covered by financial guarantees and will deal with the insurance. BAR can provide you with a list of BAR Overseas Group members, or alternatively you can search for them by county on the BAR website. All members will expect advance payment on overseas removals. emoval firms who deal with moving loads overseas.

Many companies subcontract the load to a French removals firm once it has crossed the Channel. If possible get a remover that will be with your load for the entire journey.

A great website for finding space in a van or truck for a part load is Loadup (www.loadup.co.uk) which is used by hauliers up and down the country. Hauliers would rather fill their vehicle, particularly on return journeys, at a reduced rate (backload) than leave it partly or fully empty. Private users needing to move personal goods or conduct house removals can put a message on the site free of charge.

Another possibility for saving money, and also time, is to contact a removals brokerage firm such as ET Brokers. They will contact up to 2,000 removal firms to get a quote for your full or part load. They'll give you a no obligation quote, and if you accept one of their removal companies a small fee of £30 (plus VAT at 17.5%) is charged. ET Brokers claim to get savings in the region of 50% on local quotes for European removals. They claim that their best result to date has been a saving of 90% for a client moving from Montpellier to Exeter in the UK. This client paid £500 for a full three bedroom house move as opposed to the £5,000 quote received from a local French company.

Insurance

Get several quotes and compare the differences in price and service. If a quote does include insurance then find out if you have the option of getting your own insurance. The one quoted by the removals firm is not necessarily the best deal. If you're moving items yourself then you may find it hard to get insurance as many insurance companies only provide accidental damage cover for professionally packed items rather than owner packed. As plans can change find out if there is a penalty charge for cancellation within a certain period of notice.

You will normally have to settle your account prior to dispatching your shipment so that substantial costs – such as freight charges – can be pre-paid.

Other things to consider:

1. Try to book your removals company at least three weeks in advance.

2. Try to avoid moving on a Friday because this is the busiest day of the week. Moving midweek may save money.

3. Whether you are moving items yourself or hiring a removal firm, plan where you want things to go in your new home. This makes it easier to unload when you get to the other end.

4. Give the remover a map showing the address and location of your new home along with a contact telephone number.

5. The remover will need a set of keys, location map, access points and a plan of which rooms certain belongings are going in, to take to the new house. If they arrive at the new property before you without these items, you are paying for the time they spend waiting for you.

6. On moving day leave the packing to the professionals but make sure that someone remains with them to check that nothing gets left behind.

7. Keep all your paper and important documents (passports, travel tickets, birth/marriage certificates, insurance policies, wallet, address book, mobile phones, etc.) separate. Don't let them get packed.

8. Tell your remover if there are any big or delicate objects that may need special attention.

9. Let your remover know about any awkward entrances, parking restrictions, stairs or points of access at either end.

10. Label boxes by where you want the contents to go. Your remover is not allowed to interfere with any mains services so make arrangements with gas/electricity boards well in advance.

11. Your service specification will tell you exactly what your removal company will do on your behalf and what you are expected to do yourself.

Contacts: Removals

BAR

✉ Tangent House, 62 Exchange Road, Watford, Hertfordshire, WD18 0TG
☎ +44 (0)1923 699480
Fax +44 (0)1923 699481
@ info@bar.co.uk
🖥 www.bar.co.uk

ET Brokers Limited

✉ 6 Ullswater Gardens, Kingswinford, Dudley, DY6 8DR
☎ +44 (0)870 800 3880
@ info@etbrokers-removals.com
🖥 www.etbrokers-removals.com

Loadup

🖥 www.loadup.co.uk

Anglo French Euro Removals

✉ The Mill Business Park, Maidstone Road, Hothfield, Ashford, Kent, TN26 1AE
☎ +44 (0)1233 660963 or +33 (0)5 45 30 70 08
Fax +44 (0)1233 660964
@ enquiries@anglofrench.co.uk
🖥 www.anglofrench.co.uk

Associated Moving Services

✉ 1-3 Pelham Yard, High Street, Seaford, BN25 1PQ
☎ +44 (0)1323 892934 or 020 8947 1817
Fax +44 (0) 1323 894474
@ enquiries@amsmoving.co.uk
🖥 www.amsmoving.co.uk

Cotswold Carriers

✉   Unit 2, The Walk, Hook Norton Road, Chipping Norton, Oxon, OX7 5TG
☎   +44 (0)1608 730500
Fax   +44 (0)1608 730600
@   info@cotswold-carriers.com
💻   www.cotswoldcarriers.co.uk

Ede Brothers

✉   Nightless Copse, Rusper Road, Capel, Dorking, Surrey, RH5 5HE
☎   +44 (0) 1306 711293
Fax   +44 (0) 1306 711765
@   sales@edebros.co.uk
💻   www.edebros.co.uk

Edward Baden Ltd

✉   Edward Baden House, Bell Lane, Uckfield, East Sussex, TN22 1QL
☎   +44 (0)1825 768866
Fax   +44 (0)1825 768877
💻   www.edwardbaden.co.uk

French Connexion

✉   The Old Vicarage, Leigh, Nr. Sherbourne, Dorset, DT9 6HL
☎   +44 (0)1935 872222
Fax   +44 (0)1935 873094

Federation of European Movers

💻   www.fedemac.com

Interview with a property buyer

Roger bought a house in Deux Sevres and discovered the hospitality of his neighbours.

Q. *Did you know France well before moving there?*

A. After the children had grown up and stopped coming away with us we swapped from caravanning to touring in a campervan. With the freedom a campervan gave us we took our holidays in Europe, in France particularly. Our second trip to France was a tour of the Loire valley starting near Orleans and heading west as far as Angers before heading north to the ferry port of Le Havre. The next trip saw us carry on from Angers towards the sea and then down the west coast to La Rochelle. In between times we had 5 or 10 day breaks mainly in Normandy and up to Pas de Calais.

Q. *When did you start thinking about buying a house in France?*

A. In 2000 we put the camper on the ferry to Bilbao, spent a week in the Picos mountains before crossing the Pyrenees at Bielsa and into France through the tunnel. We then spent the next two weeks making our way back to Le Havre visiting Lourdes, Auch, Agen, the Lot, Cahors, Rocamadour and Perigeux on the way. In Perigeux we started thinking about the possibility of buying a place in France and even went into an immobilier to view some properties. They didn't treat us as serious buyers and we continued our holiday.

Q. *How did you go about starting the search?*

A. Back home I started giving the idea more thought and did a lot of research on the web, looking at French agency sites and some of the English companies who specialise in France. I persuaded my wife that we should return in January on a house hunting mission as any fool can buy a place when the sun is shining. I planned our itinerary in the camper and made appointments to see specific houses and asked the agencies to include other properties within our price bracket and to our specification. Our price band was very flexible, £20,000 to £45,000, and the area Saumur down to Perigeux and La Rochelle across to Ruffec. Broadly, Poitou-Charentes and parts of Aquitaine.

Q. *When you got over to France, how did the search go?*

A. We left Lancashire on Boxing Day arriving at Le Havre 8.00am on 27th December 2001. Our first appointment was at 2.00pm with an agent in Parthenay. We arrived at 2.30 to find the office shut. Eventually it opened but the lady with whom I had made the appointment failed to arrive. She had thought I was going to confirm the arrangement. She arrived in time to show us a couple of houses, one of which I had chosen to view, the other her idea of our requirements. By this time it was dark and difficult to see any other properties.

We spent the night and several others at a friend's house in St Lin south of Parthenay. It was bitterly cold in the house as it had been shut up since October and even the log fire couldn't warm it through. We finally gave up trying to get warm and slept in the campervan.

Day followed day and merged into one as we toured the countryside with different agents roaring along country lanes in search of the right house. Most agents didn't speak English. All of them tried to show us places which were outside our price range and some which needed complete rebuilds. We had specified that we wanted a house which was habitable straight away.

Q. *How did you find your house eventually?*

A. The weather was atrocious and two properties were unreachable owing to flooded roads. (You wouldn't have known that in the summer). For some reason, even though we hadn't been there, I was taken with the area around Bressuire in Deux-Sèvres. We had made appointments with two agencies in Bressuire and had seen about six houses between the two. The agence immobilière which we eventually bought through was Cabinet Papin in Bressuire and the contact was Charly Blanchard, a youngish man with quite good English. We went to the property three times in all, twice with Charly and once on our own to see if we could find it again.

Q. *How did the actual purchase go?*

A. On the last Saturday before we left for home we decided on the house, went to see Charly, signed the necessary forms and agreed that we would come back on March 15th to do the *acte*. Just before 12.00pm we went across the road to the Credit Agricole and opened a bank account with 200 francs, all the cash I had in my pocket. The manager of the CA branch spoke no English but we managed and he made absolutely sure that we had understood what he had told us. We decided that a cheque book would be more advantageous than a cash card which attracts a monthly charge of more than £5 per month insurance and fee.

We duly made a booking on the ferry for the 15th March and spent the intervening period collecting items of furniture from auctions and small ads. We bought a new double bed and loaded it all into a colleague's Mercedes Sprinter.

Q. *Was moving in easy?*

A. After the *acte* was completed and the cheques handed over, we were given the keys and we drove off to our new home in France. The sellers arrived an hour later to show us how things worked and to collect a cheque for a proportion of the *taxe habitation* which they had prepaid to the following January. The *immobilier* had told us that it was normal.

The house has its own well so the only utility we needed in our name was the electricity and the immobilier had also arranged that with the local office. We unloaded the van, assembled the bed, plugged in the electric heaters and prepared some food before going to sleep for the first time chez nous en France.

During that 5 day visit I assembled and fitted the pre-packed kitchen units we had brought over from B&Q. The previous owners had left nothing in the kitchen save the double sink unit and drainer. The weather was again damp and cold but we got the log fire working and the oil fired range in the kitchen so it was soon quite snug. The house had been empty since at least the September before and there were quite a few damp and mildew areas. Some of the guttering was missing as were some downspouts, so water was seeping in as well as dampness from the windows having been closed for so long. Whilst we had the use of the van we bought some items of furniture and a gas cooker. That 5 day visit was over too soon and we returned to the UK.

Q. *How have you found the neighbours?*

A. We had seen one neighbour, whom I had spoken to briefly whilst standing in the pouring rain in the lane outside our house. He is a chicken farmer raising thousands of day old chicks ready for the table. Surprisingly we neither hear nor smell them.

We returned in June for a three week holiday: my wife, my older daughter and I. Our immobilier had told me to invite my neighbours for an aperitif as soon as possible. So, prior to leaving home, I printed off some invitations for the following Saturday evening. There are only 15 dwellings so on Friday night I walked around the village door knocking. When I got a reply I introduced myself and asked in my halting French if they would join us the following day at 6.00pm. Where there was no answer I left an invitation in the letter box.

Saturday at 6.00 saw us waiting in the kitchen with a table full of snacks, ice, drinks glasses ready and no villagers. Just after five past the courtyard gates opened and about 30 people streamed towards the kitchen. We shook hands exchanged kisses and set about charging glasses. When all had a drink one of the villagers raised a glass and welcomed us to the village. They brought a presentation box of three bottles of wine, potted plants and a bunch of cut flowers. The session went very well. At seven or so a young couple arrived and we heard someone say "ah the new neighbours". We were amazed, they had lived in the village a year and had not introduced themselves as we had done. The immobilier's advice had been very good.

Q. *How have things been going since then?*

A. Since then we have made good friends and have had many aperitif sessions. The old lady behind us brings us fresh veg from her garden and invites us around for coffee. Mainly to show off her latest grandchild or some other family news. The villagers hold a picnic every year and it has been timed to ensure we can be there.

9

Living in France

Visa requirements

Entry and residence of EU nationals

EU nationals entering France need to be supported by a valid ten-year passport. No visa is required.

Carte de séjour

Until recently EU citizens were obliged to apply for a *carte de séjour* (residency permit) if they intended staying in France for longer than 90 days. Since 26th November 2003 this is no longer the case and such a permit is no longer required. Although, be aware that such knowledge may not yet have percolated down to all local *mairies* in the country. Non-EU nationals will, however, need to apply for the permit.

Entry and residence of non-EU nationals

US and non-EU citizens will be able to enter and stay in France for a maximum of one month if they have with them a ten-year passport. Non-EU nationals are not allowed to take up employment in France, even temporary work, paid or unpaid, unless they have obtained a work permit before arriving in France. If they wish to stay longer than a month then they will also need to apply for a visa. There are several types of short (30-90 days) and long (90+ days) term visas. There are also a number of job-specific visas such as those for au pairs, teachers, university professors and researchers.

The website for the French embassy in the United States has a lot of good advice and information on visa application procedures for both US and non-US citizens:

🖥   www.info-france-usa.org

Long-stay work visas

Foreigners must obtain a work contract approved by the *Direction Départementale du Travail, de l'Emploi et de la Formation Professionnelle* (the local division of the Labour department in France) and a special long-stay visa issued by the *Consulate* before leaving for France. This rule also applies to transfers to subsidiaries of foreign companies in France. Employees of diplomatic or consular missions, members of international organisations, heads of French subsidiaries, scientists, artists and sailors working on ships stationed at French seaports follow other procedures and are requested to contact their local *Consulate*.

Foreign workers must secure a job offer from an employer in France or be proposed for a transfer to France by their non-EU employer. The employer in

France then applies for the *Autorisation de Travail* (work permit) at the *Office des Migrations Internationales* (OMI).

When the hiring or transfer of the foreign worker is approved, the OMI sends the file to the French *Consulate* and a letter to the applicant to inform them that the file has been transferred.

The applicant contacts the *Consulate* to obtain the visa. The applicant must submit:

1. a **passport** valid for a period of three months beyond the applicant's last day of stay;

2. four legibly filled out long-stay visa **application forms**. This can be downloaded from: 🖳 www.diplomatie.gouv.fr/venir/visas/pdf/visalon.pdf

3. two passport size **photographs** glued on the form; and the

4. **visa fee** (see below).

After arriving in France, and preferably within one week, the applicant must request a *carte de séjour* at the local *Préfecture*. (see below). They will also have to undergo a medical examination in France.

Office des Migrations Internationales (OMI)

✉ 48, Boulevard de la Bastille, 75012 Paris
☎ +33 (0)1 53 02 25 50
🖳 www.omi.social.fr

Carte de séjour

Application for a *carte de séjour* should be made at the *Préfecture* or *mairie* of your place of residence. You will be given a form to fill in with all your personal details and you must register as either employed, self-employed, retired or self-sufficient. This form must be returned accompanied by a number of documents.

The documents required are as follows:

1. A **valid passport.**

2. A **birth certificate.**

3. A **marriage certificate**. (If divorced, then divorce papers will be required. If you are divorced and have children with you then you may be asked for a custody order.)

4. **Proof of residence**. Your accommodation can be either rented or owned. If rented you must be able to produce a copy of your lease or rent statement. If owned you need an extract from the title deeds of your property or a certificate from your *notaire*. If you are staying with a friend then they must sign an *attestation d'hébergement* (proof of lodging).

5. A **gas, electricity or phone bill**.

6. Proof of **financial resources** (if not intending to work) in the form of bank statements and letters. Many *préfectures* ask for a letter from your bank confirming that there is regular money going into your account. *S.*

7. Four passport **photographs.**

Further details that may be required:

- If you are **employed**: a contract of employment or the necessary authorisations from the *Chamber of Commerce* in the case of self-employment.

- If you are **retired**: proof that you receive a state pension (from France or your home country) or that you have a sufficient income.

- If you are **student**: proof that you have registered with a French University.

- If you are **married to a French national**: a copy of your marriage certificate.

Sometimes they will ask you for an official translation of your birth and marriage certificates. Prior to leaving France you should contact your local French *Consulate* or a lawyer in France and they will make up and stamp an official translated copy of the document for you. You may be asked for proof of your date of entry into France, so save your travel tickets just in case. You may also be asked to give the full names, dates and places of birth of your parents and even your grandparents. Most French people have all this documentation.

Note: Some *préfectures* are very laid back about issuing the *carte* although others will examine every piece of document and ask you to supplement the application with others! Unfortunately there doesn't seem to be any uniformity in the guidelines offered, or documents requested by, different *préfectures* and *mairies*. They each seem to have their own rules and requirements, so it's best to take the information given here as general and approach your local officials directly to find out exactly what they need before you apply.

Once you have applied you have to wait several weeks before you receive the *carte de séjour*, although some applicants have been known to wait several months. If you are staying for a limited duration, a *carte de séjour* will be issued for this period of time only, after which your situation will be re-examined. If you plan to stay permanently, a *carte de séjour* will be issued for five years and after these five years, it can be renewed for a further ten years if you are still employed on a permanent basis. Residency rights – granted with the *carte de séjour* – can be extended to: the permit holder's spouse; dependant descendants under 21; dependant's ascendants; and also the spouse's ascendants.

Non-employed and retired people will need to prove that they have adequate income or the financial resources to live in France. Some *départements* require an up to date *attestation* from the applicant's bank stating that their account is regularly provisioned. If you have a large sum of money in your savings account then some *départements* will see this as sufficient proof that you have enough to live on, whereas others may tell you that a lump sum is not enough as the money could run out.

Short-stay work visas

The employer does not need to contact the OMI, but should provide the worker with a contract which has been approved by a *Direction Départementale du travail, de l'Emploi et de la Formation Professionnelle* (DDTEFP). The applicant should fill out a short-stay visa application form, provide one photograph which is glued on the form, a valid passport, a proof of health insurance with worldwide coverage plus one copy, the contract countersigned by DDTEFP plus one copy, and the visa fee.

Further details can be found on the French Consulate in the New York's website: 🖥 www.info-france-usa.org

You are also able to download the necessary application forms from this site.

Application fee for visas

Your application will not be examined until you have paid these fees. If your visa application is turned down you will not be reimbursed this money, but if accepted there won't be any further payments to make. The tariffs are payable in euros.

Table 9.1 – Application fees for visas

Category	Cost (€)
Visa de court séjour (jusqu'à 30 jours) Short-term visa (up to 30 days)	35
Visa de court séjour (de 31 à 90 jours), une entrée Short-term visa (from 31 to 90 days), one entry	35
Visa de court séjour (de 31 à 90 jours), plusieurs entrées, d'une durée de validité maximale de six mois Short-term visa (31 to 90 days) allowing more than one entry, valid for 6 months	35
Visa de court séjour (de 31 à 90 jours), plusieurs entrées, d'une durée de validité d'un an Short-term visa (31 to 90 days) allowing more than one entry, valid for one year	35
Visa de court séjour (de 31 à 90 jours), plusieurs entrées, d'une durée de validité de 2 à 5 ans Short-term visa (31 to 90 days), several entries, valid between 2 to 5 years	35
Visa de long séjour (plus de 90 jours) Long-stay visa (more than 90 days)	99

Currency

The Euro

On 1st January 2002, Euro banknotes and coins were introduced to twelve Member States of the European Union. In France the Euro replaced the French Franc, which ceased being legal tender on 17th February 2002. Most die-hard retail outlets (including estate agents) continue to display in Francs in parenthesis next to the official Euro.

1 Euro = 6.55957 Francs

The seven different banknotes and eight coins are issued by the European Central Bank. The new coins have one side common to all twelve countries and a reverse side specific to each country, while the banknotes look the same throughout the Euro area.

Coins

Some facts about the coins:

- The eight denominations of coins vary in size, colour and thickness according to their values, which are 1, 2, 5, 10, 20 and 50 cent or €1 and €2.
- One Euro is divided into 100 cents.
- Euro coins can be used anywhere in the euro area, regardless of what country the coin originated.
- Milled edges make it easier, especially for those with impaired sight, to recognise different values.
- Sophisticated metal technology has been incorporated into the €1 and €2 coins which, together with lettering around the edge of the €2 coin, prevents counterfeiting.

Banknotes

Some facts about the banknotes:

- On the front of the banknotes, the windows and gateways symbolise the European spirit of openness and co-operation and the twelve stars of the European Union represent the 'dynamism and harmony' between European nations.
- To complement these designs, the reverse of each banknote features a bridge. The bridges symbolise the 'close co-operation and communication' between Europe and the rest of the world.

- Various security features have been incorporated into the Euro banknotes. The print is raised to give the banknotes a unique feel and if a note is held up to the light the watermark, security thread and a see-through register will be visible. All three features can be seen from the front and the reverse side of genuine banknotes.

- If you tilt the banknote you can see on the front side a shifting image on the hologram foil stripe (on the low-value banknotes) or the hologram foil patch (on the high-value banknotes).

The Euro symbol

The European Commission's design of the Euro symbol – € – had to satisfy three simple criteria:

1. to be a highly recognisable symbol of Europe;

2. to be easily written by hand; and

3. to be an aesthetically pleasing design.

The symbol finally chosen was inspired by the Greek letter epsilon, harking back to classical times and the cradle of European civilisation. The symbol also refers to the first letter of the word 'Europe'. The two parallel lines indicate the stability of the Euro. The official abbreviation for the Euro is EUR and this has been registered with the International Organisation for Standardisation (ISO).

To familiarise yourself with the look of the Euro coins and notes there are helpful images on the European Central Bank's website: 🖳 www.euro.ecb.int

Banks

La Banque de France

Within the framework of European Economic and Monetary Union, France has an independent central bank, the Banque de France, which was established in 1800 by Napoleon Bonaparte.

Over the last Century the bank has seen plenty of reform. In 1936 a new law transformed the bank's organisation in order to strengthen the government's authority over the monetary institute. This reform was the prelude to the nationalisation of the central bank, which came in December 1945 after the Liberation. All changed again in 1993, when the Banque de France, which previously operated as a state bank, became independent. Its current independent status formally prohibits it from authorising overdrafts or granting any other type of credit to the *Trésor public* (public revenue department) or any other public body or enterprise. It does however continue to maintain the current accounts of the *Trésor public*, contribute to the management of government debt and hold the current accounts of government bills. It also draws up the nation's balance of payments.

French banks

There are more than 500 commercial, co-operative or mutual banks in France with 26,000 branches (not including the 17,000 post offices that also provide banking facilities) across the country. Banks play a major role in the French economy, employing 500,000 people that service 48 million customers. The main banking groups are among the largest French companies. The network of Caisses d'Epargne (savings bank) has a strong presence in France with 451 local offices, but their range of services is limited compared to the commercial and co-operative banks.

A recent history of mergers and consolidation

Since the early 1960s the banking sector has witnessed some major upheavals, starting with the blurring of the traditional distinction between the deposit bank and the merchant bank. The former began to invest in industry and the latter was allowed to develop a network of retail branches. Former merchant banks, such as Paribas and Indosuez, continued to deal mainly with corporate investments and had control of a good number of French and foreign companies through a complex framework of cross-holdings. Since the mid 80s there has been a new wave of change, with continuous mergers and takeovers resulting in huge conglomerations of these former deposit and merchant banks. BNP and Paribas merged in 1999 to become BNP Paribas and Indosuez is now part of the Crédit Agricole group. The tie-up in early 2003 between the Crédit Lyonnais and its main shareholder, the Crédit Agricole, looks like it could relaunch the momentum towards consolidation, and trigger expansion beyond France. No doubt, the creation of a new colossus will force other big players in the banking sector to speed up their thoughts on other merging possibilities.

Growing internationalisation

Many banks such as Crédit Mutuel, Crédit Agricole and Banque Populaire, started off as regional, co-operative outlets but now have a national, and in most cases, an international presence. Banking activities have become increasingly international, thanks to the globalisation of trade and freedom of movement of capital within the European Union, which came into effect on 1st July 1990. Nowadays these banks attempt to reconcile a strong co-operative culture with a listed-company approach, in order to provide resources necessary to pursue international growth objectives and to conclude acquisitions.

In recent years French banks have computerised most of their services and are encouraging customers to use debit cards rather than cheques that cost more to process. Several banks have created subsidiaries specialising in life insurance in order to diversify their activities and broaden their client base.

La Banque Postale

La Poste has never been just somewhere to lick the occasional stamp or send a package. It has long provided a popular banking service and manages 28 million savings accounts. With 17,028 customer outlets, La Poste's financial arm makes up Europe's most widespread and dense local service network. It also has the third-largest and fastest growing ATM (automated teller machine) network in France.

In the early 2000s, the poor performance of the stockmarket and traumatic international events triggered by 9/11, worked in La Poste's favour. Traditional savings products such as the *Livret A* and tax-advantaged passbook accounts have been as popular as ever. In the somewhat subdued market, La Poste also strengthened its position in home financing products, attracting deposits of over €1 billion.

In January 2006, La Poste took a massive step forward by broadening its services even further and turning its banking division into an official bank: La Banque Postale. This has caused a furore in French banking. Other major banks have complained that there's no room in the market for this new bank and that it will have an unfair competitive advantage. For instance, they argue that La Poste will not charge its banking arm enough for its infrastructure and that the pensions of the new bank's 1,000 employees will be subsidised by the State.

La Poste's most popular banking product to date, with over 21 million accounts, is the Livret A savings account. You need just €1.50 to open a *Livret A* (an account which can also be opened at Caisses d'Epargne, who have 24.5 million *Livret A* account holders, and Crédit Mutuel) and you can save up to €15,245. These savings are not taxed and you are not at risk of losing money as the interest, currently 2%, is set by the State. Savers can withdraw money whenever they wish. Deposits are channelled to the Caisse de Dépôts et Consignations, a state-controlled bank, to finance social housing. Previously it was necessary to go to the post office to withdraw funds, but in 2001 a modern passbook formula was introduced that includes a bank statement, and a card which can be used at ATM machines was launched.

The other major banks might get their one-up on La Banque Postale. Currently they are not allowed to run the *Livret A*, but if they are granted the right to do so, they say they would charge the government 0.8% for running *Livret A*, against La Poste's 1.3% and Caisse d'Epargne's 1.1%.

At the time of writing the competition commissioner is considering whether the duopoly distorts the French banking market.

La Banque Postale

🖥 www.labanquepostale.fr

(site has several pages of information in English, see link 'Help for English Speakers')

English-speaking banking services

More and more French banks are offering a dedicated English-speaking service. Many of these concentrate mostly on offering mortgages, although others offer a broad range of products.

A very popular dedicated English-speaking banking service for private customers, with over 10,000 account holders, is CA-Britline, based at the banking branch of Crédit Agricole of Calvados in Caen, Normandy. All their staff are either British or speak English. As well as providing a full range of banking services, they can provide mortgages and property-related insurance. To open an account with CA Britline you will need a copy of your passport, an original of a recent utilities bill showing your main address and copies of your last two month's bank statements.

Contacts: English-speaking banking services

Barclays

☎ +44 20 8973 2906
From the UK call: 0845 6755544
💻 www.barclays.fr

CA Britline

✉ Credit Agricole of Calvados, 15, Esplanade Brillaud de Laujardière, 14050 Caen
☎ +33 (0)2 31 55 67 89
Fax +33 (0)2 31 55 63 99
@ britline@ca-normandie.fr
💻 www.britline.com

Crédit Foncier

☎ +33 (0)153 33 28 30
@ buying-france@creditfoncier.fr
💻 www.credit-foncier.fr

Groupe CIC

☎ +33 (0)3 83 97 89 87
@ filbprod@cic.fr
💻 www.cic.fr

Société Générale

✉ International Private Customer Branch, 29, Boulevard Hausmann, 75009 Paris
☎ +33 (0)1 53 30 87 10
Fax +33 (0)1 53 30 87 30
💻 www.societegenerale.com

Contacts: Other french banks and credit institutions

- AXA Banque (💻 www.axabanque.fr)
- Banque Populaire (💻 www.banquepopulaire.fr)
- BNP Paribas (💻 www.bnpparibas.fr)
- Caisse d'Epargne (💻 www.caisse-epargne.fr)
- Crédit Agricole (💻 www.credit-agricole.fr)
- Crédit Cetelem (💻 www.cetelem.fr)
- Crédit du Nord (💻 www.credit-du-nord.fr)

- Crédit Foncier (▭ www.credit-foncier.fr)
- Crédit Mutuel (▭ www.creditmutuel.fr)
- Groupe CIC (▭ www.cic-banques.fr)
- HSBC France (▭ www.hsbc.fr)
- Le Crédit Lyonnais (▭ www.lcl.fr)

Other banking links

- ▭ www.banques.fr – the website of The French Banking Federation (FBF) which is the professional body of all French banks. Some English pages.

- ▭ www.lemoneymag.fr – a good online magazine and consumer guide about personal financing. Lots of articles and FAQs. French only.

Choosing your bank

An English-speaking bank is ideal if you lack confidence or aptitude in speaking French, but it's important that you don't dismiss the banks that are close to where you'll be living. Many people find that local branches, or often a particular manager or cashier at a branch, will go out of their way to help and even assist them in English if they are able to do so.

When looking for a bank make sure that you read all the small print in your application pack and find out exactly *what* tariffs you will have to pay and *how much* these are. Some banks charge for services that others provide for free, for example:

- for internet banking;
- for direct debits;
- for having a cash-dispensing card; or
- for having a cheque book sent to you.

Also, find out if, and how much, you are charged for having money transferred into your French bank from your UK bank. If you are saving, find out how much interest you will be paid and make comparisons. Your bank should be clear about all these charges from the start and should provide a list of tariffs in writing at your request.

> *Note*: **French banks are good at making you apply for debt insurance, unemployment insurance, loss of chequebook insurance and all sorts of other insurance that you may not need.**

Opening a bank account

Even if you don't intend becoming a resident in the country, you will need to set up a French bank account prior to buying a house there. This account will be needed for you to deposit the large sum of Euros just prior to purchasing the property, and for all subsequent related transactions. Following completion the account will be useful for the future payment of bills, such as local taxes and utilities and for paying out your mortgage in Euros. If you're not going to be around all the time, you'll be able to set up direct debits to pay bills and monthly mortgage payments. Many banks will be happy to send statements and chequebooks to your home address if it is outside France.

If you are a non-resident, your account will be a *compte non-résident*. You will be able to get loans or mortgages but you will not be permitted an overdraft facility (although overdrafts are not usual in France). You can change the account to a resident's account, once you have a residence permit (*carte de séjour).*

To open a bank account in France you must be eighteen and able to present a piece of identification such as your passport and a proof of address. Under eighteens can open accounts but they need the authorisation of their parents. From the age of twelve children can have a savings account and a withdrawal card.

On opening the account you'll be given a *relevé d'identité bancaire (RIB)* which is an identity slip giving details of your account number and sort code. This can be used when setting up standing orders and organising direct debits (e.g. to pay phone and electricity bills). You can have several accounts with the same bank and it is also possible to have a joint account.

Each month you will receive the *relevé des operations bancaires*, a statement showing all your ingoings and outgoings. At any time you can ask the bank for a list of recent transactions (*relevé de compte*) and you can check your account at any time via Minitel, the internet or by telephone.

A current account in France is called a *découvert*. Most employees pay salaries directly into a bank or post office account by direct transfer. As it is illegal for banks in France to pay interest on current accounts many people also keep a small amount in a savings account – *compte d'épargne*. The *découvert* will have more outgoings than ingoings and from this account the bank will withdraw interest – a sum called *agios*. It's possible to negotiate with banks on the amount of this sum.

 Tip: Prior to going to France get about six photocopies of everything: your birth certificate; marriage certificate, bank statements, utility bills, etc and get a number of passport photographs. This will save you lots of hassle, such as trips to photocopying services and photo booths, later on.

Chequebooks

You won't be sent a chequebook until two or three weeks after opening the account. Some banks will make you wait until your account has been operating for a couple of months. Chequebooks are generally free although there are some banks that make you pay. All stores accept cheques and as there are no cheque guarantee cards you are normally asked to produce some sort of identification such as your passport or *carte de séjour*.

Cheques take a long time to clear, often up to ten days.

Note: Never write a cheque out unless you are absolutely sure there is money in your account (even if you know money is due to go into your account).

It is illegal to write out a cheque when funds are not available (*chèque sans provision*) and the bank will take stringent measures against you. You'll immediately be informed by a letter that is usually titled '*Interdiction d'Emmettre des cheques*'. From the date of this letter, your details will have been entered on the *Banque de France* national database and you'll be prevented from issuing any further cheques from any French banks. You can also be '*Interdit Bancaire*' which prevents you from writing a cheque or using a *carte bleue* for five years. Getting blacklisted in this way will make life difficult and, as every lender checks these details before lending, it may prevent you from getting loans or mortgages. It's best to make payments rapidly and directly to avoid this.

The payer of the cheque may remedy the situation, and have the '*interdiction*' removed provided that the full amount of the cheque is paid to the payee and a receipt must be obtained as proof. A fine must also be paid to the '*Tresor Public*' of an amount in proportion to the cheque. The *interdiction* will only be removed if it is the first offence of the year and if it is corrected within a month. The fine can be doubled after three incidents in the twelve months following the first. If the problem is not resolved then the '*Interdiction Bancaire*' has to be maintained by law for a period of five years.

Carte bleue

As well as a chequebook you should also request a *carte bleue*, which is a debit card similar to Maestro. Most traders use an automated swipe facility to check the funds and status of the card, and prefer this method of payment to cheques. You are given a PIN (Personal Identity Number) which you tap into the machine when using the card. Funds can be debited from your current account immediately (*débit immediat*) or at the end of the month (*débit différé*). There are different types of *carte bleue*: the CB Nationale can only be used in France, but the Plus Card can be used internationally, and there are a number of cards that can be combined with Visa.

It used to be very popular for people to withdraw money by cashing cheques but banks are now discouraging this as it is costlier to process. Most people today withdraw money using their cards at ATM machines. If you are using your card to withdraw cash then your account will be debited immediately. Some cards – *la carte de retrait* – can only be used for withdrawing money.

Transferring money

Transferring money can be an expensive business. The globalisation of banks can bring some benefits: for instance if you have worldwide accounts with HSBC, then money transfer between your accounts is free. Alternatively, money can be transferred from your UK to your French bank account in the following ways. The first two examples are popular, but they are not the most economical.

Bankers draft

Banks can draw drafts on accounts that they maintain with banks throughout the world, in the currency of the country concerned. Alternatively, drafts may be drawn in Sterling or another currency (e.g. US Dollars) which are negotiable in most countries.

When requesting drafts, customers should always quote the currency that they want the draft raised in and also the country that they will be using the draft in to ensure that an appropriate draft is issued – this is especially important when ordering a draft in Euros.

S.W.I.F.T.

The S.W.I.F.T. (Society for Worldwide Interbank Financial Telecommunications) system is a computer-based system used by most international banks as a method of making overseas payments. The minimum information that is required to make a S.W.I.F.T. transfer is the account number, the name and address of the receiving bank and the name of the beneficiary. In addition all banks have a S.W.I.F.T. code and if this is known for the recipient bank it should be quoted. S.W.I.F.T. payments can be made in Sterling or local currency so the customer is allowed to make the decision on which exchange rate is used, either the UK rate or the receiving country's rate. S.W.I.F.T. transfers take 3-5 days. Banks charge up to £30 for this form of transfer, with some taking a 3-5% margin of the sum as commission.

Eurogiro

An inexpensive way of transferring money from the UK to France is to open a personal account at Alliance and Leicester Commercial Bank in the UK and La Banque Postale in France and transfer via Eurogiro. Eurogiro is a direct electronic transferral system created to give the participating postal and giro (Britain's National Girobank was taken over by the Alliance and Leicester group in 1990 and has operated under the new name – Alliance and Leicester Commercial Bank – since 2003) institutions a competitive edge in the area of cross-border handling. Funds take just 3-4 business days to transfer (although they can send urgent payments for you via Western Union). Sending a payment by Eurogiro costs a fixed fee of just £7.50 and the amount you can transfer is unlimited. Make sure you ask for Eurogiro, a S.W.I.F.T. transfer with them will set you back £17.50. It is also possible to make Eurogiro payments through Visa Europe, although check with your bank about any charges.

Eurogiro

🖥 www.eurogiro.com

Alliance and Leicester Commercial Bank

🖥 www.alliance-leicestercommercialbank.co.uk
☎ 0800 015 4116

La Banque Postale

🖥 www.labanquepostale.fr

TIPANET

TIPANET is an automated transferal system operating among co-operative banks in Belgium, France, Germany, Italy, Netherlands, Spain, Canada and the USA. The Co-operative Bank is the UK's representative. TIPANET is an automated system that enables payments to be routed to recipient Bank accounts, via the destination country's automated clearing house (e.g. BACS in the UK). TIPANET represents a cost-effective method of making non-urgent payments, £8 total costs with no recipient charges and the transfer takes 5 working days.

TIPANET transfers are always converted and received in Euros, unless to the US where US Dollars are sent. Rates of exchange will be set at the time the transfer is made. The exchange rate the bank uses may differ from the market rate and takes into account their commission charge for buying and selling the currency.

Each country has a limit that you are allowed to transfer; in France it is €50,000.

Customers wishing to use the TIPANET service must ensure they have all the account details in each country. If customers do not have all the details required, the transfer would have to go through as a non-urgent S.W.I.F.T. with the relevant costs.

For a TIPANET transfer to France you'll need:

- Bank code (5 digits)
- Branch code (5 digits)
- Account no. (11 digits)
- Check no. (2 digits)
- Beneficiary bank's name and address
- Beneficiary account holder's name
- Eeference (if you need to send one)
- Amount

The Co-operative Bank

- ✉ PO Box 200, Delf House, Southway, Skelmersdale, Lancs, WN8 6GH
- ☎ 08457 212 212 from UK or +44 1695 53760 from outside UK
- @ customerservice@co-operativebank.co.uk
- ⌨ www.co-operativebank.co.uk

You will also need to make sure that the transfer gets there in time for the mortgage payment leaving your account. Some banks are slower than others at transferring funds overseas. You do not want to face the strict penalty involved for inadvertently going into overdraft if money leaves your French account before its equivalent arrives from the UK (see section on bank accounts).

The above methods are ideal for the odd one-off payments but for large payments, such as the deposit or entire sum for buying your property, it is vital that you carefully consider the currency exchange rate. Serious planning is needed when transferring one or several large sums of money for payment of your property in France.

Currency exchange

Volatility in the currency markets can potentially have a big impact on the cost of the property you are buying. If you agree to buy an overseas property without fixing the exchange rate at the outset, you are taking a gamble.

During the months between signing the preliminary contract and handing over the entire sum, the price that you have agreed upon in Euros will not change, however the relative Sterling price probably will. If Sterling strengthens against the Euro then the cost will decline, but if the Euro strengthens then the price will increase.

> ### Example – currency fluctuations
> Halewood, a company that helps both corporate and private clients navigate the risky world of currency exchange, explains:
>
> A property priced at €200,000 would have cost a UK buyer:
>
> - **£129,870** in January 2003
> - **£142,850** by May 2003, an increase in cost of £12,980 (10% more in just 5 months)

Note: **A stronger Euro means that your property will be more expensive!**

It's particularly risky if your property is *sur plan* and you are paying in stages. If you buy the Euros each time you are required to send a payment to the developer, then it means you have no idea what the property is going to cost. If you're on a tight budget this high-risk way of buying would certainly cause sleepless nights.

Buying currency at the spot rate

The risk-free solution is to buy all of the Euros before finding a property or at least on the day of signing the preliminary contract. By doing this you are fixing the cost at the outset, which is called buying currency for 'spot'. You can then deposit the bought currency into a French savings account to earn some interest and send payments to the developer as requested.

Buying currency forward

It could be that you do not have access to all or part of the money at the outset (you could be financing part of the purchase with a re-mortgage of your UK home for instance). If you want to play safe but don't as yet have all the money, a solution could be to buy a 'forward contract'. A forward contract means that you buy the currency now at a rate that is fixed, but only pay a portion of the cost upfront. This is a solution used constantly by international businesses to protect their profit margins. It is also a solution that is made available to many by currency brokers such as Halewood and Currencies4Less.

> ### Example – buying currency forward
> Halewood offers a scheme whereby you pay a 10% deposit in the first instance and the 90% balance upon the maturity of the contract. They explain:
>
> *"For example, if you wish to buy £50,000 worth of Euros but do not need to send them for 3 months, you can agree the exchange rate now, place a £5,000 deposit, and pay the remaining £45,000 balance in 3 months. If the exchange rate moves at all in that 3-month period this will not affect you at all, as you have bought currency at the originally agreed rate. You may actually fix a rate on all your currency requirements up to 18 months forward."*

Currency fluctuations and monthly mortgage payments

Currency fluctuations will also dictate the amount you need to transfer into your French bank account each month, so you'll have to be on top of the currency rate at all times. Although the amount of Euros leaving your French account may not change if you have a fixed rate mortgage, the amount of Sterling that you have to pay into your French account will vary.

Through their Overseas Mortgage Payment Plan (OMPP), The 4Less Group offers a way of dealing with this monthly instability by fixing your exchange rate in advance. They also allow you to benefit from commercial exchange rates even for modest amounts. There is an annual fee of £50 and monthly transfer charges of £7.50. No other charges apply. They cannot guarantee the rate of exchange for the 'Fixing Day' in advance.

The deposit requirement of every OMPP means that you will be paying the equivalent of approximately two months in advance at the outset but will be paying less on month eleven and nothing on month twelve.

You can also pay by cheque by sending twelve pre-dated cheques payable to Currencies4Less with the amounts stated on the schedule, which will be sent to you after the fixing. On or around the 20th day of your application month, you will receive a statement clearly detailing how much you will be paying each month for your OMPP. This statement will display your schedule for the entire year.

Even if you don't have a mortgage, an OMPP can be used for sending any small but regular amounts of monies to a foreign country. All monies are released from The 4Less Group on the 28th of each month (except February), allowing 48 to 72 hours to clear on your foreign account.

For peace of mind it's well worth looking at such an option.

Contacts: Currency brokers

Currencies4Less

✉ Brompton Road, London, SW3 1HW
☎ +44 (0)20 7594 0594
Fax +44 (0)20 7584 4404
@ info@currencies4less.com
▫ www.currencies4less.com

HIFX (Halewood International Foreign Exchange) Plc

✉ Morgan House, Madeira Walk, Windsor, Berkshire, SL4 1EP
☎ +44 (0) 1753 859159
Fax +44 (0) 1753 859169
@ pcbs@hifx.co.uk
▫ www.hifx.co.uk

Sucden (UK) Limited

✉ 5 London Bridge Street, London, SE1 9SG
☎ +44 (0) 20 7940 9400/9680
Fax +44 (0) 20 7940 9500
@ pcs@sucden.co.uk
▫ www.sucden.co.uk

Overseas Mortgage Payment Plan

✉ 100 Brompton Road, London, SW3 1HW
☎ +44 (0)20 7594 0594
Fax +44 (0)20 7584 4404
@ info@ompp.co.uk
▫ www.ompp.co.uk

Currency charts

Figure 9.1 – US Dollar [USD] v Euro [EUR]

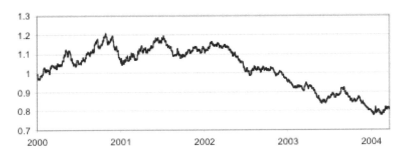

Figure 9.2 – Sterling [GBP] v Euro [EUR]

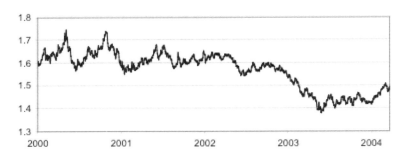

Figure 9.3 – Australian Dollar [USD] v Euro [EUR]

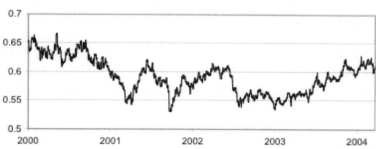

AUD/EUR

Figure 9.4 – Euro [EUR] v Japanese Yen

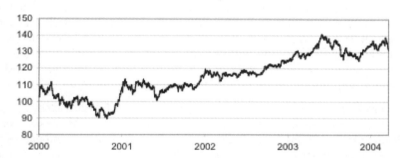

EUR/JPY

Tax

Individuals are taxed on the entire income of French or foreign sources in so far as they are domiciled in France. Those domiciled in France, regardless of their nationality, are taxed on their worldwide income and those not domiciled in France are taxed in France on their income from French sources only. These 'French sources' include rent from letting your property in France and income from assets or any professional activities, whether employment or not.

According to the French tax code, the following persons are deemed to be domiciled in France for tax purposes:

- any person who has his or her home or main abode in France, that is they spend over 183 days or more in France each year; or
- any person who carries on a professional activity in France, whether as an employee or not, unless he or she proves that this activity is carried on therein incidentally; or
- any person whose centre of economic interest lies in France.

Income tax paid by non-residents of France is assessed on a notional income (*revenu forfaitaire*) equal to three times the real rental value of home(s) available to them in France when their income from French sources is less than the notional assessment basis. This notional assessment does not apply to persons of French or foreign nationality resident in a State or territory that has signed a convention with France for the avoidance of double taxation.

The countries that have a double taxation agreement with France include all EU members, Australia, Canada, China, India, Israel, Japan, Malaysia, New Zealand, Pakistan, Philippines, Singapore, Sri Lanka, Switzerland and the USA. Double taxation treaties ensure that income that has already been taxed in one country isn't taxed again in another sharing the treaty.

Moving to France permanently

Before moving permanently to France make sure you notify the tax authorities in the country you are leaving. Some tax authorities will require evidence of you leaving the country such as evidence of a new job or proof of the house you have bought.

Those leaving the UK will have to inform HM Revenue and Customs about their departure by completing a form P85.

🖳 www.hmrc.gov.uk/cnr/p85.pdf

HM Revenue and Customs have lots of other advice on their website.

As soon as you move to France to start a job or a business, you must register at your *Centre des Impôts* (local tax centre). Once you have registered you will be sent a tax return (*déclaration fiscal*) every year. Unlike in the UK, income tax – known as *Impôt sur le revenu des Personnes Physiques* – isn't deducted at source and each individual is responsible for making their own declaration. Income tax is assessed once a year on the taxable income which a household (explained further below) derives during the previous calendar year. The tax year in France runs from 1st January to 31st December (unlike the UK, where the tax year is April to April).

You must fill in the *déclaration fiscal* and return it by a given date (or face a penalty even if the form arrives late by just a day). The tax forms are very complicated (even to the French) so it's important that you seek professional advice if you are unclear on anything. If you declare online then you are given a €20 reduction.

Several months after you have sent in your declaration, you'll receive a bill of net tax in the form of a tax notice (*avis d'imposition*), indicating the amount you must pay and the date you must pay it by (*date de mise en recouvrement*). Most people pay their tax in two instalments, in February and May, followed by payment of the balance in September. Taxpayers may also opt to pay in ten monthly instalments.

Income tax

Prior to 2006 the amount of income tax (*impôt sur le revenu*) you paid was judged according to where your salary fitted into a series of seven tax bands. 2006 brings a major reform to the system with the number of bands being reduced from seven to five. The top rate of 40% now compares with maximum rates in the United Kingdom (40%), Italy (43%), and Germany (45%). The following table shows the *barème* for 2006.

Table 9.2 – French income tax 2006

Income band (€)	Rate (%)
Below 5,515	0.00
5,515 – 11,000	5.50
11,000 – 24,432	14.0
24,432 – 65,500	30.0
Over 65,500	40.0

Source: www.impots.gouv.fr

The table below shows the older model from 2005.

Table 9.3 – French income tax 2005 (on 2004 income)

Income band (€)	Rate (%)
Below 4,334	0.00
4,334 – 8,524	6.83
8,524 – 15,004	19.14
15,004 – 24,294	28.26
24,294 – 39,529	37.38
39,529 – 48,747	42.62
Over 48,747	48.09

Source: www.impots.gouv.fr

The percentages for 2005 seem, at first sight, extortionate – not just to high earners but even to those taking home a low annual pay packet. Fortunately the computation method of income tax is not based on the above scale alone, but takes into account many provisions that reduce the percentage of tax to be paid and that allow for a highly personalised taxation.

Firstly, income tax is based on the total income of a household rather than on the income of each individual. This household could mean, for example, a family entity consisting of a single person, two married partners or those having concluded a civil solidarity pact, and their children or other dependants. In order to lift the burden of the progressive tax scale the net income figure is divided into parts, the number of which correspond to how many people there are in the household, and each part is separately taxed according to the scale. Called the *quotient familial*, the parts are worked out as follows:

- One part for a single person with no children.
- Two parts for a married couple with no children.
- Two and a half parts for a married couple with one child.
- An extra half part for each additional child.

(A married couple with four children will divide the net income into four.)

By children, the above means those dependants that are under 18. Children over 18 can ask to remain within their parents' tax threshold without condition until the age of 21, and until 25 if they are students living at home. Disabled or infirm children or ascendants can remain within the tax threshold at any age they may be.

Unmarried couples pay more tax than married or 'PACS-ed' couples. If the unmarried couple has children then each child can figure on one or the other parent's declaration but not on both.

Note: French taxation works very much in favour of the family unit. Therefore, it's not unusual for parents to encourage children to remain living at home throughout college.

As well as the reduction in tax based on the *quotient familial*, there are also numerous further allowances, deductions and credits. For example, there are allowances for childcare and domestic help, household expenses, business expenses that have not been reimbursed such as travel to and from work and business rent.

Once all the allowances and the *quotient familial* is worked into their declarations, many families on an average wage take home more money after tax than those from other European countries, including the UK. Large families in France pay the lowest tax in Europe but for those without children taxation can hit quite hard.

At the time of writing it is not fully clear to what extent existing exemptions, abatements and the distribution of tax paid in the household will be effected in future years by the simplification of the tax bands. However, it is clear that changes have been made to benefit high earners. As well as the lowering of tax, a new capping system has been introduced, so that the total amount of tax paid by individuals, including income, wealth and local taxes, must not exceed 60% of their income. If the ceiling is breached, taxpayers will be entitled to claim a refund.

Capital gains tax

Capital gains tax (*impôt sur les plus values*) is tax paid from the profit of sales of certain property in France including antiques, art, jewellery, securities and real estate.

The new France-UK double tax treaty signed in January 2004 agrees that the capital gains on the sale of UK real estate will become taxable in France with a tax credit for capital gain tax paid in the UK (which will normally be nil). The existing treaty confers on the UK the right to tax such capital gains, but, under UK domestic tax law, capital gains tax does not apply if you are not ordinarily resident in the UK (and not a temporary non-UK-resident). In consequence, for those moving permanently to France, such gains currently escape tax on both sides of the Channel. Under the new treaty they will be free of capital gains tax only when the property has been owned for at least fifteen years. Note, that as of January 2006 the treaty has not yet been ratified.

Currently, capital gains tax on real estate in France for French residents, works in the following way: tax is not paid on the sale of the taxpayer's main home (*résidence principale*) or on profit from the first sale of a residential building (*immeuble destiné à l'habitation*). Properties that have been owned by the same person for 22 years are exempt and those who are selling their second home, but do not own their main residence (i.e. they are tenants or lease holders), are also exempt.

Assessment of capital gains tax is based on the difference between the price of transfer and the acquisition price. When a property is sold less than two years after the acquisition then a short-term capital gains tax of 33.3% of any profit must be paid. After two years the capital gains tax is reduced by 5% for each subsequent year up to 22 years, and multiplied by an index linked multiplier of the sale price.

All bills relating to renovation, restoration and general improvements (although not painting and decorating) should be kept as this can be offset against the profit. The legal fees and agents fees relating to the sale can also be deducted from the tax.

 Note: Don't forget that if you move permanently to France and decide to keep a property in the UK, you will become liable to capital gains tax on it if you decide to sell it at a later date.

The capital gains payment is normally calculated by the *notaire* handling the sale. The *notaire* will appoint a tax representative (*agent fiscal accredité*) to act on your behalf concerning the tax payments. This agent will charge up to 1% plus VAT of the selling price.

Once the capital gains tax has been deducted, the remaining gains are subject to further taxation as part of the owner's income tax.

Income from property

Certain profits from property made by individuals domiciled outside France are subject to a 50% levy discharging income tax liability.

These are:

- profits made by property dealers;
- profits made by persons on transfer of real property they have built or have had built and of the real property rights pertaining thereto; and
- profits made by persons who sell land divided in plots intended to be developed.

Wealth tax

In France wealth tax (*impôt sur la fortune*) is payable by people whose assets exceed (in 2006) €750,000.

The first band of tax is only 0.55% and the bands only reach 1% at €2.3m. The threshold figure of €750,000 is calculated on net assets, that is mortgage and loans are deducted, but is calculated on family assets rather than individual assets, so that a husband and wife's assets are aggregated. The onus is on you the taxpayer to put the correct current market value on your assets. You can reduce the value of your principal residence by 20% and can value your home contents at either their real value or set them at 5% of your total assets. Any liabilities you have are then deducted, such as outstanding loans or tax bills.

Very few assets are exempt from wealth tax, with the main ones being antiques, fine art and 'business assets'. Until recently, if you were domiciled in France then the wealth tax was based on your worldwide fortunes, whereas if you were resident in France but not domiciled there, the value was based on your assets in France alone. This, however, is about to change. The French Government has recently agreed to add into the provisions of the new double tax treaty with Britain, signed in January 2004, a temporary exemption from wealth tax for British nationals resident in France, of any 'property' outside France, during their first five years of French residence. In the sixth year, it will be extended to include worldwide assets. If the UK national leaves France for at least three years, a further five-year exemption will start again from the date of his return to France. At the time of writing (January 2006), however, the new tax treaty has yet to be ratified, so it will not be in force for some time yet and the wealth tax exemption will only begin from the year following the year of ratification.

Note: Watch out, as French domicile laws are rather different to those in England and Wales. For example, you can be what is called 'fiscally domiciled' in France if your centre of economic activity is there, whether or not you live there.

Taxe sur la valeur ajoutée TVA (VAT)

TVA is applicable on almost everything in France and is one of the principle sources of revenue for the French treasury. The standard rate of VAT in France is set at 19.6%. There is a reduced rate of 5.5% for most food and agricultural products, certain types of animal food, medical drugs not reimbursed by social security, books and certain services (mainly accommodation supply, meals supply to company and hospital canteens, passenger transportation and certain entertainments).

The 5.5% rate applies also to the costs of improvement, converting and maintenance works for dwelling premises.

A special rate of 2.1% is charged on particular press publications and medical drugs reimbursed by social security.

Tax on pensions

Under most double taxation agreements pensions are only taxed in the country where you are resident. There are, however, some exceptions to this. In particular, under many agreements pensions paid for Government service (including, for example, service in the armed forces) are taxed only in the country which is paying the pension.

If there is no relief available to you under a double taxation agreement, you may be able to claim personal allowances. Tax will normally be deducted from your pension before it is paid to you – whether it is paid by your former UK employer or by an insurance company.

If you were not resident in the UK when you were an employee, your pension from that employment may not be liable to UK tax in certain circumstances.

Local taxes

Taxe foncière and *taxe d'habitation*

In the UK our local tax is 'council tax', which is based on the value of the property and the number of people living in it. The equivalent to this in France would be the combination of the two separate taxes *taxe foncière* (a property/land tax) and *taxe d'habitation* (a residence tax). The owner of the property is liable for the *taxe foncière*, while the occupier is liable for the *taxe d'habitation*; if you are an owner-occupier then you are liable for both taxes. In the case of a house being sold, the person owning the house as of 1st January is liable for the full year's *taxe foncière*. However, if a house is purchased partway through the year, the *taxe d'habitation* is often split between the buyer and the seller. If you do not confirm this (in writing) at the time of the initial contract (*Compromis de Vente*), you may be required at the time of the final contract (*Acte de Vente*) to refund to the vendor the *taxe d'habitation* that they've already paid for the balance of the year.

This tax varies from region to region, so identical properties can have very different levels of such tax depending on where they are located. A city property will be taxed more than the equivalent property in a village or the countryside. Both taxes are based on the notional rental value of the property, so the more comfortable and well-equipped it is, the more you can expect to pay. *Taxe d'habitation* also depends on the number of people living in the property.

New builds and rural conversions are exempt from *taxe foncière* for two years. Value can change, especially if the property has been improved or renovated. The French have long tried to evade such tax, for instance, by building a swimming pool so that it's hidden at the end of the garden or converting a garage so that the windows look over the garden.

People on low incomes, those over 60 years, widowers and widows not paying income tax, and those on disability benefits are exempt from such taxes.

Your notaire will have informed the relevant tax authorities of the change in ownership, so once you move into the property you can sit back and expect the bills to arrive in due course. It is possible to pay online through www.impots.gouv.fr.

The following is a list of tax specialists in the UK

Contacts: tax advice

Anthony & Cie

⬚   Villantipolis 11 – 473 route des Dollines, 06560 Sophia Antipolis, France
☎   +33 (0)4 93 65 32 23
Fax +33 (0)4 93 65 42 45
@   info@antco.com
⌨   www.antco.com

Blake Lapthorn Linnell

✉ Holbrook House, 14 Great Queen Street, London, WC2B 5DG
☎ +44 (0) 207 4301709
Fax +44 (0) 207 8314441
@ info@bllaw.co.uk
🖥 www.bllaw.co.uk

CBA Law

✉ 27 St Helens Street, Ipswich, Suffolk, IP4 1HH
☎ +44 (0)1473 384870
Fax +44 (0)1473 384878
@ emma.morris@cba-law.co.uk
🖥 www.riddellcroft.com

John Siddall Financial Services Limited

✉ Lothian House, 22 High Street, Fareham, Hampshire, PO16 7AE
☎ +44 (0)1329 288641
Fax +44 (0)1329 281157
@ france@johnsiddalls.co.uk
🖥 www.siddalls.net

PKF Ampersand

✉ 47 rue de Liège, 75008 Paris, France
☎ +33 (1) 43 87 97 33
Fax +33 (1) 42 94 13 34
@ info@pkf-ampersand.fr
🖥 www.pkf-ampersand.fr

Sykes Anderson

✉ Bury House, 31 Bury Street, London EC3A 5JJ
☎ +44 (0)20 7398 4700
Fax +44 (0)20 7283 6585
@ solicitors@sykesanderson.com
🖥 www.sykesanderson.com

Inheritance

Wills

A will made in the UK will cover your UK-based real estate and moveable goods but will not cover your property in France.

Most legal professionals recommend that you make a second, separate will (*testament*) in France to cover your French property. This can be made up by a *notaire* in France or by a legal representative in the UK. Most English and French wills contain the clause "I revoke all former wills . . . " so be careful to make sure that one will doesn't unwittingly cancel the other.

There are three types of will in France:

- **Testament olographe**
  The holographic will is the most common type of will. It is written by hand by the person making the will and must be signed and dated by them. No witnesses are required. Once the will is completed it must be registered at the central will registry (*fichier de derniéres volontés*).

- **Testament authentique**
  This is drawn up by the *notaire* in the form of a notarial document. It is dictated by the person making the will and must be witnessed by two *notaires* or a *notaire* and two other witnesses. This is automatically registered in the central will registry.

- **Testament mystique**
  This is a secret will and is very rarely used in France. This will is written by or for the person making the will. It is inserted and sealed in an envelope in the presence of two witnesses and then given to a *notaire* who will record on the envelope a note confirming that it contains a will and that the person who wrote the will handed it to him or her.

The *notaire's* fees for helping with the will are €46 if written up in the *notaire's* office, €69 if the *notaire* is called outside his or her office, and €92 if it is after office hours.

French succession law

Unlike UK law in which you are able to leave your property to whomever you please, French succession laws will apply to your property. This means that your children cannot be left out of your will in favour of your spouse and authorities will make sure that your children get their share even if you don't.

If the deceased leaves one child that child will claim half of his or her estate, if the deceased leaves two children then they will claim two thirds of the estate and if three or more children are left then three quarters of the estate will be divided between them. If you have no children, then it will be left to any surviving parents and to your siblings. The remaining portion is known as the *quotité disponible* and can be left to anyone the deceased pleases (usually their spouse) although it must be clearly outlined in a will. If you have no will, French law will make almost no provision for the widow(er) or surviving partner.

Until recently there was very little protection offered to the surviving spouse, which was often a problem, especially for many women whose working partner had bought the property in his name. Such women could have been evicted from the property by their own children. Fortunately the situation has been improved and in cases where the surviving spouse has not inherited the property, they will retain usufruct (*usufruit*) – that is the right to live in the property – for a year following the death.

Inheritance tax

The following chart shows the scale of inheritance tax (2005) to be paid. Between spouses there is a tax-free allowance of €76,000 and for children there is a tax-free allowance of €50,000. The amount in excess of this is taxed according to the following table.

Table 9.4 – French inheritance tax 2005

In direct line	Between spouses	Tax (%)
Not exceeding 7,600 EUR	Not exceeding 7,600 EUR	5
Between 7,600 and 11,400 EUR	Between 7,600 and 15,000 EUR	10
Between 11,400 EUR and 15,000 EUR	Between 15,000 and 30,000 EUR	15
Between 15,000 and 520,000 EUR	Between 30,000 and 520,000 EUR	20
Between 520,000 EUR and 850,000 EUR	Between 520,000 and 850,000 EUR	30
Between 850,000 EUR and 1,700,000 EUR	Between 850,000 and 1,700,000 EUR	35
Over 1,700,000 EUR	Over 1,700,000 EUR	40

Source: www.impots.gouv.fr

For more distant relatives the tax allowances are less and the tax rates higher.

Ownership *en indivision*

If you are joint buyers then the *notaire*, unless instructed otherwise, will state in your documentation that you have bought the property *en division*. This means that when one of you dies, the deceased's share of the estate will not go to the survivor but to the deceased's heirs. If there are children from a previous marriage then the surviving spouse may be left awkwardly sharing the property with step-children they hardly know.

Arrangements can be made in advance of the death of one owner so that the survivor retains rights to the property.

Note: **If your partner dies and you are left sharing a property with an infant then you will be unable to sell that property until that child reaches the age of seventeen.**

Clause Tontine

It is possible to have a *Clause Tontine* inserted into your *contrat de vente*. Owning a property *en tontine* roughly equates with joint tenancy in English law and will mean that when the first spouse dies, the survivor will be considered as having owned the property from the start and the rights to inhabit the property will belong to them.

For both ownership *en tontine* and ownership *en division*, inheritance tax will have to be paid on half of the property on the first death. The surviving spouse has an inheritance allowance of €76,000 and on the remaining amount after this the tax goes up in increments from 5% to as much as 40% (as shown in table 9.4).

Change of matrimonial regime

For most married couples a change of matrimonial regime would be the best way to avoid inheritance tax during both their lifetimes. When the French get married, they often sign a marriage contract which determines how their property is dealt with on their death. The regime of *communauté universelle* ensures that on the first death, all the property of the marriage is owned by the survivor. Unless this regime is actively adopted by English married couples then they will be deemed to be married under the regime of separation of goods. By inserting into the new regime a *clause d'attribution de communauté au conjoint survivant,* a couple cannot only allow all shared property to pass to the surviving spouse on the first death but also defer any French inheritance tax until the second death. All that is payable on the first death is a 1% registration duty.

It should be noted that the law provides protection for children of previous marriages who might otherwise lose out under such a change of matrimonial regime. They have a right known as *en rentranchement* to limit the rights of the surviving spouse so that they can apply only the *quotité disponible* of the forced inheritance rights – in other words they can retain their forced inheritance rights. For a couple with children from previous marriages, this means that a change of matrimonial regime may not be the best option, although the tax advantages may still make it viable in the case of very large estates.

If couples wish to change their regime then they must have been married or have had their current regime for the previous two years and the change must be 'in the interest of the family'. The change has to be submitted to the Court for homologation which can mean that the process becomes quite expensive once legal fees have to be dished out.

Lifetime gifts

It is possible to make a lifetime gift (*donation*) of your French estate to one or several of your family, thus preventing title to real estate vesting heirs you wish to exclude. These heirs are instead entitled to a cash equivalent of their percentage entitlement. The main advantage is that, if you survive a gift by more than ten years, the asset does not form part of your French estate for French inheritance tax purposes. You can also reserve a life interest (*usufruit*) enabling you or your spouse to use the French realty in your lifetimes.

Société Civile Immobilière

A *Société Civile Immobilière* (SCI) is a good solution for those sharing a property with non-family members or if there is a complex family situation such as a number of step-children. An SCI is a company set up to manage property and members' own shares in the property company (the SCI) rather than the property itself. As shares are considered personal property and not real estate property, English succession law applies and shares can be left according to the deceased's wishes.

This solution provides much greater flexibility and members can freely give shares to their children or partners during their lifetime to avoid future inheritance tax liability, although such a gift must be given ten years before death. The company must have a registered address (normally the address of the property), keep accounts and hold an annual general meeting (this must be held on French soil).

Les Union Libres and PACS

Since 1999, it has been possible for same-sex and different-sex couples who wish to legally be recognised as a union, without marriage, to register a *Pacte Civil de Solidarité*. This is an agreement between two people to give each other mutual and material support and to be jointly responsible for each other's debts. There are fiscal, housing and inheritance benefits for PACS partners – although these benefits are not quite as good as those available to married couples (much to the disappointment of homosexual couples who feel they are being denied the same rights as heterosexuals).

PACS also benefits young couples who are civil servants and who often have no choice over where they are placed. With a PACS the couple will be placed in the same town as each other. Partners register their PACS at the local court. A Pacs can easily be dissolved by informing the authorities. Once the authorities have been informed then the couple will have to wait three months until the dissolution. If one partner objects to the dissolution, then the other has to have a bailiff's letter served on them. PACS has been very much opposed by the Roman Catholic Church.

Social security

The French social security system, commonly known as *le Sécu*, deals with distributing the benefits related to healthcare, maternity, family income support, unemployment, pensions, death, industrial accidents, old-age and widowhood.

Contributions are collected together by the URSSAF (*Union de recouvrement des cotisations de sécurité sociale et d'allocations familiales*), which is controlled by the Ministry of Labour and the Ministry of Social Affairs and run by representatives of labour unions and the State.

The URSSAF then passes the money on to the ACOSS (*Agence centrale des organismes de sécurité sociale*), which distributes it to the various funds, called *caisses*, which are responsible for paying out benefits.

Hiring a new employee involves filing a 'declaration of hiring' (*déclaration unique d'embauche* – DUE) which has to be sent to the URSSAF branch nearest to the company's location. It must be sent within eight days of the employee starting work. Based on the DUE, URSSAF completes all the formalities required, such as registering the employee for social security, unemployment insurance, etc. A company can make the declaration through the website: www.due.fr. (New employees are subjected to a mandatory medical check-up.) Social security contributions are then automatically deducted from the employee's salary each month. The employee is required to provide the employer with a French social security number.

The national healthcare *caisse* for salaried employees is the CNAMTS (*Caisse nationale d'assurance maladie des travailleurs salariés*) and reimbursements for medical treatment are paid out by the CPAM (*Caisses primaires d'assurance maladie*). Family income support is paid out by the CAF (*Caisses d'allocations familiales*). The basic CAF payment is for any family with more than one child, but there many additional benefits such as the annual payment distributed at the start of the school year to help cover back-to-school expenses, and contributions towards the hiring of an *assistante maternelle* for childcare. See: www.caf.fr to see what your family is eligible for.

If you are self-employed, you'll have to register directly with the URSSAF to pay your charges. The URSSAF has 105 offices around the country and you'll have to contact the one closest to you. Be warned, the social security system in France is a minefield of bureaucracy, with numerous agencies and their obligatory acronyms involved.

www.urssaf.fr

Healthcare

Even though contributions to social security are very high, social security does not cover you 100%. You are covered for 100% of the cost of treatment for 30 of the most serious illnesses and diseases, and for almost everything else (including your doctor's consultation fee) you are covered for around 70%. The remaining 30% must be paid directly by yourself or by a private top-up insurance called a *mutuelle*. Even if you are young or in good health, it is certainly worth getting a *mutuelle* as, if you are in an accident or get an unexpected illness, medical costs can be extremely high.

EU citizens and the E111

From 1st January 2006, the European Health Insurance Card (EHIC) replaced the E111 form, which entitles EU citizens to reduced cost, sometimes free, medical treatment when they're in any European Economic Area (EEA) country or Switzerland.

The EHIC is normally valid for three to five years and covers any medical treatment that becomes necessary during your trip, because of either illness or an accident. The card gives access to state-provided medical treatment only, and you'll be treated on the same basis as an 'insured' person living in the country you're visiting. Remember, this might not cover all the things you'd expect to get free of charge from the NHS in the UK and you may have to make a contribution to the cost of your care.

The EHIC won't cover you if getting medical treatment is the main purpose of your trip. You are advised to take out comprehensive private insurance for visits to all countries, regardless of whether you are covered by your EHIC.

For more information on the EHIC and to apply online:

💻 www.dh.gov.uk

 Note: An E111 can be used to provide proof that you have health cover, when you apply for your *carte de séjour.*

If you end up living permanently in France (i.e. living there more than three consecutive months) but do not work, then you will need to apply for an:

*   **E106** if you are below UK retirement age; or an
*   **E121** if over retirement age.

If you receive a State pension, widow's benefit or long-term incapacity benefits from the UK you will be entitled to the health services of the sickness insurance scheme of France, under the same conditions as French nationals, with the costs normally met by the UK. More information can be found on The Pension Service website:

💻 www.thepensionservice.gov.uk

The E106 will only entitle the holder to healthcare for a limited period (usually two years). This time will depend on the amount of National Insurance contributions that they have made during their working life in the UK. With the E106 and E121 you will be able to register with CPAM (the *Caisse Primaire Assurance Maladie*). Most expatriates living in France, particularly retired people, register with the CPAM of which there is a nationwide network. Expatriates employed in France will be registered with another social security fund.

To get an E106 or E121 you will need to contact the:

Medical Benefits Section of the Pensions and Overseas Benefits Directorate

☎ +44 (0)191 218 7547

If you have been resident in France for longer than three months, you can apply to be covered by Universal Health Cover (*Couverture Maladie Universelle* or CMU) whether you have an E-form or not. The CMU is a medical health cover scheme designed to ensure that everyone is covered by social security for basic medical costs.

Other forms that could be relevant to you include the E128 that covers you for medical treatment up to twelve months and which is generally used by students or those on short-term work contracts, or there's the E112 which you'll need if you're going to the country specifically to benefit from that country's medical treatment. (The E112 typically covers cases such as those going abroad for heart-lung transplantation, unusual eye and skin conditions, cancer, rare hereditary conditions and brain injuries.)

Visiting a doctor

The process of visiting a doctor is much easier in France than in the UK. It is not necessary to make an appointment in advance and mostly the French just turn up at their local surgery and simply wait to be seen. Waiting rooms are normally half empty and in them you will notice a list – a bit like a restaurant menu – of tariffs. The cost for a general consultation is normally around €20.

Ensure that the doctor or dentist is *conventionné*, that is, they work within the French health system and, if you have an E-form, obtain a signed statement of the treatment given (*feuille de soins*) as you cannot claim a refund without it. You will be charged for the treatment you receive, as well as for any prescribed medicines, and the amount(s) should be shown on the *feuille*.

When getting prescribed medicines, the pharmacist will hand you back your prescription and you should attach it to the *feuille* in order to claim a refund. Medicine containers also carry detachable labels (vignettes), showing the name and price of the contents. Stick these in the appropriate place on the *feuille*, and sign and date the form at the end. The cost of common remedies and items such as bandages are refunded at the lower rate. The cost of medicines marked with a Δ on the vignette is not recoverable.

Refunds

If you have an E-form you will need to send your application for a refund by sending the *feuille de soins*, any prescription and your E-form to the nearest sickness insurance office called a CPAM while you are still in France. The refund will be sent to your home address later, but it may be subject to a bank charge. Before sending the money order, the French authorities will send you an itemised statement of the amount to be refunded. This refund process normally takes around two months.

Once you belong to a *caisse* (social security fund) you will not have to go through the same reimbursement procedures as E-form holders. The *caisse* to which you have registered will have supplied you with a *Carte Vitale,* which is an electronic card containing all the administrative information about your entitlements. It is not a payment card and contains no details about your medical situation (such as your blood type or vaccinations), it simply enables a swift reimbursement procedure. You do not need to fill in any forms and send off any application forms for reimbursement as it will all be done for you and reimbursement will take up to five days.

Learning French

If you are planning on buying a property in France then you will certainly need at least a basic proficiency in French. Of course, some brave (perhaps foolish) people do take the plunge without speaking a word of the language, but life will be a great deal easier, and you'll be less likely to encounter problems, if you learn the basics first.

Some people are naturally better at picking up languages than others, so it's impossible to say how long it takes to learn. It very much depends on how many hours you are willing to put in each week and also on your determination to learn. You won't become fluent until you have lived in France for a while and speak the language almost all the time.

If you've already got a decent but rusty proficiency in the language then you can spend some time polishing up by listening to French radio or watching French television while in the UK. Most areas of the UK can pick up French radio (you can also listen to French radio via the internet), and if you have a satellite dish it's likely you'll be able to access to French television. Hire lots of French videos and DVDs.

There are also a number of French clubs you can join (see *Alliance Française* below). Londoners can actually have a taste of living in France without even passing the Eurostar terminal . . . visit 💻 www.franceinlondon.co.uk which lists the numerous French shops, cafés and bistros about town, as well as film showings and exhibitions by French artists. The site also lists French markets that are held throughout the UK.

Evening courses

Many people learn foreign languages in their home country by taking up evening courses at local government funded colleges, universities and adult education centres. These courses usually run throughout the year, in three or four month blocks, starting in September, January or April. If you are on a course that lasts one or two years then it is likely you'll be able to take an exam at the end such as a GCSE or an A-level. Such exams will take place around May and June.

Evening language courses tend to attract people from all ages and backgrounds, as well as many people who are intending to make the move to France so it's a good place to meet people making similar plans to yourself.

A good place to start looking for such a course is in your local library, which will have reference copies of prospectuses for all the adult and further education courses in your neighbourhood. Look out on the library's notice boards or leaflets section for information on classes and tuition. Londoners should get hold of a copy of the Floodlight guide, which can be bought at most newsagents and is found in most London libraries, and lists all the part and full-time courses in all London boroughs. For nationwide information on courses contact Hotcourses or Learn Direct. Learn Direct give free and impartial advice on over 500,000 courses nationwide, as well as information on funding and childcare.

Learn Direct

☎   (Freephone UK): 0800 100 900

💻   www.learndirect.co.uk

Floodlight

💻   www.floodlight.co.uk

Hotcourses

💻   www.hotcourses.com

Specialised centres

Institut Français

Institut Français is the official centre of French language and culture, managed by the French Ministry of Foreign Affairs. Worldwide there are 150 centres in over 50 countries. The language centre in London teaches over 6,000 students a year.

There are short and long, intensive and part-time courses. Their courses are more expensive than evening classes at local adult education centres but are of a guaranteed high quality and the classes are small. Students also benefit from their fantastic facilities which includes the *Ciné Lumière* (showing French films every day), a two-storey multi-media library with a vast choice of French books, newspapers, periodicals, videos and CDs and a special multi-media children's library. The centre has a regular program of talks (from French writers, film-makers and other cultural observers), debates and wine tastings. There is a French bistro on site offering authentic regional dishes, snacks and a wine list.

Alliance Française

Alliance Française, which works alongside the Institut Française, is a cultural and educational association with over 1,000 teaching centres across the world. In the UK there are 13 centres in Bath, Belfast, Bristol, Cambridge, East Midlands, Exeter, Glasgow, Jersey, London, Milton Keynes, Manchester, Oxford and York providing courses for all levels and needs, for instance 'French for Business'. Before signing up for a course you can have a free assessment at the Alliance Française in London to find out what level you are at. Students can study for the *Alliance Française de Paris diplomas* which are officially recognised by the French Ministry of Education and internationally recognised by governments, organisations, companies and universities. They also offer customised corporate and private tuition.

Alliance Française also co-ordinates French clubs in towns all over the UK which involve get-togethers of Francophiles and French residents for cheese and wine evenings, film showings, and talks by experts on diverse subjects such as the history of chocolate or the life of Toulouse-Lautrec. The Alliance also organises excursions to France, such as a three-day trip to study the architecture of Burgundy or a 10-day trip to study art and history in Provence.

Contacts: French cultural institutes

Institut Française

⊠   17 Queensberry Place, London, SW7 2DT
☎   +44 (0)20 7581 2701
@   language-centre@ambafrance.org.uk
🖳   www.institut-francais.org.uk

Alliance Française

⊠   1 Dorset Square, London, NW1 6PU
☎   +44 (0)20 7723 6439
@   network@alliancefrancaise.org.uk
🖳   www.alliancefrancaise.org.uk

Private tutoring

Check advertisements in your local press and signs in newsagents' windows for information on private French tutors. For conversational French a good idea is to put a notice up in a local university or English language school. There are plenty of foreign students out there in dire need of a little extra cash – so such a scheme could benefit all! You could even mutually benefit each other, for instance an hour spent chatting in French could follow an hour spent chatting in English.

Self-study

Some people find it a drag having to go to evening classes after a hard day at work or in the cold winter evenings when all you want to do is go home and have a hot bath. Others are simply terrified of the classroom atmosphere. Don't worry, there are plenty of opportunities for studying in private, in the comfort of your own home and at your own pace:

Audio courses

The following are popular and widely recommended audio courses, many of which come as either CDs or tapes. An audio course is ideal because you can play the tape/CD during your commute to work, on a long drive to France or while you're doing the housework.

French with Michel Thomas Complete Course CD

This collection of eight one hour long CDs by language guru Michel Thomas is good for learning a wide French vocabulary very quickly. The course places you in an imaginary classroom alongside two French students and you are introduced to a selection of words and phrases whch you must repeat. Thomas has a clever way of building up a student's confidence, firstly by teaching them all the French words that are spelt exactly the same in English. This helps students to concentrate on pronunciation without having to memorise. So, after the first hour you already feel as though you have learnt a great deal. Memorising or note-taking is not encouraged and learning is made to feel like a far from arduous process. In no time you are putting together phrases and by the end of the CD you are negotiating restaurant reservations.

⌨   www.michelthomas.com

The BBC French Experience

Whereas some packages only cover or concentrate on certain skills, these BBC packs cover all the skills: from reading, writing, listening and speaking. Colourful, clearly laid out books are accompanied by audio cassettes and CDs. There are also television programmes that accompany the package, but these are normally broadcast during the most unsociable hours so you will need to have a video recorder at hand. All twenty programmes are also available on two 180 minute video cassettes which can either be borrowed from your library or bought.

⌨   www.bbclanguages.com

Linguaphone

Established in 1901, Linguaphone was one of the pioneers in self-study language learning. Linguaphone offer a very wide range of portable audio and book materials.

    www.linguaphone.co.uk

Online courses

BBC languages French Steps

The excellent, free online course French Steps at   www.bbc.co.uk/languages is certainly a good place to start learning French. The course introduces beginners to simple, spoken French language. It's made up of 24 short units which should be followed in sequence and include basic conversational situations such as taking a taxi, asking for directions, introducing yourself, ordering a meal, etc. It has been devised to be used in short sessions so that you can fit it around your own schedule, whenever and for however long it suits you. The whole syllabus matches the Common European Framework Level One, which is recognised across Europe as a benchmark for simple conversational language.

    www.bbc.co.uk/languages

Telephone tutorials

Frenchclasses.com

Not only does Frenchclasses.com offer a CD Rom of 108 lessons (36 beginners, 36 intermediate, 36 advanced), they also offer tuition by telephone. Teaching comprises eight 40-minute sessions in which the teacher calls you at a pre-arranged time (the cost of the call is included in the price) and discusses pre-decided themes in French. Themes include 'French for Business', 'The Life and Work of Françoise Sagan', and, ideal for those moving to France, 'Getting Along in France'. This is a great idea to improve listening and aural skills. The complete CD Rom set costs €65 and the eight phone call sessions cost €360.

    www.frenchclasses.com

Bilingual magazines and books

If you've tried reading a French newspaper or magazines as a way of learning, but find that your enjoyment is hampered by constantly having to pick up and fumble through a dictionary, then a solution is at hand with the following magazines.

Champs-Elysées

If you find keeping up with French radio for more than 30 seconds close to impossible, then *Champs-Elysées* could be a way to improve your listening skills. The monthly audio-magazine on CD or cassette is sent accompanied by a 70-page word-for-word transcript of the audio with a detailed glossary. Presented by Georges Lang, a well-known radio personality in France, each hour long programme covers news, interviews and features on topics ranging from current affairs, politics, travel, film and sport. This lively magazine is aimed at students of an intermediate to advanced level. Difficult words are highlighted on the transcript in bold and defined in an extensive French/English glossary. The glossary also contains explanations of tricky grammatical constructions and background information on people, places and issues discussed. A five month subscription (five CDs) is £69.

Champs-Elysées (UK) Ltd

✉ Spike Island, 133 Cumberland Road, Bristol, BS1 6UG
☎ (UK Freephone): 0800 833 257 or +44 (0) 117 929 2318
Fax +44 (0)117 929 2426
@ ukorders@champs-elysees.com
🖥 www.champs-elysees.com

They also have an office in the USA. See website for details.

Concorde French Language Publications

Le Rendez-Vous Française

This magazine, published in the UK but sent worldwide, is for relative (although not absolute) beginners. The six-issue, 36-page magazine is a way of both learning about France and learning the language. The publisher says it's 'designed for rapid vocabulary building and for sustaining interest and motivation'. The articles in easy French are about tourism, current affairs, French life and culture. There are tips on grammar plus exercises based on the articles. There are word games such as crosswords, vocabulary tests, etc. Dialogues are printed in two columns, one in French and one in English with useful phrases for you to use in everyday situations. An optional audio version of the magazine (on cassette) can accompany it as a way of improving your spoken and listening skills.

La Vie Outre-Manche

Concorde's other magazine *La Vie Outre-Manche*, is for intermediate/advanced learners of French, with the emphasis on improving your conversational French. The magazine has similar content to the beginner's magazine, but at an advanced level. The magazine is sent free with the audio cassettes and CDs.

You can visit their website for page samples from each of these magazines.

Concorde French Language Publications

✉ 8 Skye Close, Maidstone, ME15 9SK
☎ +44 (0)1622 749 167
Fax +44 (0)1622 744 508
@ enquiries@concordefrench.com
▭ www.concordefrench.com

Learning French in France

The French Ministry of Foreign Affairs provides a long list of French universities and colleges that provide full, part-time and summer school courses. Many of these institutions also provide homestay accommodation, where you stay in a private room in a French family's home and join them for meals.

Cactus

Cactus offers courses for all levels at centres in eleven cities in France. The courses involve 20-30 lessons of 45 minute lessons per week in classes with a maximum of twelve students plus either four or eight private lessons. Alternatively you can be taught privately, on a course individually tailored to your needs. Courses last between one and four weeks, although you can stay longer if need be. Accommodation can be with a host family or in your own studio apartment. Breakfast and an evening meal is included if you stay with the host family, as well as the opportunity to carry on bantering in French in the evenings (although after all those lessons you may well just want to crash out).

▭ www.cactuslanguage.com

Eurolingua

The Eurolingua Institute offers a whole range of short and long courses throughout the year, for all levels, at their premises in Montpelier. They can also provide homestay accommodation. Eurolingua also provide other opportunities for learning, including the chance to stay with a teaching host or taking on a work placement.

Eurolingua also represent teaching hosts based all over France and in former French colonies. This is a very intensive way of learning the lanuguage, as you get to live in the home of the person who is teaching you. Your host gives you one-to-one lessons for either 10, 15, or 20 hours a week and also takes you on excursions. You can stay with a host for as long as you like. One week seems too short but four weeks with the same host/teacher could (depending on the chemistry between you and the amount of time you get to yourself!) get quite oppressive.

Work placements

If, like myself, you spent all your teenage holidays working in the catering trade, you will recoil in horror at the thought of the three or six month work placements in the hotel and catering trade being offered by Eurolingua as a way to learn the language. Outside of the 42 hour week working as waiter/waitress, kitchen hand or cleaner (and, if you're lucky, a receptionist) in a family or chain two or four star hotel, you somehow have to find the energy to take fifteen hours of group classes and five private classes. Clearly the co-ordinators at Eurolingua have never experienced hour upon relentless hour of dodging axe-wielding chefs, pacifying obnoxious guests, burning hands on hot plates, then flopping into bed well past two in the morning still stinking of food and sweat but too exhausted to take a shower.

Having said this, it would certainly be a fast track way of learning and could also provide a valuable insight (eye-opener!) into the behind-the-scenes of the French catering and hotel industry if you are thinking of running such a business yourself. For those that cannot afford to take classes as a leisure pursuit, it provides an opportunity to study. Workers get paid €200 a week and also get staff accommodation and meals provided. On top of this you have to pay for the classes outside of your working hours – the fee for three months is €750 and for six months €950. Clearly this means that there won't be enough pocket money to go flitting about the Riviera in your free time but that's okay, as there won't be any time. . . on your two days off each week, you'll be studying.

The work placement programmes are for 18-35 year olds only. Skills and previous experience are not essential but a minimum level of spoken French is required. Remember most of what you'll be learning, you'll be learning on your feet – your poor aching blistered feet!

Eurolingua Institute SA

⊠   5 rue Henri Guinier, 34000 Montpellier, France
☎   +33 (0)4 67 58 20 17
⊠   Eurolingua House, 61 Bollin Drive, Altrincham, WA14 5QW
☎   +44 161 972 0225
@   info@eurolingua.com
🖳   www.eurolingua.com

EduFrance

Moving to France need not just involve a change of habitat. You could also combine it, as many do, with a complete career overhaul. A satisfying way to change a career is to go back to college and there are thousands of superb universities and specialised educational centres in France that offer both the chance to learn a new skill or subject while developing your language skills in the process. These universities offer academic, technical and professional degree programs in all disciplines, preparing students for careers in research and professional practice in every imaginable field. If you don't feel capable of studying in French full time then don't worry – as there are many courses listed by agency EduFrance that are taught either all or partly in English.

EduFrance is a public body created in 1998 by the French ministries of education and foreign affairs, to promote French higher education to international students. Over 10% of students in French universities are foreign. Many of these international students found out about the courses through the advice of EduFrance, which provides free information to international students on living and studying in France.

University enrolment is open to any student holding a French *baccalauréate* or its foreign equivalent – that is, a qualification that entitles the holder to begin university study in his or her home country.

There are dedicated language courses as well as all sorts of other courses such as business studies, marketing, tourism studies, physics, cinematography, textile design and computer science.

Of course you don't just have to go to university to study for a new vocation. There are plenty of courses where you can simply indulge in the pleasure of learning.

EduFrance summer universities

EduFrance are also involved in organising summer programs that combine language learning with discovery of French life and culture, along with a subject of personal interest to the student, such as engineering, art, history or hotel management. There are two one-month intensive summer sessions each year, one in January-February (corresponding to summer in the southern hemisphere), and one in June-September.

Agence Edufrance

✉ 173, boulevard Saint-Germain, 75006 Paris, France
☎ +33 (0)1 53 63 35 00
💻 www.edufrance.fr

L'Etudiant

L'Etudiant is the website of the best known student magazine in France, which has been in publication for the last 25 years. *L'Etudiant's* monthly updates provide a huge range of information on studies, courses, student life and careers. There are also many models of covering letters and CVs.

💻   www.letudiant.fr

Children's education

Young children tend to adapt very quickly to a foreign education and pick up the language within months. Adolescents (those aged 11+) have a more difficult time and take much longer to adapt.

Family exchanges

If your move to France is in the more distant future, then a good idea would be to send your older child on a long-term exchange to France, to help them adapt and give them a taste of French life. En Famille International is an organisation that arranges six month exchanges for 9-13 year olds. Two children of different nationalities spend a year together: six months are spent with the exchange partner in their own country and six months with their exchange partner in his or her own country. They attend the exchange partner's school and live with the exchange partner's family, being treated as one of the family.

En Famille International

@ infos@enfamille.com

🖳 www.enfamille.com

Education in France

Education in France is very different to that in the UK. There is less emphasis on the child as a creative individual and less of a drive to make education feel like 'fun' as there is in the UK. Many British parents complain about French education being too formulaic and rigid. Music education starts with years of learning to read music and understand musical theory before even picking up an instrument. Some parents feel that not enough priority is given to arts subjects, many of which are regarded as extra-curricular activities.

If your child has a learning disability check that the school has facilities and teachers with the skills to handle the child appropriately. Parents of dyslexic children have complained that schools are unsympathetic or don't understand their children's needs. If you cannot find a school that can cater for your child's distinct needs then you should probably reconsider your move.

State schools or private?

One of your first choices will be whether to send your child to a state-run (*école publique*) or private (*école privée*) establishment.

State schools

The Ministry of Education runs the state schools and sets the guidelines for the curriculum. Teachers at state schools are civil servants and undergo rigorous training. They are highly respected but badly paid. Unlike in the UK, the teachers do not apply for positions at schools of their choice but are sent to a school by the Ministry of Education. Compared to many other countries, the head teacher (*le directeur* or *la directrice*) has little control over how the school is developed, in terms of the type of staff recruited. State-run schools are free, although parents have to pay for text books and stationary. The advantage of a state school is that they are generally close to where you live so provide a good opportunity for your children to meet local French children from all sorts of backgrounds.

Sending the children to the local school is a way of throwing them in at the deep end, and it's certainly the fast track way to getting them to learn French and to meeting local kids. It also helps the parents integrate into their local community – you'll meet other people your age when you pick your child up from school, at children's parties, open days, etc.

Private schools

Private schools are either:

- **Sous contrat**: whereby the government pays the teachers' salaries and the school follows the national curriculum and schedule. Such schools ask parents to contribute a modest annual fee (sometimes as little as €500).

- **Hors contrat**: which means they are not subsidised by the government and have annual fees that range between €5,000 to €12,000 per year (the more expensive tend to include boarding).

Private schools have smaller classes and give more individual attention. Private 'international' schools are those which offer a bilingual education and often offer the curriculum available in your country of origin. These tend to be based in major cities in France. In Paris, there are several American or British establishments and even some some state schools that offer a bilingual education. An international school is ideal if you are only moving abroad for a short period of time. International schools are very expensive although many do have scholarships and schemes for very bright children and those from less well-off backgrounds.

An advantage of choosing an international school is that you can have more involvement with your child's education. If your child's education is in a language that you cannot fully understand then there is always the concern that even though the child has picked up the new language, their grammar is not correct or their vocabulary is lazy (you might not even know when your child is swearing). Some parents dislike the sense of detachment and disempowerment that comes from not even being able to help their child with their homework because it's in a foreign language.

A major disadvantage of sending your children to an international school is that it prevents them from integrating more fully into French culture, learning French and meeting local French children. Another problem with private schools – especially the expensive *hors contrat* schools – is that your child will end up ghettoised, mixing with children from only one socio-economic background. Local state schools tend to attract children from all sorts of backgrounds.

Registering your child with a state-run school

Registering your child with a state-run school involves contacting the *Service des Écoles* at the *mairie* (town council). You will need to take along certain official documents. These are:

1. An official translation of the child's **birth certificate** (*extrait de l'acte de naissance*), or the child's passport.

2. Both **parents' identity papers**. French families normally take along their *Livret de Famille*, which is a records book or folder containing an extract of their marriage certificate, extract of birth certificates (and, where relevant, extracts of children's or spouse's death certificate).

3. A **carnet de santé** (an official booklet containing health records of children born in France), or other official health records to show that the child has had all the necessary vaccinations for its age (tuberculosis, diphtheria, tetanus, pertussis and polio).

The *maire* will give you a certificate to say that the child has been registered and you must take this, along with your *Livret de Famille*, to the headmaster or mistress of the school. It is no longer necessary to prove where you are domiciled, although some town halls and schools will ask to see your *carte de séjour*. Non-French children should not be discriminated against when it comes to placing children in schools.

The stages of school

École maternelle (nursery school)

Most children start the *école maternelle* at age three, although the official starting age is two. As the obligatory age for children to start school is six, attendance at an *école maternelle* is optional. Most villages will have an *école maternelle*.

Each period of the child's education constitutes a cycle and each cycle has a different objective. The *école maternelle* constitutes a child's first three year cycle – Cycle 1 – the *cycle des apprentissages premiers*. The objective of Cycle 1 is for the child to learn how to deal with social situations and to become more autonomous.

The *école maternelle* is divided into three years – *petite*, *moyen* and *grand*, (small, medium and big). The last year is part of Cycle 2 and activities are geared toward preparing the child for elementary, or primary school. So, even though it is not obligatory, you may feel your child would get a better head start if they at least attend the final year of the *école maternelle*.

School hours are generally from 8.30am to 11.30am and 1.30pm to 4.30pm, except Wednesday, which is a half-day. Some schools have no school on a Wednesday, but a half-day on Saturday. Children may return home for lunch or remain at school to have lunch in the canteen.

Note: **It is very important for parents to plan their childrens' entry into each school well in advance as the better schools tend to fill up quickly. Certain elementary schools feed into certain *collèges*, and certain *collèges* feed into certain *lycées* (high schools).**

École primaire (primary school)

Children start their *école primaire* at the age of 6 or 7. The first years of *école primaire* are *Cours Préparatoire* (CP), followed by *Cours Elémentaire, première année* (CE1). These two years, together with the previous year in *maternelle,* completes Cycle 2. Cycle 2 is the *Cycle des apprentissages fondamentaux* which, according to the Ministry of Education, is:

"to ensure the acquisition of the basic tools of knowledge: oral and written expression, reading and arithmetic. It stimulates the development of the intelligence, artistic sensibility, manual and physical skills and sporting abilities. It provides a grounding in the plastic and musical arts, and, in conjunction with the family, undertakes the child's moral and civil education."

The child then moves into Cycle 3 taking *Cours Elémentaire, deuxième année* (CE2), followed by *Cours moyen première année* (CM1) and then *Cours moyen deuxième anné (*CM2). The next three years constitute the *Cycle des approfondissements*.

The required 26 hours per week of classes follow approximately the same schedule as for the *maternelle*.

Collège (secondary school)

The first two years of secondary school, 6ème and 5ème, are called the *Cycles d'observation* and the next two years, 4ème and 3ème, are called the *Cycles d'orientation*. In 6ème, the students begin learning a foreign language (usually English), and start a second foreign language in 4ème. During the 4ème, teachers meet periodically in a class council to consider each student's aptitudes or interests in order to guide the students in the type of education best suited to them. If the parents follow the advice of the guidance council, then the student, at the end of 5ème and at the end of 3ème, enters the recommended section of education. A teacher may recommend that a student repeats a year if they feel that the student lacks the maturity or the scholastic ability to pass into the following grade. This is called a *redoublement* and is not at all uncommon in primary, secondary or high school in France, where there is a great deal of pressure for high performance and the work load is sometimes very demanding.

Lycée (high school/sixth form)

Students then move on to the *lycée* where they study for the well-respected *baccalauréat* diploma. The *lycée* is divided into two cycles, the first of which is the *cycle de détermination* where the child attends the classes of *Seconde générale and technologique*. The *cycle de détermination* consists of seven main subjects from which the student decides which he or she would like to take at *baccalauréat* level. During the class of *Seconde* the student decides which *baccalauréat* to choose. There are seven types of *baccalauréat* divided into two groups:

1. **Baccalauréat général**: Literature, Economics and Social Sciences, Science, Science and Medical and Social Sciences.

2. **Baccalauréat technologique**: Science and Tertiary Technologies, Science and Industrial Technologies, Science and Laboratory Technologies.

Alternatively the student can choose to take a technical or vocational option.

At the end of the third trimester (summer term) the student indicates which sections of *Première* interest him or her and the members of the *Conseil de classe* examine the request and respond with either a *proposition d'orientation* or a less positive *proposition de redoublement*.

Each *bac* involves a number of obligatory subjects, as well as seventeen optional subjects from which to choose. The lessons must add up to a total of 29.5 to 32.5 hours per week.

The *Cycle terminal,* which consists of the classes of *Première* and *Terminale,* lead to the end-of-school diploma of *Baccalauréat général* or *Baccalauréat technologique*. This is the child's final year of obligatory education.

University

Following the *Baccalauréat général* or *Baccalauréat technologique* the student can apply for university. Universities are either private institutes or state-run establishments. The prestigious *grandes écoles* offer mainly three year vocational courses (for instance in business or engineering) and have their own entrance examinations on top of the *bac*.

Contacts: Education

Ministre de la jeunesse, de l'éducation nationale et de la recherche

The official website of the *Ministre de la jeunesse, de l'éducation nationale et de la recherche* has plenty of information on the education system in France (in French).

🖳 www.education.gouv.fr

The ministry also runs local centres called *Centres d'information et d'orientation* (CIO) which offer orientation advice free of charge.

For information on schools contact your local *mairie*. Your *mairie* will give you published information guides on education and will tell you about other educational and children's leisure activities in your area.

Centre d'information et de documentation l'enseignement (C.I.D.E.)

This centre provides information and documentation concerning all private schools in France, as well as advisory services.

✉ 6 rue Monsigny, 75002 Paris, France
☎ +33 (0)1 44 55 34 80
🖳 www.cide.fr

European Council of International Schools

This has a directory of international schools throughout France.

🖳 www.ecis.org

American School of Paris

✉ 41 Rue Pasteur, 92210, Saint Cloud, France
☎ +33 (0)1 41 12 82 82
Fax +33 (0)1 46 02 23 90
@ mcalon@asparis.org
🖳 www.asparis.org

Bordeaux International School

✉ 525 Rue Judaique, 33000, Bordeaux, France
☎ +33 (0)5 57 87 02 11
Fax +33 (0)5 56 79 00 47
@ bis@bordeaux-school.com
💻 www.bordeaux-school.com

British School of Paris

✉ 38 Quai de l'Ecluse, 78290, Croissy sur Seine, France
☎ +33 (0)1 34 80 45 94
Fax +33 (0)1 39 76 12 69
@ bspprincipal@wanadoo.fr
💻 www.ecis.org/bsp

Energy in France

Electricité de France (EDF)

France (the world's fourth highest energy consumer) is the largest producer of nuclear energy in Europe and 85% of its national supply, provided by the state-owned public utility Electricité de France (EDF), comes from 58 nuclear reactors dotted around the country. With this cheap and abundant supply of energy France dominates the export of electricity, especially that supplied to the UK and the Netherlands. Switzerland is France's biggest client and a net exporter to Italy, so a major destination for French electricity is Italy. Under French law, which encourages competition in the market, EDF negotiates as if it is a private company, and owns a number of electricity providers throughout the world, including the UK's London Electricity, SWEB, Seeboard and Virgin Home.

Strangely enough, despite having this abundant supply and raking in vast profits from its international trade in energy, electricity in France is not cheap. At the time of writing the difference between the average cost per kWh in France and UK is marginal and, whereas the cost of electricity in the UK in the last decade has remained steady, in France it has climbed steeply.

Nuclear energy

Environmental groups such as Greenpeace (see their English language pdf on www.electricitedeforce.com) try to raise awareness about the problems of nuclear energy. (You may remember that in 1985 France blew up Greenpeace ship Rainbow Warrior in Auckland harbour in an attempt to derail the organisation's campaign against nuclear testing on the Polynesian island Moruroa, killing one person on board.)

Today, Greenpeace attempts to highlight the important, but widely ignored, issue that there is no technology available for dealing safely with the radioactive waste from nuclear power plants and that this waste remains radioactive for thousands of years. While French electricity is exported to neighbouring countries, the nuclear waste remains in France as a French responsibility and public hazard. There is no contractual obligation to purchasers of French electricity to share this burden.

There is also a huge risk of illness to people living close to nuclear power plants. It's been proved that there is fourteen times the national leukaemia rates in children that live close to these sites. If you are concerned about living close to a nuclear power plant then you can check their locations by looking at their map in the corporate pages of the EDF website www.insc.anl.gov/pwrmaps/map/france.php). The majority of France's nuclear reactors are on main rivers or beside the coast. The Cotenin Peninsula in Normandy is an area to avoid as it is here that nuclear waster is dumped.

EDF is also involved in France's hydroelectric programme. Rivers have been dammed to produce electricity, resulting in the creation of huge recreational lakes but the destruction of the natural habitats of much wildlife. High voltage power lines are a blight on much of France's countryside and thousands of birds of prey are electrocuted each year.

Alternatives to electricity

For heating, hot water and cooking you do not have to use EDF. There are plenty of alternatives, albeit fossil fuel guzzling, such as gas, oil, wood and coal burning. The best alternative energy is of course wind and solar, and there are subsidies available to help you get equipped. Take advantage of these subsidies in the next couple of years as they won't be around forever.

Electricity

Circuits and wiring

Properties in France have either *triphase* or *monophase* circuits:

1. A powerful **triphase** supply is normally found in older agricultural buildings, where more power is needed to drive farm machinery and appliances. A large property with one or more *gîtes*, a heated pool and air conditioning will need a higher current, so a *triphase* may be needed here.

2. Modern domestic appliances are designed for use at 220 volts and therefore, in most average family homes, a **monophase** (single-supply) is sufficient.

Earthing

Plugs in France are round, some have two pins and others have three including an earth. Not every socket is earthed as in some countries. Older properties are seldomly, if at all, earthed. If the ground is rocky, earthing plates are recommended. They need to be set in a trench of a minimum depth of one metre. All new lighting circuits need to be earthed, as do all metallic points in the bathroom.

Radial circuits

Wiring in France is in the form of radial circuits, that is where each 'leg' is taken back to a *tableau d'electricité* individually. You can run up to eight lights or up to eight socket outlets off a radial circuit. Ring mains (as used in the UK) are not permitted. In a property where most of the wiring is adequate and only one or two rooms, e.g. a kitchen and bathroom, are being refitted, only those radials need rewiring. Don't forget to incorporate a different switch to the *tableau* for kitchen and bathroom appliances. Legrand and Hager are two of France's leading electrical material suppliers and sell *tableau d'electricité* in pre-arranged units according to the size of the installation.

EDF power levels

EDF offers a range of domestic supply/power tariffs from 3kw (lighting, fridge, tv, etc) to 36kw. An average three bedroom house without electric heating can comfortably manage on 9kw. An 18kw monophase supply is recommended for an all-electric house. If your supply is too low, an overload can occur when a water heater is running and a toaster, kettle and microwave are then switched on.

EDF calculates that in an average home 50% of the cost of electricity goes to heating, 17% to hot water and 5% to cooking. When you are considering what size water tank to get, bear in mind that on average one person uses 50 litres of water a day.

Installation

EDF is not responsible for the installation of your electricity, although they can give you details of a local registered electrician. If you have a new system put in it will need to be certified by Promotelec, a non-profit, independent organisation that promotes and certifies quality installations. Promotelec will arrange for an inspector to check the building, electrical installation, heating equipment and management, hot water output and insulation. Before electricity is connected in a new or renovated property you will need to obtain a *Promotelec Habitat Existant* label.

Promotelec

✉   Tour Chantecoq, 5, rue de Chantecoq, 92808 Puteaux, France
☎   +33 (0)1 41 97 42 22
💻   www.promotelec.com

Electric central heating

Vivrelec is the latest central heating system introduced by EDF. This is a new system of managing your heating which is installed in many new and renovated properties. It defines the temperature in each room depending on the usage throughout the day and night. Rooms of the house can be grouped into zones. *Zone Jour* can be for rooms used during the day (e.g. the sitting room, dining room and kitchen) and *Zone Nuit* for the bedrooms. A third zone can be added to regulate another area of the house, such as the bathrooms, if you know you are going to use it at certain times of the day.

The timer has six positions:

1. *Confort* – corresponds to the temperature you wish to have in each of the rooms when you are present. You regulate this temperature by the level of the button on the thermostat.

2. *Médio* – is 1°C less than *Confort*

3. *Moderato* – 2°C less than *Confort*

4. *Eco* – permits a reduction of 3-4°C of the temperature of *Confort* when you are absent.

5. *Hors-Gel* – maintains a temperature of 8°C when you are away for several days.

6. *Arrêt* – the stop function for turning it off completely at certain times.

Electricity tariffs

Opening an electric contract will cost €13.55. You will also have to choose the type of tariff. Several are available:

1. **Option Base**

   For use between 3 and 18kVa. This is a simple tariff for those who use little electricity.

2. **Option heures pleines/creuses**

   With this tariff the price per kWh is reduced for 8 hours out of every 24, generally during the night. This is why many people in France programme heating and washing machines to come on during the night. The reduced hours are called the *heures creuses* and the more expensive hours are *heures pleines*.

3. **Option Tempo**

   This is a popular tariff system that has been available since 1996. The price per kWh changes according to the weather on particular days and also according to hours of use. It is regulated by a national weather centre in Toulouse. In each year there are:

   • 300 blue days when the price is advantageous. Every Sunday is a blue day.

   • 43 white days which are equivalent to *heures creuses*. Possible on Saturdays.

   • 22 red days when the price is lifted to *heures pleines*. These will be particularly cold days between 1st November and 31st March. Red days can occur between Monday and Friday and never at weekends or public holidays. Their number of consecutive days can never exceed five days. The red days encourage people to reduce consumption during these days. For instance waiting to use dishwashers and dryers. You can join for a minimum of one year – starting on the 1st September until 31st August the following year. The most modern meters will tell you between 22h00 and 22h30 at night the colour of the following day. You will also be able to find out the colour of the current and previous day, as well as tables for previous months and years on the website 🖥️   www.tempo.tm.fr.

Electricity bills (*factures*)

Bills are sent either every three or six months. Generally, your meter will be read every six months and between each reading you will receive a bill which is an estimate of the electricity you have used. It is possible to pay for the exact amount of electricity you have used by applying for the *Service Relevé Confiance* which will involve reading the meter yourself. Every two months you will receive a card. You must fill in the figures and return it within nine days (if it's not returned within this time then an estimate will be given). It is also possible to do this online. You are unable to do this if you pay monthly or if your tariff is the Tempo option.

A tariff is part fixed and part variable. The variable part is proportionate to your needs and is determined by the nature of your equipment and whether it functions simultaneously. Included in your bill there will be a municipal tax of 8% and departmental tax of 4%. You will be refunded 2% of your bill if there is a power cut lasting more than six consecutive hours.

On your bill you will see a couple of extra costs, explained below. These were added to bills from early 2003 onwards, 'in the interests of transparency'. In other words the figures were included in your bill before (if you were receiving bills before this time) but not separately itemised, so it is not a new or added cost.

- *Le cout d'acheminement*
  This is the cost of transmitting electricity from the place of production to the consumer. It includes costs of construction and exploration, and the management of electricity lines necessary to transport the electricity. The tariff is fixed by the State.

- *Autres Prestations*
  At the back of your bill there is a line *Contribution Service Public d'electricité*. This is the proportion of your payment that contributes to electricity used by the public services.

Contacts: Electricity

- EDF (🖳 www.edf.fr)
- Promotelec (🖳 www.promotelec.com)
- Fédération de Electriciens et Electoniciens (🖳 www.fedelec.fr)
- Fédération Francaise des Installateurs Electriciens (🖳 www.ffie.fr)

Gaz de ville (mains gas)

Until recently mains gas was only supplied by the State-owned Gaz de France (GDF), part of the EDF group. The new EU directives for opening up Europe's electricity and gas markets were adopted in 2003, and, at least in theory, industrial consumers have been able to freely chose their supplier since the 1st July 2004. It is hoped that the GDF monopolisation will be dismantled by 1st July 2007 and the public will have access to other providers.

Unlike electricity mains there isn't an obligation to distribute natural gas to every home, although the number of communes that have access to gas has doubled in the last 5 years. Today gas is supplied to 16,000 of the largest French communes, making a total of 75%.of the French population with access to mains gas. If moving into a property with mains gas supply you must contact Gaz de France (GDF) to have it switched on or to have the meter read and get it changed to your name. The price of gas varies according to location. If your gas is supplied by GDF then it will be on the same bill as your EDF electricity bill.

Tariffs

- **Tariff Base**
  A simple tariff if you only use the gas for your cooking. Your annual consumption is less than 1,000 kWh.
- **Tariff B0**
  If you use it for cooking and heating water. Your annual consumption is between 1,000 and 6,000 kWh.
- **Tariff B1**
  You use gas for heating your home, cooking and hot water. Your annual consumption is between 6,000 and 30,000 kWh.

If you live in an apartment block owned by a *copropriété* and you use mains gas for cooking then it's likely that a standard charge will be included in your service charge.

Paying gas or electric bills

Make sure you pay your bills on time as the suppliers have a no nonsense cut-off policy. You can pay your bill in the following ways:

1. Send a **cheque** from your bank account. Make sure you give plenty of time to allow for delays in the post.

2. Pay by **direct debit** (*prélèvement*). You will need to complete a direct debit mandate (*autorisation de prélèvement*) provided by the utility company. Send the mandate to the utility company with a *relevé d'identité bancaire* (RIB), a document provided by your bank showing your full bank and account details. The yearly amount will be paid over ten equal monthly payments and the amount you pay will be determined by the equipment you use. If a meter reading proves that you are not paying enough, then after the first ten payments, the following one or two payments will be regulated. If you pay too much you will be reimbursed in fifteen days. If you want to choose the date that the money leaves your account then you must pay a fee of €1.36.

3. The third option involves signing and dating the tear-off portion of the bill you receive. You return this to the utility company with your *relevé d'identité bancaire* (RIB) and the utility company will debit your bank account automatically. Future bills should show your bank account details so there should not be a need to send an RIB each time.

    Some local tax offices and water companies may not accept payment other than by cheque.

4. Pay online. Go to the company website and follow their instructions.

Gaz au citerne (tank in the garden)

Where mains gas is not available, many rural properties use gas from a tank (*gaz au citerne*) which is installed on the property.

This gas can be used for cooking, hot water and heating. Tanks are hired or bought from gas suppliers such as Primagaz, Butagaz, Antargaz and Totalgaz in return for a contract to provide gas for a fixed period. The tank can come in various sizes depending on your needs – for instance Antargaz provide tanks of 500kg, 1,100kg, and 1,750kg.

The tank can be buried underground (*enterre*) or above ground (*aerienne*). The tank must be at least one metre away from your neighbour's property and if above ground it must be white. You can try to disguise it by placing large plants around it but you cannot paint it and you must leave 60cm free around it. Having a gas tank on your property will increase your insurance premiums. Burying the tank will cost a small extra sum, although this is not always charged. If you want to build around the tank then there must be a radius of 3 metres for an above-ground tank and 1.5 metres for a buried one.

You will need a qualified plumber to connect the gas to the house and to install central heating. All installation must be certified by the independent organisation responsible for quality control, Qualigaz (💻 www.qualigaz.com). They will consign you the appropriate certification – *le Certificat de Conformité d'Installation*. If you want to move the tank it will have to be emptied first and this will cost as much per ton as for delivery. It will need a maintenance check every three years.

Note: **Some owners will try to get you to pay the deposit although this should be included in the price of the house.**

With most suppliers it is possible to make one payment or to pay direct debit every three months.

Example – Gaz au citerne
As an example of costs:

- To hire a buried tank from Total will cost **€180** a year or a one-off payment of **€1,073**.

- If you choose to have the tank above ground the costs are **€90** a year to rent or **€623** as a one-off payment.

- To get a 1,400kg tank filled would cost **€895** (tax-inclusive). This fill should last a year for an average home, or two (and perhaps more) if the home is used only for holidays.

Bottled gas

Many rural homes use bottled gas for cooking and sometimes for water heating. As many people prefer cooking on gas stoves it is possible to have an electric cooker and bottled gas rings. For an average sized family a 13kg bottle used for cooking should last about six to eight weeks.

You can buy it at most petrol stations, hypermarkets, DIY and specialist shops. It's cheaper to trade in an empty bottle for a new one. To buy a new bottle you will need to pay a deposit costing around €20-25 and a fill will cost €10-15. The colours vary according to the brand. For example, Elfi by Antargaz use red for butane and gold for propane, whereas other companies use completely different colours. Propane gas is best for all year round use whereas butane has a higher condensation point and needs to be kept warm in the winter.

Gas bottles must not be stored in cellars or anywhere that is hermetically sealed. Propane must be stored outside the house. They can be used in *copropriété* owned buildings but you must have sufficient ventilation. They must be 1 metre away from your neighbour's property unless a wall separates you.

A rubber pipe will take the gas from the bottle to the stove. Officially the pipe mustn't be more than 2 metres long, but most suppliers advise on a maximum of 1.5 metres.

These are the sizes of bottles recommended for different needs:

- 3-12 kg – suitable for cooking
- 12kg + – cooking and hot water
- 35kg + – cooking, hot water and heating

Suppliers of bottled and tank gas

Antargaz

🖥 www.antargaz.fr

Useful site with images of tanks. They provide tanks of 500kg, 1,100kg or 1,750kg.

Butagaz

🖥 www.butagaz.fr

They also supply a number of related products such as outdoor heating parasols and barbeques. Their website has a useful FAQs page.

Primagaz

🖥 www.primagaz.fr

Totalgaz

🖥 www.totalgaz.fr

Their website includes a very useful dedicated English-language section.

Solar energy

Thanks to various grants over the last five years solar energy has become increasingly popular in France. From January 2005 a tax credit of 50% has been in place on the cost of solar equipment (not including the installation cost). There's a platform of €8,000 for a single occupier and €16,000 per couple (with an extra amount for each child). The systems installed must have the certification of Solar Keymark and CSTBat.

When looking at the possibility of installing solar energy systems you'll find that you have two choices:

- **Chauffe-eau solaire individuel (CESI)**
  Provides between 50 and 70% of a family's hot water (showers, baths, cooking). Generally you will need 3-5 metres of solar panels which are usually put on your roof and a hot water tank of between 200 and 400 litres (depending on the size of your family).

- **Système Solaire Combiné**
  For the production of hot water and heating. Grants for this only apply if the property is your principal residence.

The performance of the solar panel is proportional to the area's sunshine. France has four climatic zones. The zones in the north get 30-40% less sunshine than the zone adjacent to the Mediterranean. This means that homes in the northern zones will need a larger area of solar panels to collect the heat.

Agence de l'Environnement et de la Maîtrise de l'Energie

🖥 www.ademe.fr

Syndicat des Energies Renouvelables

🖥 www.enr.fr

Using your fireplace

If you buy an older property you will probably have a number of open fireplaces. If you want to use them you first have to make sure that there is plenty of ventilation. Make sure that you have an air vent, or you may need air bricks in the external walls. Your chimney will dictate what type of fuel can be used; discuss this with your builder (*maçon*) or plumber (*plombier*). The *maçon* will deal with all the brickwork and the construction of the flue and the plumber will deal with the metal (usually stainless steel) lining. If you have opted for a wood-burning stove (*poêle à bois*), you'll have to call in a chimney sweep (*ramoneur*) to check that it is clear and to provide a certificate or invoice which is vital for insurance purposes. If you don't have this documentation as proof then your insurance company could deny liability in the event of a claim due to a house fire.

If you use wood it will have to be seasoned and dry, otherwise emissions and residues such as tar and creosote are released which can build up in the flue adding to the risk of fire and structural problems. Some wood burners are unable to burn coal.

Heating with oil

Heating oil *(L'huile à chauffage)* is widely known as *mazout* in France. Just like the gas tanks, the oil is kept in a tank in the garden. It is cheaper than gas but can be messier.

🖥 www.chaleurfioul.com

Tip: **The importance of good insulation is widely recognised in France and is an essential consideration when you are building or renovating your home. Your home will be a much more comfortable place and your energy bills will be reduced if your home is well-insulated. An example of a very well-insulated home is one that has, for instance, double glazing, 8 inches of glass fibre in the roof, 4 inches of fibre glass in the walls, and a 6cm layer of compacted polystyrene under the floor.**

Cost comparisons

If cost is the deciding factor in how you choose your energy then you can look at comparative statistics on the cost of domestic energy in France on the MINEFI (*Ministère de l'Économie, des Finances et de l'Industrie*) website:

🖥 www.industrie.gouv.fr.

Cars

Taking your car to France

You are allowed to drive on 'foreign' plates as a tourist for just three months. After three months, if you plan to stay, you will need French number plates for your vehicle. From the moment you obtain your residence permit (if you need one – see previous section on residency), you have a month in which to re-register your foreign car. It is possible to begin the procedure early while still under tourist status, but evidence of a fixed address is needed.

If you're from a European Union (EU) member state and your car is a standard model that conforms to French norms (i.e. those currently on sale in France), then re-registration should be uncomplicated. The process can prove time-consuming and expensive if you're bringing in a car from outside the EU, and in this case you might well find that buying a new car in France is a better option.

Registration

Registration is called *immatriculation* and involves first going to your nearest local *préfecture* or *sous-préfecture* (chief, or sub-regional administration centre) to collect a form called *demande de certificat d'immatriculation* to fill in. You must then follow this procedure:

Car registration step 1 – Visit to the tax office

There are no customs formalities if you're bringing a vehicle to France from another EU member state, but you must go to your local *Centre d'Impots* (tax office) for a *certificat de régularité fiscale*, which shows that you've already paid VAT on the car at home. If the VAT has not been paid, you'll be liable to pay VAT in France.

If your car was bought privately and second-hand, there is no VAT to pay on it in France whether you come from within or outside the EU, but make sure you have receipts from this sale.

If you are from a non-EU country, you'll need to obtain certificate 846A from *le service des douanes* – the customs services office – to show that you have complied with French customs requirements (ask them for specific information concerning the country from which the car was imported).

Car registration step 2 – *Contrôle technique*

All cars over four years old have to pass a mechanical and safety check-up called a *contrôle technique* before they can be re-registered. The vehicle then has to be submitted for the test every two years. The *contrôle technique* is a compulsory test for roadworthiness, similar to the UK MOT, and applies to passenger cars, motorcycles and transport vehicles with a gross weight not exceeding 3.5 tonnes.

Note: Collectable cars (*véhicules de collection*) – those older than 25 years – may be exempt from a *contrôle technique* if a specific application is made and it is declared on the *Carte Grise*. Further information is available (in French) from the *Fédération Française des Véhicules d'Epoque* (FFVE). (Contact details on page 261.)

The first *contrôle* of a new vehicle should be done within the six-month period following the car's fourth anniversary. The test generally takes no more than an hour and must be done at a *centre de contrôle agréé* (recognised technical centre). Prices may vary from centre to centre but it's generally around €45. If the vehicle passes the test, the centre will give you a document that marks, among other things, the date the next test is due.

If the vehicle fails the test, you will have a specified period in which the problems can be fixed before the vehicle becomes unroadworthy. The control centre will advise you. You will be fined if your vehicle is not roadworthy.

Frequent reasons for failure:

- Worn tyre tread
- Lights not all working
- Emissions too high
- Shock absorbers faulty/worn
- Faulty/worn brakes
- Wheel alignment faulty
- Some aspects of damaged bodywork, for example if a door cannot open
- Some aspects that could impair safety, including the condition of the mirrors, windscreen and wipers

Car registration step 3 – *Attestation de conformité (certificate of conformity)*

You will also need to request an *attestation de conformité* (certificate of conformity) from the vehicle manufacturer or a certified representative. This identifies that the vehicle is of a recognised type in France or in the European Union. This *attestation* can also be obtained from the *Direction Régionale de l'Industrie et de la Recherche* (DRIRE) although it's likely they'll ask to inspect the car. DRIRE handles all the technical aspects of re-registration. It's much easier to ask the manufacturer directly, simply by calling or writing to their *Service Homologation* office.

Car registration step 4

If all has gone smoothly with the above steps then you will now have all the necessary documentation for registration. Take the completed *demande de certificat d'immatriculation* back to the motor registration (*carte grise*) office at your *préfecture* or *sous-préfecture* along with:

1. Proof of your identity (passport or *carte de séjour*).

2. Proof of your residence (EDF or telephone bill).

3. A copy of your foreign registration certificate.

4. A copy of the *attestation de conformité* (issued by the manufacturer or their agent).

5. A copy of the certificate of purchase and customs clearance certificate (issued by the *Centre d'Impots*).

6. *Côntrole technique* certificate if required.

 Tip: Remember to photocopy all the paperwork just in case anything goes astray.

Your documents may be sent to the *Service des Mines* or DRIRE to verify that your vehicle's make, year and chassis number corresponds to French homologation standards, *La fiche d'homologation*. This process can take two or three weeks.

If all goes well, you will be notified when you should return to the *préfecture* or *sous-préfecture*, to collect your registration document, the *carte grise* and your new registration number.

A tax is payable at the *préfecture*, which is calculated according to the engine power of the vehicle, and this sum varies slightly in each *département*. Once you've got your *carte grise*, you can go to your local garage and get your licence plates (*plaques d'immatriculation*) made up (this will cost around €20). Re-registering a car will cost around €220. The process can take anything up to two months to complete.

Re-registering collector's vehicles

Collector's vehicles over 25 years old are in a special category and can be re-registered without being taken to the DRIRE. In this case, you need to first put the vehicle through a *contrôle technique* then go to the *Fédération Française des Véhicules d'Epoque* (French federation of classic cars) where you can obtain a document that enables you to register the vehicle at the *préfecture* as a *véhicule de collection*, or collector's car.

Unless you are specially authorised to do otherwise, you're only allowed to drive a *véhicule de collection* in the *département* in which it is registered and in neighbouring *départements*.

Fédération Française des Véhicules d'Epoque

✉ BP 50603, 91, rue de Paris, 35006 RENNES Cedex, France
☎ +33 02 23 20 14 14
Fax: +33 02 23 20 14 15
@ secretariat@ffve.org
🖥 www.ffve.org

Buying a car in France

In France, second-hand cars must undergo a *contrôle technique* within the six months preceding any sale. A *certificat de situation* is also required, which shows that no unpaid parking or other fines apply and that there is no outstanding debt on the vehicle. Some garages selling second-hand cars also arrange the *carte grise*.

If you're buying a new car, the dealer usually obtains the *carte grise* for you.

The benefit of buying a new car is that the left-hand vehicle will be safer for you to drive. It will also be easier to sell on at a later stage.

Driving licences

If you're an EU member, you no longer need to exchange your licence for a French one within a year of obtaining your *carte de séjour* (residence permit). You can continue to drive on it until it expires. You can also record an EU licence at the local *préfecture* for no charge and will receive an *attestation* that will make the issuing of a replacement licence in the case of loss or theft much easier.

Anyone committing an offence in France that leads to a loss of points or withdrawal of their licence will have to exchange their licence for a French one. Exchanging your licence costs around €22. Although, there have been calls recently by French politicians to assign points on a UK licence in the event of an offence committed in France.

If you're a non-EU member, you are allowed to drive on your foreign licence for a year from receiving your *carte de séjour*, after which you must get a French licence.

If French licences are recognised in your country of origin, you can simply exchange your licence for a French one without taking a French driving test. But if your country of origin doesn't allow a simple licence exchange for French citizens, you'll have to take a French driving test.

If you're a US citizen, the situation varies depending on which state you come from. If your state of origin allows the exchange of a French licence for a US one, you can simply exchange it. If it doesn't, you'll need to take a French driving test.

Queries about driving licences should be addressed to your local *préfecture* or *sous préfecture* (ask for the *service des permis de conduire*).

Vehicle insurance

Vehicle insurance for unlimited third-party liability – *assurance responsabiltié civile* – is compulsory in France. Premiums are expensive because of the large number of accidents and car theft. The French Finance Minister has recently called on insurance companies to reduce their premiums to reflect the decrease in the accident rate in France, but for some reason, the insurance industry is dragging its heels on this.

As well as the *assurance responsabiltié civile* (which covers damage and medical costs sustained by the third party), you can choose policies that include fire and theft (*vol et incendie*) windscreen damages (*bris de glaces*) and accidental damage (*dommages à votre vehicule*).

Assurance touts risques is a comprehensive insurance covering all possibilities. As with all insurance policies, read the small print carefully to be absolutely sure of what you are being covered for.

Contacts: Car insurance

DRIRE

The website has full listings of the documents required for re-registration.

⌨ www.drire.gouv.fr

Ministère de l'Equipement, des Transports et du Logement

✉ Arche de la Défence, 92055 La Defense, CEDEX, France
☎ +33 (0)1 40 81 21 22
⌨ www.equipement.gouv.fr

Taking pets abroad

Dogs and cats

Dogs and cats are allowed to travel between the UK and France, without quarantine, if they are certified by The Pet Travel Scheme (PETS).

The Pet Travel Scheme (PETS)

This scheme was introduced in the UK and other European countries on 28th February 2000, and has since been extended to countries further afield including the USA and Canada. A maximum of three cats and/or dogs per person can be taken into France (this means that two people can bring in six animals, four people can take twelve etc.) Of the three animals, only one may be a puppy. The minimum age of the animal is three months.

To avoid quarantine, make sure you travel to England on an authorised route with an approved transport company.

> *Note*: **The pet can leave the UK from anywhere and by any means of transport, but it can only come back into the UK by an approved route and carrier.**

The following ports will allow entry:

- *Seaports:* Dover (Eastern Docks), Harwich (Parkeston Quay), Hull, Portsmouth and Southampton.
- *Airports:* Birmingham, Edinburgh, Gatwick, Glasgow, Heathrow, Leeds, Manchester and Prestwick.
- *Rail:* Coquelles (Eurotunnel).

It's important that you check the availability, cost and procedures of travelling with your pet to England with your preferred transport company before making a booking.

Qualifying for PETS

To qualify for PETS, the animal must, in this order, be:

1. fitted with a microchip;
2. vaccinated against rabies; and then
3. blood-tested to show the vaccine has worked.

The certificate must be issued by a Local Veterinary Inspector (LVI). It's likely that your own vet is an LVI but if not your local Department for Environment, Food and Rural Affairs (DEFRA) office will give you a list of LVIs in your area.

PETS documentation

For importing and exporting your pet cats and dogs between the UK and France the following four PETS documents are needed:

PETS 1

This is a certificate in which your vet identifies the animal and confirms that it is protected against rabies. It also gives the period of validity. This is the time from which the animal may re-enter the UK (six months after its blood test) to the time when this permission expires (which is the time it needs its first booster vaccination against rabies).

The procedure for getting the above certification is as follows:

The animal must be inserted with a microchip and vaccinated. The microchip used must be International Standards Office (ISO) standard 11784 or 11785, so that it can be scanned at the port when the animal leaves and comes back into the country. Before vaccination, the microchip is scanned to ensure that it is functioning and to ensure correct identification. A blood sample is taken about 30 days after the vaccination, for testing, to see if the vaccine has taken effect. The test is sent away and carried out in a laboratory approved by DEFRA. If the animal has a high enough level of the antibody in its blood then it is issued with the PETS certification and can leave the country immediately.

PETS 2

This is a certificate in which a vet confirms that the animal has been treated against ticks and tapeworms that it may have picked up while abroad. This certificate is issued by a vet in the foreign country before you come home not less than 24 hours and not more than 48 hours before re-entering the UK. All drugs must be licensed in the UK (e.g. Frontline) and the anti-tapeworm drug must contain praziquantel (e.g. Drontal). The owner must have a PETS 2 certificate signed by a vet to prove that this has been done.

Make sure you organise the appointment with the vet well in advance so that there is no disappointment.

If you are just on a day trip abroad, it is completed by a vet in the UK.

PETS 3

This is a certificate in which the owner confirms that while the animal has been abroad it has not travelled to a country outside the Pet Travel Scheme.

(There is no PETS 4 certificate)

PETS 5

Some countries in the scheme also request an export health certificate for the animal's entry. France simply requests a document called 'Export of a Pet Dog or Cat to France in accordance with the Pet Travel Scheme' (PETS 5), which is basically an exact copy of the PETS 1 certificate, but in French. This can be automatically issued when a PETS 1 is issued. If you already have a current PETS 1 certificate (perhaps previously obtained when visiting another country in the Scheme), you can get a PETS 5 certificate from any LVI on production of your PETS 1 certificate. The PETS 5 is valid from the day the LVI signs it.

Returning to the UK

Unless you are on a day trip, the dog or cat can only re-enter the UK at least six months after the date of its blood test. After the vaccination the animal will retain a high level of the rabies antibody in its blood for up to six months. However, there is always the risk that it was infected with rabies while out of the UK. If the animal has a high antibody level because of infection, it would develop clinical signs of rabies during these six months. If it has not done so, it is safe to assume that the high antibody level must have been due to the vaccine. The six month period starts on the day the sample was taken, not when the result comes back from the lab. If the owner wants the pet to come back before the six months is up, it would have to go into quarantine.

The PETS certificate is valid until the next rabies vaccine is due. This will be one to three years from the date of the previous vaccine injection, depending on the make of vaccine and the information on the manufacturer's data sheet. If the animal is to become a resident in France a vaccine for only one year is necessary as it is compulsory to have a vaccination annually in France. The animal in the UK will then receive its booster and be issued with a new certificate, valid for the next one, two or three years. However, if the pet goes over the period for re-vaccination, even by one day, it will have to be blood tested again and will have another six-month wait before being allowed back into the UK.

Getting an animal PETS certified is not cheap and will cost, in total, around £200.

Note: Once you have forked out all this money it's very likely that there won't be anyone on either end to check your expensive piece of paper. But, annoyingly, it's better to be safe than sorry!

Renewing a PETS certificate or preparing a pet for PETS in France

If you propose to renew a PETS certificate in France your pet must have received annual vaccinations against rabies. There is a requirement in France for pets to have an annual rabies vaccination, and the vet would be entitled under French law to refuse to issue a PETS renewal certificate following a gap of more than one year between vaccinations. In such a situation, your pet would have to be vaccinated, have a blood sample taken and, assuming a satisfactory result, wait six months before being able to enter the UK. To avoid this, and if your pet is unable to meet the annual vaccination requirement, you are advised to have it re-vaccinated in the UK if at all possible.

Dogs and cats becoming residents

If your dog or cat stays in France for more than three months it will become a resident of the country and must be identified and registered on a national database.

Pets in France are identified by either a tattoo or a microchip. Until recently they were both tattooed and microchipped in order to comply with the PETS scheme, but French authorities have now changed their legislation so animals no longer have to be tattooed if they are already microchipped. Non-ISO Standard microchips will not be recognised by the French authorities. If your dog or cat is certified under the PETS scheme it is probable that it already has an ISO Standard microchip. If it doesn't then the microchip will be changed by the French vet and your pet's eligibility for the UK Pet Travel Scheme may be affected. If an animal's microchip is replaced, it will then need a further vaccination against rabies, followed by another blood test and a six-month wait from the date of the blood test.

French legislation requires resident pets to be given an annual vaccination against rabies. A two-year vaccination against rabies given in the UK will not apply and the animal will have to be vaccinated, albeit unnecessarily, again.

Note: Once in France, if the animal is to STAY in an area infected by rabies (18 *départements* are concerned: Aisne, Ardennes, Aube, Doubs, Jura, Marne, Haute-Marne, Meurthe-et-Moselle, Meuse, Moselle, Nord, Oise, Bas-Rhin, Haut-Rhin, Haute-Saône, Vosges, Territoire de Belfort, Val d'Oise), an anti-rabies vaccination will be compulsory. If driving through such an area, the animal can be taken outside only if leashed and muzzled or carried in a basket.

Taking your horse or pony to France

On 14th February 2002 the Government announced that, with effect from the end of 2003, all horses and ponies (and other forms of equidae) will need to have a passport identifying the animal.

Passports

You can get a passport by applying to one of the organisations that have been authorised by DEFRA to issue horse passports. Some of these organisations deal with only one particular breed of horse, others will issue passports for all types. The list of these societies can be found on the DEFRA website.

Passports last for the lifetime of the animal. EU legislation requires completion of a silhouette (either a list or drawing of the colouring, markings, etc) to identify the horse. Other forms of identification, such as a microchip, can be used in addition to the silhouette but there is no legal requirement to do this. The silhouette should normally be signed either by a veterinary surgeon, or someone authorised by the society issuing the passport. Society rules may differ as to who is required to complete the silhouette.

As a rough guide, the average cost of the passport will be between £20 and £30. The cost is the responsibility of the private sector organisations that have been authorised to issue them. The horse will be given a Unique Equine Life Number (UELN) which appears on the passport and which identifies the horse. This number will be supplied by the organisation that issues the passport.

Export Health Certificate

As well as a passport, to move horses between the Member States of the EU you will need an Export Health Certificate. An inspection is carried out by a veterinarian within 48 hours of loading and signed by a veterinarian on behalf of DEFRA. As well as checking that the animal meets all the necessary health conditions (and has the appropriate vaccinations which are listed in the passport) required for export, the vet will also have to satisfy him or herself that the vehicle or container carrying the horse will be cleaned and disinfected immediately before the loading and that it is designed in such a way to prevent leakage of droppings, litter and fodder. Once you have filled in the application form, it can take up to ten working days to process.

Other pets (including rabbits and guinea pigs)

If you wish to travel to France with your pet and it does not meet the requirements of the Pet Travel Scheme, you will need to obtain an official Export Health Certificate.

Grain-eating birds

For birds of the Psittacidae family (e.g parrots, parakeets, budgerigars, cockatoos, etc) entry is limited to two birds. The importer must declare that he or she has owned the birds for over six months and undertakes not to sell them in France, and agrees to let them be examined by a veterinary inspector, if so requested. There is a special export license for birds going to France, valid for ten years, which can be obtained by DEFRA.

Rodents

Entry without any sanitary formality is limited to two rodents per person. A general derogation exists for the importation of rabbits, hamsters, guinea-pigs, etc.

Animal welfare and the long journey

A lot of people worry more about how their animal is going to cope with the long journey to France than how they are going to cope with the move themselves. As long as you make sure that the animal is fed and watered appropriately and that it has enough space to stretch its limbs, then everything should go smoothly.

If you are travelling with a cat, take it in a dog cage which will allow it more room than the usual cat carriers. If the cage has wire sides and top (as opposed to enclosed cat carriers), then cover it with a coat or dark fabric to create a dark, cave-like area into which it can retreat. The cat will be less threatened by the movement and activity outside if it has a space to retreat into. You may be able to fit a litter tray into this cage, otherwise lay newspaper down on the surface and then the cat's bedding or blanket on top.

Make sure your pet has access to food and water throughout the journey.

It is also a good idea to put dogs in cages so that they are not a distraction to the driver, and also so that it is not a potential loose cannon in the case of a crash. Make sure you stop at least every two hours to allow the dog (and yourself!) to stretch its legs and to toilet.

Animals travelling by air must be transported in containers, crates or cages which satisfy the conditions laid down by the International Air Transport Association (IATA). If travelling by sea the conditions of the carrier must be complied with. Contact the ferry company before your journey.

Contacts: Pets

Department for Environment, Food and Rural Affairs (DEFRA)

☎ Pets Helpline: 0870 241 1710
@ pets.helpline@defra.gsi.gov.uk
🖥 www.defra.gov.uk

Your local DEFRA office may be more helpful. Find out the number by looking at the general website or calling the central number (08459 33 55 77).

Scottish Executive Environment and Rural Affairs Department

✉ Pentland House, 47 Robb's Loan, Edinburgh, EH14 1TY
☎ +44 (0)131 244 6179

National Assembly For Wales

✉ Crown Buildings, Cathays Park, Cardiff, CF1 3NQ
☎ +44 (0)2920 825 111

British Horse Society

They have lots of information about the horse passport and contact details of people to approach for the passport.

🖥 www.bhs.org.uk

IFFE – French Horse Federation

🖥 www.ffe.com

The official website of the French Horse Federation has a calendar of competitions. The Federation also keeps a database of every registered competition pony in France.

Holiday home swapping

If you're concerned that you'll get bored holidaying in the same place every year then it's worth looking into swapping schemes organised by companies such as Dial An Exchange or HomeLink.

As well as timeshare swapping, Dial An Exchange has a holiday property owner's club. They have a very large number of attractive properties – cottages, ski chalets, coastal villas – all over France. Through this club, owners can get to experience other parts of the country and also other parts of the world. You can swap a week or two (or as many weeks as you like) in your French property for a week or more in the US, Mexico, the Caribbean, South Africa, Australia, New Zealand, Thailand and Fiji. The cost is very reasonable: membership is free and you only need to pay £74 per exchange week in Europe and £89 worldwide.

Dial An Exchange Ltd

✉ 21 High Street, Gargrave, Skipton, North Yorkshire, BD23 3RA
☎ +44 (0)1756 749 966
Fax +44 (0)1756 749 928
@ info@dialanexchange.com
🖥 www.dialanexchange.com

Alternatively, you could just join an international home swapping scheme. One of the largest organisations is HomeLink, which has 13,500 listed members all over the world. The membership fee is £115 and for this you get featured in their 800 page directory and receive a copy for your own use. They also publish three full colour brochures a year.

Some of the homes look fantastic – for instance, in London there's a five-storey Notting Hill house with use of the family's 7-seater Mercedes!

HomeLink International

Contact: Caroline Connolly
✉ 7 St. Nicholas Rise, Headbourne Worthy, Winchester, SO23 7SY
☎ +44 (0)1962 886 882
@ mail@homelink.org.uk
🖥 www.homelink.org

Interview with a property buyer

Anne bought a property in Pays de la Loire with the intention of living and working there.

Q. *Tell me about yourself.*

A. We live in London. I'm a PA for London Underground and my husband is an electrical engineer. He has his own business but also works for a company.

Q. *Why did you think about moving?*

A. The intention was to have the house in France as a holiday home first of all. But since Labour has been in Government we feel as though England is letting us down. We have a son who is 17 and would have moved earlier but we need to know that he is on the right track before we leave him to fend for himself. But basically the decision was made because England is a horrible place to live.

The very first time I visited France was with the school on a day trip, I remember sitting outside a cáfe sipping Orangina from a bottle and thinking Mmm this is the life! For some reason it all felt right. When I first got together with my husband the first thing he asked me was "Where do you want to be in 10 years time?" My answer was France, and that was 10 years ago next May. Luckily enough it was exactly what he wanted to hear. Basically, we spent a few weekends over in France and one summer holiday.

Q. *How did you choose your area?*

A. We didn't choose our area, it chose us. It's in the Mayenne, in a little village called Larchamp, very close to Ernee. It's a very small village with one boulangerie and one small mini market, a church and a tabac. It also has a fishing lake and a boules pitch. We are on the outskirts, in the middle of nowhere. Just how we like it.

Q. *How long did it take to move in?*

A. We got the keys for the house in May 2000. We could only spend a weekend there that year because we were getting married in Kenya so needed all our holiday days off for that. We went to the estate agent who took us to the *notaire*, signed the papers and then went and got into our Ford Transit, opened the door and moved the furniture in. It was a baking hot day so we decided to visit Ernee for something to eat. We had dinner and then took a stroll along the high street and noticed a bar called 'Jaggers'. We thought it must be English so we took a look inside and low and behold, we knew the owners!

Q. *How long did it take to find a property?*

A. We set out to find a property over the course of about four days. We had lots to look at (or so we thought). We were sent over by an English agent. We arrived for the first appointment three hours late (as the journey took twice as long as the agent had advised). When we walked into the estate agents we found out that the guy that was going to show us around had already gone out with somebody else. We were most upset so the lady there agreed to show us something else that had literally just landed on her desk. We were just happy to be looking at something, but she only had the one. We'd agreed not to buy the first house we saw so we looked at it and thanked her. We spent that night in a hotel near Mont St Michel so that we could set off for our next appointment the following day. We got there on time and the guy took us to two different houses. One had an amazing setting, down in the valley but needed too much work and one was a village house, which we just didn't want. The following day we saw another two. One was too large (and very pink) and one was just too small. All in all we saw about six, but it was the first one that kept coming to mind.

On our last day we had an appointment in St Lo. We were told to be there by 8am. It was January and snowing. We got up about 6am to be there on time. We arrived and nobody was there. We went for a coffee and they finally turned up at 9am. We weren't very happy about this as our ferry was leaving from Calais and we had a six hour drive ahead of us.

They had nothing to show us in their 'English' books. I asked to see the 'French' books but was refused. They were the rudest people we had ever met and couldn't be bothered to take us out. To cut a very long story short, I nearly had a fight with the lady and my husband nearly had a fight with the man, and I must stress that we are not violent or short tempered people.

So the property we had decided on was the first one we saw. That was in January, we paid the deposit as soon as we returned home. We had the keys in May, so all in all it took four months.

Q. *What type of house had you been looking for?*

A. We were both looking for rural (as we live in London) and wanted it to be a house with outbuildings to convert. We didn't mind some renovation but nothing too big. It would have been nice to be near the sea but it wasn't that important.

Q. *How did you finance the house purchase?*

A. My husband had previously sold his house and with the profit bought the house in France. Our property cost £31,000 with fees and taxes taking it up to £38,000.

Q. *How is your French?*

A. We cannot speak the language. Our estate agent dealt with everything for us.

Q. *Did the house need renovating?*

A. We didn't need to renovate the house, just a few details here and there but we are renovating the barn. We've mortgaged our house in London to fund some of this. We then intend to either use friends or local men to complete the rennovation.

Q. *How have you found the locals?*

A. The locals have been fantastic. Our neighbours are in their 60s and are farmers but have just retired this month. They also have a son and a daughter who speak reasonable English. The house we bought belonged to the farmer's uncle. When we first got the keys we all went into the neighbour's for a coffee and Calvados. Our first weekend there we were invited to dinner. We ate their chickens which apparently is a good sign.

They cannot speak any English and we spent a very happy evening trying to translate things using dictionaries and drawings and miming. They have taken to us very well and are always there to help us. One morning we were due to leave for the ferry at 5.30am. Our van wouldn't start. The farmer heard our poor van coughing and spluttering. He was there 5 minutes later with a super charger to get us on our way. Another time, when we were screeding the kitchen floor, I was knocking up cement for Gary, they saw us and within 5 minutes there was a tractor with a cement mixer on it! They even took us to their uncles who we bought the house off. They opened the champagne to welcome us. They are all very lovely people.

Q. *Do you intend to work in France?*

A. When we move to France we both intend to work. My husband is a qualified electrician so hopes to continue with that. I would like my own business where I can work from home. I am at present looking at franchises for sale, hopefully to do with the travel industry. We will also be renting the *gîtes* and the apartment.

10

Working in France

Running a *gîte* or a B&B

Quitting the office job and running away to rural France to run a *gîte* complex or *chambre d'hôte* (B&B) seems to be everyone's idea of a great escape! Plenty of people have made this dream a reality, but it certainly takes some planning, and some money. It is important to be realistic about how much you'll be making, especially if you have children to support and a mortgage to pay. Many owners have some other means of making a living, or at least something to fall back on during quiet times. Running a *gîte* is ideal for people that have taken early retirement and who are free from heavy mortgage or family commitments. But the market can be fickle – Tuscany's the place to be one year, Sicily the next, Croatia the year after that. You'll certainly not be getting away from the joys and pitfalls of consumerism, as countries fall in and out of fashion in the same way clothes do.

The season

Don't expect your property or rooms to be let out all year round. On average *gîtes* are let out for 12-16 weeks of the year, mainly during July and August. There does seem to be more demand in recent years for accommodation during other seasons, but the market is so saturated in the most popular areas that it will never get to the point when a full year of bookings anywhere can be absolutely guaranteed. If you do want to attract the winter market then make sure you have good heating and maximum comfort and cosiness.

Chambre d'hôte (B&B)

Running a B&B, called a *chambre d'hôte*, can be hard work. You need to be friendly and warm at all times. You can't have an off-day, you can't even have a bad hair day or walk around in your threadbare cardigan and your most slobbish tracksuit bottoms! If you're a sociable person then it's a great way to make a small living. You'll meet people from all over the world and sometimes friendships will form and people will return year after year. It's important to be sociable (or at least be able to fake it!), as friendliness is certainly one of the keys to a good B&B.

Sometimes having strangers in your home will feel intrusive. There are guests who believe they have full rein of the house. It's not unusual for owners to come in and find them stretched out on the sofa or joining you and your family while you're all crashed out like zombies, watching your favourite soap. It can be difficult if you have a young family who insist on making a mess everywhere. To avoid this, it's a good idea to introduce guests to other rooms that they can use when you first welcome them into the house and keep doors to private family areas closed at all times. Many B&Bs have a lounge area that guests are free to use.

Most guests prefer an ensuite bathroom, or at least their own bathroom even if they have to walk down the hall. They will expect to pay a lot less if they have to share a bathroom with the family. It can be unpleasant for guest and family alike to share a bathroom. For both parties there'll be no leaving toothpaste caps off, undies on the floor and no wallowing in a bubble bath for hours on end. You'll have to clean the bath until it sparkles, and de-clog the hairs from the shower, the minute after you use them.

Tips

- Supposing you have to get up at the crack of dawn in the middle of a winter and drive 5km to the nearest *boulangerie* for fresh bread for just one guest. It can be frustrating if you're not sure when your guests will emerge in the morning, so consider serving breakfast within a narrow time frame.

- Having to be around, waiting for guests to arrive can also be frustrating. Try to find out exactly when they plan to arrive and ask them to call you if they are going to be late.

- Once they have arrived it is a good idea to give your guests keys to the property so they can let themselves in as and when they like. You don't want to wait up until your guests come in from a night on the town, or get out of bed at four in the morning to let them in. Many people dislike the idea of giving out their keys to strangers, but unless you're capable of sleeping with one eye open all night, there has to be an element of trust involved.

Gîtes

Buying a *gîte*

Location

Coastal properties are the most in demand and if you're inland it's good to have access to water in the hot summer months, such as a pool or a swimming lake. It's often suggested that a swimming pool can add an extra £100 to the weekly rental of a holiday home – but it will also add to your property tax liability and needs regular safety inspection visits.

The Dutch, Germans and those from Northern France tend to prefer the south coast, so the *gîtes* in these *régions* are the most expensive to rent and are always in demand. Languedoc-Roussillon, further around to the West, is becoming increasingly popular, and property is a lot cheaper here than in the Côte d'Azur. In recent years there has been a growing demand for places off the beaten track, such as Limousin and the Auvergne, especially with the British. Perhaps they are starting to choose completely 'get away from it all' places because Britain is so densely populated and real seclusion is hard to find. Couples without children or with groups of friends often prefer to be close to towns for eating and drinking out opportunities, but the majority of people are quite happy to cook for themselves and stay in during the evenings after a busy day.

Being a long way from a ferry or airport is not too much of a problem as many parties prefer to drive to their destinations. It is only a problem for those that want to stay for just one week and often couples with very small children who do not want long car journeys. These holidaymakers are more likely to want to stay within an hour's drive of an air or ferry port.

Finding the right property

If you can afford it, go for an established *gîte* with a good rental track record, and future bookings in place. If you can't afford it, or perhaps welcome the challenge of starting from scratch, there are many rural properties with derelict outbuildings that can be converted into suitable holiday accommodation. It may take a while before you see returns on your investment. You will probably be eligible for a grant and for tax benefits if you have a run down property you wish to convert into a residence for tourism. (See next section.)

Renovating a *gîte*

Grants and *Gîtes de France*

Gîtes de France started in the fifties with the simple idea of preserving the natural habitat which was suffering from rural exodus, by providing farmers with money to convert dilapidated farm buildings into holiday properties. The government backed the idea and since then it has been a huge success. More than 2,000 new *gîtes* are created each year thanks to the *Gîtes de France* subsidies. As well as *gîte* accommodation, grants are provided to those wishing to convert their homes into *chambres d'hôtes* or create a campsite on their land. Today *Gîtes de France* represent 42,000 owners.

Gîtes de France's average investment in a self-catering property is is €58,000. This investment includes the major works and fitting of the interior; the average investment in bed and breakfast accommodation is €10,000. They do not provide the full amount that you'll need to spend on a property, and the percentage given to you depends on many criteria such as your own means, the need for tourist accommodation in your area, the state of the property, etc. Most people require an extra source of finance such as a bank loan or even a second grant from another body, such as the EU or your local DDE.

You must apply for a *Gîtes de France* grant directly through the representative office in your *département* (*Relais Départemental des Gîtes de France*). If they decide to grant aid then your architectural plans will be checked over or written up by an architect from your local *Council d'Architecture, d'Urbanisme et d'Environnement* (CAUE). If you accept *Gîtes de France*'s assistance, then you must agree to advertise your property through them and use their reservation service for between three and ten years (the length of time depends on the *département*), and you must also adhere to their quality charter. There are stipulations in terms of facilities provided, the level of comfort and sizes of rooms. For instance, toilets cannot open onto the public sitting area and *chambres d'hôte* bedrooms must be at least 12 sqm with a sink and a bathroom or shower room on the same floor.

Gîtes de France stipulates that owners must live in close proximity to the *gîte* so that guests can be assured a good welcome. You will need to have a very good command of French in order to welcome visitors, the majority of whom will be from France. Owners with very limited French have reported difficulty in getting a grant; some have been told that French holidaymakers will not like being welcomed by foreigners in their own country who are unable to even speak the language. Hopefully though this sort of pandering to some guests' intolerance will not stop you getting aid. 80% of customers hiring *gîtes* are French, with the majority of the rest being British. The typical guests are a couple with two children.

For more information:

La Maison des Gîtes de France et du Tourisme Vert

⊠   59 rue Saint-Lazare, 75 439 PARIS Cedex 09, France
☎   +33 (0)1 49 70 75 75
Fax +33 (0)1 42 81 28 53
@   info@gites-de-france.fr
🖳   www.gîtes-de-france.fr

Tips on furnishing your *gîte*

The *gîte* market is ever-competitive so your *gîte* needs to be as attractive (inside as well as out), comfortable and well-equipped as you can possibly afford to make it.

•   Many people like a mix of modern comforts and rustic charm. Explore local antique fairs for decorative pieces of traditional furniture and old paintings. Don't have too many clashing patterns on carpets, curtains, sofas and walls. It's much better to have neutral colours that will appeal to all and will make rooms look less cluttered and more spacious.

- Choose easy-clean fabrics and robust furniture.

- It's popular (and cheap) to furnish properties with Ikea products, although it can get very samey. Some guests will find that you've decked your rustic *gîte* with the same furniture, lights and tableware as their flat in West London. Ikea has a great design sensibility and their latest ranges always look very modern, but furnishings are so 'now' that in a couple of years they'll look very dated. Think neutral classics instead.

- Lighting is very important. As well as overhead lights, make sure you provide low lighting such as side lamps to enhance a warm, cosy atmosphere.

Bedrooms

- Out of all the things you can economise on – do not economise on beds! If you use an old bed, get rid of the old metal springs and get a new base (*sommier*) and mattress (*matelas*). Look under *literie* in the *Pages Jaunes* for a local supplier. Even though mattresses can be expensive in France, a comfortable bed is extremely important and sleepless nights will ruin a guest's holiday. Make sure it's not too soft, not too hard and certainly not lumpy.

- Check that the beds are good sizes and that (unless you have a seven foot giant staying) feet don't stick out the ends. King size beds will particularly appeal to the American market.

- Get plenty of washable under-sheets, pillows, duvets and spare blankets. Many *gîte* owners ask guests to bring their own sheets, duvet covers, etc. Give them the opportunity to rent sheets from you if need be. It's a lot less work for you if they bring their own sheets.

- Every person will need a bedside table or cupboard and a reading light.

- Make sure there's adequate hanging space, drawers and shelves.

- If you have a linoleum floor in the bedroom to make for easy cleaning then do put a couple of rugs about the bed. There's nothing worse, and less homely, than putting your feet on cold sticky linoleum first thing in the morning.

- Well-lit mirrors will be needed in each room for applying make-up and hair-dressing. Make sure there's a socket nearby for the hairdryer. Also, provide a hairdryer. It's tiresome having to humbly ask the owner if you can borrow one before every night out.

- Check that there is at least one full-length mirror somewhere in the house – possibly in a well-lit hallway and close to all the rooms.

- It's more than likely that your home will have shutters. If not, make sure that the curtains shut out all the light.

Bathrooms

- Cramped showers are off-putting.

- A mat will be needed to step on after getting out of the bath and shower, so that guests don't slip on tiles and so that excess water is soaked up.

- Check that there is plenty of shelf space for the shampoos, lotions and potions of everyone staying. Provide enough toothbrush holders and a couple of glasses.

- Guests will need enough rails to hang towels and hooks to hang up dressing-gowns and clothes whilst showering or bathing.

- Provide soap. It is also a nice touch to provide guests with shampoo, conditioner and shower gel.

- If there is enough space provide a bath. Many people enjoy languishing in the bath after a long day walking or sight-seeing. It will also appeal to guests staying in the winter.

- Leave a can of air-freshener near the toilet. Also leave a toilet brush and cleaning liquid. It's a good idea to leave some rolls of toilet paper in the *gîte*, as it's an easy thing for people to forget.

- A *chambres d'hôte* will have to provide towelling. Make sure it's good quality. Another good investment is to provide luxurious towelling gowns to match the towels. Leave a notice asking guests to leave towels on the floor if they wish for them to be washed.

Lounge

- Make sure there are enough seats and sofas in the sitting room for the number of people staying in the *gîte*. If you don't mind them having friends visiting then provide some extra seats.

- A TV and satellite connection is a good idea – just in case their holiday is blighted by rain. Board games, puzzles, also some books (something to please everyone: a mix of classics and contemporary, literary fiction, blockbusters and a couple of romance and detective novels). Books on local history, architecture, wildlife, flora and fauna are certainly a good idea, as well as any regional magazines. Consider leaving a box of toys for children, but do make sure that the toys are safe for children of all ages (e.g. none that they can choke, suffocate or cut themselves on).

- If you encourage young families you need to provide stair-gates, cots and high chairs, you'll also have to make sure there aren't too many knick-knacks and ornaments around for children to break.

- If you do not mind smokers (and many of your French guests *will* be smokers) then make sure you leave plenty of ashtrays. So as to limit fire risk, it's a good idea to discourage smoking. In the summer months most people won't mind going outside to smoke. Leave an ashtray outside somewhere, as you don't want to be picking cigarette butts out of the gravel drive or from your vegetable patch.

- Even though you might be a big fan of decorative candles – don't encourage guests to play with fire by leaving these candles about the *gîte*!
- Bowls of fresh pot pourri or air freshener are always a good idea.

Dining area

- The table must be large enough and there should be enough chairs for all the guests to sit down together. Have some spare (perhaps foldable) dining chairs for any visiting guests.
- Provide table mats and possibly some protective undercloth on your dining table. The undercloth used in France is called *bulgomme* and it is sold by the metre.

Kitchen

- A dishwasher and washing machine will certainly make the *gîte* more desirable, especially to large groups.
- Accommodate international caffeine habits. The Brits will need a kettle and the Italians will need a good quality cafetiere.
- Check that there's enough cutlery and crockery. Make sure you have plenty of mugs and decent wine glasses. A cheese-cutting board is a good idea and don't forget the bottle-opener.
- Check that your kitchen is fully equipped: potato peelers, spatulas, graters, wooden spoons, weighing scales, serving spoons, salad servers, sharp knives, bread knives, etc.
- Get solid sanitaryware, taps and units. Cookers with twiddly knobs are hard to clean and the knobs start coming off after much use.
- Provide the full spectrum of pan sizes. If you have large groups staying make sure that the pans – particularly saucepans – are large enough.

Outside facilities

- An outside table and chairs will be needed, and if there's no shaded area get some sort of canapé, such as a sun umbrella.
- For cooler outdoor evenings it is also possible to buy outdoor gas fire heaters.
- Provide barbeque facilities.
- Some outdoor games are a good idea such as a sponge ball and a couple of rackets. Or, how about a set of boules for getting foreign visitors into the French spirit.

- Provide seating around the pool such as reclining chairs or sun beds as well as low tables on which to put drinks and books. Sun beds will also need umbrella shades.

Safety of guests

It is very important that you are insured against personal injury claims just in case there is an accident (or in case you are unfairly accused of an accident) on your property. Sadly we live in a compensation society where simple accidents just don't happen and there must always be someone to blame. It could be that someone gets knocked over in a local pub brawl and gets a scar on his forehead, but decides to blame it on tripping over on a paving slab in your garden a few days before. The legal fees will be phenomenal.

To avoid potential accidents, your property will have to be in a good state of repair.

- Check thoroughly that there are no loose paving slabs and that carpets on the stairs are tightly fitted, that the chairs and tables aren't wonky, and that there are no sharp corners for children to run into.
- Make sure that electrical and gas installation is sound and that all equipment is perfectly safe to use.
- Make sure the thermometer is set so that water is not scolding or that there are instructions to change its setting.
- Clear instructions should be left for guests on how to operate electricity or gas, and how to use cookers and other equipment.
- In some circumstances guests may need to know how to deal with the *fosse septique* (septic tank) or will need to know how to change the gas bottle for the cooker, so leave all the instructions they may need.
- Tell guests where the torch is kept in the event of a power cut and leave a safety kit containing antiseptic cream, plasters, bandages, scissors, cotton wool, gauze, etc. at the back of a kitchen cupboard.
- All swimming pools must, by law, now be closed in by a fence. Clearly sign where the deep and shallow ends are and mark the depth of the water. It could also be worth putting a sign up not to dive-bomb! Inspect and clean the pool regularly.

Maintenance

Don't expect people to respect the property in the way that you respect your own home and others' property. Many will leave the property in the state that they found it, but others will leave it like a pig-sty. Consider asking for a deposit of, say, €100 to cover any damages.

Changeover days tend to be on a Saturday – so expect your weekends to be consumed with saying farewell, then rushing around cleaning, followed by waiting around for the next guests to arrive. In the summer months you will have no weekends free and it's doubtful you'll be able to have your holidays at the same time as everyone else.

Find out what time your guests are arriving – if it's very late then you may be able to leave the key beneath a flower pot for them.

If you're not on hand, you'll need someone you can trust to carry out essential maintenance, changeover inspections, cleaning and laundry.

Gîte complexes

Holidaymakers staying in *gîtes* tend to look for peaceful accommodation. If you're planning on more than one *gîte*, then space them out and plan your layout to maximise privacy for the guests. If guests are sharing a pool make sure that they are aware of this in advance by putting it in the description of the property when you are advertising. Don't put restrictions on other guests – such as timetables for pool use. Most families would rather share a pool than have allocated times. Of course, problems could occur when screaming dive-bombing kids disturb a childless couple who simply want to read quietly around the pool, but most people are sympathetic to each others' needs and will work things out between themselves. If you have a number of families staying in your *gîtes* then the pool area is a great place for kids to make friends with each other. Certainly do not restrict guests from using the pool when your own family are using it. Sharing your pool with guests is part and parcel of running a *gîte* complex or B&B.

Welcoming guests

A welcome folder (that also contains a 'what not to do' list!)

Provide a welcome folder that provides some of the following information:

- A list of local things to do and attractions to visit. Collect maps and leaflets from the local tourist office,

- A list of restaurants, cafes and bars with phone numbers, addresses and opening hours. Perhaps you could give a little description and your personal rating of each.

- A list of addresses of bike rental shops and some cycling maps. (You might want to consider getting some bikes for guests to borrow or rent – although be careful as you could be liable for any accidents that could occur while they are using these bikes.)

- Numbers of taxi companies.
- Address and contact number of nearest garage and location of the nearest *station-service* (petrol station).
- Contact numbers and addresses of local doctors, hospitals and pharmacies.
- If your home is nearby perhaps leave a note saying that they can buy items from you such as sewing kits, toothbrushes, tampax, paracetamol, washing powder, shampoo and conditioner, if need be.
- Notes on how to operate equipment, such as the dishwasher, washing machine and oven and how to regulate the heating.
- You may want to include details on how to deal with the loo and the septic tank.
- Tips on lighting the wood-burning stove.
- How to change bottled gas.

Things to do if you're really good!

Before guests arrive fill a jug of meadow flowers and leave it on the dining room table. Leave them a bottle of regional wine. Leave a welcome pack with bread and local cheese, wine, teabags, coffee and hot chocolate, a jug of milk and a carton of juice.

Consider inviting long-stay guests to join your own family for a barbeque although ask very casually – you don't want them to feel pressured. Leave guests to enjoy their holiday in their own way. You'll generally sense as soon as they arrive if they are the types that like to be left alone. Some guests are shy though and will be pleased if you make the extra effort. If people warm to you, they will leave feeling as if they found friends in France and will return year after year after year!

In all circumstances make sure you're on hand at least some of the time, and especially at the beginning of their stay to offer advice. Suggest ideas to them about places to visit or things to do, but don't put them under pressure to do what you've suggested (for example, don't ask them whether they did something you suggested, they'll tell you if they did).

Advertising

Many *gîte* owners spend about 15% of their *gîte* income on advertising.

Newspapers, magazines and booking companies

It's very expensive to advertise in the travel classifieds of national newspapers or magazines such as *France* and *Living France*. Advertising with companies that publish brochures and also deal with bookings can also be expensive. Some insist on coming to inspect your *gîte* and may try to impose their ideas of quality on you. (If you're with one of these big companies you may even have to book your own time there!) If owning a *gîte* is not your full-time profession then advertising with such companies that provide a booking service is a good idea. You then don't have to hang around the phone all the time waiting for enquiry calls to come in.

The internet

The cheapest, and nowadays the best, way to advertise is on the internet. Some websites such as ⌨ www.holidaygites.co.uk will let you advertise on their site for free for the first three months before subscribing to it. After that, all you pay is the advertising fee which is just £40.00 per annum, including as many changes to your advertisement as you require. There's no commission or any other fees to be paid on top of this and clients will contact you directly.

It is also a very good idea to set up your own website. You don't need to be a computer wiz to set up a simple and informative site. Computer packages such as Frontpage are not expensive, and free web space is usually on offer from your ISP. It is worth seeking advice on how to get optimum search engine exposure. For instance, when someone types the search words '*gîte*' '*Provence*' and 'sleeps 5' into Google for example – it's good if your website comes up as one of the first listed. If your site comes up on page 23 of a search then it's almost pointless.

Keep an updated availability timetable on your website – for instance in a colour -coded calendar. It can be maddening calling around numerous *gîtes* to find they are all booked up. Check that all your contact details are correct. Put attractive photographs of both the interior and exterior of your property on the site. Don't use exterior shots you have taken in the middle of winter – there should not be a cloud in the sky, or a shadow in sight, and trees and flowers should be in full bloom. Interior shots should emphasise spaciousness and light. Put your creative writing skills to the test and make your *gîte* and the area sound as idyllic as you can. But do be honest in your descriptions, then you won't lose sleep the night before your guests arrive worrying that they'll be disappointed.

You may also wish to include some notes on the conditions of letting both on your website and on the booking forms you send your guests. Here is a sample form:

1. [Description of the property.]

2. The rental is inclusive of provision of hot water, electricity, duvets & pillows, shared use of the swimming pool & use of the games facilities. It does not include provision of toilet paper, soap, washing-up liquid, jiffy cloths, etc.

3. Optional duvet covers & pillow cases may be hired for a charge of €5 per bed/week, payable on account after your arrival, otherwise you should provide your own.

4. Likewise, towels – other than bath/bathing towels – may be hired for a charge of €1.20 per person/week, otherwise you should provide your own.

5. At your request a starter pack of essential items can be provided – bread, milk, butter, coffee, sugar, toilet paper, washing-up liquid and any other items you need.

6. Any need for waterproof mattress covers must be identified on the booking form. There is no charge for mattress covers. You may, of course, provide your own.

7. Bookings are from Friday 16h30 to a subsequent Friday noon.

8. Telephone reservations are held for seven days. Receipt of the booking form with the deposit secures the booking, confirmed by email or letter.

9. An account will be requested for the balance of the rental approximately eight weeks before the commencement of your holiday together with directions for getting here.

10. In the event of a cancellation, money will only be refunded if the property has been re-let.

11. In the interest of strict fire safety regulations no smoking is permitted in the property.

12. Damage or breakage in respect of furniture, equipment, china or glassware must be reported to the proprietor and by mutual agreement either replaced or paid for in Euros.

13. The amenities of the apartments & the facilities on the site are reserved for the exclusive use of resident guests. Exceptionally, and with the prior agreement of the proprietor, visitors may be invited and a charge of €5 a person per day will be made.

14. At the end of your stay you are requested to leave the cooker, fridge, microwave oven, basins and toilet in the same clean condition in which they were found.

15. On making a booking you will receive a holiday contract embodying the above letting conditions.

Contacts: *Gîte* rental agencies

- **Chez Nous** (💻 www.cheznous.com)
- **HolidayGites** (💻 www.holidaygites.co.uk)
- **French Country Cottages** (💻 www.cottages-in-France.co.uk)
- **Brittany Ferries** (💻 www.brittany-ferries.co.uk)
- **French Connections** (💻 www.frenchconnections.co.uk)

Advice on *gîtes* management from an experienced estate agent

Patricia and her husband Tony run Agence Hamilton, an estate agent which specialises in selling property in the Languedoc Rousillon *région*. For many years they ran *gîte* management courses and have experience of running their own *gîte* complex.

Q. *Is it possible to make a living from running one or two gîtes?*

A. For a couple whose only income will be from the *gîtes*, we recommend at least four *gîtes*.

Q. *Are some areas saturated with gîtes? What are the new areas to look out for?*

A. Yes, some areas are saturated. Languedoc is the up-and-coming area. There is still a lack of good rental properties, to the extent that some of the travel companies are offering quite sizeable cash payments to anyone who can introduce an owner who subsequently signs a letting agreement with them. A good guide to non-saturated areas is to look in any of the brochures offering self-catering accommodation. Those areas with a very small section still have scope, although obviously this must be balanced against the attractions of the area.

Q. *Is it better to buy an existng gîte business?*

A. If you want an immediate income, an existing business is a must. Apart from allowing the time to convert, a new business always takes a couple of years at least to become known. With an existing business – if it has been run properly – you have the benefit of repeat clients and reputation. After that it's up to the new owners to make sure they don't lose that advantage.

Q. *In the areas you cover as an estate agent how much would you say a house with a renovated gîte would cost? A house with an outbuilding that can be converted? A gîte complex?*

A. In our area, a house with one *gîte* in good condition is unlikely to cost less than €300,000. As outbuildings tend to come fairly large in this area, your second question is more difficult, but realistically, the absolute minimum would be €225,000. For a full up-and-running *gîte* complex you are looking at €600,000 upwards.

Q. *If you are converting a property into a gîte – how much could you expect to spend?*

A. The amount you would spend is not really quantifiable, since much depends on the condition of the property, how much work needs to be done to convert, and the sort of clientele you are aiming at, i.e. whether this is going to be basic but comfortable, or whether you intend to fully equip with washing machine, dishwasher, etc.

Q. *What are the ingredients to a successful gîte business?*

A. Main ingredient: the input of the owners and the comfort and cleanliness of the *gîtes* (by which I don't necessarily mean all mod cons). These are the things which bring clients back time after time.

Q. *What is the best way to advertise and how much should you spend on it?*

A. Whilst this was not an avenue which we pursued, I think the best and cheapest way to advertise nowadays is on the internet. Using one of the brochures such as *Chez Nous* or *Bonnes Vacances*, whilst effective, is expensive.

Q. *Can you tell me some of the highs and lows of running a gîte or gîte complex?*

A. The highs are the lovely people you meet, many of whom become friends over the years; the unexpected presents of flowers or wine from the most unlikely people and watching people who have arrived really uptight, unwind in a couple of days or sometimes even a couple of hours, usually becoming so laid back they're nearly horizontal. The lows: in a really busy season not having any time to yourselves or any time off for about six months, or just the occasional client who treats you as the hired help and expects you to run around picking things up after them.

Q. *Have you got anecdotes (such as gîte horror stories!) you'd like to share? For example, who were your 'guests from hell'?*

A. Horror stories: funnily enough even in 11 years very few. But you do have to accept that people occasionally do strange things, or do not have the same standards as you do.

Q. *What sort of rules should you give?*

A. We always kept our rules to a minimum and tried to restrict them to those concerning safety and hygiene, such as nothing breakable in the pool area and not using blankets and pillows for sunbathing. We believed that if you imposed too many rules, a) clients would not bother to read them, and b) they would either ignore or forget them.

Agence Hamilton
🖳 www.agence-hamilton.com

Employment in France

Being employed

Finding work

ANPE

The State-run *Agence Nationale Pour L'Emploi* (ANPE) has a virtual monopoly on recruitment in France and a huge network of offices throughout the country. The only other employment agencies permitted by the State are *Agences de Travail temporaire,* also called *Agences d'interim*, which fill temporary positions – jobs with contracts up to eighteen months. France has the second largest temporary job market in the world, after the USA.

ANPE's basic role is to help job-seekers find jobs and help companies fill vacancies. It also provides advice on career development and assists unemployed people in registering for social benefits. A specialised service is available for those with higher qualifications seeking managerial posts and ANPE publishes a weekly guide to executive vacancies called *A Tout Cadres*. Any EU national is entitled to use the state employment service in any other EU country, but if your French is not of a high standard then you may find that some ANPE offices will give priority to French job-seekers.

Agence Nationale Pour L'Emploi (ANPE)

🖳   www.anpe.fr

Newspapers

It's also worth looking at the employment classifieds in local and national papers. *Le Monde* and *Le Figaro* for instance, both have job sections.

Foreign companies

Another good place to start your search for a job in France is to directly contact the human resources department at one of the 8,000 foreign companies established in France. Of these, about 1,800 are British. Their activities range widely across all sectors, from retailing to financial services, food and beverages to construction and manufacture. BP, ICI, AstraZeneca, GlaxoSmithKline, Barclays and Abbey National are all very well-known British companies based in France. Britain is the third largest foreign investor in France, which in turn is the third largest foreign investor in Britain.

A useful website is  www.bottin.fr which provides an online directory of companies that you can search by business type and *région*.

EURES

It's also worth looking at the EURES online job-bank. The EURES European Employment Service is an EU network of public employment services in member states and Norway. EURES provides detailed information on job vacancies and on living and working conditions in Europe. The EURES network does not provide access to all vacancies in all EU countries.

EURES

 www.eures-jobs.com

SOS Villages

SOS Villages is a great site to look at if you're dreaming of a quiet life. This is the place where mayors of tiny communes facing depopulation invite people to come and run their post office, garage, *tabac*, bar or café. Sometimes there's an advert by a community that desperately needs a doctor. As a way of bringing new young blood into the community, many of the mayors ask for a young couple with children. It's likely that most mayors will give priority to a French applicants, but if you're happy to live somewhere that's remote and are very keen to integrate in what's probably a very small community, then it's certainly worth a try.

SOS VILLAGES

✉ Le Clos Joli,,19500 Meyssac
☎ +33 (0)5 55 84 08 70
@ info@sos-villages.asso.fr
🖥 www.sos-villages.asso.fr

CVs

A curriculum vitae in France is called an *État Civil* and runs along the same lines as CVs anywhere else in the world (i.e. two pages minimum, concise information, etc.) Make sure your language is clear and that there are no abbreviations that a French employer wouldn't understand. There are lots of sample CVs on the following websites:

🖥 www.cadremploi.fr – also includes information on finding a job, interviews and guides to the professions.

🖥 www.cadresonline.com – this site's services include a CV deposit, personality tests, job vacancies, email and text alerts. You can find out how much you're worth in terms of salary.

Employment contracts

The three commonly used employment contracts in France are:

1. **Temporary employment** contract (*Contrat temporaire ou d'intérim*)
    In this case the employee is hired and paid by a temping agency. Normally such jobs are to cover an increase in work at a company, such as seasonal work. Temporary employment contracts may be renewed once, on the condition that the total employment period doesn't exceed eighteen months.

2. **Fixed Term** contract (*contrat à durée déterminée* – CDD)
    A fixed term contract must state in writing the duration of the contract. The CDD is fixed for a defined period of time up to a maximum of two years. A probationary period is usually involved. For a contract of less than six months the probationary period may not exceed two weeks and for a contract of over six months the probationary period may not exceed one month.

3. **Permanent** contract (*contrat à durée indéterminée* – CDI)
    The permanent contract is the most common in France. It is signed by the employer and future employee, and a copy is kept by each. The contract will stipulate the job title, date of employment, social security details, the company details and the place of work, the remuneration, notice period and length of the probationary period (one to three months).

Working hours

The legal working time for a company with more than 20 employees is 35 hours per week or 1,600 hours per year. The maximum working time is 10 hours per day and 48 hours per week, with a maximum of 44 hours per week on average over a period of 12 weeks (see working time adjustment). Beyond this limit any extra time worked is considered as overtime and involves an overtime premium. Companies with less than 20 employees must start paying overtime after the 39th hour.

The 35-hour week does not apply to executives and managers whose work does not directly relate to production. Their maximum working time is set to 13 hours per day and 217 days per year.

Companies that enforce the 35-hour week benefit from lower social security contributions, on a per-employee basis. This benefit also applies to companies that settle in France.

Holiday entitlement

Employees are entitled to five weeks paid vacation, plus eleven public holidays (*jours fériés*) each year. Holidays are taken at the request of the employee, subject to the consent of the employer. An employer may refuse to let an employee go on holiday if the firm is too busy at the time. Employees are nevertheless entitled to take at least four weeks off during the period between 1st May and 31st October. The employee will be required to have worked at least one month (four weeks or 24 days) before taking their first holiday.

French employees are covered by Social Security during their maternity leave. The leave they are covered for is six weeks before giving birth and ten weeks after. On the birth of a woman's third child, the maternity period is increased to eight weeks and eighteen weeks after the birth.

Minimum pay

Your work contract must state your salary and this salary must not be less than the SMIC (*Salaire Minimum Interprofessinel de Croissance*), France's minimum wage. It can be completed with benefits and an incentive scheme. Since 1st July 2002, the minimum wage has been €6.83 per hour.

Starting a business in France

Many foreigners, especially the British, find France so alluring precisely because it is a nation of small businesses. High streets are dotted with traditional family run shops rather than dominated by the national mega-chains and superstores such as WH Smith, Boots, Debenhams, Pizza Express and Starbucks. Town centres are not drearily homogeneous with the same old shopfront Goliaths.

Entrepreneurs, and those wanting to get rich quick, will soon find this quaint traditionalism stifling however. France is much less a nation of entrepreneurs than Britain, and French consumers are slow at taking to new and innovative services and products. Most small businesses have been established for many years and have offered the same product or service, with little change, for several generations. Most businesses exist for decades at subsistence level, their owners having bought into the lifestyle. If you start a small business, even a more traditional business, you could expect to break even after a couple of years, but certainly don't presume you'll ever be making a profit!

The easiest way for an outsider to start off in business in France would be to take over an existing (and reasonably successful) business or to buy into a franchise. Starting a new business in your own country is a risky and difficult undertaking, but to start a new business without much knowledge of the language, lack of personal contacts and a sparse understanding of the business procedures would be very tough, possibly foolish.

If you have an idea for a new business the first port of call should be a *Centre de Gestion,* which is a partnership of accountants and business advisors who will help you work out whether your business is viable, put financing in place and will help launch the business.

Here are some useful websites with listings of *Centres de Gestion.*

*   *Fédération des Centres de Gestion Agréés* (FCCA) – www.fcga.fr
*   *Boutiques de Gestion* – www.boutiques-de-gestion.com

Your *Centre de Gestion* will help you write up a business plan (*étude de marché*) which you will need if you are applying for loans. Alternatively you can approach a *Junior Entreprise* (a student association based at the business schools or *grandes écoles*) to conduct market research and write up your business plan. These student associations offer very attractive prices.

> *Note*: **The French term for Small to Medium Business (SME) is** ***Petite et Moyenne Entreprise*** **(PME).**

Regulations

EU nationals can move to France to set up, or buy, a business without any prior authorisation. Non-EU nationals may require a visa and should consult the French Consulate. Such foreigners are required to make a more substantial business commitment in order to gain admittance to France. Non-EU nationals will also need to obtain a special foreign merchant's permit (*Carte de commerçant étranger*) which can take up to six months to obtain. Business registration is compulsory and involves registering with the local Chamber of Commerce or *Chamber de Métiers.*

Certain activities are regulated (e.g. estate agents, driving schools) and you must satisfy the required conditions (e.g. diplomas, experience, business cards) in order to carry them out as a business. For information, contact professional organisations. You will find their addresses and contact numbers in the directory of the *Mouvement des Entreprises de France* (MEDEF) – the French Enterprises Association.

Mouvement des Entreprises de France (MEDEF)

✉   55 avenue Bosquet, 75330 Paris, Cedex 07
☎   +33 (0)1 53 59 19 19
⌨   www.medef.fr

Registering your business

Visit your *Centre de Formalités des Entreprises* (CFE) to obtain the necessary documents and registration application form (PO for a one-man business, MO for a company).

- If your business involves **trade or industry**, the CFE you need will be located at the Chamber of Commerce and Industry.

- If your business involves **crafts** or is of the mixed type (crafts and trade) then it will be at the *Chambre de Métiers* (Guild Chamber).

- If your activity involves the **professions** then it will be at the URSSAF (Social Security Contribution Collection Office).

- If you want to carry out an activity as a **sales representative**, you need the Commercial Court Clerk's Office.

- If your business involves **farming** you will need the Chamber of Agriculture.

When you go to register it's very likely that you'll be asked to take a management training course (usually a short four-day course). Such a course is mandatory for creators of small businesses, although it can be avoided if you have suitable qualifications or professional experience.

Companies and self-employed tradesmen must provide proof that they occupy commercial premises, although they may temporarily declare their registered office as being the manager's residence (for a maximum of two years). Self-employed craftsmen do not have to provide proof that they occupy commercial premises.

Funding

In addition to commercial bank loans, financial assistance may be provided to new businesses at local, national and, for large companies, even EU level. The following agencies and websites can offer lots of advice on business contacts, funding and all sorts of opportunities for setting up a business in France.

Contacts: Company funding

Business In Europe

Their website has lots of information on regional funding as well as good industry contacts.

www.business-in-europe.com

Invest in France Agency

✉ AFII Paris, 2 avenue Vélasquez, 75008 Paris, France
☎ +33 (0)1 4074 7440
@ info@investinfrance.org
Fax +33 (0)1 4074 7329
💻 www.afii.fr

French Chamber of Commerce in Great Britain

✉ 21 Dartmouth Street, Westminster, London, SW1H 9BP
☎ +44 (0)20 7304 4040
Fax +44 (0)20 7304 4034
@ mail@ccfgb.co.uk
💻 www.ccfgb.co.uk

Agence Pour La Creation d'Entreprises

✉ 14 rue Delambre 75682 Paris Cedex 14, France
☎ +33 (0)1 42 18 58 58
Fax +33 (0)1 42 18 58 00
@ info@apce.com
💻 www.apce.com

Although mainly a French website, the APCE has many useful links in English.

OSEO

OSEO is a group that helps small to medium enterprises find funding. It also provides information on starting up a business and advice on marketing, contracts and letter types, tax regimes and how to buy or rent commercial property.

💻 www.oseo.fr

Banque Du Développement des Petites et Moyennes Entreprises

This bank is the main provider of loans for the development of small to medium enterprises. The most popular loan is the *pret PCE*, which is a loan of between €3,000 and €8,000 for businesses that are less than three years old and have resources worth less than €45,000.

💻 www.bdpme.fr

Assemblée des Chambres Françaises de Commerce et d'industrie (ACFCI)

💻 www.acfci.cci.fr

Assemblée Permanente des Chambres de métiers (APCM)

💻 www.apcm.com

Interview with a property buyer

Bob is moving to the Dordorgne to run *gîtes* and a *chambre d'hôte*.

Q. *Tell me about yourself.*

A. I live in Ilchester, Somerset, in military housing having just sold our house in Cornwall. After 28 years of working in the Royal Navy, I'm moving to France. The property we are buying will be split to provide summer rental and off-season *chambre d'hôte*. At the age of 50 we are still very active, enjoy people and having been very disappointed at the standard of a number of holiday *gîtes*, we know we can provide a quality holiday experience which people will be happy to pay for.

Q. *Why did you decide to move to France?*

A. Joint decision, obviously. Quality and pace of life. Weather. We like the French people, and as long as you make an effort to integrate and contribute to the community the move will work! After all those years in the Navy I want the time to do all the things I have not done for years and I do NOT want to work 100 hour weeks, drive 50,000 miles a year on business, living most of my time away from home.

Q. *Whereabouts are you buying?*

A. We're buying a house near Eymet, 25 kms south of Bergerac. This will be our only residence, we are moving lock, stock etc. We have toured a good deal and the further south we have gone the more we enjoy it. The area has many similarities to the gentle rolling hills of Italy which I enjoy and it bears no similarity to Cornwall where we have lived for 25 years.

We found the area first, researched property extensively on the internet through dozens of websites and then went to view as many as possible. Having owned 10 properties in the UK over the years we were sure we would know it when we saw it, and we did.

Q. *How long has the process taken?*

A. Six months. Finding the property is a nightmare. Having searched the net and spoken to agents both in this country and France to agree a visit schedule, on arrival none of them kept to the plans which is most frustrating having travelled hundreds of miles to get to the area. Then, 30-40% of properties we expected to view were also being handled by other agents and the vendor had not disclosed this, hence many were sold and the agent was unaware! Fortunately the English agents tend to have links with each other and it was through one of these links we made contact with the agent who had the house we are buying.

Q. *How many properties did you look at?*

A. We viewed 27 properties in 5 days covering 2000 miles!

Q. *What is the property you have chosen and its surroundings like?*

A. Rural but not isolated, 3kms from the town. Quality restoration already completed by current French owners of 18 years. Big house, 1 hectare plot, big pool, mature gardens and so on.

Q. *Did you need to get a mortgage at all?*

A. Small mortgage through a broker in the UK. Spoken to many, all very helpful but most charge silly fees.

Q. *Can you speak French?*

A. We speak some French but none of it is legal or technical. The agent and the mortgage broker have been extremely helpful and I work with a French Naval Officer who has been a great help.

Q. *Worst experience?*

A. Actually one of the reasons we want to move from the UK was one of the greatest causes of frustration in France: very rigid working hours. The two and a half hours for lunch meant we had to stop mid-viewing and come back later, which is fine when you live with it, but on a very tight time schedule, the lack of flexibility was most annoying. Mind you, the restaurant they recommended for lunch was excellent!

Another frustrating thing was finding the right place but having to wait to move.

Q. *Best experience?*

A. Finding the 'right place' and instantly knowing it.

Q. *Any advice for others?*

A. Plenty of research, knowing what it is you want from the move, being realistic about your expectations, acknowledging you are European as well as British, accept it is a different way of life and do not expect the French to change for you.

Visit in the winter or off season and not just when the sunflowers are in bloom and the vines are heavy with fruit.

There is always another property to see, but the market is moving quite briskly .

Appendices

- *Régions* of France
- *Région* statistics
- Glossary of property terms
- Glossary of old property styles
- Facts about France
- A brief history of France
- Public holidays
- Useful addresses – embassies and consulates
- Further reading

Régions of France

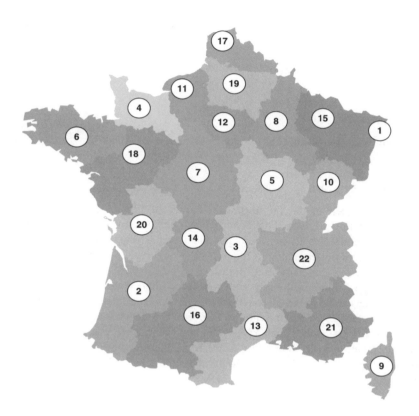

1.   Alsace
2.   Aquitaine
3.   Auvergne
4.   Basse-Normandie
5.   Bourgogne
6.   Bretagne
7.   Centre
8.   Champagne-Ardenne
9.   Corse
10. Franche-Comté
11. Haute-Normandie

12. Paris/Ile-de-France
13. Languedoc-Roussillon
14. Limousin
15. Lorraine
16. Midi-Pyrénées
17. Nord-Pas-De-Calais
18. Pays de la Loire
19. Picardie
20. Poitou-Charentes
21. Provence-Alpes-Côte d'Azur
22. Rhône-Alpes

Alsace

Population

Population: 1,734,145

Density (people per km^2): 209

Départements

Bas-Rhin (67), Haut-Rhin (68)

Région description

Alsace is situated in the far north-east corner of France and is one of the country's smallest *régions*. This beautiful and enchanting area nestles between the Vosges mountains to the west and the River Rhine, which forms a long natural border with Germany, to the east. The picturesque countryside is a mix of dense forests, rich farmland, pretty vineyards, fortified towns and quaint villages of half-timbered houses with geranium-filled window boxes. Many of these villages can be found on the *Route de Vin* which undulates for 112km along the foothills of the Vosges mountains. Summer is a good time to visit for those who enjoy Alsatian wines such as Riesling and Muscat, as a wine festival is held every weekend in a different town. Another scenic area, with its gentle rounded mountains and glacial lakes, is the 3000km^2 national park, the *Massif de Vosges*. The lush *Vallée de Munster*, home of the town Munster and its eponymous cheese, is a walker's paradise.

Alsace has often been positively described as the gateway between Latin and Germanic cultures, but its border proximity has more often than not been a millstone around the necks of the natives. In the past century, Alsatians saw their *région* annexed twice by the Germans, first from 1870 to 1918 and then again from 1940 to 1944. Even though much of the architecture, cuisine, dress and dialect is Germanic in style and the stereotype of the people matches that often held of the Germans (that is, well-organised, hard-working and tax-paying), nationalism here is rife. The people see themselves as French, but first and foremost as Alsatians. As a result of this pride, the use of their regional language has remained strong. It is spoken by four out of ten inhabitants and, although passing on less from parent to child, it has reoccurred on shop signs and menus. Known as *Elässisch*, this High German dialect, is spoken all over the *région* and by all ages, but is not taught in schools and is rarely written.

Property prices are higher than average in this *région* and fewer derelict properties are to be found as, unlike in many *régions*, there has never been a mass exodus from cities and farms. The styles of the houses are stone and half-timbered, many painted. Steep-pitched roofs and dormer windows are characteristic of the *région*. Towns such as Sauverne and Wissembourg are built in the local red sandstone.

Outsiders are attracted to the *région* for its education, cultural and economic opportunities. It's a good place to move if you're looking to stay permanently and find work. It has a relatively young population, with low unemployment. Many types of industry are represented and Strasbourg is a very important European administrative centre. Many people in this city also work in the banking sector. The *région* is a good place to base a business because it has excellent road connections and high speed TGV links to Paris (500km), plus links to Frankfurt in Germany and Basel and Zurich in Switzerland. Agriculturally, other than the vineyards, the important crops are maize, cauliflowers, mirabelles and quetsches (an Alsatian plum often made into brandy and delicious served warm in a coffee mug). Beer is also very important to the *région's* economy, and the famous bottled beer Kronenbourg is produced here.

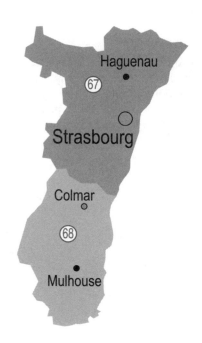

Régions

Three principal *communes*

Strasbourg (427,245)

Strasbourg is a small compact city on the River Rhine that has, in recent decades, shaken off a quaint image to take on its role as a modern European economic and administrative centre. It has developed rapidly in recent decades and is now home to the European Parliament, the European Court and the European Commission of Human Rights. There are many foreign companies located here, including the French headquarters of a number of international banks. The city offers a very high quality of life with good housing and facilities and being an important euro-centre means there are high employment possibilities for well-educated, bilingual migrants.

Mulhouse (234,445)

This is a sprawling industrial city, described in tourist brochures (not so endearingly) as France's equivalent of Manchester. Its museums focus on the city's glory days when it manufactured railways, automobiles, wallpaper and textiles. There is not much of an old town here and very little of interest to see if strolling around. Mulhouse was Swiss until 1798 when it voted to become part of France. Today many people live here and work in Basel, Switzerland.

Colmar (86,832)

The industrial sprawl surrounding this town can give visitors a bad first impression but the heart of the town is very pretty, with multi-coloured, half-timbered crooked houses along charming atmospheric alleyways. All have been extremely well-preserved. One of the most picturesque areas is the leather maker's district which has recently been restored.

Aquitaine

Population

Population: 2,900,359

Density (people per km^2): 70

Départements

Dordogne (24), Gironde (33), Landes (40), Lot-et-Garonne (47), Pyrénées-Atlantiques (64)

Région description

Aquitaine, in the south-west, is the largest *région* of France. It has a long, straight west coast, which stretches 200km from the mouth of the Gironde estuary down to the Spanish border. Along this border there are two main resorts: Biarritz in the south which, once fashionable with the glamour set of the 1930s, has recently been revived by trendy Parisians, and Arcachon to the north with its grand villas, which is popular with Bordelais weekenders. Aside from these resorts, the beautiful endless white beaches of this coastline are half-empty during the summer months, and very much unlike France's packed scorching Mediterranean coast.

The Pyrenees mountain range steadily begins to rise in the Pyrénées-Atlantiques, the southern most *département* of Aquitaine. The mountain foothills are a lush green land where the houses gradually become chalet in style. Many compare the weather here to Wales – although it is warmer, it rains a lot. Part of the Pyrénées-Atlantiques is Basque country (*Pays Basque*) where some 80,000 Basques live. The remaining 600,000 reside across the border in Spain.

The torso of Aquitaine's coastline is flanked by a large expanse of pine forests that make up most of the Landes *département*. These forests were planted in the 19th Century to stabilise drifting sands. Above Landes, the Gironde *département* around Bordeaux is home to some of the world's most celebrated vineyards, such as those in the fairly flat Medoc, west of the River Gironde, and in the increasingly hilly and pretty area around St-Emilion.

The northern, inland area of Aquitaine contains one of the most popular *départements* with the British – the Dordogne, named after what many argue is France's most beautiful river. The British call the area Dordogne, but to the French it is known as Périgord. Each area of Périgord has been assigned a descriptive colour. The south-east around Sarlat is called *Périgord Noir* because of its dense oak forests; the limestone area around the River Isle and Périgueux, capital of the région, is called *Périgord Blanc* after the light colour of its rock; *Périgord Poupre* refers to the wine-growing area around Bergerac, and the very green wooded area and pasturelands to the north is *Périgord Vert*. Apart from the lucrative tourist trade, this is an economically fragile and depopulated *région*. The two largest towns, each with populations just over 50,000, are Périgueux, known for its domed cathedral, and Bergerac, an important wine centre. Brantôme, on a bend of the water-lily covered River Dronne, much loved by British tourists.

A study of migration to the *région* by Montesquieu University Bordeaux IV found that most British ex-pats in Dordogne have been in the area for over five years, are predominantly male, above middle-age, do not live with children, and two-thirds of whom do not work. Unlike the other *départements* in Aquitaine, in which the British have either come for employment reasons or matrimonial ties, the expatriates in Dordogne are primarily there for quality of life and many first acquired their homes during the 80s property boom. This is the heartland of the stereotypical wealthy British ex-pat in France, with their own enclave of cricket teams and bridge clubs.

Agriculture has long been important to the economy and Aquitaine grows half of France's kiwi fruit, almost half its strawberries and most of its prunes. Potatoes, asparagus and maize are also important crops. Around Bergerac many tobacco fields are to be found and the forests of Landes produce a large quantity of planking for floors, roofing and wall cladding. Landes also has far-reaching fields growing succulent small carrots. Arcachon is famous throughout France for its oysters and it is possible to see the oyster beds at low tide. Although the oyster production has suffered several major setbacks, they are now flourishing again thanks to Japanese and Canadian breeding stocks.

Aquitaine's primary economic interest today is the expansion of its industrial and service sectors, especially the high-tech sector including the manufacturing of advanced materials, electronics, computer-integrated manufacturing and biotechnology.

Three principal *communes*

Bordeaux (753,931)

Despite its remoteness, Bordeaux is a bustling and cosmopolitan city. Built on the west bank of the River Garonne, it was formerly a great seaport but fell into decline after the Second World War following a drop in shipping requirements. Today it's affluent again and is home to many new technology industries. An excellent mix of communities rub shoulders, making the city a buzzing and dynamic place to be: there are thousands of students, a large North African immigrant community, and many wealthy vineyard owners who pop into town from their nearby *chateaux*. There are plenty of museums, art galleries and fine restaurants, as well as lots of good cheap eateries.

Bayonne (178,965)

Just a few minutes outside the seaside resort of Biarritz is the Basque city of Bayonne. In Basque, Bayonne means 'the good river', and in some quarters of the city you will hear as much Basque (*Euskara*) spoken as French. Bayonne is a small, pleasant city with deep narrow streets that are easy to get around on foot. The tall half-timbered houses and the shutters of the riverside buildings are painted green and red – typically Basque.

Pau (181,413)

Pau is a pretty flower-filled city with dramatic views of the Pyrenees. In the 19th Century the English discovered Pau and brought with them fox-hunting, golf (the first 18-hole golf course in France and the first to admit women is here), croquet and elegant parks with splendid vistas of the mountains. When the railways arrived it became popular with writers, artists and musicians, including the likes of Victor Hugo and Stendhal. In the 1950s, natural gas was discovered.

Auvergne

Population

Population: 1,308,878

Density (people per km^2): 50

Auvergne is one of the least populated régions in Europe, let alone France. The département of Cantal would be almost completely depopulated if it wasn't for the town Aurillac (36,096).

Départements

Allier (03), Cantal (15), Haute-Loire (43), Puy-de-Dôme (63)

Région description

Auvergne, which encompasses much of the *Massif Central*, is perhaps the least known and most remote *région* of France. With two large spectacular national parks – the dramatic *Parc Naturel Régional des Volcans d'Auvergne* and its tamer neighbour the *Parc Naturel Régional des Livradois-Forez* – it is almost entirely unspoiled and is the largest environmentally-protected area of France. Volcanic activity started here around twenty million years ago, so the *région's* mountains are older than the Alps and the Pyrenees. The youngest volcanoes around the *Puy de Dôme* are just 5,000 years old. The many extinct volcanoes that dimple the landscape make the *région* a strange, but enigmatically beautiful place. There are also spectacular gorges, and geesers, lakes, streams, rivers and thick vast forests. Hot springs and mineral cold springs attract many *curistes* who come seeking relief from rheumatism, arthritis and digestive ailments.

Auvergne's beauty wasn't, of course, enough to stem an exodus from the *région* and it is now heavily depopulated and poor. Its ageing population proves there could be some truth in its reputation for being rustic and backwards. The people also have a reputation for being taciturn and not very open to strangers – although this may be an unfair stereotype. Today the population continues to diminish, no longer because of migration to find work, but because the number of births is not greater than the number of deaths. Proportionately, the number of people over 75 matches the number under twenty. It's predicted that between 2010 and 2030 the population with diminish a further 8%.

Auvergne is the least expensive *région* for property in France but is not popular with foreign buyers. There is a tourist industry – *Le Puy-en-Velay*, with its strange volcanic skyscrapers is particularly popular – but visitors are mostly those that are passing through on autoroutes to the south or across the borders. For the very active and outdoorsy types, who can take or leave museums and restaurants, Auvergne could make a wonderful base for a second home. Even though the pace of life is slow, there are plenty of thrilling adventures to be had. It is outstanding riding, hiking and mountain climbing country and there are lakes where you can swim, sail, windsurf and fish. You can also white water raft and kayak through the gorges of the Allier and Sioule rivers. Other outdoor opportunities include paragliding and ballooning. There are several ski resorts so, for the energetic, the Auvergne is an ideal place to visit at all times of the year. Summers in Auvergne are long and warm, with temperatures often reaching 30 degrees centigrade punctuated by short sharp thunderstorms. The uplands are cooler and at altitudes of over 1,000m, snow frequently lies on the ground until May. Although much of the *région* is remote, good road and rail routes pass through and there are air connections nearby.

There is little arable land here and much of the agriculture is upland pasture. The *région* is famous around the world for its green (Puy) lentils, which have achieved AOC classification thanks to the area's rich volcanic soil. The area produces 60% of France's lentils. Other crops are corn seed and rye. Agriculture employs 15% of the working population.

Tyre production is the largest industrial sector in Auvergne, accounting for one-third of the *région's* exports and employing 130,000 people worldwide (20,000 in the *région)*. The largest manufacturer, with its headquarters in Clermont-Ferrand, is Michelin which has encouraged the development of related industries including metals and metal products, plastics, automobile equipment and mechanical construction. The company is also responsible for advancements in Auvergne's research programs, particularly in the chemicals industry.

Three principal *communes*

Clermont-Ferrand (258,541)

Clermont-Ferrand is almost encircled by wooded and grassy volcanoes. The town centre is built on top of a long extinct volcano, with the old city's main thoroughfare sloping and pedestrianised. Its reputation as the *ville noire* is not because of the industrial pollution but because of the volcanic rock used in its construction. As mentioned above, the town is the home of the Michelin tyre company. In the 1980s, when the industry went into decline, the workforce was halved and many of those who lost their jobs were Portuguese immigrants brought in to supplement the workforce. These Portuguese immigrants are now well-integrated into the community. Many young people (34,000) are attracted to university life in Clermont-Ferrand but unlike other cities they do not tend to stay following their education.

Montluçon (60,993)

The ancient town of Montluçon has a museum which houses a fine collection of hurdy-gurdies, although I'm not too sure what else the town has to offer!

Vichy (60,877)

Vichy, with its faded *fin-de-siècle* charm and grandeur, is one of the largest and most famous spa towns. It became very fashionable following visits from Napoleon III in the 1860s, but since July 1940 has been known throughout the world as the capital of Pétain's collaborationist government. The spas attract many elderly people, although attempts are now being made to rejuvenate the town by appealing to the new fitness-conscious younger generation.

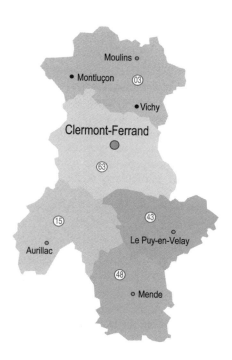

Basse-Normandie

Population

Population: 1,422,193

Density (people per km^2): 81

Départements

Calvados (14), Manche (50), Orne (61)

Région description

Basse-Normandie is located on the north-west coast of France, just to the south-west of neighbouring Haute-Normandie with which it is normally lumped together and called simply Normandy.

The seaside towns and resorts of the *région's* coast are very popular with day-tripping Parisians. Picturesque Honfleur – one of the closest seaside resorts to Paris – particularly draws the crowds. The sea here has withdrawn due to extensive siltation and the old wooden houses that once lined the seafront lie several hundred metres inland. In 1995 a 2km bridge, *Pont de Normandie*, opened across the Seine linking Honfleur with Le Havre, making it very accessible for visitors from the UK arriving into the uglier port town. Other popular seaside resorts include Trouville and Deauville which are within a stone's throw of each other and share the same *gare SNCF* and *gare routière*. Deauville, with its smart casinos and turn-of-the-century villas, was once the playground of the rich and famous, whereas Trouville is more downmarket.

Much of the north-facing coast of the Calvados *département* is lined with the D-Day beaches that claimed the lives of 100,000 soldiers on 6th June 1944. The beaches are still often referred to by their wartime code names – Sword, Juno, Gold, Omaha and Utah – and many are still deeply pitted by German bunkers and shell holes. All the coastal towns here have a war museum, although many visitors do manage to put the coast's grim history to the backs of their minds and enjoy it simply for the sand and seafood.

The Manche *département*, west of Calvados, is surrounded on three sides by the English Channel. This *département*, with its beautiful stretches of rocky coastline, has the misfortune of being known as 'Europe's nuclear dump' as, on the edge of the peninsula's western tip, is France's first uranium treatment plant. At the tip of the peninsula sits Cherbourg, a large but unappealing port town, and more appealingly to the south, beside the border with Brittany, is one of the most visited sites in France – *Mont St-Michel*. Due west of the peninsula are the

Régions

Channel islands of Jersey and Guernsey, accessible from nearby St-Malo in neighbouring Brittany.

Away from the coast the *région* is an extremely fertile land of lush meadows, rich pastures and orchards hiding small villages of half-timbered – *colombage* – houses. Around the town of St-Lô is the area known as the *bocage*, where fields are criss-crossed with tight hedgerows rooted into walls of earth over a metre high. In 1944, the Allied troops found it almost impossible to advance through this landscape. Part of the area along the River Orne, about 25km from Caen, is known as Swiss Normandie where, although not mountainous, there are cliffs, crags and wooded hills at every turn. The southern part of Basse-Normandie is a densely wooded area and is great for walkers. The *Forêt d'Ecouves*, north of Alençon, is a dense mix of spruce, pine, oak and beech and populated by deer, wild boar and wild mushrooms. In the autumn the woods attract the deer-hunters.

The main agricultural activities in the *région* are cattle, dairy and apples. Basse-Normandie is renowned for producing apples for cider and Calvados is, of course, known for its eponymous apple-flavoured liquor. Butter, cheese and milk production has suffered since EU milk quotas liquidated many small farms and stringent sanitary conditions forced many small-scale traditional cheese factories to close. Until the late 1960s, Basse-Normandie was primarily an agricultural *région* but in the past twenty years it has evolved into a more complex *région*, combining traditional output with many small and mid-sized industries and services. The *région* benefits from high GDP growth and a young population.

Three largest *communes*

Caen (199,490)

Caen is a bustling university city that has seen much expansion as its industrial suburbs have had an influx of high-tech newcomers in recent years. There is little left of the old city which was bombed on D-Day and burned for over a week before it was liberated by the Canadians and then shelled by the Germans. Little remains of the past except for ramparts around the *château* and two great abbeys built by William the Conqueror when he founded the city in the 11th Century. Caen is also the gateway for Ouistreham (15km north of Caen), a minor passenger port for Brittany Ferries to and from Portsmouth, England. For many centuries this port exported a limestone called Caen stone to England.

Cherbourg (89,704)

A port city and naval base, busy with transatlantic cargo ships and passenger ferries from England and Ireland. It has some busy pedestrian streets and some lively bars but apart from this, many visitors head straight out and onwards.

Alençon (44,382)

This is a busy but pleasant town, once renowned for its lace-making industry. During the Norman era it was an important tax-collecting centre. With its Second Empire houses and wrought-iron balconies dating from the 18th Century, it retains an atmosphere of genteel wealth.

Bourgogne

Population

Population: 1,610,067

Density (people per km^2): 51

Départements

Côte d'Or (21), Nièvre (58), Saône-et-Loire (71), Yonne (89)

Région description

Burgundy (*Bourgogne*) is a peaceful rural *région* at the heart of France, which has a rich and unique history. The Dijon-based duchy ran Burgundy for 600 years until 1477, when the *région* was jealously snatched by the kingdom of France. Evidence of the duchy's wealth and power is found everywhere, such as the many beautiful *chateaux* and lovely towns and villages. Burgundy was also a place of important religious and spiritual influence. There are two great abbeys at Vézelay and Fontenay and the ruins of a monastery at Cluny where the abbots' influence was second only to the Pope's. This monastic presence meant that during the Middle Ages Burgundy was a great church-building *région*. During the Industrial Revolution Burgundy prospered once again when, in 1838, the Schneider iron and steelworks based at Le Creusot made the first French locomotive. Today Le Creusot is not such a powerhouse; most of the workers have lost their jobs and unemployment is high.

Much of Burgundy's prosperity is now centred about the prestigious wine growing areas in the south and around Dijon. These small pockets have helped uphold the *région's* reputation as the land of great art and good living and today people visit the area to try some of France's finest wines such as Nuits-Saint-Georges, Meursault and Beaune. Most of the vineyards are found in the attractive area called the *Côte d'Or*. This is divided into the *Côtes de Nuits* and *Côtes de Beaune*, the latter is known for its whites: Meursault, Montrachet and Puligny. The reds of the *Côtes de Nuits* are considered superior as they are richer and age better. Once run by the religious orders, these vines are now owned by the seriously rich and are so lucrative they almost never come up for sale. Away from the prestigious vineyards there are less glamorous areas where the cattle outnumber people. Charolles is the heart of the cattle breeding area and is also known for its pottery.

Many visitors come to Burgundy to enjoy canal boat holidays on its inland waterways. There are 1,200km (750 miles) of rivers and canals. Cycling along the canals is also popular and there are plenty of gentle to moderately demanding walks. In the centre of the *région* is the *Parc de Morvan*, a wooded hilly area, with a number of nature trails, animal reserves and craft shops. Morvan, is an area of Burgundy with poor soil. It therefore has little means of prosperity and has always had the reputation of being the poorest and most backward area in the *région*.

Present-day Burgundy has little economic importance and few industries so it's not an ideal area for newcomers looking for work. There are poor areas but on the whole the standard of living is good. Burgundy is, surprisingly, not a popular *région* with foreign second home buyers although in recent years it has attracted more and more interest from Parisians looking for weekend retreats. Inexpensive village houses and farmhouses in need of restoration can be found. Burgundy is well connected both to the north and south by autoroutes and the TGV. It's only 100km (65 miles) south of Paris and 80km north of Lyon.

Régions

Three largest *communes*

Dijon (236, 953)

Dijon, the world's mustard capital, is a very pleasant and prosperous city. From the early 11th Century until the late 1400s it was home to the Dukes of Burgundy and was a place of tremendous wealth and power. It was also one of the greatest centres of art, learning and science. Today, thanks to its large student population, it's much more than just a heritage site and is actually a very modern-feeling town, with a bright cultural scene. If you wish to live in a small, manageable yet modern and lively city then Dijon is an ideal place to set up your home.

Chalon-sur-Saône (75,447)

This town, situated on a broad section of the River Saône, is a port and busy industrial centre. It's also a thriving business centre and there are often visiting trade fairs that take over the town. It's worth visiting during one of the town's festivals such as the carnival in March when there's a hilarious parade of giant masks or in July when there's a national festival of street artists, as well as October for the film festival.

Nevers (57,515)

This small provincial city on the confluence of the rivers Loire and Nièvre, is known for its nougatine candies and fine porcelain which are made in three workshops and sold in a few elegant, expensive shops in town. The pleasant old town dates back to the 12th Century. In the summer Nevers puts on a good open-air concert programme.

Régions

Bretagne

Population

Population: 2,906,197

Density (people per km^2): 107

Départements

Côtes d'Armor (22), Finistère (29),
Ille-et-Vilaine (35), Morbihan (56)

Région description

Brittany (*Bretagne*), the *région* occupying the rugged western tip of France, is surrounded on three sides by a long (1,110km) and varied coastline. There are rugged cliffs dotted with lighthouses, wide estuaries, islands and islets where bird life is protected, and picturesque harbours with strong maritime traditions. The many white sandy beaches and pretty coves make for wonderful bathing opportunities. Sailing and windsurfing are popular and some of the best scuba-diving in France can be found here. The climate is mild because of the Gulf Stream but its Atlantic exposure means that winters can be wet, very windy and bitterly cold.

Ferry links at Roscoff, St-Malo and the nearby ports in Normandy have made this an area very popular with UK holiday-makers and second home owners. It's also very popular with French holiday makers and in the summer months the beaches and attractive seaside towns such as Dinard, Vannes and Dinan are teeming with tourists.

The *région* is described as two lands – Armor meaning 'land of the sea' and Argoat, at the interior, meaning 'land of the woods'. Although the coastline gets plenty of visitors, much of the interior is unexplored with some parts surprisingly remote and depopulated. For those venturing inland there are plenty of lovely areas to be found, such as around Heulgoat, known for its enchanting forests, which is becoming more and more popular with second home buyers. An ideal way to explore inland Brittany is along its waterways.

Stone has always dominated the *région's* landscape. All over Brittany, stone circles and mysterious megaliths can be found. Houses in Brittany are built in the traditional pink, grey and black stones with slate roofs and the *Côte de Granit Rose* is particularly known as a land of pink stone, with pink granite rocks along the coast that have been eroded into fantastic shapes.

For many years the people of Brittany – Bretons – have seen themselves as inhabiting a country separate from France and some still speak the Breton language. Traditional Breton customs are most evident in the far western half of the peninsular, particularly in Cornouaille on the south-western tip. Breton costume is often still worn on special occasions. The eastern half (around St. Malo) has retained little in the traditional way of life.

Property is more expensive by the coast but it's certainly worth venturing inland where bargains can be found – wherever you are in Brittany, the sea is never very far away.

Brittany is considered France's number one agricultural and fishing *région*, accounting for 10% of national production. The principal crops are artichokes and cauliflowers. There's also a good deal of industrial activity and local authorities have embarked on a campaign to promote the development of advanced technologies. The capital, Rennes, is an international centre for telecommunications research, and tourism is, of course, extremely important to the *région's* economy.

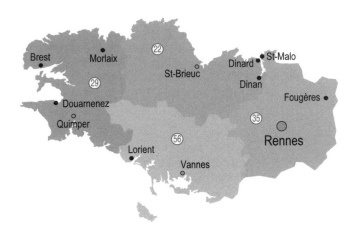

Three largest *communes*

Rennes (272, 263)

The ancient capital of Brittany, Rennes, is full of neo-classical and somewhat pompous major buildings. Enthusiasts of medieval architecture will find little to excite them here as much of Rennes was destroyed in 1720 by a major fire. It's a good place to seek employment opportunities as a great deal of development is happening in the fields of information technology, telecommunications, agro-industries, biotechnology, nutrition and the environment.

Brest (210,055)

Set in a magnificent natural harbour, Brest has had an important role in wartime and during peace it's a place of trade. The French Atlantic Fleet is based here as its dry dock accommodates ships of up to 50,000 tonnes. During World War II it was constantly bombed to prevent Germany using it as a submarine base. When it was liberated in 1944 the Americans arrived to find it destroyed beyond recognition. The post-war architecture is bleak and the town has little to offer tourists.

St-Brieuc (85,849)

This busy city is an industrial centre with few attractions for tourists, but is a good place for shopping if you live in the area. It is built in two deep wooded valleys spanned by viaducts.

Centre

Population

Population: 2,440,329

Density (people per km^2): 62

Départements

Cher (18), Eure-et-Loir (28), Indre (36), Indre-et-Loire (37), Loir-et-Cher (41), Loiret (45)

Région description

Although Centre is the name used administratively, the *région* is commonly called Central Loire, *Val de Loire*, Loire Valley or simply, the Heart of France. France's longest river (at 1,020km/628 miles), the Loire, which flows from its source in the mountains south of Saint-Etienne to the Atlantic, defines the *région's* identity. It has always been very wealthy thanks to the fertility of the land. The river is considered to be the dividing line between the cold north and warmer south and the *région* itself is temperate considering how far north it is.

The Loire Valley is a land of impressive *chateaux*, hunting lodges and cathedrals and is often visited by those with an interest in Medieval and Renaissance architecture. It's also a perfect place to walk and cycle; the flat countryside by the river is ideal for those on bikes and for simply spending lazy days picnicking by the water's edge. There are plenty of lakes and smaller rivers and the fertile landscape is covered with lush woodland, orchards and fields of maize and sunflowers.

With its impressive architectural heritage and lovely outdoor scenery it is very popular with second home owners and tourists. It is also popular with more permanent newcomers looking for a good quality of life. Although the countryside is very peaceful, there are many large *communes* such as those listed opposite, as well as the lovely towns of Chartres, Chateauroux, Blois and Montargis, and you are never far from good facilities including excellent hospitals, schools and universities. A regional focus on education has resulted in a very well-educated and well-trained labour force. The northernmost areas are also very close to Paris, so it's ideal for those working for foreign companies based in the capital who also wish for a rural home-life. Paris is easily accessible on the autoroutes and the *région* is only an hour or two's commute from the city centre.

Centre is an ideal place for those starting up a business; it has the close proximity to Paris yet significantly lower production and labour costs. Many pharmaceutical companies have invested here in recent years and local authorities support investment in small and medium-sized companies. Agriculture is important to the economy and, other than the wine grapes, the main crops are red onions, sunflowers, cucumbers, leeks and almost half of France's beetroots.

Don't expect to find many property bargains here – most were snapped up a long time ago and the average cost of property is above the majority of *régions* in France.

Three largest *communes*

Orléans (263,292)

This is the most northern city on the Loire, sitting at the apex of a huge arc in the river as it switches direction and starts to flow southwest. It was heavily bombed during WWII, but fortunately its historic centre remained intact. Many Orléanais commute to work in Paris and also spend their evenings out there. This hasn't been good for the city, and it has often tried to resist its subordinate status as a suburb of the capital. Over recent years the city has seen lots of building work, including a modern university district called La Source.

Tours (297, 631)

Tours is a lively, cosmopolitan place with a slightly bourgeois air, tucked between the Loire running along the town's long northern boundary and its tributary the Cher along the south. Its centre is efficiently laid out with 18th Century avenues, formal public gardens and café-lined boulevards. In the old town there are half-timbered houses and stairway towers from the 12th to 15th centuries. It has a large student population. Twice in its history it has hosted the French government – in 1870 during the Franco-Prussian war and again in 1940, with the onset on WWII. The vineyards surrounding Tours are famous for their crisp white wines – Vouvray and Montlouis – which are stored in the white tufaceous cliffs along this stretch of the river.

Bourges (91,437)

The centre of this small and pleasant town, with its impressive 12th Century Gothic cathedral, is situated on a hill rising from the River Yévre. Bourges is a lively city with a surprising number of good festivals for its size: in the Spring performers of every type of music are brought together for *Printemps de Bourges*. In the first week of June the *Festival Synthése* attracts electronic music aficionados; and in the summer *Eté a Bourges* is a celebration of theatre, music and open-air street theatre.

Champagne-Ardenne

Population

Population: 1,342,363

Density (people per km^2): 52

Départements

Ardennes (08), Aube (10), Haute-Marne (52), Marne (51)

Région description

Champagne-Ardenne borders Ile-de-France in the south-west, the industrial areas of Lorraine in the east, and Belgium in the north. Its name comes from the Romans who called it *Campania*, meaning literally 'land of the plains'. Today these plains, mostly to the south of the *région*, are where vast quantities of cereals and maize are grown. Sugar beet is a major crop (the smell from the sugar beet refineries can be overpowering so do not consider buying a property anywhere near one!) and the *région* grows more wheat and cabbage than any other. But cabbage aside, it is of course better known for a much more glamorous crop: the white grape that has produced Champagne's eponymous sparkling wine since the days of Dom Perignon. Only bubbly made from vines from limited parts of the *région* can be called champagne and these are mainly located in the Marne and Aube *départements*. Away from the glitzy vineyards surrounding the towns of Reims, Epernay and Troyes, much of rural Champagne is impoverished. Run-down hamlets with flaky, hanging-off shutters are common and, as so many *communes* lack decent facilities including shops, many inhabitants are dependent on weekly visits from grocery vans.

The rolling prairies that give the *région* its name are to the south between Reims, Epernay and Troyes. North of Reims the landscape becomes a flat chalky plain which is wet, bitterly cold and very windy during the winter. This area is an extension of the chalk subsoil that comes to the surface at Calais and forms the white cliffs of Dover on the opposite side of the Channel. Closer to the border with Belgium, the landscape becomes more rugged and deeply forested. This area is unsuitable for crops and the slateworks and ironworks of the late 20th Century closed down in the 1980s. The major investment in the *région* is a nuclear power plant. The largest artificial lake in Europe – *Lac de Der-Chatecoq* – found in the forested Ardennes, is beginning to attract tourists with an interest in walking and boating.

Agriculture is a strong force in the economy and champagne production accounts for one-third of the regional output (representing 2.3% of France's gross domestic product). In addition to traditional agricultural and manufacturing (metalworking and textiles) activities, Champagne has become a major industrial base for the agro foods industry. Other industrial sectors include packaging, automotive equipment (Citroën is a large employer), tyre manufacturing, plastics and chemicals. Companies choose this *région* for its lower wages (compared with the high wages of nearby Belgium) and, reputedly, a low level of absenteeism.

The *région* is not popular with second home buyers, but for anyone wishing to venture this way, inexpensive property can be found.

Three largest *communes*

Reims (215,581)

Reims (pronounced 'râns', as in 'ran' with 's' sounded), along with Epernay, is an important centre for champagne production. Visitors come to the town for *dégustation* at the dozen or so champagne houses such as Mumm and Taittinger. They also come to see one of the most impressive Gothic cathedrals in France – *Cathédrale Notre-Dame* – which was formerly the coronation church of the French monarchs. Much of the city was flattened by the bombs of World War I, but has since been reconstructed with great precision. It's a very orderly city with wide avenues and well-tended parks.

Troyes (128,945)

This beautiful city has one of France's finest ensembles of medieval and renaissance half-timbered houses and has been an important centre since Gallo-Roman times. It is also a lively commercial centre and there are numerous cut-price outlets specialising in brand-name clothing and accessories.

Charleville-Mézières (65,727)

The twin towns Charleville and Mézières, which spread across the meandering Meuse, are a good centre for exploring the Ardennes. Charleville is a major international puppetry centre and annually hosts one of the largest puppet festivals in the world called *Festival Mondial des Théâtres de Marionettes* where troops come from as far afield as Mali and Burma.

Corse

Population

Population: 260,196

Density (people per km^2): 30

Départements

Corse (20) divided into two zones Corse-du-Sud (2a) and Haute-Corse (2b)

Région description

Corsica is situated 160km (99miles) off the southern coast of France in the gulf of Genoa, but it is actually closer – 80km (50 miles) – to Italy and was in Italian possession until 1768 when it was purchased by France. The island's diverse coast of 1,000km (620 miles) has a mix of rugged cliffs as well as some of the finest beaches in the Mediterranean with beautiful half-moon bays and picturesque villages. There are no high-rise developments along the coast as buildings are restricted to a maximum two storeys and are not allowed to encroach too closely upon the beach.

Inland, further diverse landscapes can be found. Driving up the steep climbs and around sharp hairpin bends through the jagged mountains can be exhilarating. Half of these mountains are snow-capped for almost the entire year. The mid-level mountains are covered in *maquis* – a mix of harsh and resilient bushes including broom, gorse, juniper, laurel, lentisk and myrtle mixed with strong aroma-giving plants like asphodel, cistus, heather, lavender, thyme and sage (which provide the spice in Corsican cooking). Pine and chestnut forests cover the craggy mountains and olive groves fill the valleys.

Corsicans are known for being intimate in community but very reserved to strangers and some outsiders could find the taciturn people unapproachable. The family is paramount to the people. The language *Corsu* is more closely related to Italian and many people are working to keep it alive, evidenced in the bilingual or exclusively *Corsu* street and shop signs about the island. Almost half of the population is concentrated in the two major towns, and in the interior of the country many *communes* are suffering from depopulation, with few activities outside of agriculture. The most affected are 136 *communes* in the west of the island where more than half of the population are aged over 60. *Communes* that are less deserted, but which have no shops or services, are those close to the autoroutes. The people here drive to work in the major towns.

The population's relationship with the mainland is uneasy and a nationalist movement is in constant and sometimes violent conflict with central government. It's easy to understand some of the bad feeling as the Corsicans are proud of their language, culture and traditions but, until recently, the French government neglected the island both economically and culturally, and corruption was rife. In 1998 Claude Erignac, Ajaccio's *Préfet,* was assassinated and since then the French government has adopted a tougher approach towards the corruption that dogged the island for decades. Today it's a heavily subsidised *région*, both by central government and the EU. Corsicans are exempt from social security contributions and big financial incentives are on offer to draw foreign companies to the island. The island's two major activities are agriculture and tourism. The major agricultural products are clementines (99% of France's production), almonds (42%), chestnuts (21%), kiwis (17.3%) and olive oil (12.9%).

The island is most popular with Italian holiday-home owners, although there are signs of an increased interest among those from further afield.

Régions

Three largest *communes*

Bastia (54,075)

Corsica's main business and commerce centre is this bustling town in the north of the island. There's a strong Italian vibe here and buildings have remained intact from the time when it was the seat of the Genoese government from the 15th Century. The city's name comes from *bastiglia* meaning fortress. The focal point is the long *Place St-Nicholas* and one block away from this is the fashionable shopping street *Boulevard Paoli*. The prettiest part of town is the *Vieux Port* with its tall houses with peeling plaster and coloured boat hulls. It comes alive at night when a number of waterside bars and restaurants open.

Ajaccio (52,880)

Ajaccio (Ajacciu in *Corsu*) is a pastel-coloured port city which was birthplace to Napoleon Bonaparte. Many statues and several museums are dedicated to the man. There's an open-air food market every morning and a fresh fish market in a building nearby. Restaurants are good in the summer but service and food quality is reputedly poor at other times of the year. It's a relaxing place but lacks the buzz of Bastia.

Porto-Vecchio (10,326)

Until the 1950s there was little more than a 16th Century watch tower at Porto but since the onset of tourism the little town has expanded a great deal. It has profited from tourism because of its proximity to the mountains and the *maquis*, the picturesque pink village of Piana, some stunning gorges and the *Forêt d'Aïtone* with its strings of natural swimming pools. Consequently the town, popular with German tourists, is packed during the summer months.

Franche-Comté

Population

Population: 1,117,059

Density (people per km^2): 69

Départements

Doubs (25), Haute-Saône (70), Jura (39), Territoire-de-Belfort (90)

Région description

This little known *région* borders Switzerland and shares much of its architecture, cuisine and culture with its neighbour. Between the Vosges range of mountains to the north and the Jura (Gaulish word meaning 'forest') range to the south, the landscape consists of rolling cultivated fields, dense pine forest and rampart-like mountains. Not as majestic as the Alps, the Jura mountains are more accessible and are France's premier cross-country skiing area. It is also a superb place to hike and there are some fine nature trails on the more gentle slopes. The Doubs and Loue valleys, noted for their timbered houses perched on stilts in the river, and the high valley of Ain, are popular visitor areas. The *Région des Lacs* is a land of gorges and waterfalls dotted with tiny villages, each with a domed belfry decorated with mosaics of tiles or slates or beaten from metal. The lakes are perfect for swimming. The summits of *Haute-Jura* have wonderful views across *Lac Léman* (Lake Geneva) and towards the Alps.

This area is largely ignored by foreign home buyers, which is strange as its landscape makes it perfect for both a winter and summer retreat. It has good connections with the centre and south of France, Switzerland and Germany. Its proximity to Switzerland means that it's possible to work in Switzerland whilst living in France.

40% of the *région's* GDP is dependent on manufacturing activities, and most of its production is exported. Construction of automobiles and their parts is one of the most buoyant industries here. Forestry exploitation is steadily growing and 38% of the agriculture is dairy and 17% cattle farming. The *région* has a large and lucrative cheese-making industry with 40 million tons of cheese produced here each year, much of which is made by *fruitières* (traditional cheese dairies of Franche-Comté).

Three largest *communes*

Besançon (134,376)

With large parks and clean streets, this grey-stoned town enclosed in a loop of the River Doubs and surrounded by the hills of the north Jura range, is considered one of France's 'greenest' cities. There are few tourists but, with France's largest foreign student population, it is nonetheless a cosmopolitan place. The cobbled streets of the old town are full of lively bars and places to eat. Since Gallo-Roman times it has been an important stop on the trade routes between Italy, the Alps and the Rhine. Since the 18th Century it has been an important clock-making centre and in 1890 was the birthplace of rayon (artificial silk). It was also the birthplace of novelist Victor Hugo and the film-pioneering Lumière brothers.

Montbéliard (113,059)

This historic town on the River Doubs is a pretty place, with brightly coloured houses and a very Germanic feel. It's also progressive and high-tech. Car manufacturing is an important industry and the town is home to Peugeot.

Belfort (81,524)

Just across the border from Germany and Switzerland, this city is historically part of Alsace but became part of the Franche-Comté *région* in 1921. Today the city is best known as the manufacturer of TGV trains.

Haute-Normandie

Population

Population: 1,780,192

Density (people per km^2): 145

Départements

Eure (27), Seine-Maritime (76)

Région description

Haute-Normandie, located in north-west France, is home to the major ports Le Havre and Dieppe and also to some lovely resorts such as Étretat. Le Havre, the second largest port in France, is the first port of call in Europe for imports; its commercial docks offload goods from all over the world. Dieppe is one of the nicest ports in France and popular with visitors – especially day-trippers – from the UK. On Saturdays, Dieppe hosts one of the best street markets in northern France, which spreads throughout the town's streets and sells fresh products from all over the country, including fish sold straight from the boats.

Stretching south 100km from Dieppe to Étretat is the *Côte d'Albâtre*, where pebble beaches are backed by impressive tall, white cliffs. Along this coast there are small villages and few resorts. Here, villages nestle in a succession of dry valleys, the cliffs of which are fast eroding. One such place is the fishing port of Fécamp, with its attractive seafront promenade, where a *Bénédictine* monastery was built after a few drops of Christ's blood was miraculously found. Once it was a popular destination for pilgrims but today the majority of visitors come to try the digestif Bénédictine that is still made here. Further south is the small pretty town of Étretat where the white cliffs are at their most spectacular and visitors will find unusual rock formations including arches, tunnels and a solitary 'needle' out at sea.

Inland Haute-Normandie is a land of meadows and orchards, as well as many rivers and brooks. Its half-timbered *colombage* houses are much in demand. The majority have been modernised and are second homes for both Parisians and the British. Thanks to its access to many ferry links to the south of England, the *région* is extremely popular with the British and some areas are so popular that estate agents even answer the phone in English. For Brits wishing to completely escape other Brits, Haute-Normandie is certainly not the best place for your second or permanent home!

Régions

For anyone wishing to start a business in Haute-Normandie, the best assets the *région* has to offer are its transport infrastructure (its modernised port installations, linked to all the European communications networks, symbolise the merchant power of this *région*), large energy supply and the lowest rate of local taxation per head after Ile-de-France. The level of unemployment is, however, one of the highest in France, although salaries are above average.

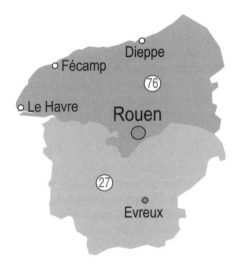

Three largest *communes*

Rouen (389,862)

Historically, Rouen, with its many spires and church towers, is an important city. It has around 200 half-timbered houses, with rough-hewn beams, posts and diagonals leaning this way and that, and a cathedral considered to be a masterpiece of French Gothic architecture, famously painted in a series by impressionist Claude Monet. Rouen was once the furthest point down river where you could cross the Seine by bridge.

Le Havre (248,547)

France's second most important port is a gateway for ferries to the UK and Ireland. At one time it was a prosperous trading post and home to great luxury liners. But WWII came and the city was obliterated by bombing raids. Redesigned by architect Auguste Perret between 1946 and 1964, it is now a regimented grid of wide, straight central streets (with the sea visible at the end of each), lined with rows of three-storey concrete buildings. Although Perret's famous dictum was "concrete is beautiful", many visitors find the buildings dreary. Le Havre was also home to Jean-Paul Sartre and it was here that he wrote *La Nausée* while teaching in a local school.

Elbeuf (75,663)

This industrial town and river port, just 70 minutes by train from Paris, is located in a tight loop on the River Seine and is surrounded by wooded hills and high cliffs. From the 16th Century the town was known as an important wool and cloth manufacturing centre, but after WWII it became heavily industrialised and is now known for producing automobile parts, electrical equipment, and chemicals. The town was badly damaged during the war when it became a point for Allied armies to cross the Seine, but it has since been restored. It has numerous churches dating from the 15th to the 17th Century.

Paris/Ile-de-France

Population

Population: 10,952,011

Density (people per km^2): 912

Départements

Essone (91), Hauts-de-Seine (92), Seine-et-Marne (77), Seine-Saint-Denis (93), Val-de-Marne (94), Val-d'Oise (95), Ville de Paris (75) and Yvelines (78)

Région description

The Ile-de-France *région* includes the city of Paris and the surrounding area. It is one of the smallest *régions* geographically, covering only 2% of the total area of France, but its 11 million inhabitants represent almost 19% of the French population, making Ile-de-France one of the most populated urban areas in Europe.

Paris is a beautiful city. It has everything a city lover could possibly desire. Chic little boutiques and huge department stores, wonderful art galleries and performance spaces, superb restaurants, and huge flea and antique markets. There are elegant squares and pretty parks and the Seine must be the most romantic waterfront in the world.

Paris is certainly an ideal place for those living in central London to have a second, albeit second *urban*, home. It's an easy weekend trip by Eurostar and bought-in-advance tickets are very cheap. For those used to London, Paris seems a lot smaller and more manageable. Even though the Metro map looks like a bowl of spaghetti, it's very fast, efficient, clean and once you get to grips with it, easy to navigate.

While Eurostar tickets can be cheap, apartments in Paris are not. It is the most expensive *région* in France and apartments in the most fashionable areas are not much cheaper than in London's most desirable areas, although it is still possible to find a studio flat in central locations for around €100,000. If you go looking for a studio flat be warned: some are no more than simply a cupboard in an attic with a dormer window, a one-unit kitchenette and a shared bathroom down a dark corridor. Unless you are buying such a studio for investment purposes, perhaps to let to students, then you'd probably have a more comfortable time staying in hotels every time you visit the city.

Régions

Ile-de-France is one of Europe's richest *régions* and accounts for 28.6% of France's GDP. It is home to many headquarters in France (38% of company headquarters, including 70% of insurance company headquarters and 96% of bank headquarters). Salary levels are also 10-15% higher on average than the rest of France. If you speak English but not a word of French, yet have good transferable professional (as well as interpersonal) skills, it's still likely that you could find a job at one of the many pan-international companies based here. And if you don't and are happy to do anything in order to make your way, there's plenty of low-skill or no-skill (but often gruelling and exploitative) work to be found, such as cleaning hotel rooms, waiting tables or dish-washing. Keep George Orwell's *Down and Out in Paris and London* in your back pocket for company though! You could also make a lucrative living teaching English.

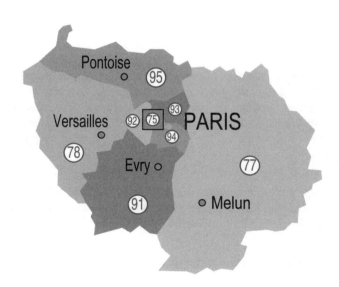

Languedoc-Roussillon

Population

Population: 2,295,648

Density (people per km^2): 87

Départements

Aude (11), Gard (30), Hérault (34), Lozère (48), Pyrénées-Orientales (66)

Région description

Languedoc-Roussillon in south-west France curves around a corner of the Mediterranean, from Provence in the east down to the borders with Spain and Andorra in the south. The modern *région* was formed when two historic provinces were merged. Languedoc takes its name from *langue d'oc*, a language closely linked to Catalan, and Roussillon in the far south was known as France's Catalonia, but today Catalonia is confined to an autonomous *région* in north-eastern Spain.

The southernmost extension of the *Massif Central* can be found in the north. Here, the *Parc Naturel Régional du Haut Languedoc* is to the west made up of deciduous forest, and to the east dry and craggy. The very isolated and mountainous *Lozère* is a wilderness where hermits and exiles have long sought refuge. To the west of the *région* are the *Grands Causses*, deep canyons above which lie limestone plateaus. The *Montagne Noire*, Corbière hills and the Cévennes are all areas of dramatic hills, mountains and deep river gorges.

The landscape flattens around the tranquil *Canal Du Midi*, which cuts across the *région's* middle with Carcassonne, a world heritage site, at its centre. South of the canal gentle rolling foothills start to ascend, climbing to the dramatic peaks of the *Pyrénnées*.

The *région's* Mediterranean coast is an area of river deltas and coastal plains. In some places there are ugly purpose-built developments but there are also some more alluring seaside places such as the picturesque port of Coullioure in Roussillon and attractive fishing villages such as Sète and Palavas. The coastline of Lower-Languedoc is cut off from the hinterland by marshy *étangs* (lagoons), which have prevented the same sort of furious development that has blighted the Côte d'Azur and the Spanish Costas.

Languedoc-Roussillon has a good mix of lively cities and picturesque medieval villages. Barcelona is an easy day-trip (and possible commute) away on the other side of the mountains and there is good autoroute and TGV access to Paris. For many years the *région* was in decline as people moved from their villages to northern cities, but now more and more people are moving back.

It is also growing in popularity with second home owners, as property is cheaper here than in Provence and Côte d'Azur, and it's easily accessible from the UK thanks to an increasing number of airports served by budget airlines. It's not the best place to find work as it has a high level of unemployment, mainly due to a population growing more rapidly than the supply of new jobs, and it is one of the least industrialised *régions* in the country with only 21% of its GDP accounted for by industry. Employment is highly service-oriented, with 68% of its workforce employed in the service sector. Telecommunications is a large industry and there are many call centres. Agriculturally, milk production from goats, sheep and cows is important and the major crops are peaches, nectarines, apricots, melon and rice. Beziers is capital of the *région's* wine industry around which some excellent wines such as Corbières, Minervois and Côtes du Roussillon are produced.

Régions

Three largest *communes*

Montpellier (287,981)

This lively, energetic and progressive city has long been an important trade centre and is today most known for being an important university city. With 60,000 students it's a youthful place – the average age is said to be just 25. The buzzing old city is almost entirely pedestrianised and has lots of bars and restaurants. This certainly should be one of the top places on the list for young people moving to France to consider. There are plenty of art galleries, theatres and music venues and to top it all off, the beach.

Perpignan (162,678)

This town, close to the Spanish border, has a distinctly southern feel and a lively street life. Most of its population is of Spanish origin, and there's also a large number of North Africans. Its heyday was in the 13th and 14th Centuries when the kings of Majorca held their court here. Unfortunately, in recent years, a relatively large percentage of the population has embraced the extreme right wing politics of Jean Marie Le Pen.

Nîmes (148 889)

This laid-back sunny city, close to the border with Provence, has the most extensive Roman remains in Europe. *Les Arènes*, the city's focal point, is the best-preserved Roman arena in the world, with seating capacity for 20,000 spectators. Once used for gladiators, today the summer crowds that flock to the arena are just as bloodthirsty, as it's the premier bull-fighting arena outside Spain. Nîmes is also known for denim, which was first manufactured in the city's textile mills and in the 19th Century exported to the southern USA to clothe the slaves. Modern Nîmes is now trying to keep up with its progressive neighbour, Montpellier, by recruiting a host of very fashionable architects and designers, including Norman Foster, Jean Nouvel and Philippe Starck, to instill it with a bit of architectural 'x' factor that's not 2,000 years old.

Limousin

Population

Population: 710,939

Density (people per km^2): 42

Départements

Corrèze (19), Creuse (23), Haute-Vienne (87)

Région description

Limousin, located in central France, is one of the most rural *régions* in the country and is perfect for those looking for tranquillity and remote, unspoiled landscapes. Its green wooded hills are dotted with old churches, castles, charming villages and *bastides*. It's an excellent territory for fishing, canoeing, kayaking and sailing, and fishing and watersports lovers will be in their element as there are deep gorges, numerous rivers and '1,000' lakes. The only large town is Limoges, a pleasant place famed for its pottery.

It's often called *France Profonde* (meaning the 'heartland of France'). Another way it's been described is as the gateway between the serious industrious north and the relaxed southern world of the Mediterranean. Property and living costs are a lot cheaper than neighbouring *régions* and this sparsely populated *région* is largely undiscovered by foreigners. Located next to the Dordogne, it is however becoming more popular with British second homebuyers. There is still plenty of run-down or deserted property to be found here, perfect for those keen on searching for restoration projects.

Limousin's major industry is agriculture but, as the soil is not particularly fertile, livestock – particularly cattle – accounts for more than 90% of total output. Several years ago, a mass exodus from agriculture resulted in the French government going so far as to advertise in the British agricultural press, offering support to British farmers wishing to go to France to revive Limousin's farming industry. The large agricultural sector has attracted the agro foods industry, with companies such as BSN, the French food conglomerate, basing themselves in the *région*. The *région* also supplies France with 25% of its gold production and 50% of its uranium.

In recent years, impoverished Limousin has been the focus of economic development and many companies have been offered incentives and subsidies for installing themselves here. New investments include a science park and research institutions, and 12,000 companies have relocated to the area. Legrand, a world leader in low-voltage electrical equipment, has located its headquarters and manufacturing centre in the area. Also, Limousin's pulp and paper industry is undergoing a good deal of expansion, as until now its 550,000 hectares of woodland have been very much an untapped resource.

All this new activity, combined with cheap property, means that this is potentially a good place for newcomers on the look-out for employment opportunities and a peaceful, green living environment.

Three largest *communes*

Limoges (173,299)

Limoge's name has been synonymous with fine porcelain since the 1770s when European artists set out to copy techniques perfected by the Chinese five centuries earlier. There are plenty of crafts museums about town showing examples of Limoges pottery but the kaolin mines are long-exhausted and any living industry is thin on the ground. The city's landmark building is *Cathédrale St-Etienne* which, built on the model of the cathedral at Amiens, is one of the few Gothic churches south of the Loire. Limoges has a lively student population and in late September there's an important gathering of writers, dramatists and musicians at the *Festival International des Théâtres Francophones*. Every other January there's a contemporary dance festival and on the third Friday of October the town's few vegetarians make exodus while everyone else hordes into the *Rue de la Boucherie* to gorge on pig's trotters, sheep's testicles and all sorts of charming offal.

Brive-la-Gallarde (65,411)

This town is a major rail junction and about as close to an industrial centre as you can get in Limousin. It's not a particularly attractive place although is very close to some of the Corrèze *région's* most beautiful villages. It's known throughout France for its champion rugby team.

Tulle (18,547)

In the Corrèze, this town is strung out for 3km along a deep narrow valley of the *département's* eponymous river. From a distance it looks bleak and grey but once you reach its heart, it's a fascinating place with lots of winding lanes and stairways bordered by very handsome houses. Firearms and lace were once the major industries of this town and it was home to France's last accordion factory.

Lorraine

Population

Population: 2,310 376

Density (people per km^2): 98

Départments

Meurthe-et-Moselle (54), Meuse (55), Moselle (57), Vosges (88)

Région description

Lorraine, in the far north-east, is often called the *Pays de Trois Frontiers* (the land of three frontiers) as it shares borders with Germany, Belgium and Luxembourg. Geologically, western Lorraine is composed of rolling hills of clay separated by the north-to-south running limestone ridges of the *Côtes de Meuse* and *Côtes de Moselle*. The heavy soils of these rolling plains support mixed farming: dairy, oats and wheat, and the ridges have worked as defensive barriers during the many times that Lorraine has been threatened with attack. The cities of Metz, Nancy, Verdun, Thionville and Toul are route centres and fortress cities defending the gaps in the ridges. Between 1871 and 1918, the *département* of Moselle in the east was annexed, along with Alsace, by Germany following France's defeat in the Franco-Prussian War. It was again controlled by Germany from 1940 to 1945. The bloodiest battle of World War I – the Battle for Verdun – took place on Lorraine's unfortunate soil. Here, hundreds of thousands of French men were brutally killed and today most of the visitors to the *région* are those on sad pilgrimages to see where their forefathers lost their lives.

Much of Lorraine's landscape has been exploited by industry. Iron ore fields of about 110km (70 miles) long and 20km (12 miles) wide, run from Nancy northward to the primary iron and steel district around Longwy, Thionville and Metz. The French part of the Saar coalfield lies for 64km (40 miles) in the east. In the south-east, Lorraine rises gradually to the summits of the Vosges. This sandstone massif has a granite core exposed in the south, where elevations exceed 1,200m (3,937ft). The political and linguistic divide between French Lorraine and the more Germanic Alsace runs along its crest.

Although the two main cities, Nancy and Metz, are very handsome, the landscape is bleak – dominated either by industry or by windswept agricultural plains, making it unpopular with second home owners. Living costs and property prices, however, are low.

Three largest *communes*

Nancy (331,363)

Nancy is an attractive and sophisticated city located on the Rhine-Marne canal which goes from Paris to Strasbourg. At the turn of the century it became an important centre of Art Nouveau. Practitioners of Art Nouveau in Nancy were visually influenced by orientalism and Baroque. This style became known as the 'School of Nancy'. There are a number of buildings around the city with decorative features in this style and, if you keep your eyes peeled, many small expressions of the movement, especially on stained glass windows and on the elaborate grillwork on entrances of homes, shops and banks. There are many fine shops to be found selling fancy goods such as chocolates and fine glass works.

Metz (322,526)

Metz (pronounced 'Mess'), the capital of Lorraine, sits on the east bank of the River Moselle and is close to the autoroute that links Paris and Strasbourg. It is a dignified city with stately public squares and lovely riverside parks with ponds, fountains, ducks and swans. It has a historic commercial centre and its large university makes it lively place. The *Théâtre* (1738-53) is France's oldest theatre building still in use.

Thionville (130,480)

Half an hour from Luxembourg and Germany this is a handsome city with many monuments. Most visitors to Thionville are those with an interest in military history.

Midi-Pyrénées

Population

Population: 2,551,687

Density (people per km^2): 56

Départements

Arège (09), Aveyron (12), Gers (32), Haute-Garonne (31), Hautes-Pyrénées (65), Lot (46), Tarn (81) and Tarn-et-Garonne (82)

Région description

In the south-west, the Midi-Pyrénées, which lies between Aquitaine to the west and Languedoc-Roussillon to the east, is a large *région* with a size almost equivalent to Switzerland and Luxembourg put together. It has eight *départements*, each with its own strong character. Magnificent mountain scenery can be found both to the north and south of the *région*. The north east encompasses part of the *Causses* which is high plateau country. This is a land of plains dotted with hillocks, sandy stretches, moors and pine woods, desolate plateaux and little valleys covered with impenetrable forests. Birds and small animals feed on the thyme and juniper growing wild in the chalky soil and as a result are hunted for their delicious and unique flavour.

The villages and farmhouses of Aveyron, a majestically stark landscape of granite outcrops and steep ravines, are built of local rock and often mimic the rock formations to the extent that they are all but invisible to outsiders.

Lot is a *département* that has become very popular with foreign buyers, particularly the British, because it neighbours the long-popular Dordogne. Character property, particularly in the beautiful *bastides* (fortified villages), is less expensive here. The Lot is noticeably hotter and drier than the Dordogne. Here, the serpentine River Lot and its many tributaries have cut dramatic gorges into the dry limestone plateau.

The *département* of Gers, just west of Toulouse, lies at the heart of the historic province of Gascony (today often dubbed France's Tuscany). The rolling countryside is lushly green and sleepy *bastides* dominate the hilltops. Here *foie gras* is the local delicacy and Armagnac the locally produced drink. This area has only recently been discovered by foreigners and is becoming increasingly popular.

Further south, the hills rise to the dramatic *Pyrénées*. The 19th Century saw a major exodus from rural areas and Ariège, the *département* furthest south, was particularly affected, losing much of its population to the industrial north.

Today people are moving back to these once deserted areas and outsiders are realising that the Midi-Pyrénées is an ideal place for a first or second home. The white sandy beaches of the Atlantic or the golden sun-baked Mediterranean beaches are a couple of hours drive or train ride to the west or east. Then, in the winter, the ski resorts of the Pyrénées are a short drive south. When you are feeling less outdoorsy you have Toulouse, one of the finest and most attractive cities in France, with its many superb shops, museums and restaurants to explore.

The people of the Midi-Pyrénées are warm and easy-going and receptive to foreigners, as for centuries newcomers have sought exile here. During the Spanish Civil War for instance, thousands of republican refugees flowed over the frontier to settle, especially in Toulouse, instilling new blood and energy into the *région*.

Midi-Pyrénées today is divided between high-tech Toulouse and the deep countryside with its traditional agricultural products. Toulouse is the largest aerospace centre outside of Paris. The sector employs more than 56,000 workers and €13 billion worth of products are exported each year. Agriculturally, the principal crops are grapes for eating, prunes, melons, apples and sunflowers. The *région* also produces 60% of France's garlic.

Three largest *communes*

Toulouse (761,090)

Toulouse, capital of the *région,* is a beautiful and vibrant city that's often called the *Ville Rose* because of the rosy colour of its brickwork. Toulouse has long been a prosperous place. At the end of the Middle Ages, pastel, a plant used to dye cloth, became fashionable, and the *région* filled its coffers by exporting it along with goose feathers from the Gers, and wines from Ariège and Gaillac. This commerce failed in the middle of the 16th Century, due to the wars of religion. House-to-house fighting put an end to any thoughts of export. The cruelty of the papists rivalled that of the Huguenots, and the plague swept through the *région*, reducing the population significantly. Today it's prosperous once more, thanks to the aerospace industry, and is a lively, cosmopolitan place with France's second largest student population after Paris. For city-lovers moving to France, Toulouse is a fine choice.

Régions

Tarbes (77,414)

Tarbes in the south is a major commercial and administrative centre. This town has a history as a military base and it's also used as a base for pilgrims looking for miracle cures at nearby Lourdes. The local stud farm, *Les Haras*, where chivalry horses are bred, is a popular attraction.

Albi (66,231)

Albi is another red-brick city, smaller but no less interesting than Toulouse, located on the River Tarn. The mammoth red-brick cathedral of *Saint Cécile*, towers above all the other buildings and was built as a fortress to protect a cruel bishop who imposed the church on the populace. The nearby 13th Century Palace of the Archbishop (also fortified) is now a museum containing the most comprehensive collection of the works of Toulouse-Lautrec, who was born in the town. Each year Albi is host to three good festivals – jazz, theatre and classical music.

Nord-Pas-De-Calais

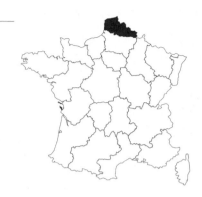

Population

Population: 3,996,588

Density (people per km²): 322

Départements

Nord (59), Pas-de-Calais (62)

Région description

One of the smallest *régions*, but with the densest population after Ile-de-France, Nord-Pas-De-Calais is largely industrialised with 35% of the population working in heavy industry, although much of this industry is in decline. Historically, the *région* has been heavily dependent on coal mines, as well as the iron, steel and metallurgical industries, which employed a high percentage of the workforce. Since the mines and many of the plants closed, unemployment has increased and remains well above the national average. A concerted effort is being made to re-employ these workers by attracting new investment to the area. This includes tax incentives, grants, free enterprise zones and low-interest loans.

Nord-Pas-De-Calais shares its border with Belgium and so there is a strong Flemish influence. Many people still speak Flemish and the locals drink more beer than wine, especially noticeable during carnivals or annual fairs.

Accessibility to northern European countries is good thanks to excellent rail and road links. There is great accessibility to the UK, via a number of passenger ports and Eurostar at Lille. Over twenty million people pass through Calais each year and it's often scoffed at by those who associate it with beer-bellied day-trippers simply stocking up on booze and fags. Most people rush away from the area as soon as they can, without discovering the spectacular 40km coastline – the *Côte d'Opale* – between Calais and Boulogne. This coast is at the narrowest stretch of *La Manche* (the English Channel) and is the closest to the white cliffs of Dover. Sandy beaches can be found at Sangatte and Wissant and, dig deeper into the countryside, and you'll find lovely woodland, river valleys, market gardens, fine golf courses and pretty villages.

The *région's* accessibility means there are many British second home owners. Prices of property in the more attractive areas are driven up because of this, although bargains can be still found. It is more expensive close to coastal areas although not extortionate compared with the coasts of other *régions*.

Only 5% of the work force is employed in agriculture. The main crops are potatoes, chicory, garden peas and green beans.

Régions

Three largest *communes*

Lille (1,000,900)

The largest city in the north, by far, is Lille, a very industrious city surrounded by a huge sprawl of suburbs and industrial plants. Some of France's worst poverty can be found here and it's also known for racial tension. Once you get through the sprawl, its *Vieux Ville* has lots of character (much of which is Flemish-influenced), and beyond the three large public squares at its centre there's a warren of red-brick terraces on cobbled lanes and passages. Lille is a prosperous commercial centre and on Saturday is jam-packed with shoppers. There are also some fine restaurants, theatres, museums and art galleries. The town has a pristine metro system and, with its Eurostar and TGV links, it has become an important transport hub in northern Europe. The town has successfully capitalised on this and has established a reputation as an international business centre.

Douai-Lens (518,727)

In the midst of mining country and only 35km south of Lille, this town although badly damaged in both world wars is surprisingly attractive and lively with streets of 18th Century houses cut through by the river and canal. It was a haven for English Catholics fleeing Protestant oppression in Tudor England.

Valenciennes (357,395)

Close to the border with Belgium, Valenciennes is a major industrial town. Its principal activities are automobile construction, mechanical engineering, railway construction and chemicals. The town, like so many in northern France, was badly damaged in the two World Wars. Today it has a large university population with over 30,000 students.

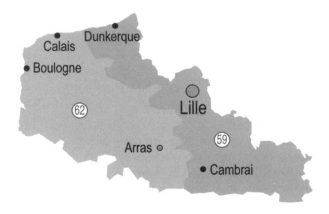

Pays de la Loire

Population

Population: 3,222,061

Density (people per km²): 100

Départements

Loire-Atlantique (44), Maine-et-Loire (49), Mayenne (53), Sarthe (72) and Vendée (85)

Région description

Pays de la Loire, in western France, has a diverse, if low-lying landscape, residing largely in the *Massif Armoricain*. The wild and rugged Atlantic coast in the west contrasts with the lush, green countryside and rivers of the Loire valley in the centre. There are vast rural areas, many devoted to agriculture, plus large urban conurbations and economic centres. It has a temperate climate with mild winters and warm summers.

Loire-Atlantique has 137km (85 miles) of rocky and sandy coastline, including 27km (17 miles) of coast dotted with resorts and known as the *Côte de Jade,* because of the green colour of the sea. Besides many scenic and rural areas, plus vineyards producing the dry Muscadet wine, the *région* is known mainly for the Nantes/Saint-Nazaire area – a major ship-building and industrial complex.

Vendée is a popular destination for tourists, with over 200km (125 miles) of sandy beaches and two offshore islands – Noirmoutier and Yeu. Cultural and 'green' tourism predominate inland. The coast is lined with woods, including the *Forêt d'Olonne*, and the *département* is bordered, north and south, with extensive salt marshes which are popular for bird-watching. Vendée's architectural heritage is evident in its impressive châteaux, abbeys and fine churches. Tourism is now the premier industry of the *département*.

Maine-et-Loire, known locally as the *Val d'Anjou*, was formed mainly from the historic province of Anjou. It is also known as the 'valley of the kings' due to its royal past and its legacy of châteaux, abbeys, romantic churches and manor houses which attract 2.3 million tourists each year.

The landscape is dominated by the Loire river and its tributaries, of which nine are navigable. The river is surrounded by a broad, fertile plain covered with lush green vegetation, market gardens, orchards and vineyards. Notable wines include Rosé d'Anjou and Saumur – available in sparkling and still varieties.

Régions

There are also fascinating troglodyte caves with 1,000km of underground tunnels – many converted into wine cellars, art galleries and mushroom farms; and large forested areas running the length of the valley – mainly *forêt domaniale*, equivalent to the British National Trust.

The most visited towns are the flowered city of Angers, with its enormous fortress of King Rene, followed by Saumur, home of the *Cadre Noir* horse-riding academy, and the Romanesque *Notre-Dame-de-Nantilly*, displaying notable 15th-17th Century tapestries. The 12th Century *Fontevrault-l'Abbaye* near Saumur is also popular, with its statues and graves of Henry II of England, his wife, Eleanor of Aquitaine, and their son Richard I (the Lion Heart).

The *département* of Sarthe consists largely of undulating fields and woodland sculpted by the Sarthe river. It has a rich architectural heritage, with numerous châteaux at Verdelles, Montmirail, Bazouges-sur-le-Loir and Le Lude. The Mayenne *département* is predominantly wooded and hilly with around 55 miles of navigable river. It is not as popular with tourists, but does have some interesting châteaux, abbeys and prehistoric caves. The cattle market at *Château-Gontier* is one of the most important in France.

Pays de la Loire is the fifth most populated *région* in France, although significant differences exist between the *départements*. Mayenne, for example has 55 inhabitants per square km, whilst Loire-Atlantique appears relatively crowded with 166 inhabitants per square km. It also has a young population, with 30% under 25 years of age.

Property prices are slightly lower than the average for France but have been rising steadily in the past few years, particularly in the coastal areas and the Loire valley, making it a good place to invest in property. There is also a high speed (two hour) TGV link between Nantes and Paris which has benefited the local economy, tourism and the property market.

The economy was traditionally based on agro foods, but today boasts an impressive and diverse economic portfolio with many small and medium sized businesses. The *région* is now the fifth wealthiest in France, and unemployment is consistently lower than the national average.

The *région* is the second largest in France for both agriculture and livestock breeding, and the fifth largest for fishing. Food processing is the leading employer in the *région's* industrial sector – primarily dairy products, biscuit manufacturing and pork products. The Nantes/Saint-Nazaire port complex is the leading French centre for ship building. Wood processing ranks number one nationally and fashion ranks second. Other strong sectors include: aeronautics and plastics (both second nationally); the automobile industry, which dominates the town of Le Mans; and the electronics and computer industry. Tourism also plays a major part in the local economy, providing 61,000 salaried jobs in the summer season.

Three largest *communes*

Nantes (406,000)

Nantes is the capital of the Loire-Atlantique *département* and the Pays de la Loire *région*.

When France developed trade with its colonies, Nantes became an important sea port and, prior to abolition, was the slave trade capital of France. Today, the Nantes/Saint-Nazaire area is a major industrial area in western France, concentrating on port activities and ship building plus sugar processing and the production of food products, tobacco, household appliances, building materials and textiles.

Significant historical buildings include the *Château des Ducs de Bretagne*, the *Saint-Pierre-et-Saint-Paul* cathedral and the *Musée des Beaux-Arts*. Notable citizens have included the politician Georges Clémenceau and the writer Jules Verne.

Angers (208,000)

Angers, capital of Maine-et-Loire, has a long history and many impressive medieval buildings, the finest being the twin-spired Cathedral of St Maurice, dating from the 12th Century. Angers is also a centre of learning. Its educational institutions host 30,000 students and provide faculties of theology, law, science, letters and agriculture, as well as a national school of arts and trades. Local industries include liqueur distillation (Cointreau) and the manufacturing of cables, ropes, electrical equipment, machinery, woollen and leather goods.

Le Mans (190,000)

Le Mans, capital of Sarthe, has many notable buildings which provide a testament to its historic past, including the Saint-Julien Cathedral (11th-15th Century), the Church of *Notre-Dame-de-la-Couture* (10th-13th Century), and the Church of *Sainte-Jeanne d'Arc* (11th Century).

Modern Le Mans is an industrial and marketing centre, home to numerous manufacturers of automobiles, railroads, textiles, plastics and tobacco products. It is also known as the 'insurance company town' of France. But it is perhaps best known for its motor sports, in particular the Le Mans *Circuit de la Sarthe*, which hosts the renowned *24 heures* automobile race.

Picardie

Population

Population: 1,857,481

Density (people per km^2): 96

Départements

Aisne (02), Oise (60), Somme (80)

Région description

This *région* in northern France borders the Ile-de-France to the south, and the Nord-Pas-de-Calais in the north. Before the last Ice Age, the *région* just south of the English Channel was attached to the chalk lands of southern England. For many people, Picardie will stand for a place where far too many men lost their lives in the wars of the last century: during World War I, it was the scene of the battles of the Somme, several of the most costly and devastating battles of the war. Agincourt, Creçy and Saint-Quentin are also well-known, poppy-carpeted battlefields. But despite its battle-weary history, Picardie is a land of peace and tranquillity.

The *région* has one of the most unspoilt stretches of coastline in the whole of France. Due to little development, the coast has kept all its original beauty and visitors will find it bathed in the half tones of light that artists such as Sisley, Degas or Seurat came to capture. The Somme estuary, which is very popular with sailing enthusiasts, is lined with pretty fishing hamlets. Le Crotoy is an estuary village that has long attracted many artists and writers and it was here that Jules Verne wrote *Twenty Thousand Leagues Under the Sea*. The dunes and marshes along the majestic Somme harbour a bird sanctuary and the area is also host to a huge range of flora and fauna.

With unspoilt shores, plains and forests, canals and rivers, the *région* is a haven for anyone who enjoys fishing and water sports. It's also an ideal place for cycling and riding. Horse riding is an important regional sport and Chantilly is the country's thoroughbred capital. The *Grandes Ecuries*, next to the racecourse, stables 240 of the country's finest horses. Archery has also been a popular sport since the Middle Ages and there's a major archery festival each spring. For golfing enthusiasts there are some of the best golf courses in the whole of France to choose from.

Picardie is the cradle of gothic art with six splendid cathedrals and numerous churches and abbeys. Amiens, Beauvais, Laon, Senlis, Noyon and Soissons are known for their massive cathedrals and the beautiful old towns of all these towns remain very much living and working places and not just heritage centres. To the south, the *châteaux* of *Chantilly* and *Compiègne* are nestled in a large forest that once extended from Paris to the eastern frontier.

Picardie is known for its dairy and beef cattle and is also a strong arable *région*. It produces 25% of all French agricultural exports and is the second largest wheat producer in the country. Grain accounts for 54% of the *région's* farm income and intensive vegetable cultivation is important, especially in the high yielding, arable land of the Somme river valley where market gardeners intensively cultivate the soil on tiny plots linked by a network of narrow canals.

This high level of agricultural activity has promoted a formidable agro foods industry and agricultural machinery sector. It is the country's largest producer of canned and frozen vegetables (through the company Findus), as well as refined sugar, and is the second largest producer of ready-to-eat convenience foods (through Herta). The agro foods industry is headed by a network of research centres, including the *Compiègne* University Biotechnology Centre, with support from the close partnership established between producers, manufacturers and distributors.

The heart of the tranquil Somme Valley is less than an hour's drive from Calais on the A16, and Beauvais, the capital of Oise, is less than an hour's drive from Paris.

Three largest *communes*

Amiens (160,815)

Amiens is dominated by the *Cathédrale Notre-Dame*, the largest gothic cathedral in Europe. The main place to hang out in Amiens is in the regenerated *St-Leu* – a medieval quarter north of the cathedral – where a very Flemish-looking network of canals can be found. This was once the centre of Amiens' textile industry. The town still produces much of the country's velvet but today the factories have moved out to the suburbs and have been replaced by loft-living and lots of fashionable restaurants, cafés and bars. On the edge of town the canals cease their role as the vistas for al fresco diners and become working waterways for a series of very fertile market gardens (called *hortillonnages*) reclaimed from the marshes. Here, the farmers travel about canals in black, high-browed punts and some still take their produce into town by boat to sell at the waterside Saturday morning market.

Creil (97,455)

Creil is a pleasant town, a short drive from Paris, surrounded by forests. The Oise river runs through the town which has long been a nautical stopover for local merchants and pleasure boaters. The town has many traditions such as the *Foire aux Marrons* (chestnut festival) which takes places each year at the beginning of November. *Creil-Montereau's* porcelain is highly sought after by collectors. Porcelain was a very lucrative industry in the 19th Century, until the factory closed its doors in 1895.

Compiègne (69,903)

This sleepy town, 80km north of Paris, has little going for it other than its opulent 17th and 18th Century royal palace at the edge of the attractive *Forêt de Compiègne*. The other pull for visitors is the start of one of the world's toughest one-day cycling races, Paris-Roubaix, on the first Sunday after Easter each year. The town's *Université de Technologie de Compiègne* (UTC) is a first-class, internationally-renowned technological college

Poitou-Charentes

Population

Population: 1,640,068

Density (people per km^2): 64

Départements

Charente (16), Charente-Maritime (17), Deux-Sévres (79) and Vienne (86)

Région description

Poitou-Charentes is a tranquil and largely unspoilt *région* halfway down the west coast. Its long Atlantic coastline has fine sandy beaches, pretty marinas and bustling resorts. There are a number of beautiful islands such as the nineteen mile long *Ile d'Oléron* which is popular with naturists and whose main industry is oyster catching. Another island, *Ile de Ré,* is known for its salt marshes and is reputed to receive more hours of sunshine than anywhere else in France away from the Mediterranean. A bridge linking it with the mainland makes it easily accessible to outsiders, to the chagrin of residents who feel that the island's previous pleasant seclusion has gone and traffic has hugely increased. On the mainland, Royan, at the southern tip of the *région*, is a busy tourist resort with five well-kept but congested beaches, or *conches* as they're referred to.

Inland Poitou-Charentes also has plenty to offer. The marshes of *Marais Poitevin* are often dubbed by tourist guides as the 'Green Venice'. The serene and lush expanse of fields can be explored by rowing boat or kayak along the canals which were built by 11th Century monks. The town of Cognac is a popular place to visit. Here, visitors can sample the world famous brandy and see how the distilling process takes place. Close to Poitiers is the Futuroscope theme park where cinema and special effects are pushed to their limit in an attempt to give an educational glimpse into the future of visual technology. It claims to have the biggest screen in Europe.

Farming is important to the economy and wheat, corn, melons and sunflowers are major crops. The dairy industry is also important and there are many cattle farms and vineyards. Away from agriculture, there are many industries producing machinery and chemicals. Niort, in the *département* of *Deux-Sèvres*, is well-known throughout France for being the main centre of the French insurance industry.

With its lovely beaches, pretty pleasant interior and mild climate, it's certainly a good place for a second or permanent home.

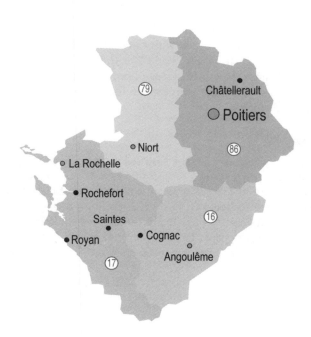

Three largest *communes*

Poitiers (119,371)

Poitiers, the ancient capital of the *région*, is perched on a hill overlooking the River Clain. The city has a captivating history involving some of the most famous French battles. The city's long history is revealed by the many historic sites such as the Roman baths and amphitheatres, the Baptistery of Saint John (4th-12th Century), the Cathedral of Saint Pierre (12th-14th Century), and the Palace of the Counts of Poitou. It has long been a reputed seat of learning with a well-established university founded in 1431, and a beautiful Romanesque cathedral. Today the town is the agricultural, industrial, and administrative centre of the *région*.

Régions

La Rochelle (116,157)

This town, known as 'the pearl of the Charente' is both an important Atlantic coast fishing port and a popular summer resort. During the 16th Century it was a centre of Huguenot resistance to the crown. Conceded by treaty to the Huguenots in 1573, the city was besieged by Cardinal Richelieu in 1627-28. The old section of the city still contains the 16th Century town hall and 14th Century towers guarding the harbour entrance. During the 18th Century, La Rochelle's port handled most of France's trade with Canada but, with the loss of Canada, port activity declined. Later, during World War II, La Rochelle was occupied by the Germans and withstood an Allied siege from September 1944 to May 1945. Today, major industries include petroleum refining and chemical, aircraft and automobile manufacturing.

Angoulême (103,746)

Deep inland, Angoulême is a lovely, fortified town built on two levels by the River Charente. The town was the subject of a fierce tussle between the English and the French in the 100 Years War and also suffered terrible damage during the 16th Century Wars of Religion. It has a rich tradition of paper-making which dates back to the 17th Century when the river water was thought to be so pure as to produce the best quality paper in the country. Angoulême also manufactures a wide variety of goods such as machinery, carpets and textiles and is a centre for the wine trade.

Provence-Alpes-Côte d'Azur

Population

Population: 4,506,151

Density (people per km^2): 144

Départements

Alpes-de-Haute-Provence (04), Hautes-Alpes (05), Alpes-Maritimes (06), Bouches-du-Rhône (13), Var (83), Vaucluse (84)

Région description

In the south-east corner of the country, stretching from the southern Alps to the French Riviera, with the border of Italy and Monaco to the east, Provence-Alpes-Côte d'Azur is a land of many contrasts. Second home owners along the coast include fast car and yacht-loving ex-film stars, over-tanned wannabies and wealthy casino-addicted pensioners from all over Europe who live in white modern villas with pools or apartment blocks clustered about resorts such as St Tropez, Cannes and St Raphäel. Further inland, the rugged Provençal scenery is inhabited by consumers of the more rustic sort of chic. Don't go searching for a wreck around here as they were all renovated years ago, not long after publication of that Peter Mayle book!

It's not difficult to see why so many people want to live in this *région*. The climate and quality of life are among the best in France. The landscape of inland Provence is alluring with stunning rock formations and rich coloured dazzling soils – don't visit the village of Roussillon in flip-flops as the bright red soil will stain your feet and ankles for days! Between the rugged hills and mountains, there are deep gorges plus fertile valleys filled with carpets of lavender, almond groves and ancient olive trees and vines. Everywhere you can smell the pleasant aromas of wild herbs such lemon verbena, rosemary, thyme and basil. This land smells so sweet that it's no wonder that perfume is a big local industry.

On the Côte d'Azur, February is a particularly lovely time when the mimosa blossoms into a vibrant array of colour and, in summer, it's heaven to sit beneath the shade of an umbrella pine and watch the blue water sparkle. It's easy to understand why the dazzling light of this area attracted so many modernist artists such as Matisse, Chagall, Picasso and Cocteau. If you want to get away from the 'playground of the rich and famous' you can visit Camargue in the west, which is an important national park with lagoons, wild white ponies and pink flamingos.

The downsides of buying a home here is that, along with Ile-de-France, it is one of the most expensive *régions* and property prices are very high. Parts of the *région*, especially those close to the coast, are heavily populated. In the summer, because it's such a popular tourist destination (especially with Northern Europeans), the beaches are packed, towns are clogged with traffic and the pretty fortified hill-top villages are full to the brim with visitors following the arrows of the *circuits touristiques*. These pretty villages are ideal places to visit or to have a second home, but not to live, as every other shop is a gift shop selling little else but postcards, pottery and pot pourri.

On the plus side, average salaries are the second highest in the country, second only to Ile-de-France. With 7.6% of the country's population (including a substantial number of retired persons), the *région* contributes 6.8% of France's GDP. Marseille, the *région's* capital, along with its satellite cities, hosts hundreds of companies in the fields of logistics (mainly in Vitrolles), computing, business services (Aix-en-Provence) and industry (Aubagne). The cities of Nice and Cannes offer the Riviera culture while Avignon and Aix-en-Provence are cities of culture and academic excellence. Agriculturally, Provence produces three-quarters of France's rice, almost two-thirds of the country's olives and half of its eating grapes. Apples, peaches, nectarines, cherries and pears are also big crops as are cut flowers (43% of France's roses and 63% of its carnations are grown here).

Three largest *communes*

Marseille-Aix-en-Provence (1,349,772)

Gregarious Marseille is France's second largest city and an important sea port, the largest European port after Rotterdam. It has a reputation for being dangerous, with drug-money laundering, racial tension, prostitution and shoot-outs, but although many social ills can be found, underworld activities flourish just as much in the ritzier parts of the Côte d'Azur. Walking around the bustling, vibrant streets is far from intimidating and it's a lot safer than most of the Western world's major cities. The *Vieux-Port* is surrounded by roads and exhaust fumes and from this port steeply climbs *Le Panier* which is the oldest part of the city. It's a charming, if slightly grotty area, but it may soon be gentrified now that rich Parisiens can make weekend trips on the recent TGV link.

Under the German occupation Marseille was a hot bed of resistance fighters, Jews and Communists, until the Germans came and gave the 20,000 inhabitants one day to evacuate before laying down dynamite and blowing the area closest to the port to smithereens. The North African area – where buckets of colourful spices, cloths and metalware are traded – is certainly worth a visit. The outskirts of Marseille's sixteen *arrondissements* are surrounded by high-rise 60s housing estates, which would look grim in the grey light of Peckham but are not such an eyesore in the sharp Mediterranean sunshine. It's hard to believe that the conglomeration extends to Aix-en-Provence, an extremely pretty but exceedingly bourgeois town with a rich cultural life and plenty of squares with ancient fountains and outdoor cafés.

Nice (888,784)

Nice is the capital of the Riviera and the fifth largest city in France. It has been one of Europe's most fashionable resorts since the 18th Century when Russian and English aristocrats built their mansions here. Later, wealthy Victorians enjoyed its winter climate. Today it's enjoyed by many heavily-perfumed old dears and their *diamanté* collar-wearing miniature poodles. The pretty old town with Italianate facades has lots of pleasant eateries and shady outdoor places to sit and watch the tourists go by. It has a pleasant enough beach, which is clean in the morning but gets dirtier throughout the day, until the evening when you can't see the pebbles for cigarette butts.

Toulon (519,640)

Half destroyed in the last war, Toulon is dominated by the military and associated industries. The arsenal that Louis XIV created is today one of the major employers in south-east France. The port is home to the French Navy's Mediterranean fleet, although the ship building yards are redundant. The town is controlled by the Front National and, compared with the many gorgeous places nearby, it is not an attractive place and its centre is somewhat run-down. Like many ports, the town is full of lively drinking holes where you can find interesting characters with plenty of stories propped against the bars.

Rhône-Alpes

Population

Population: 5,645,407

Density (people per km^2): 129

Départements

Ain (01), Ardèche (07), Drôme (26), Isère (38), Loire (42), Rhône (69), Savoie (73), Haute-Savoie (74)

Région description

Rhône-Alpes, just north of Provence-Alpes-Côte-d'Azur, is in south-east France and shares its eastern borders with Italy and Switzerland. The *région*, and particularly the *départements* Savoie and Haute-Savoie, is home to some of the most spectacular scenery in the country. The mountains rise steadily from *Lac Leman* (Lake Geneva) and keep climbing to the year-round ice-capped tip of Mont Blanc, the highest peak in Europe. In the winter it's a white-washed world of snow-capped peaks and icy lakes where everyone takes to the ski-slopes. In the summer months it's an entirely different place where you can enjoy the lowland pleasures of hiking through flower-filled meadows or swimming in the lakes. There are several national parks including the *Parc National De La Vanoise*, which is a wild mix of high mountains, steep valleys and glaciers. The area is also ideal for ambitious walkers, with 500km of marked trails. A holiday home here would be ideal for breaks at all times of the year and if let out could bring a year-round guaranteed rental income, especially if it's based in the swish ski resorts such as Chamonix and Val d'Isere. While visitors flock to the ski resorts each winter, in the remote valleys such as the Haute-Maurienne, rural life still goes on as it has for centuries, with the inhabitants hardened to the harsh climate and constant threat of avalanches.

The Alps can no longer be called a wilderness as there are many densely populated pockets. Building tends to be on the south-facing slopes that are warmer. Unfortunately air pollution caused by heavy traffic, tourism and the concentration of heavy industries (chemicals and metallurgy) has been a problem in the area.

One of the prettiest towns in the *région* is Annecy, capital of the Haute-Savoie, with its colonnaded streets and the tributaries of the *Canal de Thiou* lined with railings overflowing with geraniums. Annecy is surrounded by charming villages

Régions

and, next to *Lac d'Annecy,* there are plenty of water sports and beaches on which to picnic and bathe.

Not all the *région* is quite as dramatic as its eastern *départements*. The Beaujolais area north of Lyon is a land of pastures and forests. This area is mostly famous for its wines. The vineyards are found along a 60km narrow strip of terraces on the right bank of the River Saône. Beaujolais also produces many oils – not just olive oil, but pecan nut, almond and pine kernel oil. The *Parc Naturel du Pilat*, south of Lyon, offers stunning panoramic views across the Rhône Valley. The less explored Ardèche *département* is a great place for outdoor enthusiasts, especially walkers, cyclists and canoeists. Here is a land of deep chestnut forests, where eagles nest in the cliffs of steep gorges sliced by the tributaries of the River Saône.

Unemployment in the Rhone-Alpes is lower than the national average and average salaries rank among the top three highest paid *régions*. The Rhône Valley is France's highest-producing nuclear energy *région* and there are five nuclear power stations along the banks of the river.

Three largest *communes*

Lyon (1,348,832)

Lyon is widely considered to be the second most important city in France. It is a truly modern city and an important commercial, industrial and banking centre. It's also a majestic place with first class museums, a strong cultural life, a rich and varied entertainment scene (there are fifteen cinemas in town), an important university, classy shops and buzzing pedestrian malls. A line of impressive public squares is at the heart of the bustling city centre and the picture-postcard Renaissance old town, with 300 restored medieval and renaissance houses, is a UNESCO heritage site. In the late 1400s it became an important publishing centre with several hundred resident printers. It has also been a textile centre and by the 18th Century was Europe's silk-weaving capital. Since the 18th Century, Lyon has been an important centre of scientific research. A lively cosmopolitan and sophisticated place within a very short distance of hills, lakes and vineyards, Lyon would be a first-class city in which to set up home. It also has the advantage of a number of international schools.

Grenoble (419,334)

This city sits in a broad valley surrounded by mountains. Once renowned for its glove-making, today it is an important centre for nuclear research and home to chemicals and micro-electronic companies. There are a number of huge laboratories run by the Atomic Energy Commission on the banks of the River Drac. Grenoble has some good festivals throughout the year: jazz in March, rock in June and European theatre in June and July. It's a cosmopolitan place to eat and drink and, as a resort, it's a lot less flashy than some of the higher altitude resorts nearby. Lots of Arab and immigrant workers, a number of large foreign companies and a huge student population make for a modern, lively city with a good cultural mix.

Saint-Etienne (291,960)

Surrounded by warehouses, mine works and chimneys, St Etienne is an industrial town that has fallen on hard times. It's not quite as appealing as the other large towns of the *région*.

Appendices

Statistic	Average	Alsace	Aquitaine	Auvergne	Basse-Normandie	Bourgogne	Bretagne	Centre	Champagne-Ardenne	Corse	Franche-Comté
Region											
Region area, km	24,725	8,280	41,309	26,013	17,589	31,582	27,209	39,151	25,606	8,680	16,202
Population											
Population at last census	2,659,927	1,734,145	2,908,359	1,308,878	1,422,193	1,610,067	2,906,197	2,440,329	1,342,363	260,196	1,117,059
Population density, people per km	108	209	70	50	81	51	107	62	52	30	69
Population growth, %	2.9	6.8	4.0	-0.9	2.2	0.0	4.0	2.9	-0.4	3.9	1.8
% of population under 20 years old	24.1	24.9	22.2	21.5	25.2	23.3	24.1	24.1	25.3	22.1	25.2
% of population 60 plus years old	22.6	19.1	24.9	25.6	22.8	24.7	23.8	23.3	20.9	24.9	21.2
Life expectancy, men	74.9	75.3	75.6	74.4	74.8	74.6	74.0	75.5	74.3	74.7	75.5
Life expectancy, women	82.6	82.0	83.2	82.4	82.9	82.7	82.3	82.8	82.2	82.1	82.8
Business & Economy											
Gross domestic production, Û per person	21,963	24,844	21,931	20,622	20,582	21,958	21,063	21,791	22,589	18,359	21,235
No. of start-up establishments, total per 1000 pop	45	39	51	45	40	41	41	38	36	75	39
Employment & Salaries											
% of people in salaried employment	89.9	94.3	88.3	86.6	88.3	89.5	88.3	90.9	90.5	85.9	91.3
% of people in non-salaried employment	10.1	5.7	11.7	13.4	11.7	10.5	11.7	9.1	9.5	14.1	8.7
Quarterly unemployment level, % of regional pop	9.1	7.1	9.3	7.9	8.8	8.0	7.8	7.9	9.3	10.2	7.7
Average annual net salary, men, Û	18,876	20,195	18,677	17,734	17,638	18,326	18,195	18,963	18,332	17,273	18,224
Average annual net salary, women, Û	14,393	14,320	14,233	14,085	13,848	13,979	13,809	14,504	14,272	14,255	13,671
Property Prices											
Period property, average price, Û	102,238	143,208	121,491	75,177	86,494	85,354	107,072	92,858	97,354	24,808	98,662
New houses, average price, Û	117,661	157,183	128,031	11,148	109,304	115,005	131,608	116,832	110,433		116,952
Building land, average price, Û	23,136	53,006	36,717	22,159	19,575	21,276	29,143	24,328	26,063		2,334
Period property, average price, % divergence from average		40.1	18.8	-26.5	-15.4	-16.5	4.7	-9.2	-4.8		-3.5
New houses, average price, % divergence from average		33.6	8.8	-90.5	-7.1	-2.3	11.9	-0.7	-6.1		-0.6
Health											
Private hospital beds, short stay, per 1000 pop	1.4	1.5	1.8	1.4	1.0	1.4	1.2	1.1	1.3	2.2	0.8
Private hospital beds, continuing care and rehabilitation, per 1000 pop	0.9	1.1	1.3	0.8	0.8	0.7	0.9	0.7	0.2	1.6	0.6
Public hospital beds, short stay, per 1000 pop	2.8	3.1	2.6	3.0	3.5	3.1	2.8	2.6	3.1	2.7	3.4
Public hospital beds, continuing care and rehabilitation, per 1000 pop	0.7	0.5	0.6	1.0	0.5	0.8	0.8	0.6	0.7	0.6	0.7
Medical consultants/specialists, per 100,000 pop	66	78	100	67	55		69	64	58	102	56
Dental surgeons, per 100,000 pop	52	70	76	64	40		64	48	50	82	48
General practitioners, per 100,000 pop	98	112	128	112	99		111	96	102	128	111
State qualified nurses, per 100,000 pop	89	60	136	102	84		119	67	59	237	63
Tourism & Leisure											
Accommodation capacity of authorised hotels, total per 1000 pop	10.6	11.2	10.4	13.2	9.7	9.3	8.3	7.9	6.0	40.7	6.7
Accommodation capacity of authorised hotels, 4 star and luxury, % of total hotels	4.8	6.2	5.4	1.9	7.1	4.6	3.5	3.2	3.4	3.7	0.9
Accommodation capacity of camping sites, total per 1000 pop	20.1	6.7	36.2	18.4	20.3	9.0	30.0	9.4	5.9	78.2	12.4
Annual visitors to authorised hotels, overnight stays, total per 1000 pop	3,102	3,420	2,917	2,626	2,898	2,769	2,164	2,419	1,827	12,114	1,868
Annual visitors to authorised hotels, overnight stays, of which foreigners, % of total	29	43	19	11	35	38	23	29	37	30	22
No. of cinemas, per 100,000 pop	8.5	7.7	10.2	7.4	9.5	9.4	8.5	6.0	5.4	12.7	9.3
Cinema admissions, per person per year	2.3	2.6	2.8	1.9	2.3	1.9	2.2	1.8	1.6	1.5	2.0

Statistic	Haute-Normandie	Parisîle-de-France	Languedoc-Roussillon	Limousin	Lorraine	Midi-Pyrénées	Nord-Pas-de-Calais	Pays de la Loire	Picardie	Poitou-Charentes	Provence-Alpes-Côte d'Azur	Rhône-Alpes
Region												
Region area, km	12,318	12,011	27,376	16,942	23,547	45,349	12,413	32,082	19,399	25,809	31,400	43,698
Population												
Population at last census	1,780,192	10,952,011	2,295,648	710,939	2,310,376	2,551,687	3,996,588	3,222,061	1,857,481	1,640,068	4,506,151	5,645,407
Population density, people per km	145	912	84	42	98	56	322	100	96	64	144	129
Population growth, %	2.5	2.7	8.5	-1.7	0.2	5.0	0.8	5.3	2.6	2.8	5.8	5.5
% of population under 20 years old	26.6	25.2	22.9	19.5	25.1	21.8	28.0	25.4	26.9	22.5	23.2	25.3
% of population 60 plus years old	19.5	16.6	25.1	29.4	20.9	25.0	18.7	21.8	19.1	25.9	24.1	20.0
Life expectancy, men	74.2	76.5	74.9	74.8	74.0	76.6	72.0	75.4	73.5	75.9	75.8	76.3
Life expectancy, women	82.2	83.1	82.7	83.2	81.7	83.1	80.6	83.3	81.5	83.3	83.0	83.2
Business & Economy												
Gross domestic production, Û per person	22,473	37,756	18,680	19,611	19,875	21,788	19,332	21,830	19,818	20,027	22,182	24,832
No. of start-up establishments, total per 1000 pop	35	61	56	43	34	52	30	40	32	42	63	52
Employment & Salaries												
% of people in salaried employment	92.4	94.1	87.4	86.6	93.1	87.0	93.3	90.1	91.9	87.8	89.5	91.0
% of people in non-salaried employment	7.6	5.9	12.6	13.4	6.9	13.0	6.7	9.9	8.1	12.2	10.5	9.0
Quarterly unemployment level, % of regional pop	10.0	9.1	13.7	6.9	8.9	9.4	12.0	7.8	10.0	8.7	11.7	8.3
Average annual net salary, men, Û	19,467	26,462	17,881	17,552	18,708	18,930	18,428	18,269	18,969	17,516	19,442	20,096
Average annual net salary, women, Û	14,535	19,144	13,911	14,388	13,924	14,278	14,109	13,569	14,668	13,938	14,687	14,510
Property Prices												
Period property, average price, Û	99,233		12,356	67,802	101,232	110,183	92,525	102,613	93,128	86,757	224,381	146,871
New houses, average price, Û	120,421		129,256	121,332	130,352	121,196	125,795	115,457	11,669	108,652	199,961	172,629
Building land, average price, Û	5,352	16,649	32,974	3,423	31,988	29,384	2,402	26,186	6,522	48,431		
Period property, average price, % divergence from average	-2.9		-87.9	-33.7	-1.0	7.8	-9.5	-8.9	-8.9	-15.1	119.5	43.7
New houses, average price, % divergence from average	2.3		9.9	3.1	10.8	3.0	6.9	-1.9	-90.1	-7.7	69.9	46.7
Health												
Private hospital beds, short stay, per 1000 pop	1.1	1.9	1.9	1.3	2.0	1.7	1.5	1.2	0.8	0.9	2.0	1.2
Private hospital beds, continuing care and rehabilitation, per 1000 pop	0.7	0.5	1.9	0.5	0.8	1.1	0.5	0.7	0.7	0.6	2.1	1.0
Public hospital beds, short stay, per 1000 pop	2.5	2.4	2.3	3.7	2.9	2.4	2.4	2.5	2.8	2.7	2.4	2.8
Public hospital beds, continuing care and rehabilitation, per 1000 pop	0.5	0.6	0.5	1.1	0.6	0.7	0.6	0.8	0.7	0.7	0.4	0.8
Medical consultants/specialists, per 100,000 pop	61	121	102		62	104	58	61	46	63	133	
Dental surgeons, per 100,000 pop	38	79	75		57	79	44	54	41	51	87	
General practitioners, per 100,000 pop	101	114	141		105	132	114	105	99	115	141	
State qualified nurses, per 100,000 pop	64	62	200		61	184	65	66	62	85	179	
Tourism & Leisure												
Accommodation capacity of authorised hotels, total per 1000 pop	5.0	12.9	11.5	7.4	5.9	16.1	4.0	6.1	4.1	9.9	15.2	12.6
Accommodation capacity of authorised hotels, 4 star and luxury, % of total hotels	1.1	16.7	2.7	1.0	0.6	3.1	5.5	3.6	5.3	2.4	17.0	6.7
Accommodation capacity of camping sites, total per 1000 pop	5.8	1.5	52.3	18.0	7.3	16.5	9.1	26.1	11.1	34.4	21.1	13.2
Annual visitors to authorised hotels, overnight stays, total per 1000 pop	1,499	5,450	3,239	1,829	1,567	3,622	1,493	1,634	1,290	3,016	5,276	3,296
Annual visitors to authorised hotels, overnight stays, of which foreigners, % of total	31	59	24	12	28	34	33	15	32	13	45	29
No. of cinemas, per 100,000 pop	5.6	7.6	9.9	9.1	7.7	9.2	7.1	9.2	5.8	10.4	9.7	10.3
Cinema admissions, per person per year	2.2	4.1	2.6	1.9	2.4	2.5	2.4	2.4	1.7	2.2	3.2	2.7

Appendices

Source:

Population and agriculture statistics are from, INSEE – the Institut National de la Statistique et des Etudes Economiques (the French National Statistics office).

INSEE's population statisticss come from France's last census which was undertaken in 1999, the results were published in March 2003.

Agricultural statistics were gathered on many different dates ranging from 1999 to 2003

Industry statistics are from the Business in Europe website www.business-in-europe.com A website built in partnership with the Ministere de L'Economie, des Finances et de l'Industrie (French Ministry for the Economy) local economic development agencies and Chambers of Commerce and Industry, INSEE, Ernst & Young France and many others. The website's aim is to promote France to outside investors and to provide them with relevant information, statistics andcontact details.

Glossary of property terms

Achat – a purchase

Accompte – deposit

Acquéreur – buyer

Acte – legal deed

Acte authentique – the final contract for a sale of a property drawn up by a *notaire*

Acte en main – the final cost of a proeprty including agent and *notaire* fees

Acte de vente – deed of sale prior to conveyancing procedures

Administration fiscale – tax authorities

Agence immobilière – estate agency

Agent immobilier – estate agent

Aggrandir – to extend (i.e. roof conversion, kitchen extension)

Agrandissement – extension or enlargement

Aménagé/aménageable – converted

Appartement – flat/apartment

Appartement bourgeois – spacious apartment with separate servant's quarters

Appartement de standing – a luxury (usually modern) apartment

Appentis – lean-to

Are – 100 square metres

Arrhes – refundable deposit

Arrièr–pays – hinterland, area lying behind i.e. just inland from the coast

Arrondissement – administrative district in Paris and Lyon

Ascenseur – elevator

Assurance décès – life insurance

Assurance décès, invalidité et en général et incapacité – insurance covering death, invalidity and incapacity to work

Assurance multirisques habitation – fully comprehensive household insurance

Assurance perte d'emploi – insurance covering mortgage payments in the event of you becoming unemployed

Atelier – workshop/artist's studio

Attestation d'acquisition – proof of purchase

Attestation de confomité aux règles de sécurité – certificate of safety standards

Appendices

Attestation de propriété – proof of ownership of a property

Attribution de juridication – the formal signing of a purchase contract

Authentique – a document authorised by a *notaire*

Autorisation de Prélèvement Automatique – direct debit

Autorisation provisoire de travail – temporary work permit

Avec travaux – for renovation

Bail – lease

Bail commercial – commercial lease

Bailleur – lessor/landlord

Balcon – balcony

Ballon d'eau chaude – hot water tank

Banlieue – suburb

Bas-côté – side hallway

Bastide – fortified stone house

Bâtiment – building

Bergerie – sheepfold

Biens mobiliers – moveable

Bilan (de santé immobilier) – survey (house)

Bornage – kilometre marker

Bi–propriété – shared ownership

Bois/boiserie – wood/woodwork

Bon état – good state

Bord de la mer – by the sea

Bourg – small town or large village

Bricolage – building and DIY supplies

Brique – brick

Buanderie – wash house, laundry or utility room

Bûcher – woodshed

Bureau – study

Bureau de vente – sales office

Cabinet – small room

Cabinet WC – toilet

Cadastre – land registry

Campagne – countryside

Carneau/conduit de cheminée – chimney flue

Carte de retrait – withdrawal card

Carte de commerçant étranger – business permit (foreign resident)

Carte de séjour de l'Union Européenne – resident permit for EU nationals

Caution – guarantee or security deposit

Cave – cellar

Cave voûté – vaulted cellar

Cellier – store room for wine or food

Centre des impôts – tax office

Centre d'affaires – business centre

Certificate d'Urbanisme – town planning permit

Cession – transfer of ownership or rights

Chai – wine cellar

Chambre – bedroom

Chartreuse – monastery

Château – large mansion, manor house or castle

Chantier – building site

Chaudière – boiler

Chauffage – heating

Chauffage central – central heating

Chauffage collectif – communal or shared heating

Chauffage par le sol – underfloor heating

Chauffage par le plafond – ceiling

Chauffe-eau – hot water tank

Chaume – thatch

Chaumière – thatched cottage

Cheminée – chimney/fireplace

Chéquier – checkbook

Citerne apparente – gas tank above ground

Citerne enfouie – gas tank buried

Appendices

Clause particulière – special condition

Clause pénale – a penalty clause in a sales contract

Clause suspensive – a conditional clause in a contract that must be met in order for the sale to reach completion

Climatisation – air-conditioning

Clôture – a fence

Code du Travail – French employment laws

Colombage – half-timbering typical of Normandy

Colombier – pigeon house or dovecote

Comble – loft

Commision compris (C/C) – agent's commission included

Commission non compris – commission not included

Communauté – joint estate of a husband and wife

Communauté universelle – a marriage regime where all assets are jointly owned

Compromis de vente – preliminary contract for the sale of a property

Comptant – buying in cash with no loans

Compte – a bank account

Compte joint – joint account

Comptable – accountant

Compte séquestre – a deposit held in a special escrow account pending fulfilment of certain conditions

Compteur – meter for gas, electricity, water

Concierge – caretaker or porter of an apartment block

Concurrence – when two *notaires* are involved with a sale but only one can execute the deed

Conditions particulières – special conditions

Conditions suspensives – conditions in a contract which allow one or both parties to declare the contract null if they are met

Congélateur – freezer

Conseiller juridique – professional legal adviser

Conseiller fiscal – financial or tax adviser

Constat d'huissier – a factual statement prepared by a baillif which is irrefuatable in court

Constructable – land available for building on

Construire – construct

Contrat à durée indéterminée (CDI) – employment contract of unspecified duration

Contrat à durée déterminée (CDD) – employment contract of specified duration

Contrat préliminaire – preliminary contract

Contrat de réservation – contract to buy an off-plan property before it's built

Convention – agreement

Convention collective – sector-specific collective agreement on employment relations

Contrat de prêt – mortgage contract

Copropriété – co–ownership of a communal property (US: condominium)

Corps de bâtiments – group of buildings

Cour – yard or courtyard

Cour de ferme – farmyard

Couvert – covered

Couvreur – roofer

Cuisine – kitchen

Cuisine américaine – kitchen with all the most up-to-date mod cons

Cuisine meublée – kitchen with fixed cooker, fridge, etc.

Cuisinière – cooker/stove

Date de livraison prévue – estimated date of completion

Débarras – lumber room (where wood is kept), boxroom or cupboard

Décennale – ten year warranty provided by a registered builder

Déclaration de sincérité – formal acceptance of purchase price

Décorée – decorated and fitted ready for occupation

Dédit – penalty provided for in a contract should either party default: i.e. the buyer will lose his deposit or the seller will have to repay the deposit as well as a penalty equal to the same sum

Délabré – delapidated

Démenagement – moving house

Demeure – any building, but often used when referring to a grand house with large grounds

Dépannage – emergency repair service

Département – administrative area within a *région*

Dépendance – outbuilding

Dépôt de garantie – deposit paid when buying or renting a property

Appendices

Dernière étage – top floor

Devis – a written quotation

Direction Départmentale de l'Équipement (DDE) – departmental surveyors, land planning and public works department

Disjoncteur – electricity overload trip switch or circuit breaker

Domicile fiscal – main residence for tax purposes

Douche – shower

Droit de passage – right of way

Droit de Préemption – rights (usually by town hall) to pre-empt the sale

Droits d'enregistrement – stamp duty paid by the buyer of a property

Droits de succession – inheritance rights

Duplex – an apartment on two floors

Durée – duration of a mortgage

E

Eau chaude collective – shared hot water supply in an apartment block

Eaux usées – drain or waste water

Écurie – pigsty/stable

Égout – sewer

Emolumentsd'actes – *notaire's* fixed scale of fees

Emoluments de négociation – fees for introducing the buyer

Électricien – electrician

Emprunt – loan

Emprunteur – borrower

Enregistrement – stamp duty

Entrée – hallway

Entrepreneur – contractor or building consortium

Entretien – maintenance

Escalier – staircase

Étable – stable or cowshed

Étage – floor/storey

Étang – lake or pond

État hypothécaire – land registry search

Étude – a *notaire's* office

Expert de bâtiment – surveyor

Expert géomètre – land surveyor

Expertise – valuation appraisal

Escalier – stairway/staircase

Épargne – saving

Etage – storey

Facteur – bill

Fenêtre – window

Fenêtre en baie – bay window

Ferme – farm

Fermette – small farm of small holding

FNAIM – abbreviation for the *Fédération Nationale des Agents Immobiliers et Mandataires*, a national association of French estate agents

Forfait – fixed price

Fosse septique – septic tank

Fosse septique à toutes eaux – an all-pupose septic tank able to handle a wide range of waste products

Fosse traditionelle – traditional septic tank for bathroom waste only

Four – oven

Four à pain – bread oven or bakehouse

Foyer principal – main home

Frais – fees

Frais compris – fees included

Frais de dossier – credit society's arrangement fee for a mortgage

Garantie d'achèvement – guarantee that the property purchased off-plan will be completed

Gardien – guardian or caretaker

Gaz en bouteille – bottled gas

Gaz au citerne – tanked gas

Gaz de ville – mains gas

Gentilhommière – small manor house

Gîte – self–catering accommodation

Appendices

Grange – barn

Gouttière – gutter

Grénier – attic

Gros oeuvre – major building works until completion of basic shell of house

Habitation – dwelling

Hameau – hamlet

Hectare – 10,000 square metres or 2.471 acres

Honoraires – *notaire's* fees which aren't fixed by an official scale

Hors frais – fees not included

Hors taxes – tax not included

Hôtel de ville – town hall in a large town or city

Hôtel particulier – elegent townhouse or mansion

Huissier – an officer of court equivalent to a baillif and whose statements are irrefutable by law

Hypotheque – a mortgage or loan on a property

Homme de métier – specialist

Immeuble – apartment block (also legal term for immovable property)

Immobilier – estate agent (abbreviation of agent immobilier)

Impôt – tax

Impôt locaux – local taxes

Impôt sur la fortune – wealth tax

Impôt sur les plus-values – capital gains tax

Impôt sur le revenu – income tax

Indemnité de l'immobilisation – down payment on a preliminary contract of sale – usually 10% of the price

Indivision – joint ownership of a property or tenancy in common

Inscription – registered charge

Installation – fixture or fitting

Inventaire détaillé/état des lieux – a detailed inventory of the contents and condition of a property

Jardin – garden

Jardinier – gardener

Jouissance – possession or tenure

Jouissance libre – vacant possession

Jumelle – semi-detached house

Laverie – laundry room

Livrets d'epargne – savings book of sums deposited

Location – tenancy

Location vente – renting a property while buying some of the equity value

Locataire – tenant

Logement – lodging, accommodation

Logis – manor house

Lotissement – housing estate

Louer – to rent or let

Loyer – rental

Lucarne – skylight, dormer window

Larguer – width, breadth

Maçon – builder such as a stonemason or bricklayer

Maçonnerie – masonry, stone or brick work

Mainlevée – release or withdrawal from mortage

Maison – house

Mainson à étage – a two storey house

Mainson d'amis – holiday home

Maison bourgeoise – imposing period house from the 19th Century

Maison paysanne – farmhouse

Maison de campagne – house in the country

Maison de caractère – period property with character

Maison en carré – house built around a courtyard

Maison de chasse – hunting lodge usually located at the edge of a forest

Maison de maître – imposing period property

Maison mitoyenne – semi-detached property

Maison neuve – new house

Maison paysanne – farmhouse

Maison secondaire – holiday home

Maison de viticulture – winegrower's house

Maisonette – cottage

Maire – mayor

Mairie – town hall or, in a smaller commune, mayor's office

Maître – polite title used when addressing the *notaire*

Maître d'œuvre – a master builder or someone who manages the works

Mandat de vente – sales mandate

Mandat exclusif – an exclusive mandate to an estate agent to sell a property

Mandat de recherche – an agreement with an agent to find a property

Mandat simple – a non-exclusive mandate for an agent to sell a property, meaning a vendor can also sell through other agents

Manteau de cheminée – chimney-breast

Manoir – manor house

Marchand de biens – property developer

Marquise – porch

Mas – a Provençal-style farmhouse

Menuiserie – joining/carpentry

Menuisier – joiner/carpenter

Métier – trade

Mètre – metre (measurement)

Mètre carré – square metre

Meublé – furnished (unfurnished is *nonmeublé*)

Meubles – furniture

Mode de paiement – method of payment

Moquette – carpet

Multirisques habitation – buildings and content insurance

Mur – wall

Mur mitoyen – a party wall shared by another property

Nantissment – collateral or security for a loan

Net vendeur – the amount the vendor receives excluding agent's fees

Nonmeublé – unfurnished

Notaire – notary, the legal professional who handles the conveyancing

Nouvelle propriété – sale and leaseback

Nu-propriété – rights of owner set aside during a tenant's lifetime

Offre d'achat/offre de vente – a formal offer to purchase a property

Offre préalable – a conditional offer, for example, of a mortgage

Operation – transaction

Paiement comptant – paid in cash

Pailleur – barn for storing straw

Palier – landing at the top of stairs

Parcelle – plot of land

Parquet – wooden flooring

Parties communes – communal parts of a building, e.g. lifts and hallways

Pavillon – small detached house

Pays – a country or countryside

Pelouse – lawn

Pépinière – garden centre

Période d'anticipation – pre-completion period (especially for off–plan)

Permis de construire – building permit

Perron – flight of steps in front of a mansion

Pièce – room

Pièce de garantie – financial guarantee of a bonded estate agent

Pigeonnier – pigeon tower

Pignon – gable

Piscine – swimming pool

Plage – beach

Appendices

Appendices

Plain pied – single storey

Plafond – ceiling

Plan d'amortissement – schedule for mortgage payments

Plan cadastral – plans showing property's land area dimensions

Plan du terrain – ground plan

Plancher – wooden floor

Plomberie – plumbing

Plombier – plumber

Poêle à bois – wood-burning stove

Potager – kitchen garden

Presbytère – presbytery

Prêt immobilier – mortgage

Prêt relais – bridging loan

Prêteur – lender

Prêts capés – capped rate

Prélèver – withdraw

Prix fermé – fixed and non-negotiable price

Promesse unilatérale d'achat – preliminary or promissary contract to *buy* a property

Promesse unilatérale de vente – preliminary or promissary contract to *sell* a property

Programmateur – timer (such as for washing machine)

Propriétaire – owner

Propriété – property

Propriété baties – developed or built property

Propriétés en ruines – property in ruins

Puits – well

Quartier – neighbourhood

Quincaillerie – hardware store, ironmongers

Quittance – receipt

Ramoneur – chimney sweep

Rangement – storage area

Ravalement – restoration

Rayou caoutchouc – rubber pipe

Réfection – reconstruction

Réfrigérateur – refrigerator (usually shortened to *frigo*)

Réglement de copropriété – documents containing the rules and regulations of a communal building

Remise des clefs – handing over keys to the new owner

Relevé d'identité bancaire (RIB) – a bank statement

Relevé des operations bancaires – monthly bank statement

Rénovation – renovation

Réservoir – water tank

Résidence principal – main or principal home

Résidence secondaire – second or holiday home

Responsabilité civile propriétaire – third party liability of homeowners for which insurance is mandatory

Restaurer – to restore

Revêtement – surface

Révision de loyer – a revision or review of the rent payable on a property

Renouvellement – renewel of a rental contract

Rez-de-chaussée – ground floor

Salle – room

Salle de bains – bathroom

Salle d'eau – shower room

Salle à manger – dining room

Salle de séjour – sitting room

Salon – sitting or drawing room

Salarié – salaried employee

Sanitaire – bathroom or plumbing

Sanitation – bathroom or main drainage

Sans travaux – no work needed, ready to occupy

Séjour – living room

Séjour principal – main residence

Séparation des biens – separation of property (in a marriage regime each spouse retains legal ownership of his or her assets)

Servitudes – rights of way or easements restricting use or development of a property

Société anonyme (SA) – stock company

Société à responsabilité limitée (SARL) – limited liability company

Société civile – non-trading partnership

Société civile immobilière (SCI) – a partnership holding shares in a property

Société en commandite par actions – partnership limited by shares

Société en nom collectif – general partnership

Société par actions simplifiée (SAS) – simplified corporation

Sol – ground

Souche – chimney stack

Source – spring

Sommes débitées – sums withdrawn

Sommes créditées – sums credited/deposited

Sous-seing – preliminary contract

Sous-sol – underground/cellar

Studio – a one-roomed apartment

Surface habitable – habitable area excluding balconies, cellars, storerooms

T

Tapis – carpet or rug

Taxe d'habitation – tax based on occupancy, but not ownership, of a property

Taxe foncière – local property tax

Taxe professionnelle – business tax

Témoin – show house or apartment

Terrain – grounds or land

Terrain à bâtir – building site for sale

Terrasse – terrace

Testament – will

Titre de propriété – title deed

Toilettes – toilets

Toit – roof

Toiture – roofing

Toiture-terrasse – roof terrace

Tontine – ownership in joint tenancy under which the assets pass to the survivor

Tout l'egout – main drainage system

Toutes taxes– including taxes

Travaux – building works

Triplex – maisonette on three floors

TVA/Tax sur la Valeur Ajouté – value added tax

Urbanisme – town planning

Urgence – emergency

Usufruit – usufruct, the legal term for a life interest in a property

Valeur vénale – market value

Vendeur – vendor or seller

Vente à l'état futur d'achèvement – buying a property off-plan before it's built

Vente à tenure – sale of usufruct

Véranda – conservatory, sun-room

Verger – orchard

Vieille maison – old house

Villa – a modern detached house

Ville – town

Volet – shutter

Visa de long séjour – long-term visa

Glossary of old property styles

The following list details a number of property descriptions that you're likely to encounter if you are searching for an older property. Several of the terms refer to properties that weren't previously used for residential purposes but which can be converted, such as buildings where silk worms were incubated, old cow-sheds, or little buildings where wine was once stored and fermented.

Bergerie

These are secluded goat or sheepfold buildings located on steppes or heaths. They have a rectangular ground-plan and, depending on the *région*, canal tiles, slate or stone slabs on the gabled roof. The materials depended very much on what was immediately available on the land surrounding the site, for instance *bergeries* on the Lazarc plateau, at the south-west of the Massif Central, have 1.5 metre walls made of thick limestone slabs. Windows of *bergeries* tend to be very small. Today herds of at least 300 animals are kept, so the *bergeries*, which were only big enough for 50 animals, are pretty much redundant agriculturally. Many farmers have taken advantage of the subsidies available and converted these little buildings into *gîtes*.

Belle demeure

This is a fairly general term that refers to elegant period properties.

Chais

Larger properties in southern France often have this rectangular building which, composed of only one room, was used to store and ferment the wine. Originally they had no flooring but bare earth, the humidity of which contributed to the fermentation of the wine. Converting such a property into a comfortable residential building means a lot of work: drainage, floor insulation and renovation of the walls. The *chais* is sometimes found located in areas where viniculture no longer exists.

Chartreuse

A chartreuse is a long building used as a monastery built in the gothic style, with rows of many tiny rooms where the monks slept. Today there are only 200 of these buildings are left. Originally they were completely secluded. In south-west France people also call secluded cottages 'chartreuse'. So be sure exactly which version you're going to look at when the *agent immobilier* offers to show you one . . . a monastery may mean an entire life commited to DIY!

Chaumière

Chaumière is a thatched cottage. The thatched roof is normally found on *colombage* structures typical of Haute-Normandie. Original chaumières are becoming hard to find because the roofs which were once straw stubble (*chaume*) made from cereal such as wheat (*blé*) or rye (*siegle*), have been replaced by reed (*roseau*), slate (*l'ardoise*) or clay tiles (*tuiles d'argile*) – materials which are stronger and less expensive. Originally these cottages were built by farmers with little money who simply used the earth, wood, stones and water from the land around them to build their homes. Inhabitants today tend to be wealthy Parisian weekenders who get their materials from the local Mr Bricolage.

Colombage

These buildings were made by assembling wooden beams (*putres*) of oak (*chêne*) into a structure and filling the area between the beams with a mixture of straw, mud, clay and water, called *torchis*. France possesses a long tradition of using wood. Wood is natural, renewable, resistant, light and insulating. Contrary to popular opinion, wood is actually good at resisting fire and bad weather and it does not deteriorate in the sun. The floor of the house was made of flint, an impervious stone that prevented the earth's humidity from rising and infiltrating the walls. Colombage can be found all over northern France and particularly in Normandy (although not the Falaise *département*). It is rare to find an unrestored colombage property although unfortunately many of them haven't been restored very well and have often been completely stripped of their internal character. Strangely, properties that have been shoddily restored go for the same price as those that have been beautifully restored (although the former do take longer to sell).

Chalet (Swiss-French expression)

Chalets were normally built on the side of the mountain that gets the sunlight and were always located at higher levels.

In the often harsh environment of the mountains, the buildings were constructed to shelter both men and the animals which had to live there during the long months when the pastures were covered in snow. Most of the 'chalets' were two or three storeys high. On the ground floor was the cheese cellar and cowshed. The first floor was used as living quarters, and the top floor was the barn where hay was stored. The hay, as well as keeping the animals fed in the winter, was also useful as insulation against the freezing conditions – much in the same way that we insulate the lofts of modern houses today. In two-storey chalets, the cowshed, cheese cellar and living quarters were all on the same floor, with the hay barn above.

Chalets in the Savoie are characterised by having large balconies, which were used to air-dry hemp and corn harvests and wood for the fire. These covered balconies also allowed people to move freely about the chalet without getting wet. Some balconies have an external stairway to the upper floors.

Three colours were used to explain the precise function: the dark grey-brown for the barn, white for the part that is lived in, often situated on the first floor, and the grey for the ground floor, the cowshed.

Chalets were either constructed from wood (*chalet en bois*) or wood with mostly slates and stone slabs. In a *chalet en bois* the floor is made of slabs of stone joined by a mortar of sand (*sable*) and lime (*chaux*) and the walls are formed by tree trunks of the same width, slotted horizontally on top of each other. The walls are sometimes then covered by *tavaillons*, small tiles of wood which served to protect against the rain and strong winds. The shutters are often coloured, particularly in the northern Alps.

Colombier/Pigeonnier

These quirky little buildings were status symbols in the 17th and 18th Centuries. Often designed by the same architect and at the same time as the main house, they were sometimes as elaborate as the house and came in all sorts of styles with many different ground plans (such as round or octagonal). Small holes allowed the pigeons to fly in and out and shelves were built in the interior walls for nesting. Owners often had up to 2,000 pairs of pigeons which weren't used for racing, delivering messages and seldomly as a gourmet delicacy, but for their excrement which was used to fertilise the vineyards.

Donjon

Donjons are towers that are attached, or were previously attached, to buildings dating back to the 11th Century. They were the most solid construction of a castle, built with thick walls, small windows and no entrance on the ground floor, and so most have outlived the other part of the building. The earlier donjons had rectangular floor plans but later on round, hexagonal or octagonal plans were introduced.

Fermes (farms)

Early farms consisted of one room in which man and beast co-habited and throughout the centuries farms got larger as many farmers got wealthier. The larger farms consisted of a building to live in and further outbuildings, which were used for agricultural purposes. There are dozens of architectural styles, which often are influenced by the climate and the availability of material above anything else. Depending on the local relief, the walls are made of different stones: in Auvergne you'll find hewn stones of granite or basalt, in the Lot and Dordogne lime is common, in and around Toulouse red-brick and dry clay, and in Cévennes slate or thick lime slabs from the Causses de Larzac. Buildings were arranged often with the climate in mind, for instance the sides that faced the main winds are either protected or blind, and locations on hills protected against floods.

Ferme à cour fermée (farm with an enclosed courtyard)

Farms with enclosed courtyards are widespread in the cereal-growing *régions* north of the river Loire as far as the Belgian frontier. Outside Northern France, they are encountered only individually or in isolated groups. The typical enclosed courtyard farm consists of a yard surrounded on all four sides by buildings or walls, the only access being through a monumental-looking cart entrance combined with a pedestrian entrance. The dwelling quarters are on the side opposite the entrance and the cowsheds or stables occupy the sides that are perpendicular to the farmhouse, while the barn is located on the side in which the courtyard entrance is placed. This sort of farm was the centre of an agricultural estate run by an owner-occupant or a tenant-farmer (*le maître*) supervising numerous staff. Prior to the 18th Century, this enclosed space may have evolved from the need to protect and defend noble or church property. Later on, its sole rationale was to offer protection against the elements or outside curiosity while remaining synonymous with economic power and social prestige.

Ferme à cour ouverte (farm with an open courtyard)

Buildings are detached, instead of conjoined, with open intervals at the four angles. This layout is typical of large cattle farms, where passageways between the buildings allow for the cattle's easy access. Often these farms were originally *longères* or a *salle-hautes* that had grown into farms. Open-courtyard farms can be found in all Western *régions* (Normandy, Brittany, Maine, Anjou) and across France from Poitou to Charolles. Elsewhere, this type of farm only occurs in small isolated clusters.

Gentilhommière

This was the luxurious summer residence of a nobleman (*gentilhomme*). It is often a one or two-storey building with a large surface area and has big openings to let in light. The *manoir de gentilhomme* is often a juxtoposition of styles.

Hotel Particulier

A spacious mansion, built from the 17th Century onwards by nobles or clerics, later by the bourgoisies and wealthy. They were often very tasteful with a large inner courtyard and separate buildings for the employees. In large cities you often find they are now embassies or chambers of commerce, and in smaller cities they are law offices or small museums.

Magnanerie

These stone buildings located in southern France (particularly Cévenne, Drôme and in Provence) were built for the cultivation of silk worms. 'Magnan' is the provençal word for silk worm (*vers a soie*). The buildings are very narrow and have several floors, sometimes with large arcades. Many are surrounded by the old mulberry trees on which the silk worms were reared. Cultivating silk worms in the 18th and 19th Century was an important source of wealth for many villages. It's very rare to find these buildings today, especially ones that haven't been converted.

Appendices

Maison Bourgeoise

A maison bourgeoise is a spacious and solidly-built village house with a walled or fenced park. Such houses are often found in the better suburbs of towns.

Mas

Mas is the name for the one or two-storey farms, with barn and stables, found in south-east France. The buildings have a rectangular ground plan and some have a tower-shaped *pigeonnier* attached. The walls are made of field stones and the edges and arcades are sometimes decorated with hewn stones. Elongated roofs have a gentle pitch (one facing south) and are often clad in pink-red roman canal tiles. Original buildings had floors made of clay slabs that easily crack when removed. The mas, especially those that are isolated on plateaux or mountains, have an austere and defensive character. Newly built *provençal* villas built in this style are also called *mas*.

Maison de Mâitre

Located either rurally or in small towns, this spacious manor house has 3-5 rows of windows and a fenced-in park. The standard surface area was 200 square metres or less over three floors with reception rooms on the ground floor, private rooms on the upper floors and domestic servants quarters under the roof. From the 1850s the rich bourgeoisie added small towers and various chintzy additions, in order to compete with the status symbols of the nobles. The building materials and styles depend on the *régions* although roofs are more steeply pitched the further north you go. Well-renovated properties can fetch large sums, but it's still possible to find unrenovated properties at very low prices. This is often because, if they are in a bad condition, renovation is very costly. Heating, up-to-date sanitation, electricity and so on, will need to be considered. You also have to be careful about location: many are found on busy main roads which, when the house was originally built, were dirt tracks for ox carts and horse-drawn carriages.

Manoir

Manoirs were solidly built residences in locations where approaching enemies could easily be seen. These residences were built by feudal lords, who had not been permitted by royalty to build castles with watch towers. The buildings were not powerful enough to withstand attack or siege. Driveways lined with trees were the privileges of such nobles.

Moulin

Disused mills are very hard to come by as most have been snapped up and renovated long ago. If you can find one, then you're guaranteed a home full of character, often with the benefits of a pleasant waterside garden. Be careful when you are buying a water mill – check that the river is not prone to flooding.

Chateaux – Roman, Gothique and Renaissance

Roman

Roman (not to be confused with *Romain* which is Roman in French) is known in Britain as Norman. This early medieval architectural style from the 11th Century has squat, rounded forms and arches and naïve sculptures. Walls are very thick and windows are tiny. Nothing is visible on the outside, and there's an equal lack of ornamentation on the inside.

Gothique

The round arcades of Romanesque architecture were later substituted with pointed arches. Ceilings in the rooms were higher and the windows were taller. Chapels and cathedrals became more decorative, often with large stained glass windows. The 'rose' or wheel window is an early example. Ribbed vaulted ceilings and spires became popular. Because of the growing power of the church at this time, the gothic architectural style became more and more important in Europe from the beginning of the 13th Century and remained a dominant architectural style until the 16th Century. The best examples of gothic architecture can be found in Normandy.

Renaissance Palaces

Following a series of invasions on Italy, French sovereigns brought back with them new ideas about art and architecture and the 15th Century saw the rebirth of classical Greek and Roman culture. Decorative motifs such as flamboyant columns, domes, tunnel vaults and round arches became very popular. While French architects were packed off to train in Italy, Italian architects and artists such as Michelangelo and Leonardo da Vinci (who built the *Château de Chambord* in the Loire Valley where he was buried after his death in Amboise) were brought in. As gangs of thieves became less common, architecture became more open and orientated towards exterior elements like parks, ornate gardens, etc. The moats that surrounded the *residences de plaisir* were now decorative rather than defensive, and watch towers now became residential towers. Wing constructions also became very popular.

Appendices

391

Facts about France

General

Official name	République Française
National Anthem	La Marseillaise
Motto	Liberté, Egalité, Fraternité
Currency	Euro
Capital	Paris
Internet domain	Fr
International dialling code	33
Visas	Nationals of the EU, the USA, Canada, Australia, New Zealand and Israel do not need visas to visit France as tourists for up to three months.
Time	GMT/UTC +1 (Central European Time)
Electricity	220V, 50Hz
National holiday	Bastille Day, 14 July

Geography

Area	551,000 sq km – Largest country in Western Europe (almost one fifth of the total area of the European Union).
Land boundaries	Total: 2,889km
	Border countries: Andorra 56.6km, Belgium 620km, Germany 451km, Italy 488km, Luxembourg 73km, Monaco 4.4km, Spain 623km, Switzerland 573km.
Coastline	3,427km.
Elevation extremes	Lowest point: Rhone River delta -2m Highest point: Mont Blanc 4,807km.
Climate	Oceanic in the West, Mediterranean in the South, Continental in Central and Eastern France.
Environment	Farms and forests cover 48 million hectares, i.e. 82% of the total area of France.
	Some 26% of French territory is covered by forests, ranking France third in the European Union for the amount of forestland, behind Sweden and Finland. Forest area in France has increased by 35% since 1945 and continues to grow by about 30,000 hectares each year. France possesses 136 different kinds of trees. Most trees are deciduous (two thirds), while the remaining third consists of conifers.
Environmental issues	Some forest damage from acid rain (major forest damage occurred as a result of severe December 1999 windstorm); air pollution from industrial and vehicle emissions; water pollution from urban wastes, agricultural run-off.
Natural resources	Coal, iron ore, bauxite, zinc, potash, timber, fish.

Appendices

Population

Population	In 2000, Metropolitan and Overseas France had 60.4 million inhabitants, including 4 million foreign residents of whom 1.5 million were European Union nationals. France accounts for 16% of the European Union's population.
Largest cities	Paris 9.8 million, Lyon 1.4 million, Marseille-Aix-en-Provence 1.4 million, Lille 1.2 million, Toulouse 1.1 million.
Fertility rate	1.77 children per woman
Life expectancy	74 years (men); 82 years (women).
Languages	100% French, declining regional dialects and languages (Provencal, Breton, Alsatian, Corsican, Catalan, Basque, Flemish).

Society

Marriages	Since the start of the 1990s, the number of married couples has fallen while the number of non-married couples has risen from 1.5 million in 1990 to 2.4 million – one couple in six today.
Structure of households	Couple with at least one child: 33.5%
	Couple without children: 26.8%
	Single: 30.4%
	Single-parent families: 7.3%
Religion	Catholics: 47,000,000, 81.4% of the population
	Muslims: 4,000,000, 6.89% of the population
	Protestants: 950,000, 1.64% of the population
	Jews: 50,000, 1.29% of the population
Employment	Farmers, farm workers: 682,000 (2.6% of the total labour force)
	Self-employed non-professionals shopkeepers, heads of businesses: 1,595,000 (6.1%)
	Managerial and professional occupations: 3,008,000 (11.5%)
	Intermediate occupations: 4,759,000 (18.3%)
	Clerical, white-collar workers: 6,512,000 (25%)
	Manual workers: 5,972,000 (23%)
	Unemployed people (10%)
Education	Pupil/teacher ratio (schools): 16 to 1
	Pupil/teacher ratio (universities): 17 to 1
Standard of living	Net average annual earnings: €19,938
	Gross average household savings: €1,829, or 15.6% of disposable income.
Average salaries	Executives, management staff: €38,722
	Professionals: €70,126
	Farmers, farm workers: €21,114
	Technical and supervisory personnel: €21,409
	Other intermediate professions: €21,220
	Skilled workers: €15,482
	Clerical, white collar workers: €14,661
	Unskilled workers: €13,217

Appendices

Trade unions	Approximately two million people in France – 8% of the working population – are union members, the lowest percentage in the European Union.
Social security (where it goes . . .)	Pensions (49.2%) Health (27.2%) Family allowances (12.8%) Employment aid (8.4%)
Poverty	Percentage below the poverty line: 6.4%
Health	Health is a major concern of the French: in 1998, they spent 110.6 billion euros on medical care and goods. 75% of this was covered by the social security system, with an increasing proportion being met by households and insurance companies.

Culture

Newspapers	36% of French people read a daily newspaper every day. There are seven national newspapers and 160 regional papers (dailies and weeklies).
Books	50,000 books are published every year: half are new works and half reprints. In 2002, 331 publishing houses printed 423 million copies.
Periodicals	Among the top 100, six have a circulation of over one million and eight over 500,000 copies. With 1,350 copies sold for every 1,000 residents, France ranks first in the world for magazine readership.
Television	Watching television remains the favourite leisure activity of the French, with an average of 3 hours 15 minutes per person per day. There are over 130 television channels.
Computers	While computers are considered primarily as tools for work and are used as such by 52% of the French, an increasing proportion, currently 35.9%, of French households now have one.
Cinema	200 films were produced in 2002, making France second in the world for film investment.
Music and dance	France is the home of some 11,300 dramatic artists and dancers, 16,200 musicians and singers, 250 music, opera and dance festivals, 8,700 variety performers.
Theatre	A total audience of 8 million is drawn to some 50,000 performances put on by theatres each year. Over a thousand independent theatre companies have sprung up in recent years.
Sport	Participation in sporting activities has grown rapidly in recent years. Almost 10 million people are enrolled in sports federations, with soccer and tennis the largest. Judo, pétanque, horse riding, badminton and golf have recorded notable success in recent years.

Economy

Overview	France is the world's fourth largest economic power in terms of GDP. In 1999 France had a trade surplus of 18.9 billion euros; it is the world's fourth largest exporter of goods (mainly durables) and ranks second in services and agriculture (cereals and agri-foodstuffs in particular). It is the leading producer and exporter of farm products in Europe.

Gross domestic product (GDP) in 1999: 1,346.58 billion euros
GDP growth (1999): 2.9%
Inflation (1999): 1.3%
Trade surplus (1999): 18.9 billion euros

Agriculture
Farms: 680,000
Farmers/farm workers: 910,000
Utilised agricultural area: 54% of the area of metropolitan France

Products
Cereals 1st in the EU, 5th in the world (68 million metric tons, including 38 million tons of soft wheat and 15 million tons of grain maize)
Wine 2nd in the world and EU after Italy (52 million hectolitres)
Milk 2nd in the EU, after Germany and 5th in the world (23 million litres)

Energy consumption
Oil: 31.7%
Electricity: 35.5% (of which 76% is nuclear generated)
Gas: 13.6% Coal: 6.4%
Renewable energies: 4.7%

Leading industrial sectors
Agri-foodstuffs: 108.2 (annual turnover, billion euros)
Construction and civil engineering: 93.2
Automobiles: 86.6
Chemicals: 70.1
Telecommunications: 67.2
Materials processing: 42.8
Fashion and luxury goods: 31.4
Pharmaceuticals: 28.4
Aerospace: 19.9

Leading export markets
Germany: 14.7%
UK: 9.8%
Spain: 9.6%
Italy: 8.8%

Leading import markets
Germany: 16.7%
Italy: 9.1%
US: 8.9%
UK: 7.5%

Stock market
Market capitalisation of shares listed on the Paris stock exchange totals 844.4 billion euros, 50% of French GDP, ranking Paris seventh in the world.

Banks
The leading French banks are Crédit Agricole, Société Générale and Banque Nationale de Paris (BNP).

Insurance
The French insurance sector has consolidated its position as the fourth largest in the world, with a turnover of 167.9 billion euros. Axa, Europe's largest insurance company, CNP and AGF are the three main French insurance companies.

Appendices

Tourism | With 70 million foreign tourists annually, France is the most visited country in the world. France has 20,000 hotels, 8,000 camping sites, 860 holiday villages, 224 youth hostels, 41,000 *gîtes* and 21,440 *chambres d'hôtes* (bed and breakfast). France's income from tourism (25.6 million euros) is the third largest in the world, after the United States and Italy. The trade surplus in this sector is over 10.67 billion euros.

Transport

Road network | Densest in the world and longest in the EU with a total of 965,916 km of local, secondary and main roads and motorways, including 9,011 km of motorways (second in Europe).
While 76% of freight is carried by road, use of combined transport is sharply increasing.

Rail network | In 2000, 31,770km of track. France holds the world speed record (515km/h) with its high-speed train (TGV), which runs on 1,281 kilometres of special track allowing trains in normal commercial operation to travel at 270km/h or more.
Annual traffic: 295 million passengers on the main network, 71 million on the TGV network, 528 million on the Ile-de France regional network.

Waterways | 14,932km (6,969km heavily traveled).

Aviation | Each year over 100 million passengers and 4.8 billion tons-kilometers of freight are carried. 904 aircraft (planes and helicopters) fly under the French flag.

Merchant fleet | Annually 210 ships transport 91.5 million tons of freight. France's fleet ranks 28th in the world in tonnage. Marseille is the largest port in France and on the Mediterranean, and the third largest in Europe.

Sources: CIA World Factbook, Embassy of France in the US, INSEE, Economist, BBC, Lonely Planet

A brief history of France

58BC – 481AD	Roman conquest of Celtic Gaul. Gallo-Roman civilisation.
481-987	Merovingian and Carolingian dynasties. Sweeping invasions from the east. Hugh Capet, elected King of France, founds the Capetian dynasty.
11th-13th centuries	Development of agriculture and trade. Emergence of towns. Royal power gains ground over feudal lords. Economic and cultural role of the great monastic orders. Crusades.
14th-15th centuries	Epidemics (Black Death, 1397), famine and civil wars. Rivalry between France and England: Hundred Years' War, epic of Joan of Arc (1425-1431).
16th Century	The Reformation. Religious wars between Catholics and Protestants. Reign of Henry IV (1589-1610). Edict of Nantes grants freedom of conscience and worship (1598).
1610-1715	Reigns of Louis XIII and Louis XIV. Royal power at its peak; France dominates Europe, French culture spreads. Start of large-scale sea trade.
18th Century	Reigns of Louis XV and Louis XVI. Economic and demographic growth. Age of Enlightenment.
1789-1799	French Revolution. Declaration of the Rights of Man and the Citizen (1789). Abolition of the monarchy (1792). First Republic.
1799-1815	Rise of Napoleon Bonaparte, Emperor of the French (1804). Establishment of modern administrative institutions. European wars lead to abdication of the Emperor.
1815-1848	Restoration and constitutional monarchy (Louis XVIII, Charles X). Revolution of 1830. Reign of Louis-Philippe. Economic prosperity. First colonies established.
1848-1852	Revolution. Second Republic. First laws on labour, the press and education.
1852-1870	Coup d'Etat by Louis-Napoleon Bonaparte, nephew of Napoleon I. Second Empire. Political liberalisation (1860). Period of strong growth and colonial expansion.
1870-1875	Franco-Prussian war resulting in the loss of Alsace and Lorraine and the fall of Napoleon III. Paris Commune (1871). Third Republic.
1875-1914	Parliamentary power at its peak. Separation of church and state (1905).
1914-1918	First World War. Allied victory. Alsace and Lorraine revert to France. Peace treaties.
1919-1939	Reconstruction. Paris attracts artists from all parts of the world. Great Depression.
1939-1945	Second World War. Defeat and occupation. General de Gaulle leads the Resistance from London and Algiers. Allied victory.
1946-1957	Fourth Republic. Reconstruction. Demographic and economic growth. Decolonisation. Founding of the European Communities (Treaty of Rome, 1957).
1958-1968	General de Gaulle returns to power. Constitution of the Fifth Republic (1958). Common Market becomes a reality (1959). Signature of Evian Agreements ends war in Algeria (1962). Social crisis (May 1968).
1969-1981	Georges Pompidou's presidency (1969-1974). Presidency of Valéry Giscard d'Estaing (1974-1981). European Monetary System set up (1979). Right to vote at age 18 introduced. Abortion law promoted by Simone Veil is adopted (1975).

1981-1995	Presidency of François Mitterrand (elected 1981, re-elected 1988). Death penalty abolished (1981). Decentralisation laws passed (1982). Rules governing radio and television stations are liberalised (1982).
1986-1988	First cohabitation: The 1986 general election resulted in a parliamentary majority for the two main right-wing parties, RPR and UDF. Jacques Chirac is appointed Prime Minister by President François Mitterrand. This first cohabitation ended with François Mitterrand's re-election in 1988.
1993-1995	Second cohabitation: Edouard Balladur is appointed Prime Minister by François Mitterrand after the 1993 General Election. This cohabitation ended with Jacques Chirac's election as President of the Republic in 1995.
1995	Jacques Chirac is elected President of the Republic. Alain Juppé is appointed Prime Minister.
1997	Dissolution of the National Assembly and General Elections resulting in a left-wing majority and thus the third cohabitation. Lionel Jospin is appointed Prime Minister.
2000	In a referendum, 73 percent of the French people voted in favor of shortening the presidential term from 7 to 5 years. The 5-year term will be effective after the presidential elections of 2002.
2002	Euro bills and coins are introduced. Jacques Chirac is re-elected President of the Republic and appoints Jean-Pierre Raffarin as Prime Minister. It is the end of the third cohabitation.

Source: Embassy of France in the United States

Public holidays

French public holidays in 2006

- 1 January – *New Year's Day*
- 6 April – *Easter*
- 7 April – *Easter Monday*
- 1 May – *Labour Day*
- 8 May – *Fête de la Victoire 1945 (VE Day – WWII Victory Day)*
- 25 May – *Ascension Day*
- 4 June – *Whit Sunday (Pentecost)*
- 5 June – *Whit Monday*
- 14 July – *Bastille Day*
- 15 August – *Assumption of the Blessed Virgin Mary*
- 1 November – *All Saints' Day*
- 11 November – *Armistice Day*
- 25 December – *Christmas Day*

French school holidays

French schools across the country are divided into three geographical zones. The school holidays for each zone are slightly staggered, to lessen the impact on holiday traffic.

A calendar of school holidays, for the next few years, can be found at the website of the French Ministry of Education at:

www.education.gouv.fr/prat/calendrier/calendrier.php

Appendices

Useful addresses – embassies and consulates

Major foreign embassies

Australia

✉ 4, rue Jean Rey – 75015 Paris
☎ +33 (0)1.40.59.33.00
Fax +33 (0)1.40.59.33.10
@ Information.Paris@dfat.gov.au
💻 www.france.embassy.gov.au

Canada

✉ 35, avenue Montaigne – 75008 Paris
☎ +33 (0)1.44.43.29.00
Fax +33 (0)1.44.43.29.99
@ paris@dfait-maeci.gc.ca
💻 www.international.gc.ca/canada-europa/france/

Eire

✉ 4, rue Rude – 75116 Paris
☎ +33 (0)1.44.17.67.00
Fax +33 (0)1.44.17.67.60
@ paris@iveagh.irlgov.ie

Great Britain

✉ 35, rue du Faubourg Saint-Honoré – 75008 Paris, France
☎ +33 (0)1.44.51.31.00
Fax +33 (0)1.44.51.34.83
💻 www.amb-grandebretagne.fr

Japan

✉ 7, avenue Hoche – 75008 Paris
☎ +33 (0)1.48.88.62.00
Fax +33 (0)1.42.27.50.81
@ info-fr@amb-japon.fr
💻 www.fr.emb-japan.go.jp

Netherlands

✉ 7, rue Eblé – 75007 Paris
☎ 01.40.62.33.00 / 33.92
Fax 01.40.62.34.56
@ ambassade@amb-pays-bas.fr
💻 www.amb-pays-bas.fr

United States

- ✉ 2, avenue Gabriel – 75008 Paris
- ☎ +33 (0)1.43.12.22.22
- *Fax* +33 (0)1.42.66.97.83
- @ webmaster@amb-usa.fr
- 💻 www.amb-usa.fr

British consulates in France

Paris

Section Consulaire
- ✉ 16, rue d'Anjou – 75008 Paris
- ☎ +33 (0)1.44.51.31.00
- *Fax* +33 (0)1.44.51.31.27

Bordeaux

Consulat general
- ✉ 353, boulevard du Président Wilson, 33073 Bordeaux
- ☎ +33 (0)5.57.22.21.10
- *Fax* +33 (0)5.56.08.33.12

Lille

Consulat general
- ✉ 11, square Dutilleul – 59800 Lille
- ☎ +33 (0)3.20.12.82.72
- *Fax* +33 (0)3.20.54.88.16

Lyon

Consulat general
- ✉ 24, rue Childebert – 69002 Lyon
- ☎ +33 (0)4.72.77.81.70
- *Fax* +33 (0)4.72.77.81.79

Marseille

Consulat general
- ✉ 24, avenue du Prado – 13006 Marseille
- ☎ 04.91.15.72.10
- *Fax* 04.91.37.47.06

Source: www.expatries.diplomatie.fr

Appendices

Further reading

Life in France

Sixty Million Frenchmen Can't Be Wrong, Why we love France but not the French, Jean-Benoit Nadeau, Julie Barlow, Sourcebooks, 2003

On Rue Tatin: the Simple Pleasures of a Small French Town, Susan Hermann Loomis, Harper Collins, 2002

A House In The Sunflowers, Allison & Bus Ltd, 1997

A Normandy Tapestry, A Portrait of Rural France, Alan Biggins, Kirkdale Publishing, 1996

Instructions for Visitor, Helen Stevenson, Black Swan, 2002

Life in a Postcard: Escape to the French Pyrenees, Rosemary Bailey, Bantam UK, 2002

A Harvest Of Sunflowers: Living the Dream in the South of France, Allison & Bus Ltd, 1999

French Letters, More tall tales from the mill of the flea the bestselling author of Home & Dry in France, George East, La Puce Publishing, 1999

René and Me, George East, La Puce Publishing, 1998

French Cricket, George East, La Puce Publishing

From Here, You Can't See Paris, Seasons of a French village and its restaurant, Bantam UK, 2004

A Year in Provence, Peter Mayle, Penguin Books, 2000

Toujours Provence, Peter Mayle, Penguin Books, 2001

Encore Provence, Peter Mayle, Penguin Books, 2001

Tour De Provence, Julian More, Pavilion Books, 2001

Down & Out in Paris and London, George Orwell, Penguin Books, 1986

French language

Learning the language

French With Michel Thomas Complete Course CD (AUDIOBOOK), Michel Thomas, Hodder & Stoughton, 2000

French Language Builder (AUDIOBOOK), Michel Thomas, Hodder & Stoughton, 2001

Appendices

Dictionaries and glossaries

The Compact Oxford-Hachette French Dictionary, Marie-Hélène Corréard, Oxford University Press (Academic), 1995

CD-Rom: Concise Oxford-Hachette French Dictionary, Oxford University Press, 2001

Mini French Dictionary, Chambers Harrap, 2003

Glossary of House Purchase and Renovation Terms, Alan S. Lindsey, Hadley Pager, 2000

Concise Dictionary of House Building Terms, Alan S. Lindsey, Hadley Pager, 2001

Glossary of Medical, Health and Pharmacy Terms, Alan S. Lindsey, Hadley Pager, 2003

Hadley's Conversational French Phrase Book, Alan S. Lindsey, Hadley Pager, 1997

Glossary of French Legal Terms, Alan S. Lindsey, Hadley Pager, 1999

101 French Proverbs, Jean-Marie Cassagne, Contemporary Books, 1998

101 French Idioms, Understanding French Language and Culture Through Popular Idioms, Jean-Marie Cassagne, Contemporary Books, 1995

Pardon My French!, Chambers Harrap, 2003

Dictionary of French Slang and Colloquial Expressions, Henry Strutz, Barrons, 1999

Eating Out In Five Languages, Bloomsbury Publishing, 2004

Food and drink

La France Gourmande, Marolyn Charpentier, Pavilion Books, 2002

Languedoc-Roussillon: The Wines and Winemakers, Paul Strang, Mitchell Beazley, 2002

Touring in Wine Country: The Loire, Hubrecht Duijker, Mitchell Beazley, 1997

French Cheeses, The visual guide to more than 350 cheeses from every région of France, Kazuko Masui, Dorling Kindersley, 2000

Diary of a French Herb Garden, Geraldine Holt, Pavilion Books

Bordeaux – the Definitive Guide to France's Premier Wine Région, Robert Parker, Dorling Kindersley, 2000

Business, tax and law

Practical Guide To French Business, Melanie Hawthorne, Writers Club Press, 2003

Taxation in France 2004, Charles Parkinson, Pannell Kerr Forster, 2004

Letting French Property Successfully, Charles Parkinson and Stephen Smith, Pannell Kerr Forster, 2002

Letting French Property Successfully, Charles Parkinson and Stephen Smith, Pannell Kerr Forster, 2003

Glossary of French Legal Terms, Alan S. Lindsey, Hadley Pager, 1999

Appendices

Travel guides

France

The Rough Guide to France, Kate Baillie, **Ruth Blackmore**, James McConnachieRough Guides, 2005

French Bed and Breakfast, Ann Cooke-Yarborough and Alastair Sawday, Alastair Sawday Publishing, 2004

French Holiday Homes, Clare Hargreaves, Alastair Sawday Publishing

Régions

The Rough Guide to Dordogne and The Lot, Jan Dodd, Rough Guides, 2005

The Rough Guide to Brittany and Normandy, Greg Ward, Rough Guides, 2005

The Rough Guide to Languedoc and Roussillon, Brian Catlos, Rough Guides, 2004

Vacances: Poitou-Charentes & the Vendee, Christine Legrand and Bertrand Lauzanne-Maigret, Hachette Vacances, 2000

The Loire country and regional guide, Nicola Williams, Lonely Planet, 2002

Provence and the Cote D'Azur travel guide, Nicola Williams, Lonely Planet, 2005

Calais, Boulogne and the North of France, Patricia Fenn, Bloomsbury Publishing, 2002

Chateaux of the Loire – Michelin Green Guide, Michelin Guides, 2000

Atlantic Coast – Michelin Green Guide, From the Loire to the Pyrenees, Michelin Guides, 2001

French Riviera – Michelin Green Guide, Michelin Guides, 2001

Burgundy and Jura – Michelin Green Guide, Michelin Guides, 2000

Alsace Lorraine Champagne – Michelin Green Guide, Michelin Guides, 2001

All the books above can be ordered from:

🖥 www.booksonfrance.com

Magazines

French News

✉ SARL Brussac, BP 4042, 225 route d'Angoulême, F-24004 Périgueux Cedex, France

☎ +33 (0)5 53 06 84 40

Fax +33 (0)5 53 06 84 41

@ subs@french-news.com

💻 www.french-news.com

Living France

✉ Archant Life, Archant House, Oriel Road, Cheltenham, Gloucester, GL50 1BB

☎ +44 (0)1242 216050

@ subscriptions@livingfrance.com

💻 www.livingfrance.com

France Magazine

✉ Archant Life, Archant House, Oriel Road, Cheltenham, Gloucester, GL50 1BB

☎ +44 (0)1242 216080

Fax: +44 (0)1242 216084

@ subscriptions@francemag.com

💻 www.francemag.com

French Property News

✉ 6 Burgess Mews, Wimbledon, London, SW19 1UF

☎ +44 (0)20 8543 3113

Fax: +44 (0)20 8540 4815

@ info@french-property-news.com

💻 www.french-property-news.com

Index

Index

A

B

Index

U

V

W

Z

Index